Regional Integration, Development, and Governance in Mesoamerica

Alina Gamboa

Regional Integration, Development, and Governance in Mesoamerica

palgrave
macmillan

Alina Gamboa
Universidad Anahuac México
Mexico City, Mexico

ISBN 978-3-030-25349-3 ISBN 978-3-030-25350-9 (eBook)
https://doi.org/10.1007/978-3-030-25350-9

Cover design by Akihiro Nakayama

This Palgrave Macmillan imprint is published by the registered company Springer Nature Switzerland AG
The registered company address is: Gewerbestrasse 11, 6330 Cham, Switzerland

Preface

September 2010, I had sent in the final version of Ph.D. dissertation "Regionalism, Regionalisation and Governance: The Case of the Plan Puebla Panama," after a long process that included research, travel, and personal growth. I had returned to school to do my master's after eight years in the workforce and continued to do a Ph.D. because I had a subject of research that I could not ignore. I began the process as a single mom in a foreign country. During the years that ensued, the process combined study, work, teaching, travel, move, marriage, another move, baby, then another. I ended the process back in Mexico City, with a teenager, a toddler, and a 6-month-old baby.

As I finished up the final text, I remember a moment of frustration while on the phone with my supervisor, I wanted to change something, and he said, "save it for your book." I laughed off the comment, thinking "that will never happen." The next day after turning everything in, I shoved all my notes, notebooks, books to the back of the bookshelf, thinking I might never look at them again. I was exhausted, sleep-deprived, and tired of staring at a computer screen. I spend the next five years raising kids and working in my family's human resources firm. Away from academia except for collaborating on a chapter about education.

Fast forward to 2016; I accepted to teach part-time at Anahuac University. There I realised that the topic of my dissertation sparked interest, and I began toying with the idea of revisiting my research.

The US election of 2016 caused great worry in Mexico and Central America; many regional issues were once again at the forefront of debates. US–Mexico relations were uneasy since the president-elect had vowed to eliminate the North American Free Trade Agreement (NAFTA), build a wall on the US–Mexico border to stop illegal immigrants from entering the United States (mainly from Mexico and Central America) and considerably reduce foreign aid if specific security issues were not addressed. Mexico's President responded to the accusations and agreed to renegotiate NAFTA, however, there was much discussion in Mexico on the need to diversify trade and to strengthen both diplomatic and economic relations with its neighbours to the South. It is in the context of this discussion that I decided to revisit the possibility of publishing my research. Even though I had researched a specific regional development project in Mesoamerica, the Plan Puebla Panama (2001–2007); the lessons learned during its 7-year existence are relevant to current regional relations and the geopolitical context.

The transition from dissertation to this book was not an easy one; it had already been challenging to condense thousands of pages of research into a 300-page dissertation, even more challenging to cut out entire sections to tie it into our current context and integrate new developments and literature. My first reaction was to try and replicate the field research that took place in 2006–2008. However, time and budget constraints would not permit it. Getting permissions for the interviews that took place back then was also tricky since the contact details I have for most of the interviewees no longer work, organisations have disappeared, government offices were reorganised, or at least have new personnel. All interviewees gave their spoken (recorded) consent for their interviews to be used in my dissertation, knowing that dissertations are available publicly. However, since I was unable to contact most of the interviewees for renewed permissions for the specific use of this book, I have omitted their names and only left the position they held at the time.

In this work, I try not to lose sight of the fact that the people that were in favour of the Plan Puebla Panama regional project, as were as those against are people. Some with more to gain, some with much to lose, but people all the same. And I believe that the same is true for all development programmes, no one has perfect information, not one team has all the answers, not one external advisor group will come up with the only solution. Each group, each new government, each new team has a new diagnosis and new treatment, and mistakes will be made.

I do not have perfect information; I was an observer and investigator, and raconteur. This work is not intended to be normative, (although social science is hardly neutral), it is following for a period of time, the making and possibly unmaking of the Mesoamerican region, searching for patterns, insights, and trying to make some sense out of the regional networks that take place in one of the most amazing areas of the world. I hope this book gives you a glimpse of the complexity, beauty, and importance that this corner called Mesoamerica has for regional and global interactions.

Mexico City, Mexico Alina Gamboa

Acknowledgements

I thank God for the opportunities I have had, for giving me strength and for my wonderful family. I dedicate this book to my parents, that began this long journey with me (specially my mom, editor, and babysitter), and my husband, who supports me through thick and thin, I love you more than you will ever know. Andony, Matías, and Alexa, I love you to the moon and back....Always.

I want to thank Prof. Shaun Breslin, Prof. Benedicte Bull, and Prof. Ben Rosamond for all your feedback on my Ph.D. dissertation. You will note that I returned to my "eclectic approach to theory," it's what makes more sense to me. I also want to thank Prof. Caroline Linse for her help and encouragement.

Contents

List of Tables

CHAPTER 1

Introduction

Mesoamerican regionalism began as an effort to tackle the shared problems of this area. As a relatively new construct based on an ancient identity, the Mesoamerican Region (MAR) showcases several of the debates present today in the study of regionalism and regionalisation. Although regional borders in the Americas have never been defined to the satisfaction of all (see Phillips 2004), most literature on regionalism has divided the Americas into "North," "Central" and "South." Mesoamerica overlaps parts of North America and Central America, however, in lieu of being formed independently from the previous boundaries, Mesoamerica is directly involved, interdependent with, and linked to the political economy of these regions. In other words, the North and Central American regions were not dismantled, nor did they regroup to make room for this new region; instead, the MAR overlaps the previous spaces. This overlapping is not a new phenomenon in Latin America; for example, geographically Mexico has always been considered as part of North America, but culturally, it is included into the cultural-linguistic region of "Latin America," which includes everything from Mexico to Argentina and Chile. In light of this multiple categorising, it is unlikely that Mesoamerican regional processes will ever be independent of North, Central American, and Caribbean integration processes. This reinvention of Mesoamerica, sparked in 2001 by the Plan Puebla Panama (PPP) and other projects, heightened the awareness of the region and its role in the political economy of the Americas (see Villafuerte 2004; Lopez-Calva and

A. Gamboa, *Regional Integration, Development, and Governance in Mesoamerica*,
https://doi.org/10.1007/978-3-030-25350-9_1

Lustig 2003; Pisani and Wayne 2003). Fuelled in part as a response to the (then) forthcoming Free Trade Area of the Americas Agreement (FTAA), the PPP continued even after the collapse of FTAA negotiations in 2005. However, the project and the region underwent many changes during its seven-year existence. This case exemplifies how regions are continually shifting, changing direction, and adapting their geographical span.

Regionalism provides fertile ground for analysis in the International Political Economy (IPE) field of enquiry. The increasing number of regions and the ever-changing scope and nature of these has raised several questions for scholars of IPE, particularly the significance that this trend has on world order (Payne and Gamble 1996). The PPP (2001–2008) was one of the regional projects that shared the MAR space. It launched amidst a large amount of media hype and controversy; over its seven-year span, it was relaunched, restructured, and finally replaced with a new regional project. Nevertheless, regionalisation—the deepened economic or political relationship that can result from regionalism (Hettne 2000)—did not occur to the extent expected.

My research, which consists of a case study of the PPP, exemplifies the difficulty of implementing regional projects in Mesoamerica. By approaching the case study using the notions of regionalism, regionalisation, and governance, we can see the role of the PPP as a multidimensional regional development project, in shaping the Mesoamerican region. Dismissing the PPP as a failed project without a thorough analysis runs the risk of missing an enriching debate on the making (or unmaking) (Söderbaum 2016) of this region. My research will approach the case of the PPP, seeking to identify the cracks that caused the demise of the project and the effects it had on shaping the MAR. I argue that the PPP was not implemented in its entirety due to a weak and fragmented system of governance at all levels.

For this reason, the PPP should not be evaluated solely on the policies or projects it encompassed. Upon reviewing the institutional changes made for the transition from PPP to *Proyecto Mesoamérica*, the regional institutional structure shows a positive transformation. However, my analysis shows that this structure was only ONE aspect of the governance structure needed to implement a multifaceted regional project. Changes did not occur at other levels of governance. Out of the 99 projects proposed at the inception of the PPP, only large infrastructure projects advanced, projects that were overseen by fewer government actors. Many considered that the PPP failed since it did not complete many of its objectives or make a significant impact on poverty reduction. But, that is not the whole story, the PPP shaped the making of the MAR in other ways, mainly through the networking of non-governmental groups that opposed many of the components of the PPP. Although the original networks are no longer in place, they set a precedent, and enrich our understanding of regionalism—that which occurs outside of formal institutions.

1.1 Brief History of the Plan Puebla Panamá

The year 2000 marked a new expectancy in Mexican politics. After a historic defeat of the political party that governed during seven decades, a president from the opposition party took office. This defeat promised to change the modus operandi of Mexican politics, as well as bring forth desired development and growth. One of the issues discussed during the presidential campaign was the notable inequality existing in the nation. Not just between the rich and the poor throughout the country, but also between the north that had seemingly benefited from the increasing trade and investment promoted by the North American Free Trade Agreement (NAFTA) and the south-southeast which remained lagging. During Vicente Fox's Presidential campaign, he asserted that during the six years NAFTA had been in place, this inequality had increased instead of diminishing with the increased trade and growth as measured in terms of Gross Domestic Product (GDP) (CG-PPP 2002: 4–5). President-Elect Vicente Fox and his transition team[1] worked from the moment of their victorious July election to formulate a plan that would help integrate the weaker southern Mexican states into the rest of the national economy, promote development, and boost the welfare of its inhabitants.

The governments of Central America were working on another development plan as a response to the devastation that had occurred during Hurricane Mitch in 1998. They created, together with the IDB, the Central American Business School (INCAE), and the Economic Commission for Latin America and the Caribbean (ECLAC/CEPAL), a study, presented in Madrid in 2000 named "Central America facing

[1] Mexican elections are held in early July each six years and a winner is declared shortly thereafter; the elected candidate takes office during the December 1st inaugural ceremony, leaving a five-month "transition" gap. Starting in 2024, presidents will be inaugurated on 1 October, closing the gap to around 3 months.

the twenty-first Century" (CG-PPP 2002: 9–10), it is also known as the "Madrid Agenda." During an extraordinary meeting of the Tuxtla Mechanism for Cooperation and Dialogue (hereafter Tuxtla Mechanism)—the instrument for addressing issues conjointly between Mexico and Central America—the then Mexican President-Elect Vicente Fox proposed to unify both development plans highlighting the similarities of the conditions found in the southern parts of Mexico with those of Central America. The unification of the development plans was considered a novel idea for regional development (see Declaración Extraordinaria 2001). It was, however, not the first proposal for a regional project, since during the Tuxtla Mechanism meeting held in Guatemala (year 2000), the concept of a "Mesoamerican Region" or a "Mesoamerican Community of Nations" had already been suggested.[2]

The idea was that a joint development plan, coupled with the existing Free Trade Agreements (FTAs) between Mexico and some of the Central American countries, would be able to tackle regional problems and issues effectively. The Plan Puebla Panama, known as the PPP, was named after the geographic span it covered: from the central Mexican state of Puebla through to Panamá. Mexico and the Central American countries worked separately on the diagnostic chapters and proposals for the plan and then, in March of 2001, presented them as the blueprint for development for the region (CG-PPP 2002: 7–9).

The PPP came under scrutiny by academics, politicians, and pressure groups from the time it was first announced. Many critics attacked the use of the term "Mesoamerica" to describe the physical geography covered by the plan. Others criticised the similarities it had with proposals presented by the previous administration.[3] Debates grew about whose interests were prioritised in this development project and who would benefit. Most critics agreed that little help would reach the poorest inhabitants of the region, those whose interests were supposedly at the forefront. Throughout its first year of life, the PPP was at the centre of debates, criticisms, and protests held by academics, non-governmental organisations (NGOs), civil society groups, indigenous groups, and

[2] See www.sgsica.org/reuniondepresidentes/documentos/declara-tuxtla-IV.html.

[3] See the section on predecessors to the PPP later in this chapter. The administration previous to Vicente Fox belonged to the Institutional Revolutionary Party (PRI) which had ruled for over 70 years, a fact which illustrates why Fox's victory was considered a historical win by his National Action Party (PAN).

opposing political parties. These critics claimed vindication each time the PPP fell into a crisis.

As a result, the 2002 report on the advance of the PPP included an extensive section on changes made on the focus and structure of the Plan. This report stated that the initial document was a "first explanation of objectives and strategies, along with a set of projects made up mainly of infrastructure projects. Because of this, it was deemed necessary to reinforce the social and environmental aspects of the Plan and, in general, the whole sustainable development strategy for the region" (CG-PPP 2002: 1). In addition to presenting the advances of the PPP after one year of its existence, the project coordinators acknowledged the criticisms that had been made and began a series of adjustments to the Plan.

The PPP went through an initial institutional restructuring within each of the individual participating governments. Thus in 2003, the PPP was back in the limelight with a relaunch proposal promising to bring forth a more efficient plan with tangible results. Each member state was assigned one of the eight initiatives of the PPP (see Table 1.1) and was to designate a presidential commissioner to head that initiative and to coordinate with the other member states and internal departments. For example, Guatemala received the Mesoamerican electrical connectivity initiative, so the Guatemalan President appointed his commissioner from the National Electricity Institute (INDE). Also, each of the ministries of foreign affairs (MFAs) were encouraged to include the PPP as a critical aspect to foreign policy and to become active players in the projects. In practice, however, it was felt that several presidents appointed a commissioner out of political considerations and not necessarily according to who would be best suited for the position (Interview 27: 2006).

Notwithstanding the institutional reforms and the change in discourse by the Mexican government, sceptics thought the PPP was doomed to failure and would disappear after national elections changed governments, in particular, the Mexican presidency at the end of 2006. Initially, the PPP had been spearheaded through the President's Office for Strategic Planning and Regional Development (OPEDR), specially created by President Fox for this purpose (later declared unconstitutional by the Congress). This office housed the General Coordination of the Plan Puebla Panamá (CG-PPP) and was responsible for publishing project initiatives and reports. An example of a publication written during that time, the "Informe de Avances y Perspectivas Junio 2002," focuses mainly on Mexico and gives the impression that the Central American

Table 1.1 The Mesoamerican initiatives

1. ***Sustainable development—to promote the conservation and sustainable use of natural resources and participating parties, particularly local communities, in environmental conservation. Country in Charge: Nicaragua***
The first initiative will work closely together with the Mesoamerican Biological Corridor (MBC), as it has little budget of its own. This initiative reiterates the nations' commitment to the MBC and gives it and other environmental initiatives their full support. The PPP Nations also agree to coordinate environmental laws and to invest in research which will enable the profitable but sustainable use of national natural resources. The Mesoamerican Fund for sustainable development will be set up as part of this initiative, providing small projects with necessary funding
2. ***Human development—to reduce poverty, enable vulnerable elements of society access to basic social services and contribute to the full development of Mesoamerican peoples. Country in charge: Mexico***
The scope of the Human Development initiative is quite ample. Within this initiative fall projects for; worker training, education and literacy, local development projects, indigenous communities, environmental education for indigenous people and farmers, statistics on migration, health, and demography, as well as further statistical work to evaluate the conditions of the people in the region
Worker training or retraining for the most part will occur within manufacturing, where the new investments will provide training for potential employees, however, each state should emphasise local education, particularly in rural areas where there is a higher illiteracy rate. Bilingual primary education will be an integral part of the Plan, where the indigenous populations will be taught in both Spanish and their native language to foment the richness of the indigenous languages while enabling students to continue into secondary education which is still mainly taught in Spanish. Health issues will be tackled both through local health providers, but also through cooperation over threats that transcend borders (tropical diseases, AIDS, etc.). Educational campaigns on health and hygiene are also part of this initiative
The Human Development initiative will be funded through the local governments of each country, though the national governments may allocate further funding towards some projects, most of the initiative does not include separate funding

3. *Disaster prevention and mitigation—to promote the prevention and mitigation of natural disasters and incorporate the consideration of the elements of risk in projects by all actors involved. Country in Charge: Panama*
   This initiative is closely tied to the UNDP and CEPAL joint project to assist with disaster prevention and mitigation. In addition to a commitment to the results of this project and full cooperation thereof, PPP nations will heighten efforts to educate people on ways to prevent natural disasters, but also on how they can protect themselves and their families from potential risk
   As insurance markets are still not fully developed in the region, the initiative will facilitate the entrance of insurance companies, particularly those versed in catastrophe risk mitigation
   As part of the initiative, further funding will be given to meteorological centres and emergency response systems will be evaluated.
   The main recognition of this initiative is that in such a small and vulnerable area, disasters tend to hit more than one country at a time, therefore coordinated efforts will enable rescue teams to cover damaged areas quicker
4. *Promotion of tourism—to promote the development of ecological, cultural and historical tourism, through regional actions that will be benefit from complementarities, economies of scale and tourism's chains of production. Country in Charge: Belize*
   Stemming from the success of the coordinated tourist corridor "Mundo Maya," this initiative will continue to support standing projects, but also seeks to find new projects for the area. Tourism is already an important economic activity; however, research in the diagnostic documents for the PPP identified further untapped potential for tourism in the area. Ecotourism (successfully managed in some Mexican states and in Costa Rica) could be further developed in the region as many potential areas have been identified as suitable for ecotourism development. Since natural areas transcend borders (just like the cultural Maya route), integral circuits could be developed for rainforests or reef exploration. As part of the initiative, standards will be agreed upon to decide when a project is sustainable and official certificates will be given to all sustainable establishments. Indigenous communities will be invited to participate in the proposed projects
5. *Enabling of commercial exchange—to foment commercial exchange in the region through reducing transaction costs between countries and promote the participation of small and medium enterprises in regional exports. Country in Charge: Honduras*
   The plan includes constructing six different "development zones" which will be made up of a variety of industries. Although private and foreign investment is a key element for production in the PPP, the commercial exchange initiative focuses on the transaction processes between the nations. Identified as inefficient in the diagnostic chapters of the PPP, border transactions are targeted as processes that need to be modernized and simplified. Programs to support the small and medium enterprises in the region will also be in place, particularly since investment ventures will attract and strengthen large multinational companies
   Although commercial treaties and free trade agreements are not a priority for the PPP as numerous trade coalitions are already in existence, in some instances the treaties are overlapping or contradictory. The fifth initiative of the PPP will establish a mechanism to analyse existing commercial agreements and recommend homologising aspects of the treaties between the PPP countries

(continued)

Table 1.1 (continued)

6. *Transport—to promote the physical integration of the region to facilitate the transit of goods and peoples, and in this way lower transportation costs. Country in Charge: Costa Rica*

   The strained and inadequate transportation systems in the area, as well as the poor construction of the roads have brought this issue as one of the main priorities of the PPP. IDB and private funding have been made available for undergoing major improvements and developments in transportation, road construction, interconnectedness and an overhaul of main highways

   Under the International Mesoamerican Road Network (RICAM) heading, three highway investment programs are proposed for Mexico: The Puebla-Panama Corridor, the Atlantic Corridor, and the Mexican Interior Corridor. These corridors correspond to a Pacific route, and Atlantic route and a North-South highway system, respectively. The Transportation Corridor is a 3156-kilometre North-south Pacific Coast highway that will run through Mexico, Belize, Guatemala, Honduras, El Salvador, Nicaragua, Costa Rica, and Panama. The RICAM's main objective is to use transportation infrastructure to take advantage of the region's strategic location and enable the efficient movement of goods between the Pacific and the Gulf of Mexico

   Dry canals, or railway and highway combinations, will be running east-west to connect ports on both coasts and development zones will be constructed between the two. Initially there were five proposed dry canals located in Southern Mexico, Nicaragua, El Salvador, and Honduras. To complement the dry canals, deep-water ports will be built in order to accommodate large ocean freightliners

7. *Energy interconnection—to interconnect energy markets, particularly electrical, with a view to promotes an increase in the investments in this sector and reduce the price of electricity. Country in Charge: Guatemala*

   A large part of the industrial plan involves the installation of an energy network to facilitate production in the region. As part of the larger Electric Interconnection System for Central American Nations (SIEPAC), the energy upgrades are also meant to increase the quality of life for rural residents. A regional energy grid will be developed as part of the plan to supply the development zones with electricity and gas. Proposals include the construction of 25 hydroelectric dams and a 1830 km electrical line that will carry 230 kilowatts of power As well as an integrated energy grid, a gas line has been designed to transport natural gas through the region, from Mexico to Panama. Colombia is negotiating with the PPP countries to be included in this project

8. *Communications—to expand the supply of telecommunication services and provide universal access to them. Country in Charge: El Salvador*

   The main project under the 8th initiative is to create a regional fibre optic network to enable telecommunication services throughout the region, particularly in remote access zones. Mobile phone networks will also be expanded in order to reach the connectivity target. A secondary objective behind this initiative is to increase access to information networks for the rural population, including the internet

Sources OECD (2005) and Presidencia Documento Base (2001), ¿Qué es el Plan Puebla Panamá? Publicity leaflet

element was an afterthought. Sandoval and Salazar (2002: 9) state that the instruments of the PPP "do not leave the reader satisfied; since it emphasises on the Mexican part, leaving the remaining seven countries to one side."

To affirm the continuity and include Central America in the formulation and implementation of policies, the 2004 relaunch and set up in 2005 in San Salvador included creating a technical ministry for the PPP. This city was already home base to the General Ministry for the Central American Integration System (SG-SICA), the umbrella mechanism for Central American Integration (further explained in Chapter 4).

The change in venue ensured more attention on the Central American aspects of the PPP and that PPP directives could coordinate with their counterparts in the SG-SICA and its institutions. It also aimed to demonstrate that the PPP would be a continuous regional effort and not an imposition by Mexican policymakers, as Ornelas (2002) and Bartra (2001), have criticised as explained by Rocha (2006). The changing of location aided the Mexican Presidency in its attempt to distance the PPP from public criticism, particularly internal debates taking place in Congress and some of the south-eastern Mexican States. These internal conflicts had already weakened Mexican regional leadership.

The campaign of the 2006 Mexican elections brought the PPP out of anonymity back to the public forum. The main political parties went back and forth on the advantages of continuing with the projects, however critical they were of its track record up until then. The coalitions of left-wing political parties cried out for a PPP that would fit in with their ideology and would shift focus onto social projects instead of infrastructure. The right-wing candidate called for restructuring and increasing the institutions that looked after the project in the hope of arriving at a point where these projects would advance and bring the promised results of sustainable development in the region. During the electoral campaign and the controversial results that followed the election, the criticism of the PPP was no longer due to its proposals or lack thereof, but mainly for becoming another lost promise of development.

The PPP marched on quietly; advancing on many of its proposed infrastructure projects, although some ended up being attributed to other government or regional entities rather than to the PPP. The acceptance of Colombia, first as an honorary member and then as a full member in 2006, went almost unnoticed by the press, except for Nicaragua, where President Ortega had opposed Colombia's membership (Reforma, 11 April 2007).[4] The adhesion of the Dominican Republic also went unnoticed. The number of official projects was narrowed down again to those that were the least problematic or likely to cause protests. The newly reshaped institutions (2005) increased organisational capabilities and attempted to coordinate the relationship of the PPP with other regional organisms in Mesoamerica, after identifying cases of overlap and duplicate efforts. Shortly after Mexican President Calderón took office in 2006, he called once more for evaluating and restructuring the PPP, showing that Mexico again held the reins. In June 2008, the PPP's final progress report was presented, along with the framework for its replacement: The Mesoamerican Integration and Development Project known as *Proyecto Mesoamérica*.

It would be interesting to compare the initial 2001 diagnostic documents on Mexico and Central America to an updated version that would show what progress or results had occurred during the seven years of the PPP, but such analysis was not officially compiled.[5] Whereas the original diagnostic documents focused on poverty indicators regarding health, education, and nutrition along with statistics, including the number of households with electricity, running water, sewage and floors, only building and renewing major infrastructure within the region showed significant advancement.[6] Status reports of the PPP described the funds allocated and spent. What became noticeable during the span of the PPP is that even though multidimensional issues require a multidimensional approach, implementation mechanisms rest on the modes of governance, and if these are fragmented, so is implementation. It also highlighted the geopolitical importance of the Mesoamerican region, particularly on how differently the many issues in Mesoamerica are viewed within and outside the region.

[4]Amplía Calderón bloque regional: Integran a Colombia al Plan Puebla-Panamá pese a resistencias de Daniel Ortega; by Ernesto Nuñez and Erika Hernández Sección Nacional Periódico Reforma 11 Abril 2007.

[5]The IDB through its Office of Evaluation and Oversight published an evaluation of their participation in the PPP, in their report they state "However, the Bank's contribution to the PPP's results is difficult to determine. First, the Bank did not set up indicators to measure the impact of its regional operations. Second, the Bank did not define specific objectives to guide its involvement in, or the development of, the PPP" (OVE 2008: 22).

[6]See Plan Puebla Panamá Documento Base, Capítulo México Presidencia de la República 2001, and Plan Puebla Panamá Avances y Perspectivas Junio 2002, which points out that the main cause for the lagging of the south of Mexico was due to lack of investment in infrastructure by the Federal Government which had instead invested in the North (CG-PPP 2002: 5).

There was considerable debate on whether the PPP was a useful or detrimental mechanism for Mesoamerican development; it is not the purpose of this book to engage in this debate, neither to engage in the discussion of the usefulness of *Proyecto Mesoamérica*, although I note the different sides of the debate in chapter three. Instead, I analyse the PPP as an initial shaper of Mesoamerica within the context of the more recent wave of regionalism that began in the 1990s. The PPP created a "new concept in regional planning, … (That) ought to adapt to a new context of democratization, strengthening of the federal system, decentralisation, and higher participation of civil society in formulating and evaluating public policy" (CG-PPP 2002: 7, 41). As part of this "new concept in regional planning," it shares many of the same objectives that launched other regions into formal cooperation mechanisms.

Several of the Mesoamerican countries that participated in the PPP had recently returned to democracy and had followed the directives placed by external technical support teams to decentralise government and include other participants into their decision-making processes (Preciado Coronado and Villaruel Mora 2006; Pearce 2004). On the surface, this appears to have happened, but in practice, power and authority still reside in central governments. In fact, there are those who would waver on calling them democracies; and instead, consider them as: "the state that combines social authoritarianism, economic exclusion, and restricted civil liberties alongside political democracy" (Tedesco 2004: 36). The governance structures in the MAR that resulted from both internal changes (i.e., shifts in power structures, restoration of "democratic" governments after military rule, guerrilla activities) and external influences (i.e., technical support from World Bank, Aid agencies, the EU) are weak and fragmented. In this context, the MAR may well need a comprehensive regional development plan, but as the results of this research show, if the success of such a plan depends on the ability to implement at different levels of governance (regional, national, sub-national, and local) and requires the cooperation of other sectors outside of the government, the plan is likely to follow in the steps of the PPP.

One of the questions that directed my research stemmed from observing that large sectors of society in Mexico, and in Central America, welcomed the idea of a regional development programme with enthusiasm; and later rejected it. I wanted to find out why such a significant shift happened in a short time. Another observation that led my research was that throughout the existence of the PPP, only selected parts of the proposal were implemented. I wanted to investigate why only certain projects progressed and others lagged behind. I noticed that the various attempts to reorganise and relaunch had little success in achieving better results or acceptance.

The PPP was not the first effort of regional cooperation between Mexico and Central America; however, it is the first one that included a comprehensive agenda, with specific projects and regional institutions. The primary purpose of this book is to show how the PPP helped create a regional space now called "Mesoamerica" and observe how the PPP, along with its replacement, *Proyecto Mesoamérica*, shaped the region over the past 17 years. Using Björn Hettne's concept of "regionness" as a framework, this research observes how the PPP constructed the MAR and suggests that governance is a crucial component in the relationship between regionalism and regionalisation.

The second purpose of this book is to separate the discourse from reality. While other publications discuss whether the "development" trajectory was the right one, this study finds that implementing the social aspects of the PPP was a challenge of its own. Principally because securing funds for social projects proved difficult, and then, because the governance mechanisms needed for implementing such plans did not function adequately.

Throughout my research, the lack of contact between the PPP coordinators, government offices, and non-governmental actors was evident When the project was designed, the governmental institutions in charge did not take into account key input from external actors. Through an analysis of vertical and horizontal governance structures in the MAR, it seems that the institutional restructuring that took place was only at the regional level with a few changes at the national level. However, many of the Mesoamerican Initiatives set out by the PPP required coordination at each level of government, as well as across government and non-governmental sectors. The result was that projects requiring coordination among the regional institutions, national ministries, or through the levels of government (e.g., education proposals required that they go through to the national ministry for education, then directed through to the state mechanism, then channelled through municipal education authorities and finally reaching local schools), were left to one side in favour of projects that required little coordination.

Finally, my research findings draw out the issue of security in Mesoamerica. Security is not an issue explicitly included in either the

PPP or its replacement, *Proyecto Mesoamérica*.[7] Nonetheless, it is one of the most prominent problems in Mesoamerica today, where violence and organised crime take up a large percentage of news coverage, including abuse from state actors such as police and armed forces. Regional security has become a priority in Mesoamerica. Violence is causing people to migrate (to other Mesoamerican nations and the United States) as well as the loss of possible investment in the region. Also, the United States has expressed concern over the increasing flow of illegal migrants seeking a better life within its borders, to the point that it has threatened to restrict aid and preferential trade to Mesoamerican nations if they don't take actions to curb migration. Albeit regional security is not explicitly addressed in the PPP and *Proyecto Mesoamérica*, there is regional cooperation on the matter through other parallel mechanisms.

In this chapter, I provide the background information necessary to understand the PPP and the MAR and map out the components of the rest of the book. First, I give a brief overview of the history of Mesoamerica, its current situation, and the influence that the United States holds over the region. Secondly, I describe the PPP, its predecessors, and the use of regionalism as a form of development which will situate this case study. The last section provides the book chapter summaries.

1.2 Mesoamerica

Mesoamerica, also called Middle America, has been denominated the birthplace culture of the Americas (Woodward 1985). Mesoamerica is the nebulous area where North America ends, and South America begins, an overlapping of the two, or as a distinct "Middle" entity on its own. The exact borders of Mesoamerica have been topics for debate, particularly as until recently, it was considered mostly a cultural and historical area and not as a political entity (Bull 2005). Additionally, the cultural sphere that it referred to was attributed to pre-Columbian civilizations and not to its current inhabitants. The present political and economic mapping of the area reflect these geographical ambiguities. Throughout history, the environmentally diverse, culturally rich narrow

[7]Although one could argue that food security and avoiding natural disasters are an important component of "security" what is meant here is the concern over organised crime and violence.

isthmus between North and South America has been divided along different cultural and geographic lines, continuously shifting its borders to suit the territorial organisation at hand. When the Spaniards arrived in the Isthmus in the 1590s, they changed the original boundaries used by the native inhabitants to facilitate colonial rule. The independence movements in the 1800s shifted the borders once again to accommodate the interests of the political elite that took over power from Spain (Woodward 1988).

Initially, the newly independent countries tried to forge a union of the Central American Nations, which failed to flourish. Some areas that had formerly belonged to the Spanish territory of Guatemala were annexed by Mexico, causing discord between the two new nations. Panama was associated with Central America once it broke away from Colombia in the early twentieth century. Belize, which had also belonged to Guatemala, became part of the British Commonwealth and was not considered a part of Central America until the 1960s (Villaseñor 2006; Woodward 1985).

Mesoamerica has absconded its original archaeological definition, and it now currently refers to the geographical area that extends through nine states in the southeast of Mexico, the seven countries of Central America and Colombia.[8] These entities share many socioeconomic characteristics as well as common concerns for security and environmental issues. Although including a slightly different territory, the launch of the PPP in conjunction with the creation of the Mesoamerican Biological Corridor (MBC) rebranded "Mesoamerica" or MAR, gradually integrating it into the national and regional politics of the territory beginning in the State of Puebla in Mexico and extending through to Colombia. As the communicator between the Atlantic and Pacific Oceans, as well as one of the most culturally and bio-diverse regions in the world, the MAR isn't only a group of disorganised countries getting together to try to increase their trade influence in the Americas; it is a region that needs to find ways to safeguard its resources and to improve the welfare of its inhabitants.

The topography profoundly influences Mesoamerica. Its rich and diverse landscape makes the area interesting for those studying or

[8]Colombia was officially admitted into the PPP in 2006, previously the term Mesoamerica only included through to Panama.

travelling but complicates creating effective systems of communication needed to form political unity. Woodward (1988) gives examples from the ancient Mayan political structures to the Spanish Colonial rule and through to independence. Many attempts to create political integration in the isthmus failed due to "individual jealousies combined with geographic barriers" (Woodward 1988: 6). The Sierra Madre volcanic mountain range runs from Mexico through to Panama with breaks in the chain in Honduras, Nicaragua, and Panama. Throughout human history in the Western hemisphere, these mountains have been obstacles to communication and agriculture, although the elevation the provided, 3000–8000 feet, facilitated the development of many early civilizations (Woodward 1988). Most major cities in Central America are at the higher elevations of the Pacific mountain chain. Several fault lines run through this area, causing numerous natural disasters over the years, where earthquakes and volcanic eruptions devastate the densely populated areas.

As a small territory between the Atlantic and Pacific Oceans, hurricanes and tropical storms originating from either of these bodies of water make the Isthmus particularly vulnerable. Many lakes and streams add to the landscapes and contribute to the flourishing fauna, but rivers are not navigable enough to facilitate communication and transport. Also, during the long rainy season, smaller streams turn to rivers, frequently flooding roads and making transportation in the area more vulnerable. The task of building bridges and planning routes has improved only over the last two decades (Carr 2002; Pisani and Label 2003).

Mesoamerica has a unique biological heritage, with more than one country claiming to have the world's most diverse fauna and flora (e.g., Costa Rica and Panama claim this). Its natural ecosystems range from coral reefs to pine savannas, semi-arid woodlands, grasslands, lowland rainforests, and high mountain forests. Even though Mesoamerica covers only 2% of the earth's surface, it is home to about 12% of the planet's biological diversity, housing some 33 distinct "ecoregions" (CCAD-CBM 2003: 10). However, over the past century, these are declining at a considerable rate with eleven of these ecoregions considered in critical status and eleven more, as threatened (CCAD-CBM 2003: 10). Aggressive deforestation in the area has had severe social and ecological consequences, weighing heavily against its ability to provide jobs and potential economic gains.

Along with the flora, the fauna is also impressive; for example, Panama alone has approximately 929 known species of birds; Belize has around

150 different mammals, 540 species of birds and 152 species of amphibians and reptiles; Mexico houses 717 different reptiles and 4000 plants with potential medicinal purposes. Guatemala and Honduras host several unique medicinal plants in their high mountains, most of them endemic to the area. Along the eastern coasts, the world's second largest coral reef system runs from Mexico to Honduras, and 8% of the world's mangrove forests are in this threatened area (CCAD-CBM 2003). Finding ways of generating economic benefits from these unique ecosystems without causing environmental damage is a high priority for the region. The practice of slashing and burning rainforest, a method that is still used by many of the poorest people in the area to obtain land for agriculture is an example of a practice which is detrimental to the environment. Alternatives that enable human survival as well as for that of the environment are needed. Both the PPP and the MBC claim that responsible use of natural resources is of high priority, however, critics say that the proposed economic exploitation of these resources as set out in the PPP documents will cause further environmental degradation (Toly 2004).

The MAR does not include all of Mexico, leaving out the more industrialised arid northern region, as well as the states of the Central High Plateau. The nine states included are Campeche, Chiapas, Guerrero, Oaxaca, Puebla, Quintana Roo, Tabasco, Veracruz, and Yucatan. With a combined surface area of 502,738 km^2 (25.7% of Mexican territory), it is the home to approximately 32 million people or about 26% of the national population.[9] Nearly 75% of all Mexicans who speak an indigenous language live in these states.

The industrial sector has increased its presence in the Mexican southeast over the past decade, albeit to a lesser extent than the dramatic increases found in the north or centre of the country following the establishment of the NAFTA with the United States and Canada. However, the overall participation of south-eastern Mexico in the national GDP for manufactured goods has fallen in real terms since NAFTA's enactment (Villafuerte 2006). The increase of manufacturing and assembly plants known as *maquiladoras* make up most of the

[9]2017 population was 123,518,270, according to INEGI, however, by state the most recent statistics are from 2010, when the nine states had a population of 31,752,532 out of the total population was 114,255,555. internet.contenidos.inegi.org.mx/contenidos/Productos/prod_serv/contenidos/espanol/bvinegi/productos/nueva_estruc/AEGEUM_2017/702825097912.pdf.

industrial growth arising in the southeast region, these are owned principally by foreign companies.[10] In the early1990s, the south-eastern states had about 2900 people working in *maquiladoras*. By 2000, this figure had reached 80,000, mostly concentrated in the states of Puebla and Yucatan (Labrecque 2005).

Most of the economies in Central America and Colombia still depend heavily on agricultural commodities, although tourism is a rising industry, particularly for Costa Rica, Belize and to some extent, Panama. Panama is also positioning itself in the service market industry, in addition to its status as a financial centre. However, most of the governments are implementing policies that encourage *maquiladoras* to move to the MAR. Since the *maquiladoras* in northern Mexico are shifting their focus towards electronics and other more sophisticated manufacturing, requiring highly skilled workers, the garment industry is moving south, searching to decrease their labour expenses. The MAR is not competing with northern Mexico, but with Asia, where many *maquiladoras* moved seeking even lower costs of production (Labrecque 2005).

The *maquila* industry is a polemical issue in the MAR, where governments encourage the increase of this kind of production to foment job creation and foreign investment. However, many NGOs and labour unions (Interview 16: 2006; Interview 46: 2006; Interview 38: 2006; Interview 23: 2006), maintain that by increasing this industry, the national economies enter into a vicious cycle where wages remain low by circumventing labour and environmental laws. During field research in El Salvador, there was a great debate in the news as, once again, a textile *maquiladora* had closed suddenly, without notifying government authorities and without compensating its workers (not only concerning the cessation of work, but

[10] Initially, *maquiladoras* began in the 1960s to create factories on the northern border with the United States where they could receive raw materials or parts, assemble them in Mexico, and then, export them back across the border. Taking advantage of low wages, tax breaks, as well as lax environmental and labour laws, companies managed to increase production and profit margins overall, while the border economy grew through job creation and investment. *Maquiladoras* also invested in infrastructure such as bridges and roads, to ensure that the finished product would be able to get back across the border efficiently. NAFTA encouraged the *maquila* industry by eliminating the quotas that set the percentages of goods that *maquiladoras* had to export, which meant that they could now tap into the Mexican market. With NAFTA in place, non-American companies also established *maquiladoras* in Mexico, with the hope that their products would be considered Mexican-made and thus enter the US market tariff-free.

workers had also not been paid their week's wages). A local NGO representative interviewed the following day said that this sort of news was becoming more and more common in Central America, where national laws were not able to protect their workers (Interview 16: 2006).

Over recent decades, violence and armed conflict has plagued the MAR. Civil wars took place in Nicaragua, Guatemala, and El Salvador, but other conflicts also affected the area. The so-called soccer war between Honduras and El Salvador (1969) caused significant tension in regional relations. Mexico and Costa Rica mediated several of the conflicts and were recipients of refugees that fled the violence in their home countries. Moreover, the numerous refugee camps in Mexico created tension with local populations as they were situated in the border areas with Guatemala, mainly in the state of Chiapas, already plagued with poverty and injustice. In 1994, Chiapas had an armed uprising timed to coincide with the enactment of NAFTA. Not an isolated case, other violent uprisings in south-eastern Mexico took place in Oaxaca (2006) and Guerrero (1997, 2004). At the turn of the twenty-first century, new waves of violence have erupted in the area through drug trafficking, the illegal smuggling of migrants,[11] and street gangs known as *Maras*.

The contrast between the richness of the region with the poverty of the inhabitants of the MAR raises many questions and highlights close to two centuries of injustices, armed conflicts, devastating natural phenomena, and authoritarian governments. With few exceptions (Costa Rica and to some extent Panama), a lack of infrastructure and investment in education and health exacerbate these injustices. The PPP was proposed as a multidimensional regional development project that would mitigate the consequences of poverty, vulnerability to natural phenomena, environmental deterioration, poor infrastructure, and the lack of sustainable forms of economic productivity.

1.3 The United States

It is impossible to discuss regional politics in The Americas without mentioning the United States; this is even more evident when talking about Mexico and Central America. The past roles of the United States in the

[11] There have been many instances of Central American migrants being held hostage for money or killed during their transit through Mexico, causing diplomatic tensions; see Reforma, 30 January 2010 Reclama El Salvador muerte de migrantes.

area and the enormous influence it holds politically, commercially, and economically means that its power must not be underestimated.

Although the United States is not mentioned explicitly in any of the documents or administrative mechanisms of the PPP, critics brought the role of the United States into the debate (see Alvarez et al. 2002; Álvarez Béjar 2002a, b, c; Barreda 2002; Ornelas 2002; Sandoval Palacios 2001; and others). From the moment that President Fox announced that he had discussed the PPP with US President Bush during their first meeting in January 2001, many read between the lines. The fact that Bush reacted favourably to the proposal of the PPP, to some, meant that the project was part of a US agenda. Ornelas (2002) goes as far as to say that the PPP plays a primary role in US National Security. Considering the history of the United States in the internal affairs of several of the participating nations, mainly because the United States has regarded this area of the world as part of its "backyard," any involvement at all raises concerns (Chomsky 1985).

The United States forms part of the regional economic network overlapping in the area. Although it does not have any explicit decision-making power within the PPP, it is the dominant member of NAFTA and CAFTA-DR. Many of the concerns prioritised by the US government in the past are at least mentioned in the PPP (migration, drugs trafficking, insecurity), so some authors (i.e., Wendy 2002; Salazar Pérez 2002; Barreda 2001) consider the United States as a key player, if not THE key player in the entire project. Many of the debates that took place regarding the PPP centred on the role of the United States and its position on sensitive issues such as the militarization of the area, security concerns, and the environment. During the negotiations for the Free Trade of the Americas (FTAA, suspended in 2005), Central America and Mexico seemed to ally with the United States over the South American countries (Carranza 2000), which was not appreciated by many of the regional NGOs.

Even though claims of what the United States does in Mesoamerica are unfounded, they are readily believed due to its previous interventions in Central America during the last century.[12] US involvement in

[12]For example, Robinson Salazar's essay (2002) "El Vinculo Militar del Plan Colombia y el Plan Puebla Panamá" published in the book *Lectura Crítica del Plan Puebla Panamá*, makes strong statements about the US military involvement in the MAR. However, his evidence is weak, and supported only by websites (some of which have disappeared), and essays written by himself, as seen in his bibliography.

the independence of Panama from Colombia given in exchange for finishing the Panama Canal and controlling the territory was one of the first instances of US interference with the geopolitics of the region in pursuit of its own interests (Woodward 1985). The United States also played an active role in supporting military governments and dictatorships in the area as a strategy to prevent leftist groups from reaching power. The United States regarded the Cuban revolution's communist government as a threat to national security given that it is located only 90 miles away from its territory. Subsequent groups with ideologies resembling that of the (then) USSR or mainland China provoked the United States to prop up governments in Central America despite blatant human rights abuses, corruption and the lack of democracy. The United States provided military equipment and training to national armies that would go on to commit gross human rights violations against government opposition (i.e., El Salvador). Even as some semblance of democracy exists in Central America, much resentment towards the United States and its past involvement still remains.[13] Left-wing political parties still consider their lack of political power and electoral defeat as the work of the United States (Interview 44: 2006), claiming that the United States is involved in rigging elections to keep them out of power.[14]

1.4 Predecessors to the Plan Puebla Panamá

Mexican politics help contextualise some of the polemic surrounding the PPP. Although Central American countries are obviously key players in the process, the PPP initiated in Mexico which brought into it much of its political baggage. Without delving into too much historical and political detail, the elements of Mexican politics that many of the articles

[13]This section is intended to give a brief description of the motives behind the mistrust by several groups towards the United States, both from Mexico and from Central America. It is for background purposes only; for in-depth discussions about the US relations with Mexico and Central America please see: *Bordering on Chaos* by Andres Oppenheimer, *Central America, One Nation Divided* by Ralph Woodward 1985, Oxford University Press. *The Future of Central America, Policy Choices for the US and Mexico* by Richard R. Fagen and Olga Pellicer (eds.) 1983, Stanford University Press.

[14]The 2006 elections in Nicaragua resulting in Daniel Ortega as President, and subsequent reelections somewhat undermines these claims, nevertheless the resentment is still there.

analysing the PPP discuss at length should be noted, particularly Andrés Barreda's (2002) essay on the "Objectives of the Plan Puebla-Panama."

A vital element lies within the context of the Mexican presidential election in July 2000; Vicente Fox (Partido Acción National, PAN) ended the Revolutionary Institutional Party's (PRI) 70-year hold of the presidency. This historical victory promised change from old policies, economic stagnation, poverty, and politics. The government's "new and innovative" PPP initiative (that in its initial stage only covered the southern part of Mexico) was one of many presidential campaign issues driving Fox's victory. The election was also significant because the President's party did not hold a majority in the newly seated Congress. Therefore, the President had to negotiate with the legislative branch in order to pass any new initiatives. The "losing" PRI and PRD political parties did not concede easy victories to the new Chief of State and voted out more initiatives than they passed (Rubio 2004). President Fox had a hard time selling the PPP to the opposition parties and to the media, who were quick to find all discrepancies or weak points in the proposed project. The main points of the new development plan were discussed during the presidential campaign, so it wasn't surprising to see that discussion, including criticism and scepticism of the plan, preceded the official launch of the project.

Journalists and researchers quickly found out that the primary document for the Mexican section of the PPP, named the *Documento Base*, was heavily based on two papers written by cabinet members from the previous administration, a fact that did not go unnoticed. Álvarez Béjar (2002a, b, c), Barreda (2002), Bartra (2001), Ornelas (2002), Hiernaux-Nicolas (2002), and Chanona (2002) highlight that the recycling of previous policies showed that the new government seemed primed to continue with the same social policies that condoned the exploitation of the poor in the name of free trade and a market economy. The government of "change" seemed to be merely changing the surface of some policies without changing the content and then passing these off as new.

The two cited documents were: "The South also exists: An essay about regional development in Mexico," published in July 2000 and written by Dávila, Kessel, and Levy (Santiago Levy was Health Minister under President Fox's predecessor, Ernesto Zedillo of the PRI) and the "Initiative for the South," by Carlos Rojas, written as a government document while he was Minister for Social Development (also under Ernesto Zedillo). Some of the ideas and recommendations given in these documents turned into a series of mega projects, some of which began during the Zedillo administration while others stalled at the drawing board due to popular protest. For example, both the controversial Oaxaca-Istmo-Huatulco and the Istmo de Tehuantepec projects, initiated by the previous administration, stalled due to local protests but were later integrated into the PPP (Interview 38: 2006). Since the *Documento Base* is a by-product of these two documents, Armandro Bartra (2001) defines it as being one of "double discourse," both populist (Rojas) and neoliberal technocrat (Levy).

The PPP soon became a problematic issue in the new government. The optimism that reigned after the landslide victory of July 2000 slowly eroded by outside criticism and the failure of the Mexican President to convince the Governors in the participating states, the media, or the public, that this was a real alternative to eradicating poverty in the southeast region of Mexico. President Fox's efforts to have an "inclusive, pluralistic" government meant that he kept bureaucrats from the previous administration, including Santiago Levy (co-author of "El Sur Tambien Existe") as a Cabinet member. In addition, President Fox designated Florencio Salazar as the Presidential Commissioner in charge of the PPP, Salazar was a former PRI party member, a fact that did not go unnoticed (Call 2002).

Andrés Barreda (2001), however, traces the origins of the PPP to documents predating the two previously attributed as its foundation. He loosely identifies an additional seven sets of documents whose sources range from the IDB, the Economic Commission for Latin American and the Caribbean (CEPAL/ECLAC), documents surrounding the Mesoamerican Biological Corridor, and the World Bank, along with preparatory materials drawn up by different Mexican state governments, the Mundo Maya (Mayan World) tourism network, as well as the preliminary documents elaborated during the five-month transitional period while Fox, was still President-Elect.[15]

Mexico has passed through different models of development, from modernization, through import substitution industrialization, to neoliberal open economy, but the only common thread would seem to be the high social and environmental costs embedded in each of these (Saldivar

[15]Although Mexican elections take place every six years on the first Sunday in July, the President does not take office until 1 December.

2002). The recurring attempts to implement modernising projects in Mexico can be traced back to the nineteenth-century and have continued throughout ensuing administrations, blurring the differences among policymakers, and indicating that the political class remains the same (Lora and Sánchez 2002).

Linking the PPP to previous administrations deflated its claim to "innovativeness" and a break away from the previous PRI rule. It also raised questions on the purpose of the plan: whether the PPP was created to serve the people of the MAR, or the political classes? The Mexican government has periodically launched so-called development projects in the south-eastern part of Mexico without favourable results. The main difference between the PPP and earlier plans is that the PPP sought to connect Mexico with Central America, whereas the former strategies focused on keeping Guatemalan guerrilla groups from infiltrating Mexico (Bull 2005). A common denominator in these plans, according to Bull (2005), Salazar (2002), Sandoval (2002) and others, is that the infrastructure created as part of the projects does not attend the needs of the local population but focus on the needs of the federal government. For example, the roads built in the era of these precursor plans catered to the needs of the military partaking in border control (Salazar Pérez 2002) and had little impact on agricultural or industrial advancement in the area.

1.5 The "Plan Puebla Panamá"

From the preliminary discussions about the "new development project" for Mexico's south-southeast, the press asked questions about both the feasibility of the project as well as the social acceptance of such an endeavour. The President-Elect's transition team, and later the office of the President, gave few details before publishing the base documents in March 2001. These initial documents were divided into two chapters, the *Capítulo Mexico, Documento Base* and the *Diagnóstico Centroamérica* (*Mexico Chapter, Base Document* and *Central American Diagnosis*), and came under public scrutiny immediately after publication.

The Mexico chapter begins by highlighting the economic differences between the north and south of Mexico and states that the federal government, as a representative of society, is obliged to coordinate and guide national efforts to rid the nation of social injustice and regional inequality (Documento Base 2001). This document points out that Mexico achieved a key position in the global economy through signing FTAs with several nations and has achieved periods of high economic growth. However, it claims that pre-existing regional disparities increased through discriminatory public policies in recent years. Notably, the southeast of Mexico—the states of Campeche, Chiapas, Guerrero, Oaxaca, Puebla, Quintana Roo, Tabasco, Veracruz, and Yucatán—was economically backward when compared to the other 23 Mexican states. The document also asserts that the problems faced in this area of Mexico were structural and therefore, required an integral development programme with a long-term vision to bring about the necessary structural change. It mentions Central America as important to Mexico and as an important partner in implementing the project, particularly as "it is not enough to modernise political practices and development policy if these remain within the national borders.... this is why in a gradual but firm fashion, they [governments] have been encouraging mechanisms to intensify the region's integration processes" (Documento Base 2001: 3).

A compilation of statistics from the National Institute for Statistics and Geographical Indexes (INEGI), and the interpretation of these make up most of the document. It analyses the demography (social distribution, economic activity, indigenous population, and spacial distribution between urban and rural areas), education, health, and economic prospects. The document also describes the economic activities of the region (agriculture, fishing, export capacity), living conditions, infrastructure, transport, and telecommunications. Finally, it discusses matters of energy consumption and production, irrigation capability and across-the-board prices on public sector services. The last third of the document states the mission, vision, scope, SWOT (strengths, weaknesses, opportunities, and threats), objectives, strategies, and criteria for project selection (Documento Base 2001).

Heads of States of Belize, Costa Rica, El Salvador, Guatemala, Honduras, Mexico, Nicaragua, and Panama signed the PPP into existence on 15 June 2001, during a special summit held for the Tuxtla Mechanism in San Salvador. The leaders approved the PPP documents and agreed to accelerate integration over the next 25 years, to improve socioeconomic development between the nine Mexican States and the Central American countries. The main objective of the PPP was to obtain the "potentiality of the human richness of the MAR within a framework of sustainable development that respects cultural diversity"

(Documento Base 2001: 2). With this statement, they agreed that any project included in the plan would follow the principles of sustainable development and respect the ethnic and cultural diversity existing in Mesoamerica. However, the need for significant infrastructure improvements in southeast Mexico and Central America was the main consensus in the documents. Specific issues such as the poor quality of the region's roads and its erratic energy network were identified as the culprits for inhibiting economic advancement.

The IDB approved the eight "Mesoamerican initiatives" (Table 1.1) and promised to help fund several of the proposed projects shortly after the PPP was announced. The Mesoamerican initiatives are: sustainable human development, disaster prevention and mitigation, tourism, commercial exchange, transit integration, energy interconnection, and telecommunications. For the most part, the PPP was not an agreement that considered tariff changes or new investment rules (as most FTAs), although it sought to take better advantage of the current FTAs already in place between Mexico and Central America, and the existing Central American integration processes. The PPP argued that poverty in southeast Mexico and Central America was partially due to the lack of commercial opportunities in the region, as well as a dearth of education and practical training (Documento Base 2001).

In the original organisation, each country was responsible for spearheading one of the Mesoamerican initiatives, but the funding for these initiatives would come from a variety of sources. With an initial budget of US$10 billion, the principal lenders were the IDB, the World Bank, the European Union (EU), the Andean Development Corporation (CAF), the Central American Integration Bank (BCIE), and the development agencies in the United States, Japan, Spain, and other countries. The individual governments in the MAR would also provide funding. By June 2008, Mesoamerican governments had funded 44% of the total expenditure of the PPP (US 3518.5 m) and private investment and international loans as well as non-refundable grants financed 37% (or US 2133.5 m) (Informe Ejecutivo PPP 2008: Anexo). Private companies financed some of the infrastructure costs, as in the energy grids of Mexico and Central America, where one Spanish company (ENDESA) provided US$45.8 m out of the estimated total cost of US$405 m for the project. In such cases, the companies became co-owners of the networks (Interview 3: 2006).

A basic premise of the PPP was securing investment for infrastructure to attract industry and expand natural resource extraction, capitalising on low wages while increasing the integration between Mexico and the Central American countries. Projects involving an elaborate infrastructure of ports, highways, airports, and railways, that would support the development of the petroleum, energy, agricultural, and *maquiladora* industries used up 80% of the original budget of 80,000 million pesos (US $9 billion) leaving social projects to one side (Saldivar 2002). Infrastructure projects included complex road and rail networks to connect the Pacific Ocean to the Gulf of Mexico, regional energy distribution, and communications networks. Several differing lists of projects appeared, resulting in speculation about what would be included in the "official" PPP list. Less than 10% of the budget was assigned to social programmes included in the PPP. Critics feared that the PPP would lead to massive displacement of *campesinos* (subsistence farmers) and indigenous communities, further environmental degradation, and development with the sole goal of exporting for profit rather than as a vehicle for eliminating poverty (see Bartra 2001; Barreda 2002; Saldivar 2002; Call 2002; Villafuerte 2004, 2006).

The plan spurred debate from the offset. Academics from different areas of the social sciences, environmentalists, political reporters, indigenous groups, anti-globalisation groups, and NGOs expressed their mostly opposing, views, first through newspaper articles and websites, and later in journals and books. In 2001, two large non-government-led symposiums were organised in Mexico solely to discuss the recently announced PPP. The first, led by academics, took place at the University of Quintana Roo, and the second, organised by NGOs, civil society organisations, and indigenous groups, took place in Chiapas (the First Mesoamerican Forum). The first gathering produced a series of papers (some were later published in books) and the second resulted in a united declaration from those present at the meeting rejecting the PPP. However, both gatherings were similar in that the documents produced were highly sceptical and critical of the PPP and pointed out many of the underlying implications present in the government documents on the Plan as well as its links to other pre-existing projects. Most publications include mostly information from the Mexican element in the Plan, and its political context and policy. This imbalance is probably due to Mexico initiating the PPP, with Central America added only later, and because initially, there was more information available on the Mexican side of the plan.

Official discourse stated that the PPP was created to remedy inequality in living conditions between the northern and southern states. The Mexican states included in the project house 714 of the nations' 850 poorest municipalities (Presidencia Documento Base 2001). The nine Mexican States involved seem to have more in common with their Central American neighbouring countries than with the rest of the Mexican territory. Their demography, economy, natural resources, cultural heritage, indigenous population, and political involvement are all at similar levels and are somewhat interdependent. Similarities notwithstanding, a closer look at the region shows that this is not a homogeneous area and brings into question some of the arguments put forth in favour of carrying out the project as set out in government discourse.

Issues of debate surged around the PPP once some of the proposals included were linked to other projects in the area, such as the Mesoamerican Biological Corridor (MBC) and the Central American Integration System (SICA). As the discussions became more controversial, it was clear that the PPP was not an isolated or new project, but instead a section of a network of interrelated regional projects covering the area from southern Mexico down to Panama. Although some of the grievances that were expressed by the protesters should have been aimed at other projects or regional arrangements (such as the numerous FTAs signed between the countries involved), the PPP was perceived as the culprit of furthering unpopular proposals.

However, most groups polled or interviewed during my research did not want to see an end to tackling problems at the regional level, but rather a change in tactics. Wendy Call, of Global Exchange, states that "some [of the resistance groups] believe the PPP can be made more sustainable and humane via policy advocacy and engagement; the majority, however, feel the scheme should be rejected outright and call for its replacement with an alternative development plan that is regionally focused and not aimed at integration with northern markets" (Call 2002: 5). Many of those who adamantly opposed the plan, hoped for a replacement, not a cancellation. This was one of the core findings of the initial research leading up to the writing of this book. Based on a survey and interviews, I found that non-government groups prefer a regional approach to tackle the problems in Mesoamerica. The second core finding of my research is related to the governance mechanisms. The multilevel governance framework was introduced as a concept in

Mesoamerica through EU technical support and OECD governance reports. Recommendations from these two organisations translated into the creation of structures for decentralising government and incorporating other stakeholders into the decision-making processes. However, in practice, power was not devolved or shared among the levels of government, nor were other actors included in designing proposals or in decision-making. Even after much technical support, the panorama observed was as follows:

1. Government departments at different levels do not share information, have weak communication mechanisms, and are more interested in their own agenda than in the "bigger picture."
2. Government at the lower levels (local) was more likely to work together with other participants as they have fewer resources and a closer relationship to the people.
3. Local government was also the one most likely to be held accountable to the population.
4. Non-governmental actors do not always trust the government; the participatory mechanisms that were put in place were viewed as a masquerade to satisfy external donors and not as a means for actual participation in project design and policymaking.

However, I was encouraged to look at the micro-regions that had formed through central/regional government initiatives or the effort of local governments and other sectors. These micro-regions showed that horizontal governance is possible and can strengthen the regionalisation process.

The PPP was not implemented fully and did not achieve projected results; after seven years, a less ambitious project, *Proyecto Mesoamérica* replaced it. However, it did make four important contributions: first, an awareness of the region as a new construct; second, increased political contact between Mexico, Central America, and Colombia with a renewed sense of cooperation; third, an awareness of the difficulties of implementing a development project (OECD 2005); finally, an organised group of civil society and NGOs through the periodic Mesoamerican forums, that continued until 2011 and then dissolved, but left a legacy and a loose framework for future cooperation (Table 1.2).

Table 1.2 Proyecto Mesoamerica

The Mesoamerican Integration and Development Project is the regional integration and development mechanism that enhances complementarity and cooperation in order to implement projects that result in concrete benefits for societies in terms of economic growth, interconnectivity and social development. The PM provides the space to generate agreements and establish priorities from a regional integration perspective. The PM was launched in 2008 during the 10th Summit of the Tuxtla Mechanism for Dialogue and Coordination and as the successor to the Plan Puebla Panama. The Mesoamerican Project's main trait is the execution of specific regional impact programs

The projects are divided into two axes or pillars: Economic and Social

Economic axis or pillar includes the following lines of action:

1. Transport
    a. Highways and infrastructure (RICAM)
2. Energy
    a. SIEPAC system
    b. Biofuels and sustainable energy sources
3. Trade facilitation
    a. Modernization of customs systems and border crossings
    b. Competitiveness indexes
4. Telecommunications
    a. integration of networks

Social axis or pillar includes the following lines of action

1. Environmental Sustainability
    a. Mesoamerican environmental sustainability strategy
    b. Mesoamerican Biological Corridor
2. Public Health
    a. Mesoamerican Health initiative public–private partnership
3. Natural Disaster risk management
    a. Mesoamerican territorial information system
4. Housing
    a. Development of social housing in Central America
5. Food security (*included in 2015*)
    a. Support for family farms
    b. Distribution of seeds
    c. Rainwater collection for farm use

Source ABC of the Mesoamerican Project leaflet. Complemented with information from www.proyectomesoamerica.org (Accessed in January 2019)

1.6 Chapter Summaries

Chapter 1

In this chapter, I provide an overview of the MAR and the PPP to contextualise the findings of the research. I describe the regional setting and precursors to the PPP and give an overview of the PPP itself. I introduce the main ideas that I will discuss in the following chapters and demonstrate how the case of the PPP can be used to extract insights for the study of regionalism, development, and governance in Mesoamerica.

Chapter 2

In Chapter 2, I introduce and discuss approaches to regionalism and include the concept of governance—particularly multilevel governance—as an essential variable to this case study. Using the New Regionalism approach as a guiding framework, I discuss the relationship between regionalism and regionalisation in Mesoamerica. I bring in Governance as a variable, and explain the governance analytical framework. This chapter argues that governance is a critical component in the relationship between regionalism and regionalisation in Mesoamerica, a claim that will be supported through the evidence presented in Chapters 4–6. In Chapter 2, I also explain the methodology used in the initial research (a doctoral dissertation) and how it evolved into this book.

Chapter 3

In Chapter 3, I recount the main issues and controversies that detonated in Mesoamerica as a result of the announcement of the PPP.

I divided the chapter into two sections: underlying debates and issues. The first section, I discuss how some academics contested the idea of "Mesoamerica" as a region I also demonstrate that there was a debate whether the PPP should be considered regionalism. In the second section of the chapter, I focus on prominent issues that have been at the forefront of the debates on the MAR and its project. These issues are divided into (a) Free Trade, (b) Development, (c) Alternative Development, (d) The Environment, and (e) Security, although many of these overlap in their scope.

These issues provided the basis which guided field research inquiring into the underlying reasons as to why groups opposed the project, and what they had been expecting prior to the launch. The heated opinions uncovered evidence the geopolitical importance of Mesoamerica, as well as the impact of US policy, and the involvement that the United States has had in the region. Moreover, this book acknowledges the evidence of external interests due to the geopolitical importance of the region and factors them in as essential elements of analysis. Debates surrounding the PPP and *Proyecto Mesoamérica* highlight the importance of regional security both in Mesoamerica and to external actors.

The issues I discuss in this chapter underscore that governance does not rest solely on government but includes other sectors as well. This chapter shows the heated criticism of the PPP, as it ignored pressing issues for communities and favoured projects that would mostly benefit large companies. This convinced critics that the PPP was a mechanism for commercial interests, hiding behind the veil of a development programme.

Chapter 4

In Chapter 4, I analyse government-led regionalism in the MAR, reviewing some of the main intergovernmental regional projects. In lieu of an in-depth description of each of the projects, the chapter gives a brief overview and then explains how these projects interacted with the PPP at the regional level. In some instances, the PPP had no more influence than increasing the presence of Mexico in Central American regional mechanisms; in others, it raised conflicts of interests, and in others, there was mutual neglect. Not only did the PPP receive bad publicity, but it also caused other projects in the region to be questioned and scrutinised in a way they had never been before. Many changes were made at the institutional level throughout the duration of the PPP as a direct response to regional governance issues; however, many of these issues should have been anticipated or at least considered when the institutions were designed. Finally, in this chapter, I convey a brief description of the institutional structural changes at the regional level in the PPP's replacement, *Proyecto Mesoamérica*, and review the different regional spaces; economic, trade, development, environment, and security.

Chapter 5

Chapter 5 explores the relationship of the PPP to government institutions at the regional, national, sub-national, and local level (vertical governance). Most of Chapter 5 is based on the seminars and interviews obtained during personal field research between 2006 and 2008; however, I include recent examples and information to show that the observations are relevant some years later. In this section, I note that it is not purely a government versus non-government issue, but that intergovernmental relations within the regional projects and the MAR limited the successful implementation of the projects.

My analysis shows that *even if* the anti-government opposition were removed, and was left only with the present government structures, it would be difficult to implement projects with the proposed ambition and scope of the PPP. My research also uncovers that the different government entities follow their own agendas and oppose other levels of government.

Chapter 6

In Chapter 6, I focus on governance at the horizontal level. There has been a rise of civil society and non-governmental associations opposing regional proposals, particularly those related to mega-infrastructure projects. These groups emerged out of the frustration felt by people in the region when the promised investment failed to improve their economic and living situations but, instead, displaced people with little or no compensation. They argue that they had no input towards the approved projects and that these projects only benefit big business and those already prospering, harming those that are in a situation of poverty and are vulnerable to displacement.

In the same way, the chambers of commerce and small and medium enterprise associations that I interviewed confirmed that they were not considered when regional trade arrangements or infrastructure projects were discussed. Only a handful of big business was consulted for this purpose. They were also not aware of the tools that, supposedly, had been implemented for their benefit. Both the chambers of commerce and the regional trade union representatives that were interviewed were unaware of the existence of the "Mesoamerican Competitiveness Council" in the PPP, which was designed to help small and medium business to upgrade their methods of production so that they would be able to compete with incoming products and improve their chances of becoming exporters.

Examples from the different sectors form the argument that the mechanisms for consultation and feedback broke down. Many groups and associations felt that their only remaining option was to obstruct the reforms and projects to keep them from being implemented. Disillusioned with the government, these groups did not try to provide alternatives to government proposals or let them know what changes would need to take place before they would accept a proposal. The result was that neither governmental proposals nor alternatives were implemented. The results of a survey sent out to NGOs in the region showed that they are concerned with human development issues in the region and that these need to be addressed over those concerning trade and infrastructure. It also indicated that NGOs wanted to be included in the decision-making process and the design of development policy. In general, the concept of regional cooperation is well-received, although not in its current form. Further interviewing of NGOs and community groups brought out the interesting point that they tend to have a good rapport with local governments and have successfully completed conjoint projects. Mistrust is mostly aimed at state and national government. As I argued in Chapter 4, the research suggests that local government is the one given the least amount of power, and yet has the highest accountability to voters.

In the final chapter of the study, I review the areas of regionalism, development, and governance and revisit my research's most important conclusions.

I argue that although the Plan Puebla Panamá finished its seven-year term with a low implementation record, and the results were disappointing considering the initial optimism and hype; it should not be dismissed as a complete failure. This book highlights many useful insights that can be drawn from the implementation of the Plan Puebla Panamá.

Bibliography

Acta que institucionaliza el Mecanismo del Plan Puebla-Panamá. 2004. Accessed 3 March 2006.

Alvarez, Alejandro, Andrés Barreda, and Armando Bartra (eds.). 2002. *Economía Política del Plan Puebla Panamá*. México: Editorial Itaca.

Álvarez Béjar, Alejandro. 2002a. El Plan Puebla-Panamá en el contexto de la integración hemisférica Política y Cultura num. 18 otoño, 83–105. UNAM.

Álvarez Béjar, Alejandro. 2002b. The Puebla-Panama Plan: ¿Development of a Region or Multinational Enclave?

Álvarez Béjar, Alejandro. 2002c. Sies Factores Estructurales que explican la estrategia del Plan Puebla Panama. In *Economía Política del Plan Puebla Panamá*, ed. Alejandro Álvarez Béjar, Andrés Barreda Marín, y Armando Bartra. México: Editorial Itaca.

Barreda Marín, Andrés. 2001. Los Peligros del Plan Puebla Panama. In *Mesoamerica: Los Ríos Profundos. Alternativas Plebeyas al Plan Puebla Panamà*, ed. Armando Bartra. Mexico: RMALC/El Atajo Ediciones/Instituto "Maya", A.C.

Barreda Marín, Andrés. 2002. Los Objetivos del Plan Puebla Panamá. In *Economía Política del Plan Puebla Panamá*, ed. Alejandro Álvarez Béjar, Andrés Barreda Marín, y Armando Bartra. México: Editorial Itaca.

Bartra, Armando (ed.). 2001. SUR, Megaplanes y utopías en la América equinoccial. *Mesoamerica: Los Ríos Profundos. Alternativas Plebeyas al Plan Puebla Panamà*. México, D.F.: RMALC/El Atajo Ediciones/Instituto "Maya", A.C.

Bull, Benedicte. 2005. Between Bush and Bolivar: Change and Continuity in the Remaking of Mesoamerica. In *The Political Economy of Regions and Regionalisms*, ed. Morten Bøås, Marianne H. Marchand, and Timothy M. Shaw. Houndmills, Basingstoke, Hampshire: Palgrave Macmillan.

Call, Wendy. 2002. *Plan Puebla-Panama: Done Deal or Emerging Flashpoint*. April 9.

Carr, III Archie. 2002. A Plait of Three Colors. *Americas* 54 (July–August): 64. http://www.questia.com/.

Carranza, Mario Esteban. 2000. *South American Free Trade Area or Free Trade Area of the Americas? Open Regionalism and the Future of Regional Economic Integration in South America*. Burlington, VT: Ashgate.

CCAD-MBC. 2003. *Estrategia regional para la conservación y uso sostenible de la biodiversidad en Mesoamerica (ERB)*. Comisión Centroamericana de Ambiente y Desarrollo El Salvador.

Chanona, Alejandro. 2002. Procesos de Integración en el marco del Plan Puebla-Panamá. In *Lectura Crítica del Plan Puebla Panamá*, Eduardo Andrés Sandoval Forero, y Robinson Salazar Perez, coordinadores. Libros en Red.

Chomsky, Noam. 1985. *Turning the Tide: U.S. Intervention in Central America and the Struggle for Peace*. Boston: South End Press.

Coordinación General del Plan Puebla-Panamá (CG-PPP). 2002. *Informe de Avances y Perspectivas Plan Puebla-Panamá Junio*. Mexico: INEGI.

Declaración Extraordinaria. 2001. *Declaración Conjunta de la Cumbre extraordinaria de los paises integrantes del Mecanismo de Diálogo y Concertación de Tuxtla*. http://sieca.org.gt/publico/OACUERDOS/DECLARACION_CONJUNTA_DE_LA.

Hettne, Björn. 2000. The New Regionalism: A Prologue. In *National Perspectives on the New Regionalism in the South*, ed. Björn Hettne, Andreas Inotal, and Osvaldo Sunkel. London: McMillan Press Ltd.

Hiernaux-Nicolas, Daniel. 2002. El Plan Puebla Panamá: ¿una nueva visión del desarrollo regional? In *Lectura Crítica del Plan Puebla Panamá*, Eduardo Andrés Sandoval Forero, y Robinson Salazar Perez, coordinadores. Libros en Red.

Labrecque, Marie France. 2005. Cultural Appreciation and Economic Depreciation of the Mayas of Northern Yucatán Mexico. *Latin American Perspectives* 32 (143) (July): 87–105.

Lopez-Calva, Luis F., and Nora Lustig. 2003. *Social Protection and Inclusive Trade: Strengthening the Sources of Convergence Within FTAA*. Universidad de Las Americas Working Paper No. 2003-06.

Lora Cam, Jorge, and Jose Luis Sánchez R. 2002. La recolonización de Angelopolis, el TLC, el Plan Puebla Panamá y el ALCA. In *Lectura Crítica del Plan Puebla Panamá*, ed. Eduardo Andrés Sandoval Forero y Robinson Salazar Pérez, coordinadores. Libros en Red.

OECD Territoral Reviews. 2005. *The Mesoamerican Region: Southeastern Mexico and Central America*. OECD Publishing. http://www.sourceoecd.org/regionaldevelopment/9264021914; http://www.sourceoecd.org/governance/9264021914.

Office of Evaluation and Oversight (OVE). 2008. Interamerican Bank. *Evaluation of IDB's Support to the Plan Puebla Panama Initiative*, August. https://publications.iadb.org/en/evaluation-idbs-support-plan-puebla-panama-initiative.

Ornelas, Delgado Jaime. 2002. El Plan Puebla Panamá y la globalización neoliberal. In *Lectura Crítica del Plan Puebla Panamá*, ed. Eduardo Andrés Sandoval Forero y Robinson Salazar Pérez, coordinadores. Libros en Red.

Payne, Anthony, and Andrew Gamble. 1996. Introduction: The Political Economy of Regionalism and World Order. In *Regionalism and World Order*, ed. Andrew Gamble and Anthony Payne. London: Macmillan.

Pearce, Jenny. 2004. DEBATE Collective Action or Public Participation? Complementary or Contradictory Democratisation Strategies in Latin America? *Bulletin of Latin American Research* 23 (4): 483–504.

Phillips, Nicola. 2004. The Americas. In *The New Regional Politics of Development*, ed. Anthony Payne. Basingstoke: Palgrave Macmillan.

Pisani, Michael J., and Wayne A. Label. 2003. Plan Puebla-Panama: Toward FTAA or Regionalism? *Business Horizons* 46 (5) (September–October): 33–40.

Preciado Coronado, Jaime, and Aarón Villarruel Mora. 2006. México y Centroamérica: hegemonía mundial, resistencias y visibilidad social. In *Geoeconomía y Geopolítica en el área del Plan Puebla Panamá*, ed. Daniel Villafuerte Solis and Xochitl Leyva Solano. México: Editorial Miguel Angel Porrúa.

Presidencia de la República. 2001. *Plan Puebla-Panamá Capítulo México.* Documento Base.

Rocha, Alberto. 2006. La geopolítica de México en Centroamérica: ¿una hegemonía regional? In *Geoeconomía y Geopolítica en el área del Plan Puebla Panamá*, ed. Daniel Villafuerte Solis and Xochitl Leyva Solano. México: Editorial Miguel Angel Porrúa.

Rubio, Luis. 2004. Democratic Politics in Mexico: New Complexities. In *Mexico Under Fox*, ed. Luis Rubio and Susan Kaufman Purcell. Boulder: Lynne Rienner.

Salazar Pérez, Robinson. 2002. El vinculo militar del Plan Colombia y el Plan Puebla Panamá. In *Lectura Crítica del Plan Puebla Panamá*, ed. Eduardo Andrés Sandoval Forero y Robinson Salazar Pérez, coordinadores. Libros en Red.

Saldivar, V. Americo. 2002. El Plan Puebla Panama: Una Locomotora sin Vagones de Segunda. In *Lectura Crítica del Plan Puebla Panamá*, ed. Eduardo Andrés Sandoval Forero and Robinson Salazar Pérez, coordinadores. Libros en Red.

Sandoval Forero, Eduardo Andrés. 2002. El Plan Puebla Panamá y la globalización de los indios. In *Lectura Crítica del Plan Puebla Panamá*, ed. Eduardo Andrés Sandoval Forero and Robinson Salazar Pérez, coordinadores. Libros en Red.

Sandoval Forero, Eduardo Andrés y Robinson Salazar Pérez. 2002. *Lectura Crítica del Plan Puebla Panamá*. Libros en Red.

Sandoval Palacios, Juan Manuel. 2001. El Plan Puebla Panamá como regulador de la migración laboral mesoamericana. In *Mesoamerica: Los Ríos Profundos. Alternativas Plebeyas al Plan Puebla Panamà*, ed. Armando Bartra. Mexico: RMALC/El Atajo Ediciones/Instituto "Maya", A.C.

Söderbaum, Fredrik. 2016. *Rethinking Regionalism*. New York: Palgrave Macmillan.

Tedesco, Laura. 2004. Democracy in Latin America: Issues of Governance in the Southern Cone. *Bulletin of Latin American Research* 23 (1) (January): 30–42.

Toly, Noah J. 2004. Globalization and the Capitalization of Nature: A Political Ecology of Biodiversity in Mesoamerica. *Bulletin of Science, Technology & Society* 24 (1) (February): 47–54.

Villafuerte Solis, Daniel. 2004. Mas allá del Plan Puebla-Panamá: del TLCAN al ALCA. *Comercio Exterior* 54 (4) (abril): 283–284. revistas.bancomext.gob.mx/rce/magazines/65/2/villa0404.pdf.

Villafuerte Solis, Daniel. 2006. Integraciones en el Norte y Sur de México: del NAFTA al CAFTA. In *Geoeconomía y Geopolítica en el área del Plan Puebla Panamá*, ed. Daniel Villafuerte Solis and Xochitl Leyva Solano. México: Editorial Miguel Angel Porrúa.

Woodward, Ralph Lee, Jr. 1985. *Central America: A Nation Divided*. London: Oxford University Press.

Woodward, Ralph Lee, Jr. 1988. *Central America: Historical Perspectives on the Contemporary Crises*. New York: Greenwood Press.

Interviews

3. Director of Integration, Ministerio de Relaciones Exteriores Guatemala, 25 September 2006, Guatemala City.
16. Regional Director of CODA international, El Salvador (Project liaison with Perulapía), 6 September 2006, San Salvador, Perulapía.
23. Director of International Economic Section, Departamento de Estudios Económicos y Sociales, Fundación Salvadoreña para el Desarrollo Económico y Social. FUSADES, 5 September 2006, San Salvador.
27. PPP initiatives coordinator, Oficina local del Plan Puebla Panamá en El Salvador, Ministerio de Relaciones Exteriores El Salvador, 5 September 2006, San Salvador.
38. AMAP Director, Mexican Association for the Self-Determination of Peoples (AMAP), 22 August 2006, Mexico City.
44. Full day meeting and visit with the local government of San Bartolomé de la Perulapía municipality in El Salvador, Mayor Guillermo Sanchez, and 5 other local government representatives. All those involved in the meeting were members of the FSLN political party, 6 September 2006, El Salvador.
46. Director CODA international (Sessions at Perulapía recorded, informal background conversations not recorded), 5 and 6 September 2006, El Salvador.

Conferences Attended

"Gestión integrada de programas sociales y autoridad social: experiencias latinoamericanas", Dr. Rolando Franco, Facultad Latinoamericana de Ciencias Sociales y Centro de Estudios para el Futuro FLACSO, Tuesday 17 October 2006, San José, Costa Rica, 10:00 a.m.

"Gobernabilidad Democrática y Nuevas Orientaciones Políticas en Costa Rica: escenarios a partir de las elecciones 2006" organised by Centro de Estudios Políticos, Maestría Centroamericana de Ciencias Políticas, UCR, Facultad Latinoamericana de Ciencias Sociales y Centro de Estudios para el Futuro FLACSO, 17 October 2006, 8:00 p.m.

"Indigenous People in Mexico" presented by Lynda Martinez del Campo Fonda del Claustro, Mexico City, 17 March 2007.

"Multi-level Governance and Systems of Economic Organisation' Workshop", 17–19 May 2007, University of Warwick, Scarman House.

CHAPTER 2

Theoretical Framework

The previous chapter introduced the MAR—its challenges and influences; the PPP—giving an overview of its seven-year existence; and the transition to Proyecto Mesoamerica. This chapter presents the theoretical framework that supports the assumption made in the previous section: that governance structures in Mesoamerica were responsible for the failure to implement the PPP regional development project, particularly the social agenda. It is important to contextualise this case within the study of regions and regionalism since it can provide insight on the making and unmaking of regions, and what makes them consolidate into more cohesive polities (Söderbaum 2003).

Several authors categorised the study of regionalism into "old/classical" and "new" regionalism, a distinction that no longer makes as much sense. Söderbaum, for example, considers that although "it is plausible to distinguish between old and new regionalism in a temporal, empirical, as well as a theoretical sense…I find the identification of new patterns of regionalism (coexisting with older forms) more relevant" (Söderbaum 2016: 4). "Old" regionalism has not disappeared; interviews with officials in the SICA clearly showed the prevalence of the "old" regionalism integration models in the objectives and policymaking for Central American integration. And considering the concept "new" diminishes its significance when something "newer" takes place. In the 2018 context, we observe new paradigms in regionalism: the forthcoming exit of the United Kingdom from the European Union, the renegotiation

A. Gamboa, *Regional Integration, Development, and Governance in Mesoamerica*,
https://doi.org/10.1007/978-3-030-25350-9_2

or possible elimination of NAFTA, and restructuring of other regional organisations are sure to shake up regional studies, where the tendency to increase and deepen might shift to a tendency to break apart.

This book sets out to explore the relationship between regionalism and governance or governance structures in the MAR. Many authors note the connection between regionalism and governance, such as connections implying global governance (Hveem 2003) or economic market governance (Phillips 2002). This case study shows how governance structures can shape a project headed at the regional level, through its implementation at the national and local levels. It also reflects the increasing importance that non-government actors have in policymaking and implementation. In other words, regionalism can shape governance (through the creation of institutions), but governance shapes regionalisation.

The case of the PPP exemplifies how the various "regions" (developmental, environmental, security, trade, etc.) of Mesoamerica have matured differently. Again, due to the governance structures, certain aspects of the PPP were implemented while others were left behind or abandoned. The current governance structures in Mesoamerica evolved from several roots: first, they evolved from colonial structures to those set up after independence (retaining remnants of the colonial institutions); second, from external sources such as the post-conflict peace accords as well as structural reforms encouraged in the late 1980s and early 1990s; third, from the technical support, offered to countries transitioning back to democracy; and fourth, from reform requirements placed by international lending institutions and other regional institutions they wished to join or engage in trade (i.e., Inter-American Development Bank, World Bank, NAFTA, etc.).

This chapter discusses the key terms used throughout the book—most notably, "regions," "regionalism(s)," and "regionalisation"—and contextualise Mesoamerican regionalism. A framework of analysis explained by Hettne and Söderbaum (1998, 2000, 2008), often called the New Regionalism Approach (NRA), serves as a point of departure. Through their understanding of "regionness,"[1] it is possible to assess if the MAR

[1] Söderbaum (2016) states "Regionness is not intended as a parsimonious theory. It should be understood as a heuristic and conceptual tool for improving our thinking about the ways whereby multidimensional regions are made and unmade by different agents and institutions" (p. 14).

deepened in regionness during the seven years of the PPP. It draws out from the literature issues that are of interest to regional studies: governance (particularly multilevel governance), developmental regionalism, security regionalism, and micro regionalism.

2.1 R Regions, Regionalism, Regionalisation

Although the "regional" terms sometimes vary from author to author, they build on the same principle: that each one of these relates to something greater or forms part of something larger (Hettne 2000a: xix). Söderbaum (2003) divides regions into three categories. He refers to the historical definition of the space between the national and the local within particular states as a *micro-region*, although he acknowledges that these could also manifest cross-border between different countries. The larger territorial units or subsystems between the state and the global level are *macro-regions*. He then goes on to define the in-between point between these two as the *meso-region* or "mid-range state or non-state arrangements and processes" (Söderbaum 2003: 6). Hook and Kearns (1999) made similar distinctions with different terminology: *regional*, *sub-regional*, and *sub-subregional*. So, "the Americas" is relative to Global, "Latin America" is relative to the Americas, "Mesoamerica" is relative to Latin America, and within Mesoamerica, there can be a further breaking-down into cross-border micro-regions. Even though each of the processes mentioned can be studied independently, it is the relationship among these, from the global to the micro-regional, which generates particular interest (Breslin and Hook 2002).

Defining the scope of a specific region (whether macro or micro) in itself can be complicated; regions continually change so it is a "region in the making" (Hettne 2000a, 2003). A region does not just exist in and of itself; it is determined by a conscious process since "regions do not have fixed borders, instead they are constantly being reassessed by political actors who negotiate who is 'in' and who is 'out'" (Grugel and Hout 1999: 9). As Breslin states, "regions are formed by people; they are politically and socially constructed" (Breslin 2010: 38) so a region will shift and change according to the will of its members, as well as the changing world context.

For this book, these terms are best clarified and applied according to the following definitions: "Regions" are groups of nations or parts of nations that are identified through a common special area, political or economic alliance; "regionalism" is a programme or an ideology often associated with a specific project that includes the deliberate effort from the governmental level to deepen the economic or political relationship between the subscribing parties; and "regionalisation" is the actual process of increasing exchange, contact, and coordination resulting in an improved economic or political integration. The distinction between these concepts is of relevance to this study, however, the emphasis is on the relationship between them.

Regionalisation can result from regionalism—for example, the removal of barriers to transnational transactions by the EEC and the EU—or it can occur spontaneously at a non-governmental level, through the cross-border activities of civil societies, corporations, migratory patterns, and so on. In the same fashion, regionalisation could lead to the creation of a regionalism, whereby highly regionalised groups demand institutional frameworks to formalise their activities. Finally, "regionness" refers to the degree to which a region is interconnected and to the extent that it is perceived to constitute a coherent unit—particularly by those within the region itself (though external identification can also be necessary) (Gamble and Payne 1996; Hettne 2000b; Hveem 2003). Regionalism is sometimes expressed as being the "formal" or *de jure* region, whereas regionalisation would be the *de facto* or "real" region (Higgot and Reich 1998). Hettne considers that a region will increase in "regionness" and become a more unified polity as the formal and real regions converge (Hettne 2003).

Under these parameters, the PPP (and its successor Proyecto Mesoamerica), is considered as "regionalism" since it was created through government-led initiative. Similarly, other "formal" projects that share the same space of the PPP (though not necessarily the same borders) such as the SICA or the Mesoamerican Biological Corridor (Chapter 4 focuses on the interaction between formal regional projects) are also "regionalisms." The PPP did contribute to some regionalisation in the MAR, seen through the linking of projects at the regional level and intergovernmental cooperation. However, regionalisation also manifests through the networking of non-government sectors, particularly the NGOs and Civil Society groups (these will be developed further in Chapter 6). Regionalisation also can be seen through the networking of workers' unions, chambers of commerce, and specific trade groups throughout Mesoamerica.

Crucially, some of the regional networks emerged not as part of PPP initiatives but emerged parallel to or in opposition to the PPP proposals.

The Mesoamerican forums discussed in Chapter 6 formed in direct opposition to the PPP, and as the PPP expanded to include Colombia, the forums also expanded. Some networks in the MAR predate the PPP (workers' unions and chambers of commerce networks), however, others were created post-PPP (legislators, municipal government forums, association of the southern Mexican states' governments) to tackle issues that were not being (in their view) adequately dealt with by the regional project. All these networks help the region to become more closely linked in some ways; however, the disaggregate measure of this phenomenon questions the future of a region where regional actors are all pulling in different directions without integrating into the regions' modes of governance. As in most cases of regional integration, the relationship between regionalism and regionalisation is not a simple one-way process (in either direction). Therefore, this study identifies governance as an important element in the dual relationship between regionalism and regionalisation.

The Mesoamerican Region[2]

Mesoamerica is an example of the shifting region since it is a geographic area that shares a historical, ethnic, and social connection. However, this geographic area has changed throughout the centuries. In pre-Columbian times, archaeology shows that Central America and a large part of Mexico (reaching up to the Central States), where the Aztec and Nahua dynasties lived, were tied through trade with the Maya empire. The Mayas existed in three Mexican States (Chiapas, Yucatan, and Quintana Roo), Guatemala, Belize, and Honduras, but they mostly shared the Mayan language and culture, without having strong political ties

[2]For further reading on Latin American and Hemispheric Integration, see Carranza, Mario Esteban (2000) *South American Free Trade Area or Free Trade Area of the Americas? Open Regionalism and the Future of Regional Economic Integration in South America*, Ashgate; Blejer, Mario I. (1984) Economic Integration: An Analytical Overview in Inter-American Development Bank, *Social and Economic Progress in Latin America, Special Report: Economic Integration*, Washington, DC, pp. 5–34; Devlin, Robert, and Estevadeordal Antoni (2001) What's New in the New Regionalism in the Americas? In *Regional Integration in Latin America and the Caribbean: The Political Economy of Open Regionalism*, ed. Victor Bulmer Thomas, University of London, London; Phillips, Nicola (2003) Hemispheric Integration and Subregionalism in the Americas, *International Affairs* 79 (2): 327–349.

(Woodward 1985). During the 300 years of colonialism after the Spanish Conquest, Mexico and the Kingdom of Guatemala (part of modern Mexico and Central America, not including Panama), shifted borders depending on the political influence of the local *encomendados* (large land owners with political responsibilities) with the Spanish Crown, though they were always under the government of the "New Spain" based in Mexico City (Woodward 1985).

Borders shifted once more with independence from Spain; Central America formed part of the independent Mexican Empire under Iturbide during its brief 11-month existence. Then it seceded, with only Chiapas (which had been part of the Kingdom of Guatemala) remaining as part of Mexico. In the 1800s, there was an attempt to unite into a Central American Federation, but conflict with the British interests in Belize, coupled with disagreement over power structures, resulted in regrouping into independent states. Panama's independence from Colombia in 1903 again reshaped the region, particularly once the Panama Canal was built and had a significant impact on trade routes and the economy of the area. The modern Mesoamerica, as was defined by the PPP in 2001, included the nine south-eastern Mexican States and seven Central American countries; in 2006, it expanded once more to accommodate Colombia and the Dominican Republic in 2009.

2.2 Approaches to New Regionalism

The term "new regionalism" as used in international relations/international politics was coined during the 1990s after noting that the wave of regionalism that was taking place throughout the world "warranted a new type of analysis which went beyond classical integration theory and emphasised the social, political and cultural dimensions" (Hettne 2000a: xviii). For Mistry (2003: 136) "as economic integration cedes to regionalism, the analytical constructs provided by earlier theories of integration become obsolete, they need to be replaced by a more holistic theory of regionalism." Several volumes[3] thoroughly explained the differences between the "old" and "new" regionalism, highlighting that the new regionalism was multidimensional, the processes included efforts from "below" and "within," and were taking place in a multipolar global order

[3] See Hettne et al. (1999, 2000a, b), Söderbaum and Shaw (2003), Gamble and Payne (1996), and Fawcett and Hurrell (1995).

rather than the pre-existing bipolar world (Hettne 2000a: xx). Also, as Marchand et al. (1999) and Hettne and Söderbaum (2000) point out, regionalism should be used in the plural "regionalisms" since they observe varieties of patterns of regionalism, each distinctive from the other.

Söderbaum (2005, 2016) uses Cox's fundamental distinctions on theory to divide the theoretical approaches to his dichotomisation of the study of new regionalism into (a) problem-solving approaches and (b) critical approaches. He classifies neorealism, liberal institutionalism, and liberal economic integration as problem-solving approaches, and subdivides critical approaches into world order analyses, the NRA, and the new regionalisms/new realist approach (Söderbaum 2005: 221–222). With this distinction, Söderbaum contends that the problem-solving approaches were designed mostly for the study of core regions, mainly Western Europe, and therefore reflect scenarios that might not be applicable for regions in other parts of the world (Söderbaum 2005). In contrast, he considers that the critical approaches offer "significantly more capital for the study of areas of the world that have customarily been excluded and ignored in the debate" (Söderbaum 2005: 222).

The construction or building of a region, beyond its geographical territory, means that there is some form of coherence on a political, social, or economic scale. Building on the idea that regions are dynamic and continuously changing, it is then understood the "collective perception of identities and meanings with blurred and ever shifting boundaries" (Väyrynen 2003: 27) shape regions. In this sense, there is no beginning nor end, but instead, have a constant activity that may not even be heading in the same direction. Bull (2005: 14) states that:

> Regions are constructed, deconstructed and reconstructed – intentionally or unintentionally – in processes of global transformation. The construction of a region may give a certain spatial configuration a higher 'degree of regionness', understood as the relative convergence of dimensions such as cultural affinity, political regimes, security arrangements and economic policies.

However, the instrumental use of regionalism can be to promote specific outcomes, where actors assign functions to select units; these functions are not intrinsic, but relative to particular interests (Väyrynen 2003: 27). Emmanuel Adler has further advocated the concept of "cognitive regions" (Adler 1994: 41), underlining the significance of citizens' sense of regional awareness and identity as members of that region. This idea highlights a notion of a common culture, history, beliefs, and a common enemy, or at least what Hurrell defines as "some external 'other'" (Hurrell 1995: 41), i.e., a security threat or cultural or social obstacle. Although some might argue that constructivism puts a lesser emphasis on the intensely economic or political relations among states within a region; Wendt (1994) comments: "Constructivists are interested in the construction of identities and interests, and as such, take a more sociological than economic approach to systemic theory" (Wendt 1994: 385). Wendt goes on to say that states are "constructed by historically contingent interactions" (Wendt 1994: 385), rather than formed on more independent bases.

A consensus does not exist on the nature of regions; nevertheless, three points extracted from the literature are useful in framing this study. *First*, rethinking the role of regions at various levels of the world political economy. These levels can be the world system (order), the level of inter-regional relations, and the internal pattern of a single region (Hettne et al. 1999; Bøås et al. 2003: 203). The interaction among the different levels of region (from micro to macro) provides an abundant element for analysis as to the complex processes that take place (Gamble and Payne 1996; Breslin and Hook 2002). *Second* the state, although still an important actor (authors differ as to the degree), is not the only actor shaping the region (see Shaw 2002; Söderbaum 2003; Marchand et al. 1999); instead there is a complex "cocktail of state actors, interstate and global institutions, and non-state actors (especially multinational corporations, emerging civil society organisations, and NGOs) that have an effect upon regional outcomes….to this long list of potentially important actors we should add sub-national and local authorities" (Breslin et al. 2002: 17). *Third*, it is essential to acknowledge the coexistence of multiple forms of region (Breslin et al. 2002: 17).

I framed my research using Hettne and Söderbaum's NRA.[4] In its initial stages, the NRA over-emphasised the role of globalisation in contemporary regionalism. In retrospect, Hettne (2003) considers that state involvement should be more prominent, not that it should become once again entirely inward-looking as in previous regional analysis, however, it should be balanced. When using the NRA with a further social constructivist element to understand the regionality/regionness of Mesoamerica, it is crucial to give equal weight to the external and internal influential factors. Also, it is

[4] In some instances, it has also been called the New Regionalism Theory (NRT) (Hettne and Söderbaum 2000) but most continue to refer to it as the NRA.

essential to look at both regionalising actors and the governance structure. Another attribute of this approach is it considers that regionalisation can proceed unevenly along the dimensions of "new regionalism" with degrees of integration differing across the areas of economics, politics, culture, and security (Hettne and Söderbaum 2000: 462).

Hettne and Söderbaum (2000), based the NRA on three metatheoretical postulates: (i) global social theory, in favour of a marriage between individual strands in development theory and political economy; (ii) social constructivism, where "interests, motives, ideas and identities are not exogenously given but socially construed by reflective actors, capable of adapting to challenges imposed by the actions of others and changing contexts" (Hettne and Söderbaum 2000: 460); and (iii) comparative theory "within a globalised framework, i.e., to look upon a particular region in a world of regions, together constituting an emerging world order marked by regional peculiarities" (Hettne and Söderbaum 2000: 461). These postulates drawn from several social science disciplines are what make the NRA a flexible multidisciplinary approach.

The MAR is irregular insofar as it does not include all of Mexico; instead, it contains the sections considered to be most like the Central American States. The NRA applies to cases like these since it "does not view regions as simple aggregations of states. It recognises that the regional frontier may…cut through a particular state's territory, positioning some parts of the state within the emerging region and others outside" (Hettne and Söderbaum 2000: 462).

The NRA is a tool designed to study the "multidimensional process of regional integration, which, includes economic, political, social, and cultural aspects. It is both a positive concept, summarising certain tendencies in the world system and a normative position, arguing in favour of such tendencies as a potential new world order" (Hettne 2000b: 164). This approach describes the process of regionalisation through the degrees of "regionness." These are: regional space (geographical and ecological unit); regional complex (social system); regional society (organised cooperation); regional community (regional civil society); and region-state (acting subject) described in Table 2.1.

Classifying the degree of regionness is useful since it gives parameters for identifying where a region is and, after a change in variables, whether a difference in the degree of regionness occurs (in either direction). Mesoamerica had the characteristics of a "regional society" degree of "regionness" at the inception of the PPP. Regional society is considered

Table 2.1 Classifying regionness

Degree of regionness	*Characteristics*	*Elements that favour deepening in regionness*
Regional space	Pre-regional zone Rooted in Territory Communities linked through "pre market transactions"	Increase transactions Intensify contact between human communities
Regional complex	Widening of translocal relations between human groups Influence between cultures Exchanges are unstable short-sighted and based on self-interest Predates Westphalian state building (particularly in former colonies)	Dramatically increase degree of transnational contact Open up to external relations
Regional society	Appearance of actors apart from State Regionalisation process intensifies through formal cooperation or spontaneously Real region and formal regions form	Increasing relationship between formal and real region Institutionalisation of structures to reinforce Processes at the various levels and sectors begin to complement each other
Regional community	Is becoming an active subject with a distinct identity, institutionalised or informal actor capability Real region and formal region mutually reinforce each other Transnationalised regional civil society plays important role Regional collective identity emerges	Consolidate regional collective identity Transformation of governance structure towards an equilibrium between the levels of governance
Regional institutionalised polity/region state	Representative of the idea of the EU as outlined in the Maastricht treaty Multilevel governance More fixed structure of decision-making Strong civil society	

Based on Hettne and Söderbaum (2000: 462–468) and Hettne (2003: 28–29)

the degree where the crucial regionalisation process intensifies, where non-state actors appear. The regional actors were present, the state functions were unbundling, and there was an impetus to go forward and move into a deeper degree of regionness. At one point, the PPP directives were looking at moving towards a Mesoamerican Integration System (SIMA), which might have led to the next degree of regionness—a regional community. Mesoamerica had the necessary elements to deepen in regionness: it had the "formal" region in the PPP and the MBC, and it had the "real" region manifested in the many networks coexisting in the region (see Chapter 6) including transnationalised regional civil society in the form of the Mesoamerican forums. However, instead of reinforcing each other, they worked against each other. Even though all the elements/actors were present for deepening regionness, why did this not occur? I hypothesise that the construction of the region was fragmented due to the systems of governance so that the existing regionalism did not translate into a regionalisation within the process; instead, regionalisation took place outside the formal region.

The fifth degree of regionness described in the NRA, the regional institutionalised polity (also region-state), is still considered hypothetical and even unlikely. It suggests that decreasing nation-state capacity through higher regionalisation will give way to a multilevel governance structure where some form of equilibrium between the levels of governance will be reached (Hettne and Söderbaum 2000: 468).

The study of regionalism is about explaining the relationship between regionalism and regionalisation in the light of a multilevel, complex world, where different actors shape a region, and regions exist in multiple forms. Though authors use different terms such as "supply" and "demand" (Milner 1997; Mattli 1999) or the "deepening of regionness" (Hettne 2003), in essence, they explain what it is that provides cohesion to a region. Finding coherence is difficult even when considering only state-centred projects. At present, explanations should include the states' reactions to globalisation and financial crises, as well as include all the multiple actors that try to carve out their interests in a regional project. Furthermore, how can regional policy be formed and implemented into "multiple forms of coexisting regions"? As part of the "new regionalism," the issue of governance has been brought up as an essential key to unlocking some of these questions. In this study, the governance structure of the MAR is the element that can best explain the outcome of the PPP as a project; and, it can also explain why the region does not increase its "regionness."

New Regionalism and Governance

Several authors have linked the importance of the nodes of governance to the understanding of the success of regional integration projects. Mattli, for example, considers that when assessing a regional project there is a need to look beyond the market relationships and consider the institutional and political forces of a region, particularly in governance (Mattli 1999). Regional integration projects can contribute to regionalisation; however, when these are not implemented, it is difficult to assess how much a project added to said regionalisation.

Phillips (2001) suggests looking at regionalism as the result of "the regional reorganisation of development, capitalism, or governance" (Phillips 2001: 565, 581). Bøås et al. considered governance (along with civil society) one of the "two most prominent concepts on the contemporary agenda" (Bøås et al. 1999: 1069). Grugel (2004: 604) considers "governance is an integral component of new regionalism" but warns not to "expect the projects of governance that new regionalism encompasses to be identical" (Grugel 2004: 606). But what is governance in this context? Even though at times it is used as a synonym for "government," which in Hufty's (2009) point of view creates confusion surrounding a term that has acquired new connotations, it is now past that definition to the point where "governance without government" (Rosenau 2000) is considered possible. Scholte finds "governance is today far from reducible to the state and interstate relations. Regulatory activities in world politics now also involve substate institutions, suprastate organs, market agencies, and civil society organisations" (Scholte 2001: 24). Although governance does still imply some form of "governing" or steering mechanism, it is no longer exclusive to the state and government actors. Moreover, "Governance occurs at multiple levels of action in a variety of geographical settings within the contemporary global political economy" (Payne 2005: 75). In this sense, governance can take place on a global scale, a regional scale, a national scale, and sub-national scale. Regionalism, for example, "would have a role, as one level of governance, as a means for states to manage certain common problems that were identified as being handled best at a regional level" (Gamble and Payne 2003: 62). Hveem (2003) considers that the region could also solve some of the problems of global governance, where, the global scale is still too large. Also, the meaning of "governance" changes with regionalisation because it "brings different political variables into play, as the traditional fixed domestic and international landscapes become blurred." (Cooper et al. 2008).

In line with the idea that governance takes place at multilevels of action is what is known as multilevel governance, defined by Bache and Flinders as:

> The multi-level governance concept thus contained both vertical and horizontal dimensions. 'Multi-level' referred to the increased interdependence of governments operating at different territorial levels, while 'governance' signalled the growing interdependence between governments and non-governmental actors at various territorial levels. (Bache and Flinders 2004: 3)

Multilevel governance, as presented by several authors (Peters and Pierre 2000; Hooghe and Marks 2003), tends to move along two spheres: the vertical and the horizontal. In vertical multilevel governance, power moves simultaneously from the nation state up to the transnational level of government (regional or international) and down to local communities in a coordinated manner. "Even if the states still have a considerable level of control possibilities, this development automatically means, on the one hand, that local governments are gaining in power, including more political influence within the nation-state but to a higher extent also in an international setting" (Eckerberg and Joas 2004: 407). The horizontal sphere implies a diversification of power and responsibilities from governmental to non-governmental actors at all levels from international, regional, national, or local. However, this does not erase the government from the picture. "Frequently empirical studies of multilevel governance, especially from the local level perspective, conclude that the role of national government, even if eroded from several directions, is still central to most policymaking processes" (Eckerberg and Joas 2004: 411). "Governance still derives fundamentally from what states do" (Payne 2005: 75). Instead, the horizontal sphere implies a negotiated or cooperation form of policymaking, where these external parties are involved in policy creation and implementation.

Where Eckerberg and Joas (2004: 406) consider governance to be "a change from a traditional way of management or government into a new, modern, way of management or government," other writers would like to see a fuller definition, where the focus ceases to be government and instead a "broader, more inclusive and encompassing process of coordination than the conventional view of government" (Peters and Pierre 2001). The baseline definition of multilevel governance refers to negotiated, non-hierarchical exchanges between institutions at the transnational, national, regional, and local levels (Peters and Pierre 2001: 131).

According to Eckerberg and Joas (2004), the traditional way to see policymaking as a top-down system (from international to local) and currently academics consider using the nation state as the dominating actor out-dated, to the point of questioning the position of the nation state. They do not argue that the nation state is disappearing from the international stage, but instead that it is taking on a different role. Within multilevel governance, institutional relationships do not have to operate through intermediary levels but could take place between regional and local, bypassing the state.

The concept of multilevel governance emerged as an observation of what was taking place in the European Union, where power was dispersed from the central government to other levels of government (including the regional level) and non-state actors. What has been interesting with multilevel governance is that it shifted from being an observation to a normative project of governance, where technical support teams from the World Bank, the EU, and various UN agencies (like ECLAC) plus others, encouraged regional institutions and member states to "create" multilevel governance.

Governance and Governability

Payne (2005) distinguished between "projects of governance" and "theories of governance,"[5] whereby the first set assert normative standards and the second describe the system of rule (see page 56).

In the same document, he warns the reader to not push the distinction between projects of governance and theories of governance too far (Payne 2005: 68–69), since there will be cases where a theory can be turned into a project. Multilevel governance has been used more as a "project of governance" in Mesoamerica, a point further discussed in Chapters 4–6.

[5]Projects of governance are Entrepreneurial governance, Good governance, and Global governance; theories of governance are divided into the subfields of Public policy, International Relations, and International Political Economy (see Payne 2005: 55–71).

Several authors have been reluctant to use the term "governance" when referring to Latin America. Arce Tena (2006) considers governance to be a European concept that spread with the "White Paper on European Governance" in 2001 and prefers to refer to governability in Latin America, which he defines as the "ability to generate orderly processes within an institutional framework" or "the capacity to govern" (Arce Tena 2006: 7). However, he considers that this "governability" is to be applied with the principles of democracy, which he sees are intricately related to the "participation and cooperation of citizens for national stability" (Arce Tena 2006: 7). Considering that in many cases in Latin America the democratisation process has led to a lower capacity to govern and implement policy compared to previous authoritarian governments, Arce Tena (2006) argues throughout his book, that when citizens legitimise governments through participation, and governments are accountable to its citizens, then democratic governability takes place. While Fregosi (2008) admits that many times the problem stemmed from a translation problem where governance was at one point translated indiscriminately both into "gobernabilidad" and "gobernanza" (see Solà 2000), both he and López note that there are some underlying differences in the terms. They argue that the concept of "democratic governability" evolves through the transition from the described "ungovernability" in Latin America in the 1970s, to the use in the 1980s of "governability" as how a system manages to articulate and manage to resolve all the tensions occurring within its environment. The main difference is that democratic governability implies that civil society has access to mechanisms that allow it to participate in the functions of the state (López 2008: 215). Democratic governability then describes "the capacity of the Latin American governments to implement political decisions and functions efficiently, with legitimacy and with citizen approval" (López 2008: 214). In this sense, democratic governability remains more a national project than a tool used to observe regional governance structures.

Governance Analytical Framework

Hufty (2009) agrees that governance is frequently used as a "normative framework," particularly by institutions like the World Bank which formed a criterion directed mainly at developing countries whereby

Table 2.2 Governance analytical framework (based on Hufty 2009)

Independent variable Factor *x*	→	Intermediary variable (governance)	→	Dependent variable Impact
PPP and regional institutions (Regionalism)	→ ⇐	Horizontal and vertical governance	→ ⇐	Regionalisation

"good governance"[6] was a pre-condition to receiving loans and used as a political tool for changing societies. He defines governance as "the processes of interactions between the actors involved in a collective issue that lead to decision and the formulation of social norms" (Hufty 2009: 7). In addition, he considers governance as a social fact, something that "is" and has characteristics that can be analysed or interpreted in a non-normative or non-prescriptive way. As such, it is not a "model" to be encouraged but a fact to be described. In this understanding, different levels of governance can be analysed along with the different characteristics of the governance processes of various societies in numerous places and times through a methodology he calls the "governance analytical framework" (Hufty 2009: 7). In this framework, governance can be considered as an intermediary variable, as one that produces effects on a dependent variable and can depend on independent variables that affect it. Using governance as the intermediary variable in Mesoamerica to explain the outcome of the PPP could look like this (Table 2.2).

This framework is used to analyse cases in which the problem is the subject of a governance process or processes, and where "all the *stakeholders* (individuals or groups) are included in the analysis, whether 'formal or informal' (recognized by the authorities or not), without prejudice. For example, social networks form part of the real situation for each organised society but are not usually included in an analysis of actors…" (Hufty 2009: 11).

[6]The World Bank Institute defines governance as "the traditions and institutions by which authority in a country is exercised for the common good. This includes: (i) the process by which those in authority are selected, monitored, and replaced; (ii) the capacity of the government to effectively manage its resources and implement sound policies, and (iii) the respect of citizens and the state for the institutions that govern economic and social interactions among them." Good governance is built on the principles of openness, transparency, participation, and accountability (http://www.worldbank.org/en/topic/governance).

This study identifies the implementation of the PPP in Mesoamerica as a governance problem. The framework described is a useful tool for formulating an investigation and organising observations made on the issue and the direction of the process. In the case of Mesoamerica, both "multi-level governance" and "good governance" normative projects have been used as tools to strengthen the regional and national governments. The result of these projects has brought about hybrid forms of "good governance" and "multilevel governance" where the governments have agreed to decentralise or meet with civil society groups, but in the end, do not share any of the decision-making powers in accordance to the original models.

Recognising that governance is an essential variable in the outcome of the regional project means that it can be included as part of the analysis on the overall ability of the PPP to be implemented as a regional project. For example, the success of many of the PPP social projects (as opposed to infrastructure) depended on the ability to reach the local level. Observing the governance processes both horizontally (across sectors) and vertically (from regional to local) provides key information as to why so many aspects of the PPP were unable to be implemented. I am by no means prescribing how it "should" work; there is no right answer. Nevertheless, when actions down a chain are expected to render specific results, and when said results are not obtained, it is helpful to go back and analyse the chain to find the gap. This is what the GAF proposes.

In the same fashion, if it is assumed—as Hettne (2003) and Hveem (2003) do—that society's acceptance or rejection influence the region as a political project, then a project is only viable when "the top-down approach is reconciled with a bottom-up approach" (Hveem 2003: 81). As will be discussed particularly in Chapter 6, this has not been the case in Mesoamerica. The best way to reconcile these is through collective governance, where actors share the responsibility for making decisions and implementing them (Hveem 2003: 81).

Based on the assumption that the governance of a region is heavily dependent on the acceptance of the regional approaches at the local level, whether negotiated or imposed, local protest to a regional scheme shows a breakdown in this relationship and results therefore in a loss of governance. In Mesoamerica, the rejection of the PPP caused diminishing governance at various levels. However, several successful cross-border projects exist that can provide some insight as to what might be missing at the regional level.

Micro-regionalism

In order to deepen regionness, Hettne and Söderbaum (2000) state that the processes at the different levels of the region (micro to macro) need to become mutually reinforcing and complementary, rather than competitive and diverging, and the gap between the formal and real regions has to be narrowed (Hettne and Söderbaum 2000).

The study of micro-regionalism has evolved from being a minor observation of the dynamics of a border region within a broader context. Both the complexity of micro-regions and the deliberate creation of micro-regions to encourage development have opened up the possibility of studying micro-regionalism on its own, within the greater regional and global context. "Microregionalism refers to those processes of growing regional interconnectedness that occur below the national level, and which cut across national borders" (Breslin and Hook 2002: 8). Some of these projects are government-based, whereas other groups, such as sub-national political authorities, transnational corporations, civil society organisations, or migration patterns, promote others. Ojendal refers to the micro-regional approach as the "integrating neighbouring provinces in different states with each other in order to hasten FDI (Foreign Direct Investment), industrialization and economic growth. Microregionalism –or Growth Triangles– is partly a planned strategy, but also a more spontaneous development" (Öjendal 2000: 13). Overall, "it shares the motivation of seeking to reinscribe spatial relations in order to promote political, economic, security, cultural and other interests" (Breslin and Hook 2002: 8).

Whereas, at the regional level, Mesoamerica is facing a crisis in governance, there are instances throughout this study where cross-border micro-regions are carrying out exciting environmental and commercial projects. These projects, often involving the efforts of local government, NGOs, civil society, and local business, have shown promise of development, confirming that it is the combined efforts that make the difference. Chapter 5 explores some reasons why local governments accept this cooperation; mainly that the lack of funds transferred from central government to local governments have incentivised them to search for ways to stretch and increase their limited resources. In addition, border areas in Mesoamerica have had to strengthen cross-border cooperation to deal with issues of commerce, waterways (environment), street gangs, and migration.

As pointed out by Breslin (2000), there is a growing symbiotic relationship between the micro-regional, the sub-regional, and macro-regional. "Microregionalism, then, not only coexists with other forms of regionalism; it is inextricably linked to them" (Breslin and Hook 2002: 3). Each has its own function and space in the global context. Micro-regionalism in the MAR is linked to the rest of the processes that have taken place and are still taking place throughout the region. By giving some examples, some inferences will be drawn out as a complement to this study in the concluding chapter.

Regions and Development

PPP would fall into Hettne's (2003) category of "Developmental Regionalism," where it is not only used as a means for improving their collective bargaining position and increasing economic cooperation, but also seeks to stabilise the economy, reinforce societal viability, face common problems (i.e., natural disasters) and manage the region's environment and resources (Hettne 2000a: xxxi). In particular, periphery regions consider development the main reason for forming regional alliances. Hettne explains that for peripheral regions to become less peripheral, they need to become more regionalised, that is to increase their level of regionness (Hettne 2000a: xxi).

Even though the separate waves of regionalism in Latin America occurred under different ideologies (dependency vs. neoliberal economics), the primary goal was always "development" (see Bowles 2002). Although what precisely is meant by "development" has been contested, "it was nevertheless widely agreed that development was something which select countries had achieved but which large parts of the world still needed to experience" (Payne 2004a: 1). For several decades, the problem of development had its own discipline that was an interdisciplinary field of enquiry and debate.[7] However, as the world order has shifted, some authors have thought it best to "think afresh" what is meant by development inside the field of IPE (Hettne 1995; Payne 2004a; Payne and Phillips 2010).

[7]For a full account of the history of development studies, see Hettne, Björn (1995) *Development Theory and the Three Worlds: Towards an International Political Economy of Development*, 2nd ed., Longman, Harlowe.

Since nations do not develop (or "underdevelop") by themselves, it is necessary to look beyond the nation state to move past the debates that were stuck somewhere between it and a premature "world approach" (Hettne 1995). In order to do this and find a new approach to development, there needed to be "a marriage between certain strands of development theory and certain strands of international political economy" (Hettne et al. 1999: 354). The premise for this new approach to development is based on the realisation that "development" is not exclusive for those countries that are lagging, but that all nations pursue "development."

Governments are searching for new ways of promoting development in their nations. As regionalism has shown some success in areas of development, deliberate efforts for this kind of cooperation have increased (Payne 2004b).

Although there is a case for explaining regional agreements as a means for leverage on the multilateral forum, this does not account for the differences in the scope and structure of the various types of regional agreements and cooperation. This standpoint does not explain why a member of a larger and more robust regional group (i.e., Mexico as a member of NAFTA and Latin American Integration Association LAIA/ALADI) would want to draw up a new form of regional cooperation with the smaller economies of Central America. However, several of the PPP documents (CE-PPP 2002, 2003) refer to the accelerated development of Spain, Portugal, Greece, Italy, and Ireland as a consequence of their joining the stronger nations already in the EU, as an example of the desired outcome for Mesoamerica through the PPP.

In the attempt to be an "innovative" development programme, the PPP agreement was different from previous experiences of regional integration in Mesoamerica; it included aspects such as health and education, infrastructure, which would necessitate the involvement of various ministries, and it also implied that it would have to permeate below the national level (i.e., for health to be improved, it had to reach hospitals and medical care; for education to be improved, it had to reach the actual schools and teachers). Implementing the PPP to the extent of its proposals meant that other levels of government and, in some cases, non-government actors would have to cooperate and follow the recommendations set out in the project. This was a high expectation for a project that was signed off in a presidential summit, just as commercial treaties had been signed off in the past. The PPP faced its first roadblock: the top-down model that had worked for commercial agreements did not work for a proposal that required some form of multilevel governance, both in its preparatory stages and in its implementation stages. An integral multifaceted project, such as the PPP when designed in the same fashion as an FTA—in an office by a few "experts"—works well on paper, but in practice faces many implementation challenges.

Poor implementation is deemed as "*the* Achilles heel of developing country RTAs. It stems from various sources, such as domestic political sensitivities, lack of technical capacities in government agencies, and the cascading workload of the implementation – and negotiation – of multiple trade agreements simultaneously" (de Lombaerde et al. 2008: 2). To mitigate the sources of poor execution, de Lombaerde et al. (2008) argue that governance of regional integration is the central element of successful RTA implementation so that the intended results would come about. They consider that even though the national level is still the most critical policy level, the world is shifting in such a way that governance is taking place at different levels so that the regional level is gaining more importance (de Lombaerde et al. 2008: 4). Although these authors refer to customs unions and FTAs, the premise they develop can also be applied to cases like the PPP. They argue that to get "governance right" (a key element to implementation), there needs to be active monitoring of the processes carried out by the involved institutions, whether these are public or private.

2.3 Methodology

This book began as a doctoral study over ten years ago. The original investigation began as research on new forms of regionalism using the Plan Puebla Panamá as a case study. Most of the research took place between 2006 and 2008 and was revised once the PPP was replaced with *Proyecto Mesoamerica*.

A combination of research methods was used for the initial study (triangulation): a survey (questionnaire), interviews, and observation (Burnham et al. 2004). The scarcity of information on the PPP during the early stages of research led to broadening the scope to the entire Mesoamerican region. As more literature on the PPP was published, I scaled it back to a case study focusing on the PPP, although I included other projects if they related to the PPP and regional governance.

I did most of my theoretical and factual research through books, journals, and official publications, although I use newspaper and magazine articles for updated information. Most PPP and *Proyecto Mesoamerica* official documentation are available online, including the constitutive acts, Base Documents for Mexico and Central America, and official progress reports.[8] I was given official documents and reports when I visited regional offices. Statistics and reports from CEPAL, the World Bank, and INEGI are available online and were useful to corroborate information. Books and journals written by political analysts in Mesoamerica varied in their usefulness; I considered many of them purely opinion pieces, as they had poor or no referencing to substantiate their statistics and facts. These are included in Chapter 3 as they fuelled many of the debates about the PPP, providing useful insight into the strong opinions on the Mesoamerican projects. However, I tried to include as much local research and analysis as possible, as this realm of literature highly influenced policymaking and non-government actors' opinions within Mesoamerica.

The second stage of research consisted of sending out a questionnaire to NGOs and community-based groups working in the region. The purpose of the survey was to gather their opinions on the different projects as well as to determine how much they knew about them and see if I could draw any conclusions about the level of "regionness" of the MAR. Several authors asserted that NGOs and community-based groups were vehemently opposed to the proposed regional development plans. Some of these authors, such as Bartra (2002), Call (2002), and Bull (2005) referred to the Mesoamerican Forums as an indicator of the reactions to the projects. This assertion merited further investigation into the forums and, in general, the opinions of NGOs and Civil Society.

A useful website to start with was "Mesoamerica Resists" (mesoamericaresiste.com, no longer operational), which stated the opposing views to the PPP and contained an address book with 400 affiliated organisations. This address book, complemented with information from

[8]The original website for the PPP was eliminated in 2003 and then a provisional website was set up as part of the Mexican Ministry of Foreign Affairs. A permanent website was set up in 2006, administered by the PPP Ministry, which later remained part of the Proyecto Mesoamerica website: https://web.archive.org/web/20071029105130/www.planpuebla-panama.org/; www.proyectomesoamerica.org.

organisations that supported the NO PPP booklet, the AMAP organisation, and the Alforja group, provided the names and addresses of over 500 organisations that I compiled into one database used to send out a questionnaire. After considering several options, I opted for an online questionnaire service. The electronic tools that accompanied the service helped in mailing and tracking respondents, as well as filtering out e-mail addresses that were no longer in use. It also meant that this segment of research did not need to be done *in situ*. Out of 500 NGOs and Civil Society groups included in the database, about 400 had an electronic address. The purpose of the questionnaire was to find out whether opposition to the PPP by NGOs and Civil Society groups was to regionalism or the specific project and to see if dialogue existed between the organisations and government representatives. This was a key component since one of the conditions needed to traverse from a regional society to a regional community is the deepening of mutual trust and responsiveness between formal organisations and social institutions leading towards community and region building (Hettne and Söderbaum 2000: 466).

The questionnaire (see Annex B) was designed to take about five minutes to complete (although some organisations opted to write out long opinion pieces in the open-ended "any other comment you would like to add" option at the end); and as an incentive to answer the questionnaire, those who answered received a copy of the results.

Although an online questionnaire has its limitations, there was enough response (27%) to use the questionnaire results both for analysis and as a tool for further research. The questionnaire was sent out to 182 organisations via e-mail using www.surveymonkey.com.[9] This resulted in 61 responses, 14 declined, and the rest were non-responsive. Although the original list included more than 400 NGO's, community groups, and

[9]The final list of 182 organisations was made up of those whose e-mails appeared to be functional, although there is the possibility that not all the recipients saw it due to spam filters. Seven respondents began to answer, but only answered the first two or three questions and skipped the rest. Two of these contacted me to say that they tried to return to the questionnaire at a later time but were unable to continue since the programme identified them as already responded. Another one did not continue with the questionnaire because it is an indigenous organisation based in Panama linked to the Government and the PPP. I was able to exchange several e-mails with the contact person, but we both agreed that his answers might give misleading results. The questionnaire was sent out prior to personal field research, so several NGOs that had not responded to the questionnaire were interviewed independently to comment on some of the results obtained from this exercise.

social movements, over half of the initial questionnaires were returned as undeliverable with an expired electronic address. Later in the research, one member of FUNPADEM mentioned that many of the organisations change names when their funding runs out because many funding bodies are not able to give to the same organisation two years in a row. To circumvent this clause, they change their name and contact details, e-mail being the easiest to change (Interview 20: 2006).

This questionnaire does not reflect the viewpoint of all the NGOs in the area, as it excludes those that have limited resources and do not have access to computers or an electronic address. However, it did provide a general perception of the projects by these organisations, their primary concerns about the development of the region, and the level of cooperation among them. It also provided some information on the scope of regional social networks and the amount of communication among them and government representatives.

The questionnaire provided material for the next stage of research by bringing up further questions and interview topics. The information obtained from the survey was useful both for qualitative research design for interviewing NGO representatives and community organisations and for interviewing other participants involved in the regional development projects.

I then travelled to several key cities in Mesoamerica (2006), which facilitated observation and interviews of key actors identified in the previous stages of research. These included San Salvador and San Bartolomé de la Perulapía in El Salvador, Guatemala City in Guatemala, San José in Costa Rica, and Mexico City, as well as the states of Veracruz, Guerrero, Puebla, Yucatán, and Quintana Roo in Mexico. I chose El Salvador because it is the location of the PPP main offices, as well as the SICA office; also, representatives of an NGO invited me to visit their project in one of the poorest provinces (Perulapía) and speak with the municipal authorities. Guatemala houses the Central American Parliament, the SIECA, and several NGOs opposing the PPP and was the country overseeing one of the few successful projects of the PPP (SIEPAC). As for Costa Rica, I chose it because it is the country that has resisted integration with the rest of Central America, and I attended some conferences that were taking place in San José. During the time I was there, Congress was voting on whether to ratify the CAFTA-DR when Costa Rica was the only country missing. I met with Union representatives, think tanks, and the Central American Monetary Council. Originally Honduras was also on my agenda to visit the Mesoamerican Competitive Council (Consejo Monetario de Competitividad or CMC); however, due to time and monetary constraints, the usefulness of such a visit was reassessed. Several interviewees had dismissed the impact of the CMC, and although interviews with this organisation would have enriched the research, I decided it would not be a cost-effective visit.

In Mexico, Chiapas was left out of the agenda due to previous visits, particularly a work-related one in 1999, where I had contact with government officials (including the then governor), the press, several NGOs, the village of Acteal (where a massacre took place in 1997), and the Pohló Zapatista camp (known as *Caracol*). With this background, I considered that incorporating the development and social problems of Chiapas (and Oaxaca) would draw away from the purpose of this book. Volumes could be written just on specifics of Chiapas and Oaxaca (as well as other challenging areas in Central America). A brief overview would confuse the reader more than it would explain these problems, and it would also diverge from the primary research objectives. Instead, I chose the states of Guerrero, Veracruz, Yucatan, and Quintana Roo, as they better represent the generalised problems of the south-eastern part of Mexico (poverty, lack of services, etc.) without the added issues that are very specific to Chiapas and Oaxaca.

Most of the field research took place during the months following the controversial 2006 Mexican presidential election, so the political atmosphere made it conducive to carry out informal interviews of people off the street, such as taxi drivers, hotel employees, etc. with general questions about the PPP. Both the President-elect, Felipe Calderón, and the second-place candidate, Andrés Manuel López Obrador, had each proposed reassessing the structure of the PPP and other Mesoamerican mechanisms during their campaigns, so there was a heightened awareness about these projects that had laid dormant for several years. Amid this awareness, there were seminars taking place as well as relevant debates on local television transmissions and local newspapers, which in turn provided both pertinent information and contextual background. In Central America, there was ample news coverage on the Mexican election results since a narrow margin separated the two top candidates. Calderón was declared victorious and López Obrador demanded a recount through media-covered protests.

I interviewed representatives of the regional institutions as well as the different levels of government, trade unions, indigenous groups,

Chambers of Commerce, think tanks, NGOs, international organisations, academics, and community during the travel period of research. As a Mexican who had previously worked closely with government departments, I had expected to obtain interviews with government officials in Mexico with ease. Nevertheless, these were mostly with lower ranking officials and many times I was just given official documentation and leaflets (already obtained through other sources). Surprisingly, in the three countries visited in Central America, I obtained lengthy interviews with more relevant officials. In Guatemala, for example, the office of the PPP housed in the Ministry of Energy prepared an "official programme" for my visit. They were, however, disappointed that I arranged additional interviews on my own.

Interviews with NGOs and civil society organisations were scheduled to develop further some of the results obtained from the questionnaire. I set up meetings with business associations to see if they had any input on regional trade policy and the PPP infrastructure projects. The intent was to meet with Small and Medium Enterprises since one of the objectives of the PPP was to help them increase productivity and profits. The PPP progress reports evidenced that there was regular consultation taking place with large business associations and attempts to contact some of them showed that these were highly inaccessible for interviewing. However, there was information available both through the PPP progress reports and newspaper coverage. In the end, I only interviewed two Chambers of Commerce and one SME association after cancellations from three other business groups, two in Costa Rica and one in El Salvador. Although they did offer to reschedule, time did not permit. Unfortunately, this resulted in having minimal (first-hand) input from a business perspective. I have included information from the interviews, as this demonstrated that these groups were left out of the decision-making process. The interviewees also provided references to many business networks in the MAR that spanned the area, supporting previous observations about regionness and governance. Nevertheless, the narrow contact with business representatives in the MAR meant that generalisations about a "business sector" cannot be formed based on my research, so any inferences have to come from other studies.

I grouped the interview questions by sector; different sets of questions were designed for government officials, regional (international) organisations, NGOs, and think tanks to simplify coding. In practice, however, the interviewees tended to diverge from the questions, resulting in over 60 hours of recordings. These tangents often brought in specific insight or were frank observations that enriched the information found in written material. In addition to the structured aspects of the interviews, I gave space for unstructured discussion and dialogue. At least two hours were allotted per interview, which with the Ministry of Foreign Affairs of El Salvador was not enough time and caused tardiness to another appointment. The material obtained from these interviews was rich but complicated to code and weave into the study.

Once most of the interviews had taken place, I discovered that there had been a debate on the translation of the word "governance" into Spanish. In earlier texts and debates, the word had been translated into "gobernabilidad." However, several papers surged challenging the translation, since the word "governability" was also translated into "gobernabilidad." Some translators began to use the word "gobernanza," even though linguists argued that this was an Anglicism. However, the term "gobernanza" is now accepted by the Royal Spanish Academy of Language as a synonym for "gobernabilidad" (Solà 2000; Hufty 2009). In academia, researchers were using both; however, the connotations changed. Gobernabilidad is understood as the "ability to govern," while "gobernanza" came to mean systems of rule that were not limited to government. I did not use sections of interviews where the use of the word "gobernabilidad" was ambiguous or unclear.

The transition from study to this book was not painless. *Proyecto Mesoamerica* has now been in place for ten years; even though the case study focuses on the PPP, there have been substantial changes in regional governance structures worth noting. The Mesoamerican forums continued through 2011 but then disappeared, including the website and documents. I was able to contact a former member of RMALC (now inactive) who gave me the historical archives and explained what had happened to the organisation. I was able to get in touch with some of the people I interviewed in 2006–2008; however, most of them had changed positions and contact details. As I had permission to include their comments in the original dissertation but did not obtain signed permission for this book, I have removed their names and left only their titles for reference purposes.

2.4 Summary

The process of regionalisation of the MAR has slowed down since the "real" and "formal" regions have not been reconciled, and therefore antagonise rather than complement each other. Governance is a crucial variable in the process of regionalisation in the MAR, since it was the main stumbling block to implementing projects, particularly social projects. Multilevel governance, as a normative project, has brought about a series of hybrid systems of governance in the MAR, where the principles of power sharing across the vertical and horizontal layers of governance are supported to obtain international funding or recognition, and yet the actual powers still reside in central government.

The attempt to demonstrate "multi-level governance" and "good governance" to international funding bodies, challenged the systems of governance in the MAR to the point that neither the traditional forms of governance, nor new forms of governance were effective in implementing the regional project. Mesoamerican governments were encouraged by the OECD and IDB to decentralise power to the different territorial levels while including non-governmental actors in the governing process. In practice, however, the changes made to satisfy the recommendations given by the technical support teams and numerous restructuring exercises that have taken place throughout the vertical and horizontal spheres remained on paper, provoking some government actors to withdraw from the process altogether.

The resulting situation was that the PPP regionalism did not relate to the regionalisation that was taking place in a mutually reinforcing way. Part of the regionalisation in the MAR is a reactive process where pre-existing networks and newly formed networks did not find efficiency or inclusion in the PPP regional project and so, remained on the sidelines. Similarly, the other regionalising forces were in direct opposition to the PPP, so they also remained on the outside. Micro-regions intricately tied to the PPP experienced some success in implementing cross-border projects. A look at the governance structures in the micro-region, as well as its relationship to the MAR as a whole, could point to a regionalisation occurring at this level that could then spread to the entire region.

Bibliography

Adler, Emmanuel. 1994. Imagined (Security) Communities. Annual Meeting of the American Political Society 1–4 September, New York.

Arce Tena, Carlos A. 2006. *La gobernabilidad democrática: una perspectiva para el desarrollo*. México D.F.: Ediciones Miguel Angel Porrúa.

Bache, Ian, and Matthew Flinders. 2004. Themes and Issues in Multi-level Governance. In *Multilevel Governance*, ed. Bache Ian and Flinders Matthew. New York: Oxford University Press.

Baert, Francis, Tiziana Scaramagli, and Fredrik Söderbaum. 2014. Introduction: Intersecting Interregionalism. In *Intersecting Interregionalism, Regions, Global Governance and the EU*, ed. Francis Baert, Tiziana Scaramagli, and Fredrik Söderbaum. www.researchgate.net/publication/259580409. Downloaded 6 December 2017.

Balassa, Bela A. 1961. *The Theory of Economic Integration*. London: Allen and Unwin, 1962.

Baldwin, Richard E. 2006. Multilateralising Regionalism: Spaghetti Bowls as Building Blocas on the Path to Global Free Trade. *The World Economy* 29 (11): 1451–1518.

Barbossa, Rubens Antonio. 1991. *América Latina em perspectiva: A Integraçao Regional Da Retórica à Realidade*. Sao Paulo: Ediçoes Aduaneiras Ltda.

Bartra, Armando. 2002. Hacia una Nueva Colonización del Sureste. In *Economía Política del Plan Puebla Panamá*, ed. Alejandro Álvarez Béjar, Barreda Marín Andrés y Armando Bartra. México: Editorial Itaca.

Bauzas, Roberto, and Jaime Ros (eds.). 1994. *Economic Integration in the Western Hemisphere*. Notre Dame: University of Notre Dame Press.

Baylis, John, and Steve Smith. 2001. *The Globalization of World Politics: An Introduction to International Relations*, 2nd ed. Oxford: Oxford University Press.

Blatter, Joachim. 2004. From 'Spaces of Place' to 'Spaces of Flows'? Territorial and Functional Governance in Cross-Border Regions in Europe and North America. *International Journal of Urban and Regional Research* 28 (3) (September): 530–548.

Blejer, Mario I. 1984. Economic Integration: An Analytical Overview. In *Social and Economic Progress in Latin America, Special Report: Economic Integration*, 5–34. Washington, DC: Inter-American Development Bank.

Bøås, Morten, Marianne H. Marchand, and Timothy M. Shaw. 1999. The Weave-World: Regionalisms in the South in the New Millennium. *Third World Quarterly* 20 (5): 1061–1070.

Bøås, Morten, Marianne H. Marchand, and Timothy M. Shaw. 2003. The Weave-World: The Regional Interweaving of Economies, Ideas and Identities.

In *Theories of New Regionalism: A Palgrave Reader*, ed. Fredrik Söderbaum and Timothy M. Shaw. Basingstoke: Palgrave Macmillan.

Bøås, Morten, Marianne H. Marchand, and Timothy M. Shaw (eds.). 2005a. *The Political Economy of Regions and Regionalisms*. Basingstoke: Palgrave Macmillan.

Bøås, Morten, Marianne H. Marchand, and Timothy M. Shaw. 2005b. The Political Economy of Regions and Regionalism: An Introduction to Our Critical, Revisionist Inquiries. In *The Political Economy of Regions and Regionalisms*, ed. Morten Bøås, Marianne H. Marchand, and Timothy M. Shaw. Basingstoke: Palgrave Macmillan.

Bøås, Morten, Marianne H. Marchand, and Timothy M. Shaw. 2005c. Conclusion: Possible Projections for the Political Economy of Regions and Regionalisms. In *The Political Economy of Regions and Regionalisms*, ed. Morten Bøås, Marianne H. Marchand, and Timothy M. Shaw. Basingstoke: Palgrave Macmillan.

Bowles, Paul. 2002. Regionalism and Development After (?) the Global Financial Crises. In *New Regionalisms in the Global Political Economy: Theories and Cases*, ed. Shaun Breslin et al. London: Routledge.

Breslin, Shaun. 2000. Decentralisation, Globalisation and China's Partial Re-engagement with the Global Economy. *New Political Economy* 5 (2): 205–226.

Breslin, Shaun. 2010. Regions and Regionalism in World Politics. In *Issues in Twenty-First Century World Politics*, ed. Mark Beeson and Nick Beesley, 33–51. Basingstoke: Palgrave.

Breslin, Shaun, and Glenn D. Hook (eds.). 2002. *Microregionalism and World Order*. New York: Palgrave Macmillan.

Breslin, Shaun, Richard Higgot, and Ben Rosamond. 2002. Regions in Comparative Perspective. In *New Regionalisms in the Global Political Economy: Theories and Cases*, ed. Shaun Breslin et al. London: Routledge.

Broome, André. 2014. *Issues and Actors in the Global Political Economy*. New York: Palgrave Macmillan.

Bull, Benedicte. 2005. Between Bush and Bolivar: Change and Continuity in the Remaking of Mesoamerica. In *The Political Economy of Regions and Regionalisms*, ed. Morten Bøås, Marianne H. Marchand, and Timothy M. Shaw, 14. Basingstoke: Palgrave Macmillan.

Bull, Benedicte, and Morten Bøås. 2003. Multilateral Development Banks as Regionalising Actors: The Asian Development Bank and the Inter-American Development Bank. *New Political Economy* 8 (2) (July): 245–260.

Bulmer-Thomas, Victor. 2001. Introduction. In *Regional Integration in Latin America and the Caribbean: The Political Economy of Open Regionalism*, ed. Victor Bulmer Thomas. London: University of London.

Burnel, Peter. 2000. Democracy Assistance: The State of the Discourse. In *Democracy Assistance: International Cooperation for Democratization*, ed. Peter Burnel. London: Frank Cass.

Burnham, Peter, Karin Gilland, Wyn Grant, and Zig Layton-Henry. 2004. *Research Methods in Politics Political Analysis.* London: Palgrave-Macmillan.

Call, Wendy. 2002. Plan Puebla-Panamá: Done Deal or Emerging Flashpoint? *NACLA Report on the Americas* 35 (5, Mar/Apr): 24–25. New York: Taylor & Francis Ltd.

Carranza, Mario Esteban. 2000. *South American Free Trade Area or Free Trade Area of the Americas? Open Regionalism and the Future of Regional Economic Integration in South America*. Burlington, VT: Ashgate.

Cooper, Andrew F., Christopher W. Hughes, and Phillippe De Loambaerde. 2008. *Regionalisation and Global Governance: The Taming of Globalisation?* London and New York: Routledge.

Curly, Jon M. 2008. Cleaning Up the Spaghetti Bowl. In *Economic Integration in the Americas*, ed. Joseph A. McKinney and Stephen Gardner. London and New York: Routledge.

De Lombaerde, Philippe, and Luis Jorge Garay. 2006. New Regionalism in Latin America and the Role of the US. UN-CRIS Occasional Papers O-2006/10.

De Lombaerde, Philippe, and Luk Van Langenhove. 2004. Indicators of Regional Integration: Conceptual and Methodological Issues. UN-CRIS Occasional Papers O-2004/15.

De Lombaerde, Philippe, Antoni Estevadeordal, and Kati Suominen. 2008. Governing Regional Integration for Development: Introduction. In *Governing Regional Integration for Development*, ed. Philippe De Lombaerde, Antoni Estevadeordal, and Kati Suominen. Aldershot: Ashgate.

Devlin, Robert, and Antoni Estevadeordal. 2001. What's New in the New Regionalism in the Americas? In *Regional Integration in Latin America and the Caribbean: The Political Economy of Open Regionalism*, ed. Victor Bulmer Thomas. London: University of London.

Eckerberg, Katarina, and Marko Joas. 2004. Multi-level Environmental Governance: A Concept Under Stress? (Guest Editorial). *Local Environment* 9 (5) (October): 405–412.

Fawcett, Louise, and Andrew Hurrell (eds.). 1995. *Regionalism in World Politics: Regional Organization and International Order*. New York: Oxford University Press.

Fregosi, Renée. 2008. Gobernabilidad y Gobernanza Global: desafíos teóricos y políticos. In *II Escuela Chile-Francia: Transformaciónes del Espacio Público*, ed. Ximena Póo. Chile: Documento de Recopilación de Ponencias Cátedra Chile-Francia "Michel Foucoult".

Gamble, Andrew, and Anthony Payne. 1996. Conclusion: The New Regionalism. In *Regionalism and World Order*, ed. Andrew Gamble and Anthony Payne. London: Macmillan.

Gamble, Andrew, and Anthony Payne. 2003. The World Order Approach. In *Theories of New Regionalism: A Palgrave Reader*, ed. Fredrik Söderbaum and Timothy M. Shaw. Basingstoke: Palgrave Macmillan.

George, Stephen. 2004. Multi-level Governance and the European Union. In *Multilevel Governance*, ed. Ian Bache and Matthew Flinders. New York: Oxford University Press.

Grugel, Jean. 1996. Latin America and the Remaking of the Americas. In *Regionalism and World Order*, ed. Andrew Gamble and Anthony Payne. London: Macmillan.

Grugel, Jean B. 2004. New Regionalism and Modes of Governance—Comparing US and EU Strategies in Latin America. *European Journal of International Relations* 10 (4): 603–626.

Grugel, Jean, and Wil Hout. 1999. *Regionalism Across the North-South Divide State Strategies and Globalization*. London and New York: Routledge.

Haggard, Stephen. 1997. The Political Economy of Regionalism in Asia and the Americas. In *The Political Economy of Regionalism*, ed. Edward D. Mansfield and Helen V. Milner. New York: Columbia University Press.

Hettne, Björn. 1995. *Development Theory and the Three Worlds: Towards an International Political Economy of Development*, 2nd ed. Harlow: Longman.

Hettne, Björn. 2000a. The New Regionalism: A Prologue. In *National Perspectives on the New Regionalism in the South*, ed. Björn Hettne, Andreas Inotal, and Osvaldo Sunkel. London: Macmillan.

Hettne, Björn. 2000b. Global Market Versus Regionalism. In *The Global Transformations Reader*, ed. David Held and Anthony McGrew. Cambridge: Polity Press.

Hettne, Björn. 2003. The New Regionalism Revisited. In *Theories of New Regionalism: A Palgrave Reader*, ed. Fredrik Söderbaum and Timothy M. Shaw. Basingstoke: Palgrave Macmillan.

Hettne, Björn. 2005. Beyond the 'New' Regionalism. *New Political Economy* 10 (4): 543–571.

Hettne, Björn, and Fredrik Söderbaum. 1998. The New Regionalism Approach. www.unisa.ac.za. Last accessed 22 March 2010.

Hettne, Björn, and Fredrik Söderbaum. 2000. Theorising the Rise of Regionness. *New Political Economy* 5 (3): 457–472.

Hettne, Björn, and Fredrik Söderbaum. 2002. Theorising the Rise of Regionness. In *New Regionalisms in the Global Political Economy: Theories and Cases*, ed. Shaun Breslin et al. London: Routledge.

Hettne, Björn, and Fredrik Söderbaum. 2008. The Future of Regionalism: Old Divides, New Frontiers. www.researchgate.net/publication/259713955. Downloaded 6 December 2017.

Hettne, Björn, András Inotal, and Osvaldo Sunkel (eds.). 1999. *Globalism and the New Regionalism*. Basingstoke: Macmillan.

Hettne, Björn, Andreas Inotal, and Osvaldo Sunkel (eds.). 2000a. *National Perspectives on the New Regionalism in the South*. London: Macmillan.

Hettne, Bjorn, Andreas Inotal, and Osvaldo Sunkel (eds.). 2000b. *The New Regionalism and the Future of Security and Development*. London: Macmillan.

Higgot, Richard, and Simon Reich. 1998. *Globalisation and Sites of Conflict: Towards Definition and Taxonomy*, CSGR Working Paper. University of Warwick, Centre for the Study of Globalisation and Regionalism. Accessed 01 March 1998.

Hooghe, Liesbet, and Gary Marks. 2003. Unraveling the Central State, but How? Types of Multi-level Governance. *American Political Science Review* 97 (2) (May): 233–243.

Hufty, Marc. 2009. The Governance Analytical Framework. www.north-south.unibe.ch/content.php/publications/Infosystem/On-line%20Dokumente/Upload/GovernanceFrameworkE.pdf. Last accessed 15 July 2010.

Hurrell, Andrew. 1995. Regionalism in Theoretical Perspectiva. In *Regionalism in World Politics*, ed. Andrew Hurrell and Louise Fawcett. Oxford: Oxford University Press.

Hveem, Helge. 2003. The Regional Project in Global Governance. In *Theories of New Regionalism: A Palgrave Reader*, ed. Fredrik Söderbaum and Timothy M. Shaw. Basingstoke: Palgrave Macmillan.

Hook, Glenn, and Ian Kearns (eds.). 1999. *Subregionalism and World Order*. Basingstoke: Macmillan.

López, Miguel Angel. 2008. Gobernabilidad y Democracia en America Latina: La Institucionalización Partidiaria. In *II Escuela Chile-Francia: Transformaciónes del Espacio Público*, ed. Ximena Póo. Chile: Documento de Recopilación de Ponencias Cátedra Chile-Francia "Michel Foucoult".

Lopez-Calva, Luis F., and Nora Lustig. 2003. Social Protection and Inclusive Trade: Strengthening the Sources of Convergence Within FTAA. Universidad de Las Americas Working Paper No. 2003-06.

Malamud, Andrés. 2004. Regional Integration in Latin America: Comparative Theories and Institutions. *Sociologia* 44: 135–154. ISSN: 0873-6529.

Mansfield, Edward D., and Helen V. Milner. 1997a. The Political Economy of Regionalism: An Overview. In *The Political Economy of Regionalism*, ed. Edward D. Mansfield and Helen V. Milner. New York: Columbia University Press.

Mansfield, Edward D., and Helen V. Milner (eds.). 1997b. *The Political Economy of Regionalism*. New York: Columbia University Press.

Mansfield, Edward D., and Eric Reinhalt. 2003. Multilateral Determinants of Regionalism: The Effects of GATT/WTO on the Formation of Preferential Trading Arrangements. *International Organisation* 57 (4) (Fall): 829–862.

Marchand, Marianne H., Morten Bøås, and Timothy M. Shaw. 1999. The Political Economy of New Regionalisms. *Third World Quarterly* 20 (5): 897–910.

Mattli, Walter. 1999. *The Logic of Regional Integration: Europe and Beyond*. New York: Cambridge University Press. Net Library e-book accessed through Warwick Library.

Maxwell, Joseph A. 2005. *Qualitative Research Design: An Interactive Approach*, 2nd ed. London: Sage.

Milner, Helen. 1997. Industries, Governments, and Regional Trade Blocs. In *The Political Economy of Regionalism*, ed. Edward D. Mansfield and Helen V. Milner. New York: Columbia University Press.

Mistry, Percy S. 2000. Regional Integration and Economic Development. In *National Perspectives on the New Regionalism in the South*, ed. Bjorn Hettne, Andreas Inotal, and Osvaldo Sunkel. London: Macmillan.

Mistry, Percy S. 2003. New Regionalism and Economic Development. In *Theories of New Regionalism: A Palgrave Reader*, ed. Fredrik Söderbaum and Timothy M. Shaw. Basingstoke: Palgrave Macmillan.

Mitrany, David. 1975. *The Functional Theory of Politics*. New York: St. Martins Press.

Mittelman, James H. 1996. Rethinking the "New Regionalism" in the Context of Globalization. *Global Governance* 2: 189–213.

Neumann, Iver B. 2003. A Region-Building Approach. In *Theories of New Regionalism: A Palgrave Reader*, ed. Fredrik Söderbaum and Timothy M. Shaw. Basingstoke: Palgrave Macmillan.

Nogués, J., and R. Quintanilla. 1995. Latin America's Integration and the Multilateral Trading System. In *New Dimensions in Regional Integration*, ed. J. De Melo and A. Panagariya. New York: Cambridge University Press.

Offenheiser, Raymond C. 1998. Transforming Central America After Hurricane Mitch. *Foreign Policy* (Fall 1999), 8. http://www.questia.com/.

Öjendal, Joakim. 2000. Sharing the Good: Modes of Managing Water Resources in the Lower Mekong River Basin. Department of Peace and Development Research (PADRIGU), Göteborg University, Göteborg.

Orantes, Isaac Cohen. 1981. The Concept of Integration. In *CEPAL Review*. Santiago: Publicaciones Naciones Unidas.

Ornelas Delgado, Jaime. 2002. El Plan Puebla Panamá y la globalización neoliberal. In *Lectura Crítica del Plan Puebla Panamá*, coord. Sandoval Forero, Eduardo Andrés, and Robinson Salazar Pérez. Buenos Aires: Libros en Red.

Payne, Anthony. 1996. The United States and Its Enterprise for the Americas. In *Regionalism and World Order*, ed. Andrew Gamble and Anthony Payne. London: Macmillan.

Payne, Anthony. 2004a. Rethinking Development Inside International Political Economy. In *The New Regional Politics of Development*, ed. Anthony Payne. London: Palgrave Macmillan.

Payne, Anthony. 2004b. Concluding Thoughts and Next Steps. In *The New Regional Politics of Development*, ed. Anthony Payne. London: Palgrave Macmillan.

Payne, Anthony. 2005. The Study of Governance in a Global Political Economy. In *Globalizing International Political Economy*, ed. Nicola Phillips. New York: Palgrave Macmillan.

Payne, Anthony, and Andrew Gamble. 1996. Introduction: The Political Economy of Regionalism and World Order. In *Regionalism and World Order*, ed. Andrew Gamble and Anthony Payne. London: Macmillan.

Payne, Anthony and Nicola Phillips. 2010. *Development*. Cambridge, UK: Polity Press.

Peters, Guy B., and John Pierre. 2000. Developments in Intergovernmental Relations: Towards Multi-Level Governance. *Policy and Politics* 29: 131–135.

Peters, Guy B., and Jon Pierre. 2001. Developments in Intergovernmental Relations: Towards Multi-level Governance. *Policy and Politics* 29 (2): 131–135.

Phillips, Nicola. 2001. Regionalist Governance in the New Political Economy of Development: 'Relaunching' the Mercosur. *Third World Quarterly* 22 (4): 565–583.

Phillips, Nicola. 2002. Governance After Financial Crisis: South American Perspectives on the Reformulation of Regionalism. In *New Regionalisms in the Global Political Economy: Theories and Cases*, ed. Shaun Breslin et al. London: Routledge.

Phillips, Nicola. 2003. Hemispheric Integration and Subregionalism in the Americas. *International Affairs* 79 (2): 327–349.

Phillips, Nicola. 2004. The Americas. In *The New Regional Politics of Development*, ed. Anthony Payne. London: Palgrave Macmillan.

Phillips, Nicola (ed.). 2005. *Globalizing International Political Economy*. New York: Palgrave Macmillan.

Rosenau, James N. 2000. Governance in a Globalizing World. In *The Global Transformations Reader*, ed. David Held and Anthony McGrew. Cambridge: Polity Press.

Sanchez Bajo, Claudia. 2005. European Union-Mercosur Interregionalism: Negotiations, Civil Society and Governance. In *The Political Economy of Regions and Regionalisms*, ed. Morten Bøås, Marianne H. Marchand, and Timothy M. Shaw. Basingstoke: Palgrave Macmillan.

Santiso, Carlos. 2000. Towards Democratic Governance: The Contribution of the Multilateral Development Banks in Latin America. In *Democracy Assistance: International Cooperation for Democratization*, ed. Peter Burnel. London: Frank Cass.

Scholte, Jan Aart. 2001. The Globalization of World Politics. In *The Globalization of World Politics: An Introduction to International Relations*, ed. John Baylis and Steve Smith, 2nd ed. Oxford: Oxford University Press.

Shaw, Timothy M. 2002. New Regionalisms in Africa in the New Millennium: Comparative Perspectives on Renaissance, Realisms and/or Regressions. In *New Regionalisms in the Global Political Economy: Theories and Cases*, ed. Shaun Breslin, Christopher W. Hughes, Nicola Phillips, and Ben Rosamond. London: Routledge, Taylor & Francis Group.

Söderbaum, Fredrik. 2003. Introduction: Theories of New Regionalism. In *Theories of New Regionalism: A Palgrave Reader*, ed. Fredrik Söderbaum and Timothy M. Shaw. Basingstoke: Palgrave Macmillan.

Söderbaum, Fredrik. 2005. The International Political Economy of Regionalism. In *Globalizing International Political Economy*, ed. Nicola Phillips. New York: Palgrave Macmillan.

Söderbaum, Fredrik. 2016. *Rethinking Regionalism*. London: Palgrave.

Söderbaum, Fredrik, and Timothy M. Shaw. 2003. *Theories of New Regionalism: A Palgrave Reader*. Basingstoke: Palgrave Macmillan.

Söderbaum, Fredrik, and Timothy M. Shaw. 2003. Conclusion: What Futures for New Regionalism? In *Theories of New Regionalism: A Palgrave Reader*, ed. Fredrik Söderbaum and Timothy M. Shaw. Basingstoke: Palgrave Macmillan.

Solà, Amadeu. 2000. Colaboraciones: La traducción de governance. *Puntoycoma*, No. 65 (septiembre–octubre). www.europa.eu.int/comm/translation/bulletins/puntoycoma/65/pyc652.htm. Accessed 15 August 2009.

Sunkel, Osvaldo. 2000. Development and Regional Integration in Latin America: Another Chance for an Unfulfilled Promise? In *National Perspectives on the New Regionalism in the South*, ed. Bjorn Hettne, Andreas Inotal, and Osvaldo Sunkel. London: Macmillan.

Väyrynen, Raimo. 2003. Regionalism Old and New. *International Studies Review* 5 (1) (March): 25–51.

Viner, Jacob. 1950. *The Customs Union Issue*. New York: Carnegie Endowment of International Peace.

Welch, Stephen, and Caroline Kennedy-Pipe. 2004. Multi-level Governance and International Relations. In *Multilevel Governance*, ed. Ian Bache and Matthew Flinders. New York: Oxford University Press.

Wendt, Alexander. 1994. Collective Identity Formation and the International State. *The American Political Science Review* 88 (2): 384–396.

Woodward, Ralph Lee, Jr. 1985. *Central America: A Nation Divided*. London: Oxford University Press.

Woodward, Ralph Lee. 1988. *Central America: Historical Perspectives on the Contemporary Crises*. New York: Greenwood Press.

Interview

20. Fundación para la Democracia (FUNPADEM) Background Information Conversation nit Recorded 17, 18, 19 October, San José Costa Rica.

CHAPTER 3

Debates and Issues

3.1 Introduction

The purpose of this chapter is twofold; primarily, I give an overview of the issues discussed in the literature on the MAR and the PPP to provide a sense of the debates surrounding the projects and understand the complex relations between the governments and other interest groups in the region. Secondly, relating to the theoretical framework in the previous chapter, I will discuss the importance of regional governance for the implementation of any project in the area. Focusing only on the issues of these projects limits the analysis to current policymaking. The nodes of governance that the PPP projects rested upon were at best institutionally weak and poorly coordinated, which hindered the deepening of regionness in Mesoamerica obstructing expected results. A closer look at these levels and their problems provide greater insight into the difficulties encountered in the process of regionalisation in the MAR, beyond temporal projects.

Notwithstanding the vast amount of literature on other projects in the region, mainly those centred around SICA, NAFTA, the CAFTA-DR, and FTAA, I will focus on the debates about Mesoamerican projects or region-wide issues. However, in subsequent chapters, other projects that are either within or overlap the region are discussed, as they are relevant to the critical questions of governance and regionalisation.

A. Gamboa, *Regional Integration, Development, and Governance in Mesoamerica*,
https://doi.org/10.1007/978-3-030-25350-9_3

As the picture became more evident on what implementing the PPP was going to mean to both Mexico and the other countries involved, analysts began to look at the role of each country. Some like Armando Bartra (2001a), Sandoval (2002), and Salazar (2002), considered that the overwhelming focus on Mexico left the remaining seven countries behind. Bartra (2002) points out that the name Puebla-Panama indicates the inequality of the members. Whereas Puebla is a state within Mexico, Panama is a country, and the title placed them at the same level. Instead, Bartra suggests that the plan should have been called Puebla-Darien (referring to the most southerly province of Panama). To this point, during the negotiations for his country to join the project, Alvaro Uribe, the Colombian president, suggested changing the name to Puebla-Putamayo, the most southerly state of Colombia, and not Plan Puebla-Colombia. Bartra, Sandoval, and Salazar compared the PPP with past efforts by Mexico to annex parts of Guatemala (and the successful annexation of Chiapas and the Soconuco region), as examples of Mexico exercising hegemony in Central America (López Villicaña 2002). The PPP was considered another manifestation of Mexico in its attempt to increase its sphere of influence (Álvarez Béjar 2002b; Rocha 2006), while some saw it as a way of integrating Central America into NAFTA (Ornelas 2002).

More outspoken authors claimed that Mexico was once more playing puppet and doing the dirty work asked by the United States, particularly in the efforts to contain migration and drug trafficking (Saldívar 2002). However, most agreed that it was another triumph of neoliberal globalisation, this time over Mesoamerica, and "a project designed from above by the elite, without any basic consensus, and therefore it is vertical and authoritarian" (Saldívar 2002: 76).

The initial surge of articles and books on the PPP slowly died down after the Mexican government reorganised the administration of the PPP from the President's office to the MFA in 2003. During this time, controversial people were removed from office, and the budget was restructured. The Mexican Government's website on the PPP was removed for almost a year, as was all statistical information from the official government site (INEGI); the only official information available was through the Inter-American Development Bank (IDB). For some time, it seemed the PPP had been abandoned and left to die (Pickard 2004). However, NGO websites, as well as sites of those against the proposal, continued to denounce the negative impact of controversial infrastructure projects that remained in force (even though many no longer carried the banner of the PPP). In early 2004, President Fox relaunched the PPP after hiring a public relations firm to do a complete image makeover and carry out public opinion polls. The articles that followed became more analytical and less reactive, linking the relaunch of the PPP to the FTAA negotiations (due to consolidate by 2005) and the signing of the Central America-US Free Trade Agreement. Not only Mexican and Central American academia had a renewed interest in the PPP, but also those studying regionalism and regionalisation. Pisani and Label (2003), Villafuerte (2004a), and Bull (2005) analysed the relationship between the PPP and the (then) possibly forthcoming Free Trade Area of the Americas.

Other authors focused on the highly debated subjects surrounding the PPP, such as environmental concerns, indigenous rights, and the likelihood of the United States inserting its own agenda (i.e., immigration and drug trafficking) into the PPP. Subsequently, analysts in Mexico focused mainly on Mexican history and domestic policy, while those carried out in Central America referred mostly to the relevance of the PPP to issues of Central American integration (Rocha 2006).

To better cover the debates sparked by the PPP, I divided this chapter into four sections. In the first section, I include some of the underlying discussions on the issue, mainly the use of "Mesoamerica," and the role of the Mesoamerican projects in shaping both this region and the broader Americas. Then in the second section, I discuss the five key issues that have been at the centre of controversy and debates. The third section considers the usefulness of going beyond these debates and arguments and delving into the areas of effective regional governance in Mesoamerica. The fourth and final section, I discuss some of the new debates that appeared after the restructuring of the PPP into *Proyecto Mesoamerica*.

3.2 Underlying Debates

Notions of Mesoamerica

Initially, upon the announcement of the PPP, there were some objections to the use of the term *Mesoamerica* to designate the area covered by the project because it diverged from the previous use of the word and definition of the geographical area. Several authors credit the archaeologists Kroeber and Kirchoff (1939) as the first to use the term "Mesoamerica" describing the area depicting an interrelated set of high cultures in pre-Columbian times situated in the humid areas of Mexico, Guatemala and parts of Honduras (Romero Contreras and Ávila Ramos 1999). According to Romero Contreras and Ávila Ramos (1999), when the concept of Mesoamerica emerged it was initially based on geographical and environmental characteristics; however, as it evolved from Kroeber's original writings, the cultural element became its defining characteristic. Mesoamerica, described by Kroeber and Kirchoff in 1939 sets the borders from the Sinaloa and Pánuco rivers in Mexico to the Motagua River and Nicoya Gulf in Nicaragua, according to evidence that pre-Columbian inhabitants showed similar cultural characteristics within this defined area (Romero Contreras and Ávila Ramos 1999).

The Mesoamerica of PPP shifts the borders south. Compared to the archaeological Mesoamerica, it excludes large parts of Central Mexico, while it adds Nicaragua, Costa Rica, and Panama. Thus, the Mesoamerica of the PPP is a new construction that mixes and matches formerly established regions. It cuts Mexico in two, transgresses different Middle American regions, and brings in Panama. Bull (2005), Chanona (2002), Saldívar (2002), Bartra (2001a) and others highlight its strategic location between the Atlantic and Pacific Oceans, and improvements to infrastructure may well drive it to become more important in increasing and facilitating commerce above and beyond the Panama Canal. For Alberto Rocha (2006), Jaime Preciado and Aaron Villaruel (2006) the geopolitical and geo-economic interests of Mexico and the United States are the deciding factors on which projects formed part of the PPP, particularly those regarding electrical connection and infrastructure. Even though cultural factors should remain an essential common denominator in present-day Mesoamerica, especially the rich cultural heritage of its ten million indigenous people (18% of the population), two other factors have increased in importance: the environment and poverty (Chanona 2002).

Initially some academics and politicians were reluctant to use the term Mesoamerica, and instead used "area of the PPP" or Central America and Mexico. Abel Pacheco, the former President of Costa Rica, attempted to rename it by calling it *Grand Central America* (Notimex, Mexico, 1 June 2002). In 2006, when the Colombian Foreign Minister, Carolina Barco, was questioned about Colombia's change of status from observer to a permanent member of the PPP, she said "Colombia has always identified with Central America, with Mesoamerica, with its culture, its geography, and its history, and seeks to strengthen this integration" (Octavio Pineda, *Reforma*, 14 January 2006).

Despite this academic debate, most of the regional networks have accepted the use of the term Mesoamerica and have adopted it for their use. The director of the Mexican Association for the Self-determination of Peoples or Nations (AMAP) claims that they were the first to use the term and that the Mexican government then followed suit (Interview 38: 2006). However, Rocha (2006) points out that it was during the IV Tuxtla Mechanism Summit in Guatemala (2000) that the terms "Mesoamerican Region" and "Mesoamerican Community of Nations" was first used (page 58).

Mesoamerica Resiste (Mesoamerica Resists)—civil society and NGO network created to oppose the PPP—gives Mesoamerica the same geographical area as the project it rejects. However, it believes that what unites the peoples of Mesoamerica is that their staple food is a diet based on white corn and that they mainly descend from the Maya,[1] even though corn as a staple food runs further north in Mexico and it is also found further south, into Venezuela and Colombia. The Maya, both pre-Columbian and present day, do not extend through the whole area of the PPP, and even where they do, they are not a homogenous group. "The people we refer to as Maya speak 30 different languages, have highly varied political structures (and) have unique histories" (Labrecque 2005: 100).

Notwithstanding the above observations on its political or regional status, one interesting point is how the Mesoamerican identity continues to form. Even the polemic leader of the Zapatista National Liberation Army (EZLN), Subcomandante Marcos, addressed the inhabitants of the area as "Mesoamericanos" (as opposed to "Mexicanos" or "Guatemaltecos") during the first Mesoamerican Forum, held in Tapachula in 2001. Moreover, the ease by which current inhabitants of the PPP area have identified themselves as "Mesoamerican" brings an interesting twist to the subject and makes possible a study of Mesoamerica as a political, cultural, and environmental transnational region. As Bull (2005) argues, the current discourse on Mesoamerica is a paradigmatic case of region construction, since its borders, description, and discourse have changed and continue to shift. Bartra (2002), who initially rejected the use of the term Mesoamerica, reluctantly agreed

[1] One of the most famous Mayan legends states that the gods formed the first people out of corn, and masa (corn dough), highlighting the importance given to this food for both sustenance and culture.

to it in his 2004 article "Mesoamericanos, recalentando una identidad colectiva," noting the acceptance of the name by social groups and their fervour in adopting this identity. He finally concludes that considering the fight for social justice and against the PPP, just as the Greeks formed their identity by getting rid of the barbarians, "the peoples of Middle America, the crucial and crucified America, deep America, we are becoming Mesoamerican" (Bartra 2004: 8). Whatever the future may bring, the term Mesoamerica has outgrown its archaeological connotations and introduced into the political arena through the articulation of regional policy regimes spanning geography that extended from southern Mexico to Panama (Toly 2004: 50; Bull 2005) and has now expanded to include Colombia.

Interestingly, once the OECD published its territorial report (2005) branding the "Mesoamerican Region" or MAR, the debate on the use of the term died down. The change of name from PPP to *Proyecto Mesoamerica* in 2008 was not controversial, a sign that the term is finally accepted. The PPP and MBC projects no longer define Mesoamerica, it now has a regional identity of its own. Although "MAR" is far from being as easily recognised as, for example, "EU" or "NAFTA," Mesoamerica has begun to gain recognition as a regional space.

Regionalism and Mesoamerica

Geographically, Mesoamerica is desirably located between two major oceans and joins North with South America. Thus, it is a vital connection between most trading blocs. Also, within the defined geographic area of the PPP, several regional integration projects already exist (or coexist) and overlap. In this sense, "the PPP is virtually a crossroads of several projects of regional integration" (Chanona 2002).[2] Even though the benefits from the array of these regional arrangements are contested, "regions, then, are perceived as a necessary element of competitiveness in and integration into the fabric of the global economy" (Toly 2004: 49).

The very nature of the PPP has been questioned by several authors (Chanona 2002; Villafuerte 2004a; Álvarez Béjar 2002a), since, in Latin America, integration is still seen through the eyes of classical integration theory (i.e., Balassa 1961). Although they still consider it technically a

[2] See Chapters 2 and 4 for details.

development project, most analysts agree that it is integrationist in its nature. Alejandro Chanona explains that "the PPP is not a process of regional integration per se, but it is very close to being one" (Chanona 2002). Moreover, there is a consensus that the PPP was designed to encourage integration between Mexico and Central America through the building of infrastructure, and that it will have a role to play in both FTAs with the United States, as well as in the then possibly forthcoming FTAA.

There are diverse interpretations to the link between the PPP and the FTAA and other ambitious agreements. Authors such as Villafuerte (2004a), Saldívar (2002), and Álvarez Béjar (2002a), see the possibility of the FTAA as the main *raison d'être* of the PPP, because "the main concern of the PPP is not to compensate the great regional asymmetries that were deepened by the North American Free Trade Agreement (NAFTA), but instead to build the necessary foundations for the globalising project of the Free Trade Area of the Americas" (Villafuerte 2004a: 283). He is very sceptical of the stated purpose of ending the economic structural problems in south-eastern Mexico and believes that instead the planned infrastructure is aimed at strengthening the "weakest link" of the FTAA.

Villafuerte (2004a) sustains this argument by pointing out that the planned highway system (RICAM) does not actually link the nine Mexican States, nor the Central American countries, but instead it links cities to major market venues and ports. Similarly, Barreda (2001) considers the PPP a strategic territorial reorganisation of the region, its primary purpose being the consolidation of the FTAA. Muñoz agrees with this assertion and further adds that "the conceptualization of the PPP as a reterritorialization of capital required an analysis of the organization of space within capitalism… and the relevant role of the state in organizing space through regional agreements" (Muñoz Martínez 2004).

While these analysts consider the use of the PPP as a building block for hemispheric trade as objectionable, López-Calva and Lustig (2003) focus on the potential positive effect the PPP will have on regional convergence in the run-up to the creation of the FTAA (being negotiated at the time). Through econometric analysis and using the European experience, López-Calva and Lustig find that 70% of the convergence pattern is explained by infrastructure and 30% by human capital, expressly, by levels of education.

It was investment in these areas that brought about the convergence of the poorer countries of the European Economic Community (EEC), which was the predecessor of the European Union (EU), and its wealthier members. Their focus, similar to the government documents, is based on the disparities found between the different areas in Mexico. "The Mexican states in the south have not been able to catch up with the rest of Mexico and have followed a convergent pattern with the Central American countries. This means that the whole PPP region needs a specific policy to be able to reverse the divergent pattern from those markets that are well integrated into the world economy" (López-Calva and Lustig 2003: 23).

In other words, since south-eastern Mexico has become more like Central America and is becoming less integrated into the world economy, there is an incentive to promote a project that helps both Central America and south-eastern Mexico to engage in the world economy. Through their study, López-Calva and Lustig (2003), conclude that the investment set out by the PPP could bring about results like those experienced in the EEC.

On the other hand, Pisani and Label considered the PPP "just another vehicle to improve the lot of Central America and Mexico primarily by enhancing basic infrastructure with a call toward greater intra-regional economic liberalization" (Pisani and Label 2003: 35). Like López-Calva and Lustig (2003), their paper focuses only on the economic aspects and demonstrates how the improved infrastructure will attract regional industry. Furthermore, they do not go into detail on whether this new regional industry would bring tangible benefits to the inhabitants of the region. In contrast, Muñoz Martínez warns readers that, although infrastructure projects are considered neutral and apolitical, they are often "concealing the exploitation of labour, the political struggles, and the social implications behind their creation" (Muñoz Martínez 2004: 69).

Ornelas (2002), Salazar (2002), Álvarez Béjar (2002b) and other authors consider that the regional projects taking place in Mesoamerica were all strategically designed by the United States to continue its hegemonic rule in Latin America as well as pursue its interests, specifically anti-immigration and drug trafficking prevention. Sandoval (2002: 171) goes as far as saying "part of the analysis is the role that the PPP plays in the process of arriving at the Free Trade Agreement of the Americas (FTAA); the hegemonic control of all of Latin America by the United States; the linking of the PPP with Plan Colombia; the problem of drug trafficking; guerrillas; migration; and many other difficulties."

It is not without foundation that these authors look towards the United States to explain many of the problems and policies that take place in Mesoamerica. As I noted in the Chapter 1 of this book, the United States played an active and controversial role in the politics of many of these nations. Wounds have not healed in Nicaragua (1981–1990), where US involvement prolonged civil wars and bloodshed and in El Salvador (1980–1992). Panama still has gaping holes from the bombs reminding them of "Operation Just Cause" in the 1990s.

Trade patterns also influence policy, as more than 80% of exports from Mexico and close to 40% from Central America (SIECA 2005) end up in the massive US market. Moreover, remittances sent home by migrants in the United States to their home markets now make up a substantial proportion of GDP in Mexico and most of Central America to the point where, in 2001, El Salvador decided to forgo the use of their currency, the Colon, and change to the US dollar. It is indisputable that the United States has significant influence over Mesoamerica, and yet it is a limited viewpoint to attribute so many of the region's shortcomings or policies solely to the strategic interests of the United States or any other external influence.

Ironically, as Bull (2005) points out, even if the proponents of the PPP should fail to implement the proposed projects as envisaged, it would not mean that Mesoamerican regionalism is dead. The "regionalisation" that has developed as a result of the opposition to the PPP may play a future role in constructing Mesoamerica as a region.

Through the rhetorical emphasis on the common heritage of the Mesoamerican people and the creation of cross-border alliances, it could be the opponents of the PPP that make the Mesoamerican region a political reality (Bull 2005). The declaration resulting from the Chiapas Mesoamerican Forum in 2001 states: "We also envisage integration, but one where the people come first" (*Declaración de Tapachula* 2001). With the benefit of hindsight, what I found is that regionalisation took place hand in hand with the projects. The agenda of the Mesoamerican networks is still primarily to oppose the PPP and, since 2008, *Proyecto Mesoamerica* and the Special Economic Zones (*Zonas Económicas Especiales* [ZEE]). The opposition has seemed to work in sync with the advances in the PPP, even including Colombian civil society groups and NGOs once Colombia became a member.

Stepping back from sensitive political issues, Bull (2005) looks at the PPP through the eyes of the "new regionalism" literature (see the previous chapter). She also places it within the context of the two competing visions of Latin American regionalism: the first originating in Simon Bolivar's Pan-American vision and the second originating in the Monroe Doctrine. Bull reminds the reader that the main lesson from the critical literature is that regionalism in the disadvantaged parts of the world operates under entirely different premises than in the wealthier parts. One example is that of the increased role for not only foreign states but also international organisations, to set the agenda for the regional process. The PPP was heavily dependent on external financing, particularly that of the IDB, albeit the Central American Economic Integration Bank (BCIE), was the source for local funding. As another example, The United Nations Development Programme manages the MBC along with the Global Environment Fund (GEF) and the German Aid agency (GTZ). Moreover, she notes that it is not only the PPP that reconfigures Mesoamerica, but that the civil society and NGO networks have a regionalising effect.

Bartra (2001a) Hernández and Carlsen (2001) discuss proposals for alternative integration and development projects. They call for projects that can be achieved through grassroots movements and local cooperation to meet the needs of local communities. In other words, they propose an alternative integration designed by local communities without the input of government experts. They argue that since the needs of the local communities have been ignored in favour of the aims of big business, even if big regional projects increase GDP in the region, they will not have the desired effect on poverty reduction and community welfare.

3.3 Issues

Trade—specifically free trade—, security, development, alternative development, and the environment are some of the main issues prevalent when discussing Mesoamerica. Many authors centre around one or more of them and discuss the role given to Mesoamerican regional projects regarding these issues, or their effectiveness in dealing with them.

Free Trade: Competitive Advantage and the Neoliberal Discourse

One of the driving forces of the PPP is free trade, which along with neoliberal economics was first administered to the region through the harsh Structural Adjustment Programmes (SAP) imposed by the International

Monetary Fund (IMF) during the mid-1980s and 1990s and later adopted with fervour by a new generation of foreign-educated technocrats in Mexican and Central American governments. The introduction of these measures was anything but subtle; they meant a radical change to economic policy and, for the most part, were detrimental to local production, previously based on an import substitution model. The sudden opening of the markets meant increased trade deficits and exacerbated the inequality between the rich and the poor. Bartra (2001a), Ornelas (2002) and others question the continuance of this policy through projects like the PPP or the FTAA, claiming that the more impoverished population will always lose out with neoliberal economic policies that are inherently designed to benefit the rich.

Principles of free trade introduced half-way through the PPP's *Documento Base*, make it clear that the infrastructure projects were designed to enable the members of the PPP to make full use of the Free Trade agreements already signed between Mexico and Central American nations.[3] The roads included in the project were not meant to link up marginalised communities or intended to shorten travel from villages to markets; they were designed for the movement of goods, moving merchandise to ports, or facilitating transport of goods by land through the region (Bougher 2003). The PPP did not trace new highways; it took previously outlined projects, existing roads, and ports that were underused to "modernise" and link together as a regional system (Interview 38).

Some, like Saldívar (2002), argue that Mexico has not benefited from this model of development in real terms. Using official statistics from the ECLAC/CEPAL and INEGI organisations, Saldívar shows that Mexico only keeps one out of four dollars obtained through exporting manufactured goods (representing 80% of non-energy exports). The government, in the diagnostic PPP documents, argues that south-eastern Mexico needs to find its competitive advantage, mostly that of low labour costs, to be attractive to investors and boost MAR exports. However, not all agree that competitiveness is the answer to the region's deeply rooted economic problems. Miguel Velasco and Heredia Gonzalez (2004), concluded in their analysis of the periods from 1990–1995 to 1995–2000, that competitiveness (as understood in classical economics) is

[3] For details see http://economia.gob.mx/swb/es/economia/p_Tratados_Acuerdos.

not necessarily a factor that has caused the disparities of development between the north and south of Mexico. The south-southeast, as the area of Mexico included in the PPP, is called, showed that rates of competitiveness were in the middle ranges but had a low development rate. One of the factors that influenced the study's resulting data was the fact that the large companies on Mexico's northern border did not transfer benefits to the area, as they were mostly assembly plants with little added value. Other determining factors were geography and environment, where development led to ecological deterioration (Miguel Velasco and Heredia Gonzalez 2004).

Miguel Velasco and Heredia Gonzalez (2004) conclude that the PPP would not bring the desired benefits to the general population of the MAR; instead, it would mostly bring about benefits for big business (MNCs), and those interested in exploiting the natural resources found in the area. This fits in with what other authors have concluded (i.e., Delgadillo Macías 2006; Bartra 2001a): that for the Plan to support positive development within the region, it needs to be redefined to include the expectations of the local population.

In addition to the infrastructure initiatives, which I will discuss in the next section, the PPP also included proposals to harmonise border controls and to establish a series of labour-training projects, particularly for textiles and electronics, the main sectors of the *maquila* industry in Mexico. The PPP documents proposed including *maquiladoras* as a motor for industrial development as it had done in northern Mexico from the inception of NAFTA (*Documento Base* 2001; Barreda 2001).

As pointed out by Labrecque (2005), it seems ludicrous to continue to propose *maquiladoras* as an economic model for development. In her analysis, she recommends that Yucatan (which lured *maquiladoras* away from northern Mexico's triple wages several years before the PPP) "has been a veritable laboratory for the Puebla-Panama Plan" (Labrecque 2005). Based on the Yucatan's experience, she estimates that the rest of the region will experience similar results. Her study shows that as it becomes more challenging to compete with East Asia, wages will drop below worker's subsistence and then companies will begin to pull out leaving behind unemployed people with useless skills (Labrecque 2005). Moreover, it does little for the local economy because they do not use local materials.

Bougher (2003) raises the question, regarding the *maquilas* in El Salvador, of "whether it is better to have employment while fighting for decent wages and working conditions, or not to have the factories at all?" She points out that *maquilas* preferred to hire women as they were easier to control and less likely to unionise (Bougher 2003), heightening gender inequality and marginalisation.

Delgado-Wise (2004) considers this type of industrialisation as "import oriented," noting that even in a more sophisticated industry, such as the automotive, uses up to 90% imported components of the vehicles assembled in *maquilas* and exported to the United States. In these cases, "what is actually being sold to the outside is labour, without it leaving the country" (Delgado-Wise 2004).

Chanona (2002) states that business and political elites are more in tune with the needs of big capital than with the needs of the population around them. Therefore, they continue to push for policies favourable to their interests. According to Bartra (2001a), the PPP is export-oriented and is even limited in as far as intra-regional (MAR) trade is concerned. As I will discuss further in the next two sections, authors are quick to point out that the entire PPP, particularly the planned infrastructure, has been designed to cater to markets outside the MAR while neglecting local and regional markets. Mexico, for example, has a population of about 128 million; however, less than a third of the population has real purchasing power.

Opponents to these models call for a development programme that would focus on increasing the purchasing power of the rest of the population to shift the dependency on foreign markets to growing internal demand.

Development

The MAR needed significant improvements to infrastructure, evident before the launch of the PPP. The deteriorating quality of the region's roads and its unpredictable energy network were identified as inhibiting economic growth (Pisani and Label 2003; López-Calva and Lustig 2003), and both the CEPAL/ECLAC and the IDB cited these issues as imperative to the advancement of Central American Integration (ECLAC 1998). Advocates of the PPP believed that investing in infrastructure would attract private investment and boost exports from the region, thus encouraging the local economy. Infrastructure projects financed by the IDB, like the International Network of Mesoamerican Highways (RICAM) and the Central American Electrical Interconnection System (SIEPAC) were active components of the PPP.

Locals opposed the infrastructure aspects of the proposal; they claimed that since they did not participate in the planning process, these infrastructure projects did not consider their needs and instead catered only to the needs of big business and central government (Villafuerte 2004a). Historically, the needs of the wealthy and powerful were at the forefront of infrastructure projects in the MAR. The development of the first ports and highways during colonial times catered to the needs of the Spanish empire; the building of the railroads during the dictatorship of Porfirio Diaz (1884–1911) in Mexico benefited a small elite, with the *campesinos*, indigenous peoples, and the poor losing out (López Villicaña 2002). Centuries of building infrastructure—supposedly to promote development but then incurring high social costs—have rendered the population sceptical of such rhetoric, particularly when documents such as that of Dávila, Kessel, and Levy state that "the design of the public policies for the southeast should keep separate the objectives of poverty reduction from those of regional development" (Dávila et al. 2002). The PPP did not try to separate these objectives and instead attempted to include a series of points through the Mesoamerican initiatives that would increase cooperation between the key players as well as further integration in the area. "Development" policy centred on boosting economic growth and wagered that by achieving growth, somehow the region would develop.

The PPP was not only about infrastructure and increasing foreign investment in the area. Instead, its design resembled one of the multidimensional manifestations of regionalism considered in the New Regionalism Approach. The plan included budgets for education and health programmes, although these were later reduced due to lack of funding and coordination. It was relatively easier to secure financing for large infrastructure projects than social issues, partly because banks are more likely to lend to projects with higher visible returns, but also because there is a general agreement on such projects (Interview 7: 2006). Smaller projects and those for social improvement lacked coordination among the numerous regional bodies and were often competing for the same funds instead of pooling their resources. Chapters 4 and 6 of this book will further discuss the issues of coordination and regional governance.

Alternative Development

Upon the announcement of the PPP, Subcommandante Marcos, of the EZLN, together with representatives of 109 peasant, labour, environmental, and indigenous organisations, immediately denounced it and pledged that it would be a colossal failure. The "Declaration de Tapachula" resultant from this gathering in Chiapas, in May 2001, accused the PPP as "savage colonialism." After this, anti-PPP groups developed into a regional movement. It included, among others, the general anti-globalisation movement, various community groups, and peasant movements. Several authors mention the first three large-scale gatherings organised by civil society groups and regional networks: May 2001 in Chiapas, November 2001 in Guatemala, and July 2002 in Nicaragua,[4] each including between 250 and 350 groups. The main slogan coined by the Zapatistas was "Peace with justice, democracy, and liberty" (Sandoval Forero 2002). They do not oppose globalisation and the PPP per se, but they are against those that place the "ox behind the cart," privileging free trade and free market over social justice and the protection of the environment (Saldívar 2002).

The civil society movement presented in the Mesoamerican Forums thus far lacks a shared agenda of development; they have gathered under the shared objective of opposing the PPP and later Proyecto Mesoamerica. Even so, Bull considers that they could be pursuing what James Mittleman calls "transformative regionalism" (Mittleman 2000 in Bull 2005). However, as will be explained in Chapter 6 and the final chapter of this book, the Mesoamerican Forums that have taken place show that they remain in a more "reactive" mode than "transformative."

Bartra (2001a, 2002, 2004) and Nicolás-Hiernaeux (2002) explored the possibility of alternatives to the PPP. They rejected the notion of needing a comprehensive plan imposed upon the people and therefore proposed issues that needed to be considered by the people to construct an alternative (or several alternatives) to the PPP (Nicolás-Hiernaeux 2002). They began by identifying what they regarded as the real advantages of the region, such as the socio-diversity of its people; biodiversity that has been nurtured and cared for by its people; communal organisation; cultural richness; and diversity in social and natural spaces. These authors favoured creating an alternative project with the following characteristics: development based on tradition and the right to choose differently; development that respects the natural environment; development based on traditional forms of social organisation; that cohabits with

[4]There has been a total of eight of these gatherings, now known as the Mesoamerican Forums. The last one took place in Minatitlan Veracruz in 2011.

the earth's and people's timing; a grassroots global alternative stemming from below (Nicolás-Hierneaux 2002; Bartra 2001a).

Moreover, given the past relationships between government and opposition movements in the region, the regional networks profoundly mistrust the government representatives, an obstacle that needs addressing.

The Environment

Mesoamerica represents one of the most bio-diverse areas in the world. Its 0.5% of global mass represents 7% of registered global biodiversity (Arreola Muñoz 2006: 142). It also has one of the highest rates of deforestation and loss of animal and plant species. The model used in Mesoamerica is based on a project that began with the National Institute for Biodiversity in Costa Rica (INBio), whose purpose was to facilitate the non-damaging use of the nation's biodiversity. Created in 1989, INBio is a non-profit NGO committed to economic development. According to Meyer (1999), INBio is a unique NGO because its primary objective is to inventory the biodiversity and find a use for it within the economic activity.

The central element of the programme includes multinational corporations (mostly pharmaceuticals) which research genetic and biochemical resources in Costa Rica's conservation areas. Identifying, extracting, and using biochemical resources has become profitable as well as a means of preserving the environment, and the success of the INBio project turned it into a role model to follow as a way of fostering sustainable development (Toly 2004). The MBC, for example, is patterned after the INBio model, and expanded into the region. "In particular, Costa Rican environmental policies are being regionalized through the emergence of the PPP and the MBC" (Toly 2004: 51). But, as opposed to INBio—where "the information generated…is shared freely with non-commercial users, both national and international" (Meyer 1999)—,Toly does not consider the MBC's objectives to be transparent because it applies a commercial element. One crucial factor from the INBio experience is that it employed the local rural population, together with Costa Rican university graduates, to work on the biodiversity inventory, implementing a policy to employ mostly nationals (Meyer 1999). The MBC does not seem to have institutionalised these policies. Even though Meyer considers the INBio experience an example of "obvious success stories," she does concede that "the benefits of such NGO activity cannot be expected to be distributed equally" (Meyer 1999: 75), which contributes to the main arguments against this type of model: unsustainability and unequal distribution.

The main problem, as highlighted by Toly (2004), is that this form of development is often short lived. Initially, while the research and classification are in process, conservation of the area will be essential and therefore successful. However, once this process is complete, there may not be a reason to continue: "to the extent that a particular ecosystem does not offer ecological services, ecotourism opportunities, or genetic and biochemical resources that are highly valued by the global market, they are in danger of converting back to unsustainable uses such as timber or hydroelectricity" (Toly 2004, 52). He also points out that even if these projects result in a sustainable means of profiting from the environment, the local population is not likely to benefit from this use of natural resources; on the contrary, they may find themselves excluded from conservation areas. This occurred in the Montes Azules Biosphere in Chiapas, where people have been expelled numerous times since it was declared a National Conservation site in 1979 (Montemayor 2002). The most recent expulsion was carried out by the army because it was considered a matter of "National Security" (Álvarez Béjar 2002b). Resistance groups are therefore adamant about finding alternative paths for ecological policies that would include local communities and share benefits with them.

Though Toly (2004) gives a broader panorama of the ecological issues involved in both the PPP and the MBC, there are still several questions left unanswered. Considering the present state of the environment in the region and its daily loss of species, would continuing with the status quo pre-PPP and MBC be a better alternative to the current plans? Those rejecting the plan altogether, have yet to put forth comprehensive options that include the local population. They mostly infer that the local farmers and indigenous communities have a symbiotic relationship with nature and therefore would care for it better than a government-designed plan. Notwithstanding, this "symbiotic relationship" is not evident amid poverty and lack of education, further highlighting that the problem must be addressed from many fronts.

Although the general population better accepts the MBC, many authors (i.e., Bartra 2004; Muñoz Martínez 2004; Pickard 2004; Álvarez Béjar 2002a; Rioja Peregrina 2002; Villafuerte 2004b) consider its elements as forms of "biopiracy" and exploitation of the area. Rioja goes as far as to compare what he calls a new kind of environmental piracy with the naval pirates from the sixteenth and seventeenth centuries because, in both cases, the "pirates" had the support of their home government (Rioja Peregrina 2002). On the one hand, the actors losing out are the poor indigenous and *campesino* communities while on the other side, the ones profiting are universities, governments, agro-industry, pharmaceutical, and other multinational companies (Rioja Peregrina 2002).

Governments and companies would argue that bioprospecting, which is the official term for identifying and investigating live organisms, is not harmful to indigenous communities. Bartra (2001a), Rioja (2002), and Sandoval (2002) argue the contrary. Researchers rely on the knowledge of local communities when carrying out their investigation and then patent their final product. The investigating party is the only one that can use the patent once its registered, and the indigenous population who provided invaluable information for the research can no longer commercialise their knowledge in the future. Companies buy low and sell high whatever they extract from biogenetics; they do not share or distribute the knowledge obtained or the use or advantages with the original owners (Saldívar 2002; Rioja Peregrina 2002).

Instead, Saldívar (2002) argues that local and indigenous communities have the right to take care and make the best use of their natural resources. Nevertheless, these authors do not provide a feasible alternative. As they noted declaring the areas protected and thus not allowing any economic activity condemns the local community to poverty or clandestine operation. Letting all the communities make use of the environment as they see fit could also exacerbate deforestation and the misuse of natural resources.

Security: Migration, Drugs, and Armed Conflict

Neither the PPP nor Proyecto Mesoamerica addressed security issues as part of their initiatives. Regional cooperation for security remained mainly within the scope of the Tuxtla Mechanism (for Mexico and Central American cooperation) and other regional bodies of collaboration in the Americas. Nonetheless, security was at the forefront of debate since it is considered one of the critical issues affecting Mesoamerica.

There are two kinds of security threats in Mesoamerica: those that directly affect the people within the area (such as armed conflict, the *Maras* violent gang groups, and drug-related activity) and the issues that affect others outside Mesoamerica (Bull 2005). The United States shows a vested interest in addressing security threats in Mesoamerica as some of these threats reach its borders. The existential threats include the increasing flow of migrants from the MAR to the United States, drug trafficking, guerrillas, and paramilitary groups as well as the vulnerability of core resources such as oil and water.

According to Delgado-Wise (2004: 146), Mexican migration policy under the Fox administration shifted towards a "greater subordination of the country to the strategic, geopolitical, and geo-economic interests of the United States." Although the PPP stipulated that the main deterrent to migration was to create jobs in areas with high emigration rates, other measures have been taken to deter Central American migrants from entering Mexico and penetrating further to reach the United States (Bull 2005). Mexican officials argue that policies implemented deterring Central Americans from illegally crossing into Mexico are essential to the "national security" of Mexicans, and not of the United States. Thus, the Mexican officials reproduce the security discourse used by the Americans regarding the northern border (Bull 2005), where Mexico is trying to negotiate better treatment for illegal immigrants and a higher number of working visas for migrant workers.

Armando Bartra (2001a), states that the issue of stopping migration is the only thing that he agrees with in the whole PPP, although not for the same reasons as the government, instead, due to the social breakdown it causes. Men who migrate to the United States during peak times (*i.e.*, harvest) are gone for many months of the year, leaving behind single-parent households to care for the land and economy back home. A different viewpoint is presented by Delgado-Wise (2004), who notes that, for the most part, migrant workers do not work in primary sectors and in the case of Mexicans, hold a higher level of education than the (Mexican) national average. Migration causes Mexico to lose a substantial amount of its qualified workforce. Considering that most migrant workers spend their income on their living expenses in the United States, even with the high level of remittances back home, these directly benefit the US economy. Migrants also contribute more taxes to their host economy than they receive in benefits and public services. In the same way, the home government does not collect fiscal contributions from the workers. The only taxes the Mexican or Central American governments receive, are the taxes collected from transfer services (*i.e.*, Travelex or Western Union) compared to what they would receive from taxing full wages of the workers if they remained at home (Delgado-Wise 2004).

Sandoval (2001) is concerned with the policies that Mexico has put into place to stop Central American migrants from using Mexican territory as a route into the United States. He documents the history of Central American migration to the United States in the 1980s as a result of fleeing the military conflicts that were rampant in the region. This massive influx of migrants into the United States caused "a response of alarm towards a phenomenon that they considered a threat to their national security, which this nation (US) helped create" (Sandoval 2001: 231). Upon analysing and comparing documents emitted by the United States, Guatemala, El Salvador, and Mexican governments concerning migration, Sandoval is concerned that the United States is "regionalising its immigration policies just as it has done with its economic and political-military policies" (Sandoval 2006). He considered the PPP as a channel for imposing strict migrant controls from the southern Mexican border to stop the flow of Central Americans travelling to the United States.[5]

Military presence in the MAR increased since the announcement of the PPP, extending beyond the border areas. One extreme is the picture depicted by Salazar Perez (2002) of the plans to override the region of the PPP and Colombia with US-trained military in order to contain drug trafficking and keep track of the movements of guerrilla or dissident groups. Although this picture seems somewhat over-embellished, military presence is found in the area and has been used to patrol areas controlled by the Zapatistas, as well as the borders and landing strips. The military has also been known to burn *campesino* and indigenous community fields to get rid of alleged drug tillage. Particularly controversial was the Plan Nuevos Horizontes, stationing US troops in Nicaragua and Guatemala (NoPPP 2002; Salazar Perez 2002) and the Plan Merida, where the United States provided Mexico assistance with fighting drug trafficking and organised crime and was extended to include Central America and the Caribbean (*El Universal* 21 December 2008 and 31 January 2009).[6]

[5]In 2018, the US has threatened to condition NAFTA re-negotiations to migration issues. https://www.reuters.com/article/us-trade-nafta-mexico/mexico-dismisses-trump-threat-to-tie-nafta-to-migration-policy-idUSKBN1HU27T.

[6]"Impulsan Plan Mérida Regional," Silvia Otero, 21 December 21 2008, *El Universal*; "Guatemala ve desorden en la Iniciativa Mérida," Silvia Otero, 31 January 2009, *El Universal*.

The *Maras*, or organised (mostly youth) violent street gangs, are now a significant security issue for Central American and Mexican policymakers (Savenije 2007). Generally considered a phenomenon that initiated in the United States, the *Maras* emerged during the 1980s in the streets of Los Angeles. They were initially composed by young Central Americans living in Los Angeles that found themselves threatened by the already well organised Chicano street gangs and in response, formed their own bands (Savenije considers the possibility that some of the youth leaders actually formed part of Calle 18, a well-known Chicano gang, and later branched off). As the street gangs became a violent problem in the United States, campaigns to deport them to their countries of origin took place. Some were expelled due to criminal behaviour or illegal status, and many lost their refugee status once peace accords were signed and thus returned to their countries of origin. There the gangs reunited became stronger but continued to have links to groups in the United States and across Central America, creating transnational networks (Íñiguez 2005; Savenije 2007). As pointed out by Savenije (2007) and by Ángeles and Martínez (2006), street gangs in Central America did not initiate with the foreign-bred arrivals, but the gang culture changed with it. The gangs multiplied, becoming increasingly violent as they became more involved in drug trafficking, and developed into a regional concern. The most violent *Mara*, the *Mara Salvatrucha* or 13, has an estimated 100,000 members throughout the United States, Mexico, and Central America.[7] During the most recent Tuxtla Mechanism summits, *Maras* have been high on the agenda as a regional security concern. The permeable borders in Mexico and Central America have allowed them to roam freely, increase their membership and become more involved with organised crime. Savenije (2007) warns that the "*mano dura*" and other anti-*Mara* policies in Central America have caused the *Maras* to migrate to Mexico.

Some authors, like Ángeles and Martínez (2006), are concerned that the governments have upgraded the issue to one of "national security" and have only taken repressive measures to control the problem. Savenije (2007), compares the different experience of Nicaragua where there is a strong presence of local street gangs but not the transnational *Maras*, as

[7]An in-depth documentary on the Maras was aired on Discovery channel, 16 March 2008, summaries of this documentary can be found on http://www.tudiscovery.com/maras/index.shtml "Maras, una amenaza regional".

a reference point to guide policymaking towards the problem. Íñiguez (2005), for example, does not believe that the *Maras* pose a regional threat but instead a challenge—one to face with "intelligent and deliberate actions". Savenije (2007) cautions that while repressive measures might ensure public safety, they do not consider the social causes behind the phenomenon, and thus, it will continue to breed. Íñiguez (2005) points out that according to his research, poverty is not the decisive factor in the increase of the *Maras,* so he advises policymakers to expand their strategy beyond poverty reduction. The increasing violence experienced in Mesoamerica in *Mara* strongholds is such, that more and more migrants fleeing the region claim that remaining in their homes means certain death.[8]

Toussaint and Garzón (2017), relate the problem of the *Maras* from their origin and how poverty, inequality, marginalisation, and lack of opportunities for youth made Mesoamerica fertile ground for the proliferation of gangs and violence (Toussaint and Garzón 2017: 25). They highlight that the violence generated by the *Maras* in the border regions has become a problem of national security for Mexico, and also, it has caused stigma for Central American migrants who are perceived as delinquents, making them vulnerable to repressive acts by Mexican authorities (Toussaint and Garzón 2017: 27).

According to several opposition groups, the PPP served US security interests in another sense; namely to secure access to vital natural resources. The MAR could provide supplemental oil reserves to the United States's increasingly unreliable supply (NoPPP 2002). The Mexican states included in the PPP account for 65% of Mexico's oil reserves and 95% of its current oil production. Although illegal exploration took place in some of the virgin jungles of Guatemala during the 1990s, none of these reserves have been formally exploited. Opposition groups to the PPP feared that the project would increase oil exploration and development of oil extraction in the Petén province in Guatemala and Mesoamerica in General (NoPPP 2002). At one point, former Mexican President Vicente Fox had made plans to establish an oil refinery in Central America (possibly Costa Rica) as well as a natural gas processing

[8] "Pide Trump detener caravana migratoria" Periódico Reforma, 3 April 2018, p. 4; "Esperan por asilo en frontera de EU" Periódico Reforma 30 April 2018, p. 2; http://www.excelsior.com.mx/global/cinco-puntos-para-entender-la-caravana-migrante/1236194.

plant (Ivonne Melgar, *Reforma*, 4 November 2005) since most oil exported from Mexico is crude, however, these did not take place.[9]

3.4 Governance

Until this point in the chapter, I have discussed the issues central to the arguments used against the PPP by those critical of the project or directly opposing it. Governance is mentioned indirectly by those opposing the PPP when they point out how local communities and other important actors that were key to implementing the PPP were ignored. The unclear relationship between the PPP and the Central American Integration bodies highlighted problems in regional governance through the overlap of activities and lack of coordination. However, governance was not addressed and remained on the sidelines of the primary debates.

Conversely, in 2005, the OECD published a territorial review on the Mesoamerican Region. Like most territorial reviews, it is full of statistical information and evaluations on the region's macroeconomic performance. It evaluates potential economic opportunities that could result from improving the MAR's infrastructure, using its natural and cultural resources and increasing the *maquiladoras*, to promote industrialisation. All in all, this review has many similarities with the PPP diagnostic documents, even using the same statistical information provided by the INEGI. Like the PPP documents, it gives an accurate description of the lack of services and opportunities faced by the people living in Mesoamerica as well as the high rates of inequality among the different sectors of the population. The document stresses competitiveness as the key to obtaining a reliable source of economic growth, which would then translate into a source of development (OECD 2006: 82–143).

The second part of the territorial review, however, dealt with governance and recognised that "Governance across levels of government –or 'multilevel governance'– has become a major issue in territorial policy making" (OECD 2006: 68). The OECD (2005) report gives specific instructions on what should be done to improve governance along the lines of the "projects of governance" I introduced in the previous chapter. First, it recommended that reforming regional institutions (OECD

[9] An ongoing controversy in Mexico throughout 2008 was to allow foreign investment in the national oil company Pemex. During Peña Nieto's presidency (2012–2018) Energy reform passed to allow foreign investment.

2006: 27) so that these could then design and implement a territorial development policy. Then a meso-regional territorial information system should be created (OECD 2006: 28–29) for the MAR. It not only recommended the reform of regional institutions, but it also called for decentralisation and reforms both at national levels and sub-national levels so that each one knew its assigned role. Part of its diagnosis identified that:

> Vertical relations across levels of government are regulated by complex sets of administrative laws, which are often unknown to officials. These laws tend to assign competences for territorial development to different central level ministries without specifying how sub-national authorities should be involved. The result is that there are several areas where neither the central nor the local level act. (OECD 2006: 30)

Without repeating every recommendation given by the OECD to improve governance and to achieve functional "multi-level governance," it is essential to point out that they are all based on the reform of regional and national government institutions. Even though transparent, efficient institutions are important towards achieving effective governance, institutional restructuring through external recommendations and technical support may not be the best means by which to do this in Mesoamerica. So far, the many attempts at institutional reform coupled with internal national politics have not produced the desired results.

3.5 Post-PPP

The announcement of the restructuring of the PPP on 10 April 2007 did not significantly change the formed opinions about Mesoamerican regionalism. Japhy Wilson (2008), for example, considered that whatever restructuring might take place institutionally in the PPP, the general implications for the state of Chiapas would be to the detriment of its inhabitants, particularly the indigenous majority. The transition to *Proyecto Mesoamerica*, for the most part, did not make front page news, but there were some reactions in the media. Some interpreted the change as an effort by the Mexican Presidency to recover regional leadership (*Nación*, 28 August 2008)[10] while others considered it purely a

[10] Also see *Nación* 7 April 2007 after the extraordinary meeting of the PPP in Campeche.

name change to avert controversy (*La Jornada*, 29 June 2008). Some newspapers like *El Universal* buried the transformation into a small article about the housing credits announced during the summit (*El Universal*, 29 June 2008). The *Jornada* newspaper which had published a full supplement upon the announcement of the PPP in 2001, gave it the most amount of print space. It summed up the transformation by stating:

> (President) Calderón spurred the name change and together with his Salvadorian counterpart, Elías Antonio Saca, he made the announcement, which concludes the plan born seven years ago in the midst of controversy and that was several times declared dead by its critics due to setbacks and few achievements.[11]

Bosco Martí Ascencio (2007), none the less welcomed the idea of replacing the PPP with a new version, stating that even though the PPP had not achieved many of its objectives, many lessons had been learned and it was a project worth revising and implementing. Once *Proyecto Mesoamerica* was launched, Martí Ascencio further analysed what he considered to be the legacy of the PPP and the implications for the new project.[12] According to Martí Ascencio (2008), there are three main legacies from the PPP. The first is that it nurtured the Tuxtla Mechanism which was created after the signing of the Central American peace accords, but that had not seen effective use until the PPP. Second: Mexico's interest in Central America and Central American integration generated interest from international organisations. This interest translated into financial and technical support flowing into the region. Third: he considers that the PPP placed the south-eastern part of Mexico on the national agenda, noting the lack of previous government investment and planning (Martí Ascencio 2008: 11–12).

The rest of his article reviews the infrastructure projects completed under the PPP and then continues to explain the institutional and project reorganisation into *Proyecto Mesoamerica*. Though his evaluation

[11] Claudia Beltrán, "Sepultan en Villahermosa PPP y lo reciclan como Proyecto Mesoamérica," *La Jornada*, 28 June 2008.

[12] It is important to note, even though it is not mentioned in his articles, that Bosco Martí Ascencio, at the time of publication of these articles, was the Mexican Deputy Presidential Commissioner for *Proyecto Mesoamerica*.

regarding the legacy of the PPP brings out some valid points, because of the extensive debates that reviewed in this chapter, they are quite narrow. López Castellanos (2009) paints a bleaker picture than either Wilson or Martí Ascencio. He reiterates the assertion of previous authors that the PPP was designed exclusively for the benefit of US capital by reducing the production and transport of goods. According to Lopez Castellanos, *Proyecto Mesoamerica* is not a weaker version of the PPP but a stronger one, he states that "the novelty is the name and the incorporation of Colombia that, under the government of Álvaro Uribe, has been characterised as a military government, completely enabling the interests of the United States and that is why it is a natural ally of the PAN government in Mexico" (López Castellanos 2009: 24). He considers that the US government of Barack Obama was worrisome due to the interest it had given to the region and the increase in military bases in the region since taking office. He also considers that the military coup that took place in Honduras in 2009 was a product of US economic interests (López Castellanos 2009: 70) since the government of overthrown Manuel Zelaya was close to the left-wing governments of Bolivia and Venezuela and "threatened the Proyecto Mesoamerica or at least Honduras' participation" (López Castellanos 2009: 70).

Capdepont Balina (2011) stresses that the Proyecto Mesoamerica as a continuation of the PPP, was still relevant because it took advantage of the region's strategic location and its valuable natural resources. His historical account of Mesoamerica highlights colonial exploitation, and how external actors searched the Isthmus for new paths to cross from the Atlantic to the Pacific Ocean. He urges his readers to remember the geopolitical context leading up to the building and later, the control of the Panama Canal. It is of no surprise to him that the PPP suggested creating "dry canals" and other infrastructure focused on the movement of merchandise (Capdepont Balina 2011).

Martha Ardila (2015) considers Proyecto Mesoamerica a project of cooperative multilateralism, where Mexico and Colombia are taking on the role of regional leaders. Noting that Mexico has lost legitimacy as a regional power due to violence and drug trafficking, she considers that it is using Proyecto Mesoamerica (as well as the Pacific Alliance) to maintain presence as a regional player. Mexico's interest in Central America, however, goes beyond wanting to remain a regional power. Mexico "is worried about the instability of the Isthmus, its problems of poverty and instability.... even more today, when there are security threats present both in Central America and in large parts of Mexican territory" (Ardila 2015).

Monica Toussaint and Marisol Garzón (2017), question whether Proyecto Mesoamerica has been a success or failure noting the projects' objectives, scope, and priorities. They highlight two major issues in Mexico (they don't include Central America): migration and violence. They argue that leaving out these crucial elements render the regional cooperation agreement futile and useless.

Juan Manuel Sandoval Palacios, Raquel Alvarez de Flores, and Sara Yaneth Fernández Moreno (2011) compiled a series of essays into a book project to address another situation they felt was being ignored. Their book focuses on the displacement of peoples caused by or aggravated by *Proyecto Mesoamerica*. The appropriation of land for specific projects like dams or highways caused the displacement of peoples. Alvarez de Flores and Rivera Castellanos (2011) note that in Colombia indigenous communities on the border with Venezuela were forced off their land, first by armed guerrillas and military presence and now due to the exploration for oil and other natural resources. Fernández and Pacheco (2011) argue that agro-industry elements of Proyecto Mesoamerica and the search for natural resources have damaged the environment increasing the occurrence of natural disasters. Many displaced people in Mesoamerica have left their places of origin due to natural disasters (hurricanes, earthquakes) that have left them homeless and desolate. Displacement of people is not linked to only one cause nor does it go in only one direction, as explained by Gellert and Lynch: "Primary displacement not only refers to the movement of peoples' 'out of the way' of project development, but the movement of workers into areas where the demand for project labour outstrips the local supply" (Gellert and Lynch 2003: 17–18).

3.6 Summary

The PPP brought to light many of the most relevant issues for the MAR. These issues have been discussed thoroughly by academics and other authors resulting in a vibrant debate about the development of the region and the implications that regionalism in the form of the PPP could have had on the welfare of the inhabitants of the MAR. However, many interesting questions that arise in the literature were left unanswered. Much of the debate in favour or against the PPP highlighted the importance of addressing ongoing issues in the region, and the appropriateness (or lack thereof) of the PPP to do so.

The question posed in this book is not whether replacing the PPP had to do with its appropriateness in addressing regional issues (without minimising the essential debates on policymaking). Instead, it asks whether it was the weak and fractured levels of governance in the MAR that hindered the implementation of the PPP, and if so, could any multidimensional regional development plan succeed? Going beyond the issues and considering these more general themes could shed light on some of the roots of the problems in the MAR beyond their manifestations. Viewing the PPP in this light will also show the importance of governance in the relationship between regionalism and regionalisation. Governance at all levels will determine how much of the "regionalisation" process makes it into a formal regionalism and it will also influence whether the regionalism produces a "regionalisation" process, increasing "regionness."

The following chapters will show how the PPP helped to shape Mesoamerica as a region both by modifying existing regional structures and by encouraging regionalisation (as a part of and reaction to the project). The PPP also shed light on regional governance in Mesoamerica and how it attracted technical support to address these issues. I will argue that the PPP did not achieve its goals since from its creation, it did not include non-state actors in the design and prioritisation of projects. The next three chapters will show that the governance systems required for implementing the PPP were weak and fractured.

The following chapter, I present the network of regional projects directly within Mesoamerica and discuss the interaction with projects that overlap one or more of the countries involved. I examine the coordination mechanisms and review the cases where relations improved. I obtained most of the information presented in Chapter 4 through visits to the regional bodies and local research centres in 2006; these visits enriched my understanding of the effectiveness of these institutions and the possible outcomes of institutional reform.

Bibliography

Acta que institucionaliza el Mecanismo del Plan Puebla-Panamá. 2004. http://www.sieca.org.gt/Sitio-publico/OACUERDOS/83-1Acta.htm. Accessed 3 March 2006.

Aguirre Rojas, Carlos Antonio. 2002. A Modo de Introducción: Chiapas en Perspectiva Histórica. In *Chiapas en Perspectiva Histórica*, ed. Aguirre Rojas Carlos Antonio, Bolívar Echeverría, Carlos Montemayor, and Wallerstein Immanuel, 2nda edición. España: El Viejo Topo.

Álvarez Béjar, Alejandro. 2002a. El Plan Puebla-Panamá en el contexto de la integración hemisférica Política y Cultura Núm. 18, 83–105. UNAM, otoño.

Álvarez Béjar, Alejandro. 2002b. The Puebla-Panama Plan: Development of a Region or Multinational Enclave? In *Economía Política del Plan Puebla Panamá*, ed. Alejandro Álvarez Béjar, Andrés Barreda Marín, y Armando Bartra. México: Editorial Itaca.

Álvarez Béjar, Alejandro. 2002c. Sies Factores Estructurales que explican la estrategia del Plan Puebla Panama. In *Economía Política del Plan Puebla Panamá*, ed. Alejandro Álvarez Béjar, Andrés Barreda Marín, y Armando Bartra. México: Editorial Itaca.

Álvarez Béjar, Alejandro, Andrés Barreda, and Armando Bartra (eds.). 2002. *Economía Política del Plan Puebla Panamá*. México: Editorial Itaca.

Alvarez de Flores, Raquel, and Rivera Castellanos Luz Dary. 2011. Desplazamientos Forzados de Poblaciones Indígenas en la Frontera Colombo-Venezolana a Raíz de los Mega Proyectos de Desarrollo. In *Planes Geoestratégicos, Desplazamientos y Migraciones Forzadas en el Área del Proyecto de Desarrollo e Integración Mesoamérica*, coordinadores Juan Manuel Sandoval Palacios, Raquel Álvarez de Flores, and Sara Yaneth Fernández Moreno. México: Seminario Permanente de Estudios Chicanos y de Fronteras, DEAS-INAH; Venezuela: Centro de Estudios de Fronteras e Integración, Universidad de Los Andes-Táchira; Colombia: Departamento de Trabajo Social, Facultad de Ciencias Sociales y Humanas, Universidad de Antioquia. https://www.academia.edu/7454005/PLANES_GEOESTRAT%C3%89GICOS_DESPLAZAMIENTOS_Y_MIGRACIONES_FORZADAS_EN_EL_%C3%81REA_DEL_PROYECTO_DE_DESARROLLO_E_INTEGRACI%C3%93N_DE_MESOAM%C3%89RICA.

Ángeles Cruz, Hugo, and Santiago Martínez Junco. 2006. Violencia social y pandillas. Las maras en la región fronteriza del Soconusco, Chiapas. In *Geoeconomía y Geopolítica en el área del Plan Puebla Panamá*, ed. Daniel Villafuerte Solis and Xochitl Leyva Solano. México: Editorial Miguel Angel Porrúa.

Ardila, Martha. 2015. El regionalismo mexicano en la Alianza del Pacífico y el Proyecto Mesoamérica. *Carta Económica Regional Año* 27 (116) (Julio-Diciembre): 36–62.

Arreola Muñoz, Arturo V. 2006. Mesoamérica, el saldo actual de sus recursos naturales estratégicos. In *Geoeconomía y Geopolítica en el área del Plan Puebla Panamá*, ed. Daniel Villafuerte Solis and Xochitl Leyva Solano. México: Editorial Miguel Angel Porrúa.

Balassa, Bela A. 1961. *The Theory of Economic Integration*. London: Allen and Unwin.

Barreda Marin, Andres. 2001. Los Peligros del Plan Puebla Panama. In *Mesoamerica: Los Ríos Profundos. Alternativas Plebeyas al Plan Puebla Panamà*, ed. Armando Bartra. México: RMALC/El Atajo Ediciones/Instituto "Maya", A.C.

Barreda Marín, Andrés. 2002a. Los Objetivos del Plan Puebla Panamá. In *Economía Política del Plan Puebla Panamá*, ed. Alejandro Álvarez Béjar, Andrés Barreda Marín, y Armando Bartra. México: Editorial Itaca.

Barreda Marín, Andrés. 2002b. El Plan Puebla Panamá. *Biodiversidad* 33 (Agosto): 1–8.

Bartra, Armando (ed.). 2001a. *Mesoamerica: Los Ríos Profundos. Alternativas Plebeyas al Plan Puebla Panamà*. México: RMALC/El Atajo Ediciones/ Instituto "Maya", A.C.

Bartra, Armando. 2001b. SUR. Megaplanes y utopías en la América equinoccial. In *Mesoamerica: Los Ríos Profundos. Alternativas Plebeyas al Plan Puebla Panamà*, ed. Armando Bartra. México: RMALC/El Atajo Ediciones/ Instituto "Maya", A.C.

Bartra, Armando. 2002. Hacia una Nueva Colonización del Sureste. In *Economía Política del Plan Puebla Panamá*, ed. Alejandro Álvarez Béjar, Andrés Barreda Marín, y Armando Bartra. México: Editorial Itaca.

Bartra, Armando. 2004. Mesoamericanos: Recalentando una identidad colectiva cemos. *MEMORIA Revista Mensual de Política y Cultura Numero 183*, Mayo.

Bougher, Kathy. 2003. Women's Lives for Sale: Free Trade and Education in El Salvador. *Off Our Backs* 33 (11) (November–December): 15–18.

Bull, Benedicte. 2005. Between Bush and Bolivar: Change and Continuity in the Remaking of Mesoamerica. In *The Political Economy of Regions and Regionalisms*, ed. Morten Bøås, Marianne H. Marchand, and Timothy M. Shaw. Basingstoke: Palgrave Macmillan.

Bull, Benedicte, and Morten Bøås. 2003. Multilateral Development Banks as Regionalising Actors: The Asian Development Bank and the Inter-American Development Bank. *New Political Economy* 8 (2) (July): 245–260.

Call, Wendy. 2002. Plan Puebla-Panama: Done Deal or Emerging Flashpoint? *International Journal of Public Administration* 9 (April): 24.

Capdepont Ballina, Jorge Luis. 2011. Mesoamérica o el Proyecto Mesoamérica: La Historia como Pretexto. *Revista LiminaR. Estudios Sociales y Humanísticos año* 9 (1) (junio). ISSN: 1665-8027.

Carr, Archie III. 2002. A Plait of Three Colors. *Americas* 54 (July–August): 64. http://www.questia.com/.

Carranza, Mario Esteban. 2000. *South American Free Trade Area or Free Trade Area of the Americas? Open regionalism and the future of regional economic integration in South America* Farnham: Ashgate.

Chanona, Alejandro. 2002. Procesos de integración en el marco del Plan Puebla-Panamá (PPP). In *Lectura Crítica del Plan Puebla Panamá*, coordinadores

Eduardo Andrés Sandoval Forero y Robinson Salazar Pérez. Buenos Aires: Libros en Red.

Chomsky, Noam. 1985. *Turning the Tide: U.S. Intervention in Central America and the Struggle for Peace*. Boston: South End Press.

Coordinadora regional de los altos de Chiapas de la sociedad civil en resistencia. 2002. *Plan Puebla – Panamá: Un proyecto de "Desarrollo"...¿Para quién?* http://www.nadir.org/nadir/initativ/agp/free/colobmia/puebla/pueblapanama.htm.

Curly, Jon M. 2008. Cleaning Up the Spaghetti Bowl. In *Economic Integration in the Americas*, ed. A. McKinney Joseph and Stephen Gardner. London: Routledge.

Dávila Enrique, Kessel Georgina, y Levy Santiago. 2002. El Sur también existe: un ensayo sobre el desarrollo regional de México (originally published in Economía Mexicana, vol. XI, 202–260). In *Ensayos Sobre el Desarrollo Económico y Social de México*, compilador Santiago Levy. México: Fondo de Cultura Económica.

Declaración de Mérida. 2002. Declaración Conjunta de la quinta cumbre del Mecanismo de Diálogo y Concertación de Tuxtla, 27 y 28 de junio 2002. http://sieca.org.gt/Publico/OACUERDOS/DeclaraciondeMerida.htm.

Declaración de Guatemala. 2000. Declaración Conjunta de la IV Cumbre de los Jefes de Estado y de Gobierno de los países integrantes del Mecanismo de Diálogo y Concertación de Tuxtla, 25 de Agosto. http://www.sieca.org.gt/publico/OACUERDOS/TuxtlaIV.htm.

Declaración de Tapachula. 2001. Photocopy of Text.

Declaración de Villahermosa. 2008. *Declaración Conjunta de la décima cumbre del Mecanismo de Diálogo y Conceración de Tuxtla*, 28 de junio de 2008. http://sieca.org.gt/publico/OACUERDOS/DeclaraciondeVillahermosa.htm.

Declaración Extraordinaria. 2001. Declaración Conjunta de la Cumbre extraordinaria de los países integrantes del Mecanismo de Diálogo y Concertación de Tuxtla. http://sieca.org.gt/publico/OACUERDOS/DECLARACION_CONJUNTA_DE_LA.

Declaración Política del VII Foro Mesoamericano de los Pueblos ¡Mesoamérica en Resistencia, No al neocolonialismo del libre comercio! 2008. http://Chiapas.indymedia.org/local/webcast/uploads/declaracion_vii_mesoamericano.pdf.

Delgadillo Macías, Javier. 2006. El cálculo de un índice de desarrollo socioeconómico para la región del sur-sureste de México. In *Los espacios de reserva en la expansión global del capital: El sur-sureste mexicano da cara al Plan Puebla-Panamá*, Felipe Torres Torres y José Gasca Zamora (coordinadores). Barcelona, España: Universidad Nacional Autónoma de México y Plaza y Valdés S.A de C.V.

Delgado-Wise, Raúl. 2004. The Hidden Agenda of Mexico's Fox Administration. *Latin American Perspectives* 31 (5) (September): 146–164.

Dirección Ejecutiva Proyecto de Integración y Desarrollo de Mesoamérica. 2008. *Informe de Actividades 2008.* El Salvador. www.planpuebla-panama.org. Accessed 4 November 2008.

Edelman, Marc. 1998. Transnational Peasant Politics in Central America. *Latin American Research Review* 33 (3): 49–86.

Fernández, Sara Yaneth, y Carlos Iván Pacheco. 2011. Macroproyectos, desplazamiento y guerra en Colombia: apropiación de territorios y de los cuerpos como referentes simbólicos de dominio. In *Planes Geoestratégicos, Desplazamientos y Migraciones Forzadas en el Área del Proyecto de Desarrollo e Integración Mesoamérica*, coordinadores Juan Manuel Sandoval Palacios, Raquel Álvarez de Flores, and Sara Yaneth Fernández Moreno. México: Seminario Permanente de Estudios Chicanos y de Fronteras, DEAS-INAH; Venezuela: Centro de Estudios de Fronteras e Integración, Universidad de Los Andes-Táchira; Colombia: Departamento de Trabajo Social, Facultad de Ciencias Sociales y Humanas, Universidad de Antioquia. http://www.academia.edu/7454005/PLANES_GEOESTRATÉGICOS_DESPLAZAMIENTOS_Y_MIGRACIONES_FORZADAS_EN_EL_ÁREA_DEL_PROYECTO_DE_DESARROLLO_E_INTEGRACIÓN_DE_MESOAMÉRICA.

Fregosi, Renée. 2008. Gobernabilidad y Gobernanza Global: desafíos teóricos y políticos. In *II Escuela Chile-Francia: Transformaciónes del Espacio Público*, ed. Ximena Póo. Chile: Documento de Recopilación de Ponencias Cátedra Chile-Francia "Michel Foucoult".

Gellert, Paul K., and Barbara D. Lynch. 2003. *Mega-Projects as Displacements.* Oxford: Blackwell.

Grugel, Jean, and Wil Hout. 1999. *Regionalism Across the North-South Divide State Strategies and Globalization.* London and New York: Routledge.

Grupo Técnico Interinstitucioinal (GTI). 2001. *Plan Puebla-Panamá: Iniciativas Mesoamericanas y Proyectos.* San Salvador, El Salvador: BCIE-BID-ECLAC con el apoyo del INCAE.

Hansen, Tom. 2001. El neoliberalismo como fundamento del PPP. In *Mesoamerica: Los Ríos Profundos. Alternativas Plebeyas al Plan Puebla Panamà*, ed. Armando Bartra. México: RMALC/El Atajo Ediciones/ Instituto "Maya", A.C.

Harvey, Neil. 2006. La disputa por los recursos naturales en el área del Plan Puebla Panamá. In *Geoeconomía y Geopolítica en el área del Plan Puebla Panamá*, ed. Daniel Villafuerte Solis and Xochitl Leyva Solano. México: Editorial Miguel Ángel Porrúa.

Hernández Navarro, Luis, and Laura Carlsen. 2001. El Plan Puebla Panamá, Pueblos Indígenas y Café. In *Mesoamerica: Los Ríos Profundos. Alternativas Plebeyas al Plan Puebla Panamà*, ed. Armando Bartra. México: RMALC/El Atajo Ediciones/Instituto "Maya", A.C.

Hettne, Björn, and Fredrik Söderbaum. 2002. Theorising the Rise of Regionness. In *New Regionalisms in the Global Political Economy Theories and Cases*, ed. Shaun Breslin et al. London: Routledge.

Hufty, Marc. 2009. The Governance Analytical Framework. www.north-south.unibe.ch/content.php/publications/Infosystem/On-line%20Dokumente/Upload/GovernanceFrameworkE.pdf. Accessed 15 July 2010.

Informe Ejecutivo. 2006. El PPP: Avances retos y Perspectivas.

Informe Ejecutivo. 2008. El PPP: Avances retos y Perspectivas.

Íñiguez, Martín. 2005. Los Maras ¿Problema de seguridad pública o nacional? Territorio y Economía Número Especial 4/2005. México: Frontera Sur, Sistema de Información Regional de México, 19–26.

Labrecque, Marie France. 2005. Cultural Appreciation and Economic Depreciation of the Mayas of Northern Yucatán, México. *Latin American Perspectives* 32 (4) (July): 87–105.

Levy, Santiago (compilador). 2004. *Ensayos Sobre el Desarrollo Económico y Social de México*. México: Fondo de Cultura Económica.

Levy, Santiago, y Rodríguez Evelyne. 2003. IV. El Programa De Educación Salud y Alimentación, Progresa-Programa de Desarrollo Humano Oportunidades. In *Ensayos Sobre el Desarrollo Económico y Social de México*, compilador Santiago Levy. México: Fondo de Cultura Económica.

López-Calva, Luis F., and Nora Lustig. 2003. *Social Protection and Inclusive Trade: Strengthening the Sources of Convergence within FTAA*. Universidad de Las Americas Working Paper No. 2003-06.

López Castellanos, Nayar. 2009. *Del Plan Puebla-Panamá al Proyecto Mesoamérica: un espejo de la globalización*. México: Neoliberal Plaza y Valdés Editores.

López Villicaña, Román. 2002. El Plan Puebla-Panamá: Historia y Geopolítica. In *Lectura Crítica del Plan Puebla Panamá*, coordinadores Eduardo Andrés Sandoval Forero y Robinson Salazar Pérez. Buenos Aires: Libros en Red.

Lora Cam, Jorge, and Sanchez R. Jose Luis. 2002. La recolonización del Angelopolis, el TLC, el Plan Puebla Panamá y el ALCA. In *Lectura Crítica del Plan Puebla Panamá*, coordinadores Eduardo Andrés Sandoval Forero y Robinson Salazar Pérez. Buenos Aires: Libros en Red.

Lybecker, Donna, and Stephen P. Mumme. 2002. Decentralization and Environmental Protection on Mexico's Northern and Southern Boundaries. *Journal of Environment & Development* 11 (4) (December): 402–429.

Marras, Sergio. 1992. *América Latina: Marca Registrada*. Buenos Aires: Grupo Editorial Zeta.

Martí Ascencio, Bosco. 2007. ¿Por qué retomar y reposicionar el Plan Puebla Panamá? *Revista Bien Común* 152 (August).

Martí Ascencio, Bosco. 2008. Proyecto Mesoamérica: fortaleciendo la integración y desarrollo regional. *Revista Mexicana de Política Exterior* 83: 9–39.

Meyer, Carrie A. 1999. *The Economics and Politics of NGOs in Latin America*. Westport, CT: Praeger.

Miguel Velasco, Andrés, and Armando Heredia González. 2004. Regiones competitividad y Desarrollo en México *Problemas del Desarrollo: Revista Latinoamericana de Economía* 35 (138) (julio–septiembre).

Moguel, Julio. 2001. Claroscuros del PPP. De cómo se escamotean los derechos de los indios y se traslada el debate a los presuntos temas del desarrollo. In *Mesoamerica: Los Ríos Profundos. Alternativas Plebeyas al Plan Puebla Panamà*, ed. Armando Bartra. México: RMALC/El Atajo Ediciones/ Instituto "Maya", A.C.

Montemayor, Carlos. 2002. La Guerrilla Recurrente. In *Chiapas en perspectiva histórica*, ed. Carlos Antonio Aguirre Rojas. España: Ediciones de Intervención Cultural.

Muñoz Martínez, Hepzibah. 2004. State, Capital and "Second Nature": Re-Territorialization in the Plan Puebla Panama. *Capitalism Nature Socialism* 15 (1) (March). London: Routledge.

Nicolás-Hiernaux, Daniel. 2002. El Plan Puebla Panamá: ¿una nueva visión del desarrollo regional? In *Lectura Crítica del Plan Puebla Panamá*, coordinadores Eduardo Andrés Sandoval Forero y Robinson Salazar Pérez. Buenos Aires: Libros en Red.

NoPPP (Network Opposing the PPP). 2002 assumed date. Batalla por el Futuro de Mesoamerica, una colección de artículos. ACEJ/ACERCA—Handout available through RMALC.

OECD Territorial Reviews. 2005. *The Mesoamerican Region: Southeastern Mexico and Central America*. OECD Publishing. http://www.oecd.org/mexico/oecdterritorialreviewsthemesoamericanregionsoutheasternmexicoandcentralamerica.htm.

OECD Territorial Reviews. 2006. *The Mesoamerican Region: Southeastern Mexico and Central America*. OECD Publishing. http://www.sourceoecd.org/regionaldevelopment/9264021914; http://www.sourceoecd.org/governance/9264021914.

Orantes, Isaac Cohen. 1981. The Concept of Integration. In *CEPAL Review*. Santiago: Publicaciones Naciones Unidas.

Ornelas, Delgado Jaime. 2002. El Plan Puebla Panamá y la globalización neoliberal. In *Lectura Crítica del Plan Puebla Panamá*, coordinadores Eduardo Andrés Sandoval Forero y Robinson Salazar Pérez. Buenos Aires: Libros en Red.

Orozco, Marcela. 2011. Mesoamérica: Integración y Tratados de Libre Comercio. In *Planes Geoestratégicos, Desplazamientos y Migraciones Forzadas en el Área del Proyecto de Desarrollo e Integración Mesoamérica*, coordinadores Juan Manuel Sandoval Palacios, Raquel Álvarez de Flores, and Sara Yaneth Fernández Moreno. México: Seminario Permanente de Estudios Chicanos y de Fronteras, DEAS-INAH; Venezuela: Centro de Estudios de Fronteras e Integración, Universidad de Los Andes-Táchira; Colombia: Departamento de Trabajo Social, Facultad de Ciencias Sociales y Humanas, Universidad de Antioquia. http://www.academia.edu/7454005/PLANES_GEOESTRATÉGICOS_DESPLAZAMIENTOS_Y_MIGRACIONES_FORZADAS_EN_EL_ÁREA_DEL_PROYECTO_DE_DESARROLLO_E_INTEGRACIÓN_DE_MESOAMÉRICA.

Pacheco, Carlos. 2003. Los Callejones del desarrollo en Centroamérica: del Mitch al Plan-Puebla Panamá y el ALCA. In *Otro Desarrollo es Posible: Sistematización de experiencias y reflexiones críticas desde Centroamérica*, ed. Oscar Jara. Alforja, Costa Rica: Centro de Estudios y Publicaciones.

Pardinas, Juan. 2004. Fighting Poverty in Mexico: Policy Changes. In *Mexico Under Fox*, ed. Luis Rubio and Susan Kaufman Purcell. Boulder: Lynne Rienner.

Paz Paredes, Lorena. 2001. La Costa Grande de Guerrero, laboratorio de la promoción concertada del desarrollo regional. In *Mesoamérica: Los Ríos Profundos. Alternativas Plebeyas al Plan Puebla Panamá*, ed. Armando Bartra. México: RMALC/El Atajo Ediciones/Instituto "Maya", A.C.

Pellicer, Olga (ed.). 1998.*Regional Mechanisms and International Security in Latin America*. New York: United Nations University Press.

Pickard, Miguel. 2004. *The Plan Puebla Panama Revived: Looking Back to See What Is Ahead* La Chronique des Ameriques avril Núm. 12. www.americques.uqam.ca/pdf/Chro-0413-ppp-eng.pdf.

Pisani, Michael J., and Wayne A. Label. 2003. Plan Puebla-Panama: Toward FTAA or regionalism? *Business Horizons* (September–October): 33–40.

Ponce de León, Juana. 2001. *Our Word Is Our Weapon: Selected Writings Subcomandante Insurgente Marcos*. New York: Seven Stories Press.

Preciado Coronado, Jaime, and Aarón Villarruel Mora. 2006. México y Centroamérica: hegemonía mundial, resistencias y visibilidad social. In *Geoeconomía y Geopolítica en el área del Plan Puebla Panamá*, ed. Daniel Villafuerte Solís and Xochitl Leyva Solano. México: Editorial Miguel Ángel Porrúa.

Presidencia de la República. 2001. *Plan Puebla-Panamá Capítulo México*. Documento Base.

Rioja Peregrina, Leonardo H. 2002. Biopiratería y la lucha política en el contexto del PPP. In *Lectura Crítica del Plan Puebla* Panamá, coordinadores Eduardo Andrés Sandoval Forero y Robinson Salazar Pérez. Buenos Aires: Libros en Red.

Rocha, Alberto. 2006. La geopolítica de México en Centroamérica: ¿una hegemonía regional? In *Geoeconomía y Geopolítica en el área del Plan Puebla Panamá*, ed. Daniel Villafuerte Solís and Xochitl Leyva Solano. México: Editorial Miguel Ángel Porrúa.

Romero Contreras, Tonatiuh, and Lorena Ávila Ramos. 1999. Mesoamérica: Historia y reconsideración del Concepto. *Ciencia Ergo Sum* 6 (3): 233–242. http://redalyc.uaemex.mx/redalyc/src/inicio/ArtPdfRed.jsp?iCve=10401602.

Rozental, Andrés. 2004. Fox's Foreign Policy Agenda: Global and Regional Priorities. In *Mexico Under Fox*, ed. Luis Rubio and Susan Kaufman Purcell. Boulder: Lynne Rienner.

Rubio, Luis. 2004. Democratic Politics in Mexico: New Complexities. In *Mexico Under Fox*, ed. Luis Rubio and Susan Kaufman Purcell. Boulder: Lynne Rienner.

Salazar Pérez, Robinson. 2002. El vínculo militar del Plan Colombia y el Plan Puebla Panamá. In *Lectura Crítica del Plan Puebla Panamá*, coordinadores Eduardo Andrés Sandoval Forero y Robinson Salazar Pérez. Buenos Aires: Libros en Red.

Saldívar, V. Américo. 2002. El Plan Puebla Panamá: Una Locomotora sin Vagones de Segunda. In *Lectura Crítica del Plan Puebla Panamá*, coordinadores Eduardo Andrés Sandoval Forero y Robinson Salazar Pérez. Buenos Aires: Libros en Red.

Sandoval Forero, Eduardo Andrés. 2002. El Plan Puebla Panamá y la globalización de los indios. In *Lectura Crítica del Plan Puebla Panamá*, coordinadores Eduardo Andrés Sandoval Forero y Robinson Salazar Pérez. Buenos Aires: Libros en Red.

Sandoval García, Carlos. 2004. Contested Discourses on National Identity: Representing Nicaraguan Immigration to Costa Rica. *Bulletin of Latin American Research* 23 (4) (October): 434–445.

Sandoval Palacios, Juan Manuel. 2001. El Plan Puebla Panamá como regulador de la migración laboral mesoamericana. In *Mesoamérica: Los Ríos Profundos. Alternativas Plebeyas al Plan Puebla Panamá*, ed. Armando Bartra. México: RMALC/El Atajo Ediciones/Instituto "Maya", A.C.

Sandoval Palacios, Juan Manuel. 2006. Migración y seguridad nacional en las fronteras norte y sur de México. In *Geoeconomía y Geopolítica en el área del Plan Puebla Panamá*, ed. Daniel Villafuerte Solís and Xochitl Leyva Solano. México: Editorial Miguel Ángel Porrúa.

Sandoval Palacios, Juan Manuel. 2011. El proyecto de Integración y Desarrollo de Mesoamérica (Proyecto Mesoamérica) en el marco de la Alianza para la Seguridad y Prosperidad de América del Norte (ASPAN), la política de Seguridad Democrática y la Iniciativa Mérida. In *Planes Geoestratégicos, Desplazamientos y Migraciones Forzadas en el Área del Proyecto de Desarrollo e Integración Mesoamérica*, coordinadores Juan Manuel Sandoval Palacios and Raquel Álvarez de Flores, and Sara Yaneth Fernández Moreno. México: Seminario Permanente de Estudios Chicanos y de Fronteras, DEAS-INAH; Venezuela: Centro de Estudios de Fronteras e Integración, Universidad de Los Andes-Táchira; Colombia: Departamento de Trabajo Social, Facultad de Ciencias Sociales y Humanas, Universidad de Antioquia. http://www.academia.edu/7454005/PLANES_GEOESTRATÉGICOS_DESPLAZAMIENTOS_Y_MIGRACIONES_FORZADAS_EN_EL_

ÁREA_DEL_PROYECTO_DE_DESARROLLO_E_INTEGRACIÓN_DE_MESOAMÉRICA.

Sandoval Palacios, Juan Manuel, Álvarez de Flores, Raquel and Fernández Moreno Sara Yaneth, (Coordinadores). 2011. *Planes Geoestratégicos, Desplazamientos y Migraciones Forzadas en el Área del Proyecto de Desarrollo e Integración Mesoamérica* Published by: Seminario Permanente de Estudios Chicanos y de Fronteras, DEAS-INAH (México) Centro de Estudios de Fronteras e Integración, Universidad de los Andes-Táchira (Venezuela and Departamento de Trabajo Social, Facultad de Ciencias Sociales y Humanas, Universidad de Antioquia (Colombia). http://www.academia.edu/7454005/PLANES_GEOESTRATÉGICOS_DESPLAZAMIENTOS_Y_MIGRACIONES_FORZADAS_EN_EL_ÁREA_DEL_PROYECTO_DE_DESARROLLO_E_INTEGRACIÓN_DE_MESOAMÉRICA.

Santiso, Carlos. 2000. Towards Democratic Governance: The Contribution of the Multilateral Development Banks. In *Democracy Assistance: International Cooperation for Democratization*, ed. Peter Burnel. London: Frank.

Savenije, Wim. 2004. La mara Salvatrucha y el Barrio 18 St. Fenómenos sociales transnacionales, respuestas represivas nacionales. *Foreign Affaires en Español.* (abril–junio). http://www.foreignaffairs-esp.org/2004040401faenespessay040205/winsavenije/la-mara-salvatrucha.htm.

Savenije, Wim. 2007. Las pandillas transnacionales o "maras": violencia urbana en Centroamérica. *Foro Internacional* 47 (3) (July–September): 637–659.

Talcott, Molly. 2014. "Together We Have Power" Personal Traumas and Political Responses Among Activist Oaxaqueñas. *Latin American Perspectives* 41 (1) (January): 72–88.

Toly, Noah J. 2004. Globalization and the Capitalization of Nature: A Political Ecology of Biodiversity in Mesoamerica. *Bulletin of Science, Technology & Society* 24 (1): 47–54.

Toussaint, Mónica, and Marisol Garzón. 2017. El Proyecto Mesoamérica: ¿Éxito o Fracaso? Límites de la Cooperación de México hacia Centroamérica Entre Diversidades. *Revista de Ciencias Sociales y Humanidades* (8): 15–52.

Villafuerte Solis, Daniel. 2004a. Mas allá del Plan Puebla-Panamá: del TLCAN al ALCA. *Comercio Exterior* 54 (4): 283–284. revistas.bancomext.gob.mx/rce/magazines/65/2/villa0404.pdf.

Villafuerte Solís, Daniel. 2004b. Los problemas del desarrollo en la frontera sur. *Territorio y Economía Número Especial 3.* Chiapas Sistema de Información Regional de México, 51–59.

Villafuerte Solís, Daniel. 2006a. Integraciones en el Norte y Sur de México: del NAFTA al CAFTA. In *Geoeconomía y Geopolítica en el área del Plan Puebla Panamá*, ed. Daniel Villafuerte Solís and Xochitl Leyva Solano. México: Editorial Miguel Ángel Porrúa.

Villafuerte Solís, Daniel. 2006b. Reflexiones Finales. In *Geoeconomía y Geopolítica en el área del Plan Puebla Panamá*, ed. Daniel Villafuerte Solís and Xochitl Leyva Solano. México: Editorial Miguel Ángel Porrúa.

Villafuerte Solís, Daniel, and Xochitl Leyva Solano (eds.). 2006. *Geoeconomía y Geopolítica en el área del Plan Puebla Panamá*. México: Editorial Miguel Ángel Porrúa.

Villegas, Claudia. 2011. Vulnerabilidad Social, desastres y migración forzada: el caso de migrantes climáticos. In *Planes Geoestratégicos, Desplazamientos y Migraciones Forzadas en el Área del Proyecto de Desarrollo e Integración Mesoamérica*, coordinadores Juan Manuel Sandoval Palacios, Raquel Álvarez de Flores, and Sara Yaneth Fernández Moreno. México: Seminario Permanente de Estudios Chicanos y de Fronteras, DEAS-INAH; Venezuela: Centro de Estudios de Fronteras e Integración, Universidad de Los Andes-Táchira; Colombia: Departamento de Trabajo Social, Facultad de Ciencias Sociales y Humanas. http://www.academia.edu/7454005/PLANES_GEOESTRATÉGICOS_DESPLAZAMIENTOS_Y_MIGRACIONES_FORZADAS_EN_EL_ÁREA_DEL_PROYECTO_DE_DESARROLLO_E_INTEGRACIÓN_DE_MESOAMÉRICA.

Wilson, Japhy. 2008. The New Phase of the Plan Puebla Panama in Chiapas (Parts 1, 2, 3). *Bulletins of CIEPAC "Chiapas Day by Day"* (560), May 22. http://www.ciepac.org/boletines/chiapas_en.php?id=560.

Wilson, Japhy. 2011. Contesting the Plan Puebla Panama: Henri Lefebvre and the Politics of Space in Southern Mexico. In *Planes Geoestratégicos, Desplazamientos y Migraciones Forzadas en el Área del Proyecto de Desarrollo e Integración Mesoamérica*, coordinadores Juan Manuel Sandoval Palacios, Raquel Álvarez de Flores, and Sara Yaneth Fernández Moreno. México: Seminario Permanente de Estudios Chicanos y de Fronteras, DEAS-INAH; Venezuela: Centro de Estudios de Fronteras e Integración, Universidad de Los Andes-Táchira; Colombia: Departamento de Trabajo Social, Facultad de Ciencias Sociales y Humanas, Universidad de Antioquia. http://www.academia.edu/7454005/PLANES_GEOESTRATÉGICOS_DESPLAZAMIENTOS_Y_MIGRACIONES_FORZADAS_EN_EL_ÁREA_DEL_PROYECTO_DE_DESARROLLO_E_INTEGRACIÓN_DE_MESOAMÉRICA.

Interviews

7. Coordinator Human Development, Dirección Ejecutiva Plan Puebla Panamá,1 September 2006, San Salvador.
38. AMAP Director, Mexican Association for the Self-Determination of Peoples (AMAP), 22 August 2006, Mexico City.

CHAPTER 4

Regionalisms and Regional Governance in Mesoamerica

4.1 Introduction

In the first and third chapters of the book I presented the Mesoamerican region as a new construct and explained the controversy caused by the PPP due to the Mexican political scene at the time of its launch. I demonstrated through the literature that opposition to the PPP was because the plan had invested in areas of little interest for the communities within the MAR. Both the budget allocations and the detailed projects showed that infrastructure was prioritised over the social aspects of the PPP. In the second chapter I presented regional theory and the differences between regionalism and regionalisation, concepts that will be revisited throughout this book. Portraying "regionness" as a measuring stick for the regionalisation that is taking place, I introduced the NRA of Hettne and Söderbaum (2000, 2002), using governance as the variable in the construction of a region, primarily in how regionalism can lead to regionalisation and vice versa. Nevertheless, governance takes place at different levels (Payne 2005), and though the levels are difficult to separate, I will focus this chapter on the regional level and hone in on the formal institutions that have been formed to foment regional cooperation. The regional level is the intermediary between the "global" and the "national" however, even at this level there are different "regions" intersecting, overlapping, and "maturing" at different rates. This chapter will

A. Gamboa, *Regional Integration, Development, and Governance in Mesoamerica*,
https://doi.org/10.1007/978-3-030-25350-9_4

analyse the way the spheres of governance at the regional level influenced the implementation and progress of the PPP in Mesoamerica.

For clarity, these regions have been classified as follows: developmental region, trade and monetary region, environmental region, and security region.[1] The distinctions are not clear cut and many projects overlap over more than one of these "regions"; however, the aim of this classification is to show that commitment to regional cooperation differs by area.

In this chapter I will give an overview of the institutional structure of the Tuxtla Mechanism, the PPP, and the SICA, and how they worked together. Then I will discuss the different "regions" and how the institutional structures hindered or furthered their development and how some of the lessons learned from problems in the PPP were incorporated in the transition to Proyecto Mesoamerica.

Although the complete list of regional institutions is much longer than the one used here, by analysing a sample of the "spaghetti bowl" (the part entangled around the PPP) in Mesoamerica, the question could be shifted from: "is this regional project effective" to "can any regional project be effective" in Mesoamerica?

The interaction between the PPP and other regional entities is important to this research since one of the bottlenecks facing regional governance is rooted in the lack of coordination and communication between the different regional bodies. While there is great potential in the aggregation of efforts between all the regional institutions in practice, they compete more with each other than they work together.

4.2 Regional Institutions

Mesoamerica: The "Spaghetti Bowl"

Latin American regionalism under the LAIA/ALADI (from the 1990s) encouraged the proliferation of FTAs among its members as a form of motivating intra-regional trade. This produced what is known as the "spaghetti bowl" effect of open regionalism where there are many overlapping trading and political arrangements in a region.

Mesoamerica is a prime example of a region housing complex systems of governance (see Phillips 2002: 78). The numerous multinational

[1] The original study did not classify these regions, instead it focused on how certain institutions intersected with the PPP.

agreements existing in this region are equipped with their own institutions, norms, and scope. The "spaghetti bowl" effect up until now, was considered a harmless by-product of open regionalism, one that would eventually resolve as the World Trade Organisation (WTO) became a more efficient mechanism for multilateralism (Mansfield and Reinhalt 2003; Baldwin 2006).

Instead of "cleaning up the spaghetti bowl," Mesoamerica so far has done the opposite, creating new mechanisms where others could be either expanded or consolidated to the same effect. Whereas Curly (2008), encourages a region or regions to homogenise agreements in order to "reduce the deadweight administrative costs of overlapping and inconsistent agreements" (Curly 2008: 230), Mesoamerica has seen an increase in these kinds of agreements, not only of those that are led by the regional institutions, but also those created by other government groups (as is the case of the regional meetings between parliamentarians or municipal governments held at their own initiative).

The ability to coordinate at the regional level is crucial to the pursuit of regional development strategies using regional integration projects in Mesoamerica. A clear demarcation of the responsibilities and scope of each regional body as well as a regional vision would help to ensure that all the institutions are working towards the same goal. As projects initiated in different institutions and regional bodies sometimes overlap, it is important to make sure that they do not compete for the same funding or block the progress of other similar projects. Convergence at the regional level is an important element to consolidate a region; if there is a shared regional vision and goal, then the overlapping regional arrangements will not have a significant bearing (Hettne 2003: 29).

The MAR hosts a realm of regional projects and institutions (see Table 4.1). Furthermore, there are other more specialised regional governmental groups such as the Central American Parliamentary Presidents' Summit and the Union of Central American Municipalities (FEMICA) that meet regularly. What is most striking about the organisations that form part of SICA is that not all of them have the same members.

Mexico was a full member of the PPP (2001–2008) and currently of Proyecto Mesoamerica and is a member of the Mechanism of Tuxtla and the MBC but not of the rest of the regional mechanisms; however it is an observer in both SICA and PARLACEN (Declaración de Guatemala 2000) and is regularly involved in giving technical advice to

Table 4.1 Central American Integration System

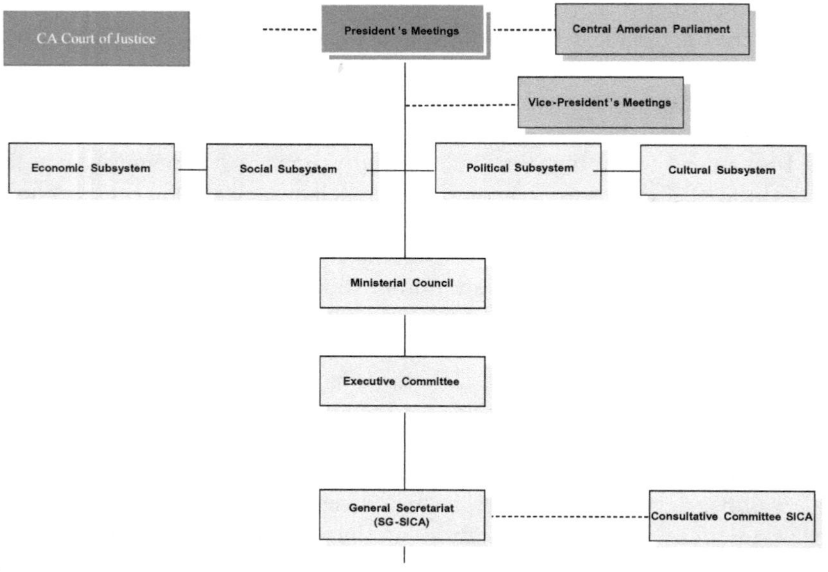

Source Secretaría de Integración Económica Centroamericana (SIECA)

organisations such as the Central American Monetary Council (CAMC). As an observer, Mexico is often invited to participate in the Presidential summits or, if a topic is scheduled in one of the regional bodies, it can request to be included. Then an invitation is extended to Mexico so that it can participate as well as include items on the agenda. For example, Mexico requested to be present during meetings of the Central American Security Commission when the issue of *Maras* (regional street gangs) was discussed (Interview 19: 2006).

The PPP was born out of the Tuxtla Mechanism of Dialogue and Cooperation between Mexico and the Central American countries and touted as an "innovative tool" for regional development (Declaración Extraordinaria 2001). Mexico had created several instruments for cooperation with Central America including; the Contadora Group, the Action Committee for the Social and Economic Development of Central America, and the Energy Economic Cooperation Program (Pacto de San José) (Figueroa Fisher 2014). The Mexican Commission for Cooperation with Central America was formed in 1990 as an inter-institutional body composed by 23 government offices and directed by the Ministry of Foreign Affairs (MFA).

The Tuxtla Mechanism grew out of the “Reunión Cumbre” (Summit Meeting) held in 1991 in Tuxtla Gutierrez, Chiapas with the participation of El Salvador, Guatemala, Honduras, Mexico, and Nicaragua, where they gathered to discuss development issues for Central America and Mexico. Formed soon after the Central American Peace accords, its main objective was to facilitate “political dialogue, consolidate peace, democracy, and regional cooperation.”[2] The mechanism was then consolidated into formal periodic meetings during the second Cumbre Tuxtla Gutierrez held in San José, Costa Rica in 1996 and was signed by the eight participating governments. The PPP did not replace the Tuxtla Mechanism it formed part of it, and it was during the annual Tuxtla Mechanism meetings that PPP progress reports were presented.[3] Other programmes such as the Programa Mesoamericano de Cooperación (PMC—Mesoamerican Cooperation Program created in 1998, specifically dealing with development issues)[4] also formed part of the Tuxtla Mechanism. The agenda of the high-level president meetings is defined beforehand and security issues are usually included under the political heading.

In addition to the Tuxtla Mechanism many other regional institutions were already in place when the PPP was announced. These institutions were not involved in the creation of the PPP and it was not clear in the initial stages of the Plan how it was to relate to them, if at all. Many of the objectives and purposes of the PPP were the same as those of existing institutions, so some academics argued that once again, governments were covering up for the failures of past attempts of the same initiatives by giving them a new name (see Bartra 2002; Chanona 2002; Saldivar 2002; and others.).

[2] http://www.sica.int/consulta/documentos.aspx?Idm=1&search=mecanismo%20tuxtla.

[3] Proyecto Mesoamerica, the PPP replacement was announced in the 2008 Tuxtla meeting, and its progress reports continue to be presented in this forum. Colombia and the Dominican Republic became official members in 2009.

[4] http://www.proyectomesoamerica.org:8088/emsa/documentos/Proyectos/IF/Presentaciones/Presentacio%CC%81n%20programa%20mesoamericano%20de%20cooperacio%CC%81n%20(oct2014).pdf.

The Plan Puebla Panama

The first chapter of the book described the origins of the PPP, its initiatives and its objectives. In this section I will describe the evolution of its institutional structure and the mechanisms that were set up to facilitate the coordination of PPP projects in Mesoamerica.

The PPP's organisational structure reflected its intergovernmental status. The highest authorities of the PPP were the regions' presidents, who then delegated work to the Executive Commission (hereafter Executive Commission) composed of delegates from each country. The Presidents met within the framework of the annual Tuxtla Mechanism regular meetings. For practical reasons, the Central American Presidents first met together for the SICA presidential summit, and the next day as part of the Tuxtla Mechanism.

Mexico was normally not invited to the SICA meetings unless there was an issue that concerned it directly (Interview 19: 2006). Once the priorities for the PPP were set for the year the follow up would be taken over by the Inter-institutional Technical Group (GTI) comprised by the IDB, the BCIE, CEPAL, SIECA, and SICA and by those in charge of each of the eight initiatives (Interview 7: 2006, see also CG-PPP 2002). "Each initiative is a world of its own; every initiative has its own technical committee which is composed basically of links with the corresponding (area) ministers. If it is not a ministry, then it is the authority it is under, like in (*the mitigation of*) natural disasters (*initiative*)" (Interview 7: 2006).

The PPP was launched as soon as the initial document was completed in order to ride on the post-election momentum even though it was still a work in progress (Interview 7: 2006). As would be the case in many other proposals (energy reform, tax reform) then President of Mexico, Vicente Fox (or his team) thought that the government ministries, congress and state governors would try to work together for the benefit of the country and further "the change" that Mexicans had voted for (Rubio 2004: 26). Instead technical and institutional issues (like having to relocate PPP to the MFA) were used as excuses to stall projects and undermine the PPP. Mexican law states that the MFA is the only government department that had the proviso for forging international agreements and thus, the point of contact for any Mexican relations with regional organisations.

The initial placement of the PPP as part of the President's office was viewed as a blatant disregard for the functions of the MFA and a lack of

Table 4.2 PPP structure 2002

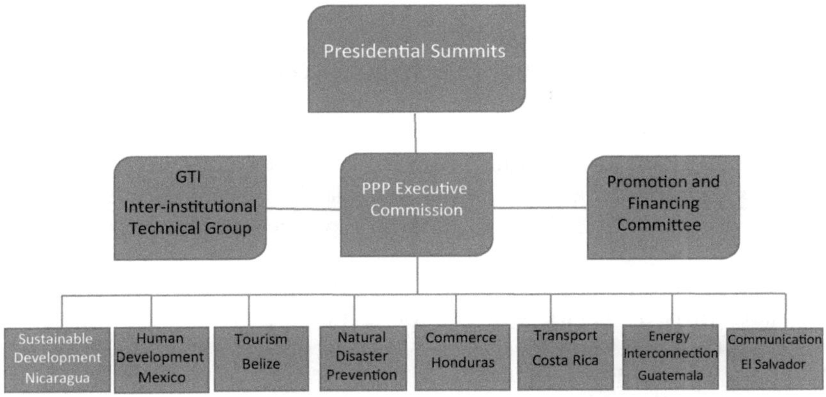

Plan Puebla Panamá, por un desarrollo equilibrado y socialmente incluyente. Gobierno de la República, Secretaría de Relaciones Exteriores (2003)

respect for national institutions. The MFA only dealt with the regional institutions officially recognised within its offices and avoided contact with the PPP until the Mexican Government agreed to relocate the PPP offices to the MFA in 2003 (based on Interviews 11 and 26: 2006). This relocation brought about an awkward moment for the PPP as it took place behind closed doors of Mexican politics. Many of the communication gaps within the PPP structures became noticeable.

It is unclear whether there were similar "territorial" disputes within Central American governments but there was a sense of disappointment in the Central American PPP offices at the lack of a strong Mexican leadership. Since Mexico had initiated the proposal to join the development plan for its southeast region with Central America's Madrid agenda, it was expected to become a driving agent for the PPP and to invest in Central America. Although a promise or framework for Mexican investment in Central America does not exist in the official PPP documentation nor in the Tuxtla Mechanism memorandum, the expectation of the investment was mentioned by five interviewees, three that worked directly with the PPP (either in national offices or ministries), one that worked with an academic body and one that worked with an international organisation (Interviews 19, 16, 27, 30, and 23). The recurrent mention of this and the manner that it was expressed by those interviewed alludes to a conclusion that this expectation was built upon a declaration or promise that was not delivered (Table 4.2).[5]

On 25 March 2004, the PPP was relaunched during the meeting of the VI Summit of the Tuxtla Mechanism in Managua, Nicaragua. During this meeting, the Heads of State of Guatemala, Honduras, Mexico and Nicaragua, as well as the representatives of Costa Rica, El Salvador, and Belize, signed an Act to institutionalise the Plan Puebla Panama, its components and structure. This established the five bodies of the PPP and clearly indicated their functions. As part of the restructuring the PPP Secretariat relocated (Acta PPP 2004) to San Salvador setting up bi-monthly meetings with the GTI in different venues A practice that was later revised due to cost. By 2006, meetings were held only when important issues arose otherwise, each department carried on what they had been previously assigned (Interview 7: 2006).

One frequent complaint by some of the veteran PPP representatives (those that had been involved for more than 2 years) was that too much time was spent bringing people up to date (Interviews 7, 11, and 13: 2006). There is high rotation in government so whenever there is a change in administration a resignation of a cabinet member, or reorganisation in a ministry, the personnel changes.

> They often arrive at a meeting just having taken over from someone else and have not had time to read all the material; they are completely lost. We must explain what is happening to them and most of the meeting is spent answering questions instead of making decisions and assigning tasks. The meetings rotate between countries, so we have to travel, spend several days and come back feeling like little was achieved. It isn't anyone's fault, it just happens. (Interview 13: 2006)

The Executive Commission of the PPP oversaw the planning, coordination, and follow up of projects and initiatives adopted within the Tuxtla dialogue. It was composed of the Presidential commissioners as well as one designated by the Prime Minister of Belize. The Executive Commission was headed by a co-presidency shared by whichever state was the President Pro-Tempore of the SICA and by Mexico (Acta PPP

[5]There is a mention in the CG-PPP 2002 document that Mexico would set up a fund as a modification of the San José Accord (for reconstruction after national disasters) (CG-PPP 2002: 13).

2004). As the SICA presidency changed every six months the co-presidency with Mexico was established to give continuity. However, during such times as the relocation of the PPP offices in Mexico or other instances when Mexico was preoccupied with internal affairs, little attention was given to the Commission. Although the IDB was not formally a member its president sat on the Executive Commission which received input from the Inter-Institutional Technical Group (GTI) and the Consulting and Divulging Programme.

Each of the delegates had been assigned one of the Mesoamerican Initiatives, albeit each of the initiatives had a technical commission in charge of assessing needs and progress (Presidencia de la República 2001; GTI 2001; Interview 19: 2006).

The supporting body for the Executive Commission was the Executive Management where a Managing Director was appointed for four years based on professional qualifications and ability to appoint support staff and consultants. The Executive Management became the Permanent Secretariat and remains the same under *Proyecto Mesoamerica* (Mesoamerica Project). What did change under the new scheme was the relationship between the Permanent Secretariat and the SICA framework.

The Promotion and Financing Commission (CPF) of the Plan Puebla Panama was created to help and support the PPP member countries with identifying and securing funding for the PPP projects. The Commission was made up of the president of the IDB, the BCIE, the CAF, and the Official Credit Institute of Spain (ICO) and coordinated by the IDB president. Financing obtained through the Commission would be subject to the fiscal legislation, institutional norms and budget availability of each of the member states (Presidencia de la República 2001). In 2004 this commission was strengthened to ensure funding for the projects. However, the link between the financial organisms and the regional organisms that requested funding was still missing. "Sometimes we are all competing for the same funding, and some of our projects are very similar, it is a problem that, instead of us cooperating to present a stronger case to the financing institutions, we end up securing a little bit of money and can only do part of a project" (Interview 7: 2006). Another problem that surfaced and affected the human development projects was that these financial institutions for the most part give loans not grants:

> ...governments are more likely to go into debt for infrastructure projects, projects that have possibility of remunerating the investment through

> business or trade, but they do not want to go into debt for human development projects, they want grants for those, and we are not obtaining grants. That is also a reason why the human development initiative is not advancing as quickly. [The other reason given was Mexico's lack of leadership] (Interview 7: 2006)

The GTI supported the Executive Commission in the process of defining the initiatives and projects included in the PPP. The GTI was made up of the BCIE, the IDB, the ECLAC/CEPAL, the INCAE, SIECA, the Secretary General of the SICA, the UNDP, the CAF, the Spanish Institute for Commerce (ICEX), ICO, the AICD, the Indigenous and Ethnic Participation Advisory Group (GAPIE), and all the regional organisations or entities determined by the Executive Commission.

The Consultative Council of the PPP was introduced in the 2004 Act. The Council's aim was to encourage the participation of organised civil society including; the private sector, development banks and Non-Governmental Organisations (NGOs) interested in promoting the Mesoamerican initiatives and the PPP. Initially the IDB oversaw liaising with these sectors and setting up monthly meetings in Washington. However, none of the NGOs or Civil Society organisations interviewed during field research had ever been specifically invited to participate in those meetings. Even though the meetings were open to all NGOs, "those meetings take place in Washington. They are for the organisations that are rich and have offices in Washington; we should not have to travel there to get informed, or to state our point of view" (Interview 38: 2006).

The Consultative Council was an example of reactive policy; it was only set up after initial protests. Being invited to join a "dialogue," only after avid protests and serious criticism did not ease relations with opposing actors. On the contrary, it appeared to make matters worse, with the "consulted" organisations saying that "they do not want to dialogue, they do not want to change anything, they just want us to approve what they already have in mind" (Comment in response to question 8 of the questionnaire; see Annex B) (Table 4.3).

Members of the PPP could request modifications or withdraw from the 2004 Act through a communiqué to the Executive Commission which would then give its approval. Similarly, aspiring members would need to present a formal application. In the case of Colombia, it was first accepted under the status of "observer" for two years before its

Table 4.3 PPP structure 2005

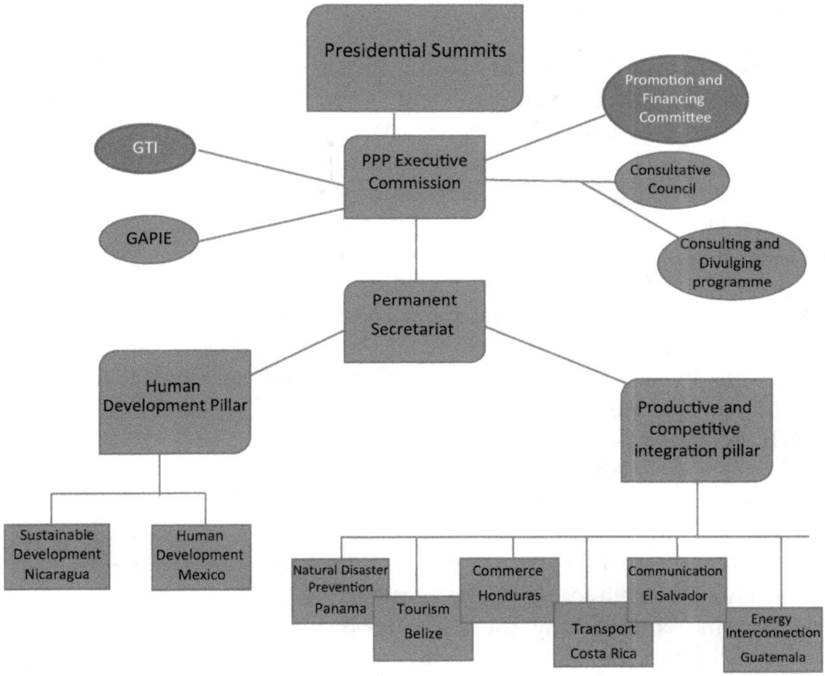

Source Informe Ejecutivo: Avances del Plan Puebla Panamá Junio 2005–Junio 2006 VIII Cumbre del Mecanismo de Diálogo y Concertación de Tuxtla. Ciudad de Panamá, Julio 2006

full membership was approved in 2006. The Dominican Republic did not present a formal request to the Executive Commission; instead it addressed the MFAs since it deemed unnecessary, being a full member of the SICA, to first become an observer (Interview 19: 2006).

The enthusiasm from the Mesoamerican Presidents about the PPP sometimes created false expectations. Soon after Colombia began the process to become a full member of the PPP the then Mexican president Vicente Fox insinuated that Peru and Ecuador could join, a prospective that horrified some members in the PPP headquarters.

> We don't even know how Colombia is going to fit in yet, even less the Dominican Republic which we know will apply. I don't think that the PPP should expand before the scheme is working properly. We will lose the

> vision of the PPP. We had clear goals and expectation and dates. If we keep inviting more countries in, then that will be lost. (Interview 19: 2006)

However, the PPP representative in El Salvador's MFA said that this expansion would be very unlikely. Colombia and the Dominican Republic were already a bit further than they had expected, "we don't want to lose the identity of Mesoamerica" (Interview 30: 2006).

As is turned out other countries did not apply to join the PPP and it seems unlikely to happen under Proyecto Mesoamerica. A final report was presented in June 2008 on the status of the PPP projects. The main purpose of the document was to establish Proyecto Mesoamerica. As with previous progress reports it was produced by the Executive Commission. Thus, there has not been an evaluation of the PPP made by an outside body. It is unlikely that such an evaluation will take place since it was "all voluntary, it is (was) based on Memorandum of Understanding, in other words 'gentlemen's pacts'" (Interview 30: 2006).

During the 10th summit of the Tuxtla Mechanism held in Villahermosa, Tabasco, Mexico on 28 June 2008, it was announced that the PPP would change its name to the Mesoamerican Development and Integration Project known as Proyecto Mesoamerica. This name change resulted from the extraordinary meeting of the Tuxtla Mechanism requested by the then newly installed Mexican President Felipe Calderón, held in April 2007. During this meeting, the participating Heads of State instructed the Executive Commission to evaluate the scope and capabilities of the PPP and devise a strategy to consolidate it into an efficient instrument for regional development. The evaluation identified four major areas in need of an overhaul: (a) institutional strengthening; (b) increased communication with other regional mechanisms; (c) selection of projects that could be included according to specific criteria; and (d) positioning and diffusion (Martí Ascencio 2008: 17). The changes made to the PPP in its transformation to Proyecto Mesoamerica were mostly institutional; however there was an important change regarding the number of projects that continued (reduced from the 99 active projects to 22) as well as the guidelines for any new projects that could be added on later.

As part of the joint declaration signed by the presidents who attended the summit, they agreed to the name change and to implement the recommendations presented in the 2008 PPP activities report. The first recommendation was to simplify the complicated institutional structure that evolved over the seven years of the PPP. Each country was instructed to formalise a National Office for Proyecto Mesoamerica and include a representative from the country's Treasury department to ensure the necessary coordination with the national budget. The BCIE, IDB, and CAF integrated into a Promotion and Financing Commission to simplify the procurement of funding and the design of proposals (Martí Ascencio 2008: 18).

As part of commercial strategy, the Mesoamerican Competitiveness Council (CMC) was restructured, and, all the FTAs that had been forged among the Mesoamerican countries were revised in order to find points of convergence and meet the objective of advancing towards a sole Mesoamerican agreement. Furthermore, the Mesoamerican Programme for Scientific and Technical Cooperation required restructuring and strengthening for it to fit in with the region's priorities and promote projects that would contribute to regional development and integration (Dirección Ejecutiva Proyecto de Integración y Desarrollo de Mesoamérica 2008).

As far as trade was concerned the report recommended converging the PTAs and FTAs that had been signed by the Mesoamerican countries into one single FTA spanning the entire region. Noting the problems that had risen from having so many PTAs with different memberships and scopes, it was decided to meld them into one. The eight Mesoamerican Initiatives were replaced by a new mechanism focused on individual projects. In order to be considered as part of the Proyecto Mesoamerica a project would have to meet at least two of the following criteria: (a) thematic areas: falling under one of the activities, areas or topics defined by the member states as specific to the project; (b) integration: contributing to regional integration by including two or more member states; (c) harmonisation: to avoid duplicating activities that were either programmed or already taking place by other regional initiatives; (d) regional focus: either taking place regionally or contributing to a regional project in the case of it being mostly in one country; or (e) regional public goods: to promote the creation of regional public goods which would benefit more than one country as a result of coordinated efforts of the countries involved (Dirección Ejecutiva Proyecto de Integración y Desarrollo de Mesoamérica 2008).

The CPF was consolidated with the IDB, BCIE, and CAF as its main partners and Finance Ministers were included into the permanent structures in the GTI. The GTI remained the same, but regular meetings

Table 4.4 Proyecto Mesoamerica structure (2016)

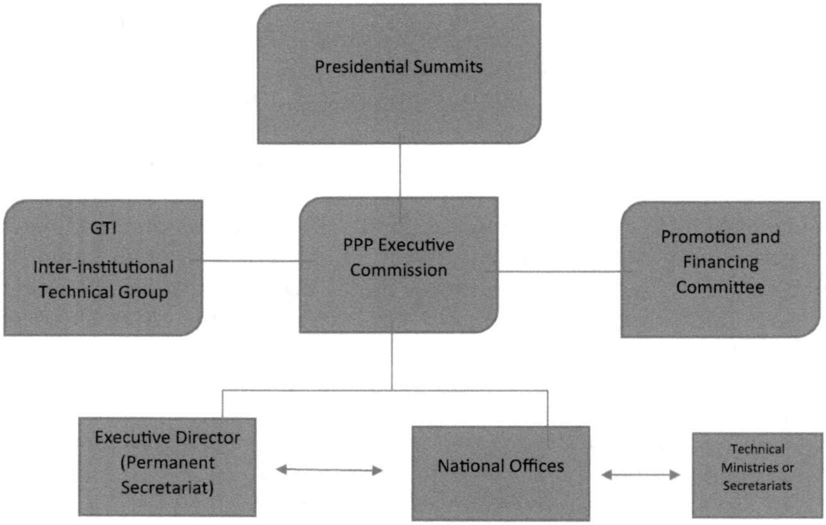

Source http://www.proyectomesoamerica.org/index.php/acerca-delpm/mecanismos-de-governanza, accessed August 2018

were set up with the SICA to consolidate cooperation between the two (Declaración de Villahermosa 2008) (Table 4.4).

Central American Integration System (SICA)

Pre-existing the PPP were two sets of institutions[6]: The first set includes the institutions that already formed part of Central American integration efforts. Though most of these organisations are exclusive to all or some of the Central American countries, some of them allow Mexico and other countries to participate as "observers." These institutions remain the most prominent in the area even though "the institutional framework created around the Central American Integration System (SICA) by the Tegucigalpa Protocol in 1991 has been hampered for years by a

[6]Though these institutions are complex and interesting entities in and of themselves, the objective of this research is to determine how they interacted with the PPP and Mesoamerica as a region, so they will be discussed solely with this purpose in mind.

lack of strategic focus and by the discrepancies between the commitments assumed in Presidential Summits and the actual policies pursued by Central American governments" (OECD Territorial Reviews 2006: 27).

Due to Central America's long history of integration efforts, the PPP was seen in some quarters as intruding on pre-existing schemes. One regional analyst stated that:

> …the PPP, first and foremost, is a project that came from Mexico and that is the feeling at the regional level and to some degree generates mistrust. The initiatives do not have a clear regional identity and the parts of the PPP that have been advancing are those that already existed to a certain extent and had some momentum, like electrical interconnection (SIEPAC). The prevailing feeling in Central America is that these projects would have continued advancing with or without Mexican support. (Interview 23: 2006)

However, with an opposing view, the director of the PPP office in El Salvador commented that: "we took projects that were already in our agendas, such as SIEPAC, and integrated them [into the PPP]. SIEPAC had been dormant, it was 20 years old, and it was the PPP that reactivated it" (Interview 30: 2006). This same government official noted in 2006, that after five years of the PPP and several changes in government the focus and projects of the PPP had not changed. Instead he states, "I think that the commitment by governments and states is getting stronger.[7] What we have seen is that with each change the commitment grows stronger; meaning that the eight countries still want to continue; even more so, both Colombia and the Dominican Republic want to join" (Interview 30: 2006).

Moreover, actions in Central America had been characterised by a sort of "Integration A la Carte," where countries opt in and out of the different integration schemes according to national interests.[8] The fact that these organisms have differing memberships hinders their ability to homogenise their goals and give the institutions any real power

[7] 2001–2006 Panama, El Salvador, Costa Rica, and Honduras had changed governments. Mexico had just had an election, though the new government did not take office until 2007 and Nicaragua was about to hold national elections.

[8] The SICA/CEPAL review of Central American Integration (2004) refers to the differing memberships and constantly has to clarify the discrepancies of membership in the different SICA institutions.

to implement regional policies. One clear case in point is the Central American Court of Justice designated by the Tegucigalpa Protocol as the legislative body for Central American integration created in 1994 by Guatemala, El Salvador, Honduras, Nicaragua, and Costa Rica. Costa Rica and Guatemala did not ratify it (Interview 25: 2006), rendering what could be a strong regional organisation very weak. Although Guatemala finally joined in 2008 Costa Rica, the Dominican Republic and Panama have not. The same can be said about the Central American Parliament (PARLACEN) where Costa Rica does not participate, arguing that it is a weak, useless, and corrupt instrument. Instead, Costa Rican senators prefer the regional association of parliamentarians of Central America for discussing matters with a regional scope (Interview 31: 2006). A PARLACEN representative, however, counteracts that argument by saying that if the governments represented do not grant real power to PARLACEN and other governments that would like to see the institution reformed remain outside of the parliament then it will continue to be limited (Interview 29: 2006).

However, this same representative argued that since the EU Parliament began as a "recommending" body instead of a "legislating" body, PARLACEN could eventually evolve in the same form. One analyst from the El Salvador Foundation for Economic and Social Development (FUSADES) said that in Central America:

> …there is much resistance to give up sovereignty. Supranational organisms do not exist as such, the Central American Court is just sitting there, stagnant; only three members have ratified; The Central American Parliament is practically inoperable; the SICA is being questioned as to its institutional effectiveness, the SIECA is an institution that cannot make regional policy, it is more of an organism that provides technical support. The problem is that the governments do not want to give up any of their sovereignty, and that is what makes it complicated. (Interview 23: 2006)

Central American Integration has been one of the oldest integration efforts in Latin America, beginning in the 1950s. During this first effort, ECLAC/CEPAL encouraged Central America to form a regional free trade area protected from the rest of the world through high tariff barriers. With technical support from ECLAC/CEPAL, the Central American Common Market (CACM) formed as a customs union between Costa Rica, El Salvador, Guatemala, Honduras, and Nicaragua. During its first decade of existence exports by member countries to their CACM partners increased from approximately 7% of the sub-region's total exports in 1960 to about 25% in 1968.

Towards the end of the sixties, the CACM began to decline as disputes rose from unequal trade patterns. Costa Rica and Guatemala had more developed industrial parks and export capacity while Honduras, and Nicaragua suffered from an increased trade deficit with its neighbours. By 1970 Honduras had pulled out due to conflict with El Salvador (known as the football war). In addition, conflicting macroeconomic policies and unilateral currency devaluations led to the imposition again, of trade restrictions by CACM's remaining members (O'Keefe 2001). In the 1980s with the problems of internal civil conflict and guerrilla activity permeating the region (Costa Rica as the exception), the CACM was all but dead.

In the early 1990s the return to democratic governments in Central America and the resurgence of other regional trading blocks around the world revived the concept of Central American integration. Once again, the presidents of Costa Rica, El Salvador, Guatemala, Honduras, and Nicaragua met intent on renewing their commitment to economic integration. In 1991 joined by the Panamanian head of state, they met in Honduras and signed the Protocol of Tegucigalpa, an addendum to the 1962 Charter of the Organization of Central American States (ODECA). It was this Protocol that established SICA as the new institutional framework that would facilitate integration efforts in Central America. Once more in 1993, the Heads of States met in Guatemala and signed the Central American Economic Integration Protocol to the General Treaty on Central American Integration of 1960, establishing the gradual move towards a customs union. This second protocol also included the gradual shift towards a joint customs authority, the eventual movement of labour and capital among the member states and possible monetary union as long-term objectives. Panama and Costa Rica, however, have remained on the sidelines of some of the parallel agreements (Interview 47: 2006).

The Protocol of Tegucigalpa established that the highest institutional body would be the Central American Presidents' meeting to be held at least twice a year. During these meetings, the Heads of State defined the broad policy objectives, and goals of the integration process and decisions would then be adopted only by unanimous consensus. Vice-Presidents' meetings also would take place to assist the Presidents

(SG-SICA 2010). These meetings were construed to enable high-level political cooperation and show that the SICA is not only committed to economic integration but also political integration (O'Keefe 2001). The next highest authority is the Council of Ministers, headed by Foreign Relations Ministers who represent the different ministries that are responsible for integration and regional development. In the Council, each country is entitled to one vote, and for the most part, a majority vote suffices for procedural matters although some decisions require a unanimous vote.

Below the Council of Ministers lies the Executive Committee composed of one representative from each member state. The country's president chooses each representative and then they meet at least once a week to oversee the daily activities of the SICA. An Executive body (SG-SICA) headquartered in San Salvador, coordinates the four specialised technical ministries.

There are a number of institutions affiliated with the Central American integration process under the umbrella of SICA such as: The Central American Bank for Economic Integration (BCIE), the Central American Court of Justice (CCAJ), the Central American Monetary Council (CMCA), the Central American Economic Integration System (SIECA) and an advisory Central American Parliament (PARLACEN). The CMCA, as a financial institution comes under the umbrella of the SG-SICA and is on the same plane as the SIECA (2006). They inform SG-SICA of their activities and SG-SICA in turn delegate activities that fall under the competence of the CMCA. The Minister of the CMCA stated that there now exists more communication with the SIECA since he often meets with his counterpart in that institution to ensure that they are working towards the same goals (Interview 6: 2006).

Just like in other areas, SG-SICA coordinates the activities among institutions within the same sector. In the financial field it mainly coordinates the Finance Ministries with Central Banks and the leading financial institutions (like BCIE, IDB). However, "multi-sector meetings hardly take place since it is challenging to get so many ministers to a single meeting. These take place at a lower level" (Interview 6: 2006).

The Presidential meetings are the most important ones resulting in unanimously signed declarations of intent. Nevertheless, it is not the Heads of State that enact the decisions. After the Presidents sign an agreement or resolution, they do not follow it up, but instead they expect their staff to pass it along to the corresponding department. When it can be passed directly to a ministry, it is more likely that action takes place, but many times there are more complications.

> Sometimes the agreements must go through Congress for approval before they can be worked on, in particular when there are elements of transnational cooperation, and those cannot be signed by the President. Trade agreements have to pass through Congress, that is why some countries that signed the CCJ have not ratified, because it has to go through their Congress, and Congress won't approve. (Interview 47: 2006)

A common misconception is that the higher level the meeting, the more likely it is that things will get done. But in Mesoamerica, this is not always the case.

> The Presidents meet twice a year and then, they meet all the time when they are going to talk to the Mexican President, or because someone has arrived.... What happens here in Central America is that they meet too often, they make too many agreements... we are undergoing a process that the decisions made by the Presidents need to be on specific matters, matters that have been thought out, developed, and proposed so that they don't just have a lot of non-binding agreements. (Interview 6: 2006)

As I will explain in further detail in the next chapter, it is not enough to involve the presidents or the regional institutions in a multifaceted project for it to come into effect. Projects and laws need to trickle down through the tiers of government for them to convert from an abstract desire to a concrete reality. As an example, the IDB's evaluation report published in 2008 noted that from 2004 to 2007 "neither finance ministers nor members of the finance ministries attended PPP meetings" (Office of Evaluation and Oversight [OVE] 2008: 23).

Both the OECD 2005 regional report and the EU 2002–2006 technical support recommend reforming the SICA (OECD Territorial Reviews 2005; European Commission 2002). Though there is an agreement to reorganise institutions into greater efficiency and effectiveness, nevertheless, up until this point, the reorganisation of the institutions resulted in increasing bureaucracies and decreasing efficacy (see SICA/CEPAL 2004). Also, the lack of national governments' commitment to fully implementing the recommendations given draws into question the purpose of maintaining these expensive operations (Table 4.5).

Table 4.5 Overlapping regionalisms in Mesoamerica

Regional project	*Date*	*Participating countries*	*Location*	*Observers*
Plan Puebla Panama (within Tuxtla Mechanism for Cooperation) Proyecto Mesoamerica (since 2008)	2001–2008	México (9 states), Guatemala, Nicaragua, Belice, Honduras, Costa Rica, El Salvador, Panamá, Colombia (2006) Dominican Republic	Permanent Secretariat San Salvador, and State Office	
Mesoamerican Biological Corridor Reinserted into Proyecto Mesoamerica	1997–2010	Mexico (5 states), Costa Rica, Guatemala, Nicaragua, Belice, Honduras, El Salvador, Panama	Representatives in each country	
Central American Economic System (SIECA)	1960	Costa Rica, El Salvador, Guatemala, Honduras, Nicaragua	Guatemala City, Guatemala	
Central American Integration System (SICA)	1962 addendum 1991	Belize, Costa Rica, El Salvador, Guatemala, Honduras, Nicaragua, Panama, Dominican Republic as an Associated State	San Salvador, El Salvador	Mexico, Chile, Brazil as Regional Observers. Taiwan, Spain, Germany as Extra-regional observers
Triangulo del Norte (Northern Triangle)		Guatemala, El Salvador, Honduras		Signed FTA with Mexico and with Colombia
Central America 4 (CA-4)	1998	Guatemala, El Salvador, Honduras, Nicaragua		
Central America 5 (CA-5)	2002	Guatemala, El Salvador, Honduras, Nicaragua, Costa Rica		
Central American Parliament (PARLACEN)	1991–	Guatemala, El Salvador, Honduras, Nicaragua, Panama (Costa Rica never ratified)	Guatemala City, Guatemala	Mexico, Dominican Republic, Special Guests
Central American Court of Justice	1994	Nicaragua, El Salvador, Honduras	Managua, Nicaragua	Costa Rica, Guatemala (pending membership)
Central America, Dominican Republic Free Trade Agreement (CAFTA-DR)	2006	United States, CA-5, Dominican Republic		

Association of Caribbean States (ACS)	1994	Antigua and Barbuda, Bahamas, Barbados, Belize, Colombia, Costa Rica, Cuba, Dominica, Dominican Republic, El Salvador, Grenada, Guatemala, Guyana, Haiti, Honduras, Jamaica, Mexico, Nicaragua, Panama, St Kitts and Nevis, St Lucia, St Vincent and the Grenadines, Suriname, Trinidad and Tobago, Venezuela.	Port of Spain, Trinidad and Tobago	Argentina, Brazil, Canada, Chile, Ecuador, Egypt, Finland, India, Italy Netherlands, Korea, Morocco, Peru, Russia, Spain, Turkey, Ukraine, and the United Kingdom. CARICOM, SELA, SICA and the SIECA in 1996. ECLAC and the Caribbean Tourism Organisation were admitted in 2000, 2001
North American Free Trade Agreement (NAFTA)	1994	Mexico, United States, Canada		
Central American Economic Integration Bank (BCIE)	1960	Founding members: Guatemala, El Salvador, Honduras, Costa Rica, Nicaragua. Panama (Non regional members: Mexico, the Republic of China, Argentina, Colombia, and Spain Beneficiary Member: Belize)	Tegucigalpa, Honduras	WB, IDB, AEO, OMC, CEPAL, USAID
Central American Monetary Council (CMCA)	1964	Costa Rica, El Salvador, Guatemala, Honduras, Nicaragua, República Dominicana	San José Costa Rica	Mexico, Colombia
Association Agreement Central America- European Union	2010	EU-Member Countries Costa Rica, El Salvador, Guatemala, Honduras, Nicaragua		

For example, more than one government official in CA and several political analysts (Interviews 23, 31, 33, and 34: 2006) considered PARLACEN to be a "resting" ground for former presidents[9] so that they could enjoy impunity for whatever they had done during their presidency. An outgoing president cannot be investigated for corruption allegations until they leave PARLACEN. As a response to the inefficacy of the PARLACEN and these allegations of corruption, legislators from each of the Central American countries have created an alternative mechanism of regional cooperation where the president of each legislature and an alternate, meet regularly at different locations to discuss matters of regional importance. Since 2007 a regional encounter of Central American legislators takes place regularly, over 50 legislators participated in the first one held in San Salvador and the second held in Panama City.[10]

On the other hand, officials at PARLACEN commented that their legislative body had little power because any decision or policy that they approve is only considered a recommendation and is not legally binding at any level (Interview 29: 2006). Unlike the European Parliament, where decisions become part of the EU's legal system and disseminated throughout the population, PARLACEN decisions are only made known to government officials who can choose to ignore them.

When issues on the allocation of funds arose where both the former PPP and SG-SICA were competing for the same resources, the SG-SICA was invited to coordinate the technical assistance for each of the eight initiatives according to each sector. SICA also organised its consultative areas to reflect the PPP initiatives and facilitate coordination between the two bodies (Interview 19: 2006). Although the restructuring took several years, this new scheme eliminated some duplication of projects and led to more effective use of funds. Nevertheless, PPP directives still maintain that

[9]Although each member-country has twenty elected representatives and replacements, Presidents and Vice-Presidents from member countries automatically become members as soon as their term is over and for a time period as determined by each national constitution (SG-SICA 2010).

[10]These encounters have been organised by the Local Development Institute of Central America (IDELCA). I was told about them in an interview when they were still being formed, and later received information through a legislative aid (Interview 21: 2006).

> …the biggest hole in the process is communication. There have been lessons learned, most of them consequences of the lack of communication. That is why the Executive office of the PPP was created in February 2005, for communication and continuity. Institutions are important, but they also create greater bureaucracy. This kind of integration is not a political system, but rather a branch of it. With SICA, the greatest challenge is to find a way to be more complementary and less competitive. (Interview 7: 2006)

In 2006 the EU carried out an assessment of the Central American integration institutions (leaving out the PPP, MBC, and Tuxtla Mechanism) as part of the Central American Regional Integration Support Programme (PAIRCA) established in 1993. The PAIRCA presented a project including institutional restructuring that local academics and political figures received with mixed reviews. Some believed that it was what Central America needed to push integration in the right direction (Interview 14: 2006). Others thought that a vast restructuring (already attempted before hurricane Mitch devastated much of Central America in 1998) would run-up a considerable expense with little positive results because those already embedded in the system wanted it to continue as it was (Interview 34: 2006).

Many of the EU proposals included the strengthening of institutions and the granting of supranational powers, that according to most government officials would never make it through their legislative assemblies since Central American Integration thus far had been purely intergovernmental and national constitutions would not permit that loss of sovereignty (Interview 3: 2006) (EC 2006). Both analysts from FLACSO and FUSADES saw, in a positive light, that the EU had been giving Central American integration institutions technical assistance, particularly guidance in forming a customs union. The EU is putting enormous pressure on Central America to negotiate as a block before they sign an FTA between the regions. Integration has been on the table for a very long time and pressure from the EU along with the impulse that Mexico gave through the PPP, helped further this integration. However, as pointed out by several regional analysts, these projects lack a clear vision of integration. "Each one has a different vision of what 'integration' means, and conjointly, as the MFAs are working towards one view of integration through the PPP, Economic Ministers are working on negotiating FTAs on their side, and those working with the multilateral forums, like the WTO, are working independently as well" (Interview 23: 2006).

The interaction among the people involved in the SICA institutions across sectors and borders was interesting. The existence of regular meetings and personal contact among the representatives was evident as was the case of SIECA and SICA, but these were limited to issues on economics. Few were optimistic about achieving integration as they envisioned it. Even though there was optimism that integration would bring forth development in the region there was a sense that they still hadn't found the magic formula required for it to consolidate.

In the economic subsystem of integration, the SIECA, the people I interviewed showed considerable optimism about the CA4 customs union (Guatemala, Honduras, El Salvador, and Nicaragua) that is in place. However, the inclusion of Costa Rica has not finalised[11] as it is not ready to commit to the free movement of people. This economic subsystem was encouraged shortly after the peace accords were signed, to solidify them through trade. The primary market for Central American products was and is still the United States; however, the internal Central American market comes in as a close second (Interview 14: 2006).[12] The main accomplishment of the SIECA in addition to the CA4 was tariff harmonisation (which is at about 94%). However, one problem that SIECA has found notable in the FTA schemes that are already operating in Central America is that since the borders are very permeable once products enter the region, they tend to circulate.

> Right now, only Central American goods are supposed to travel freely in the C4 and C5; if we bring in merchandise from China to Guatemala, then it cannot move freely, but in the end it does. Even though our border controls are still supposed to stop the free movement of goods, they don't. That is why it is important to finalise the customs union and regulate these situations. (Interview 14: 2006)

The PPP did not affect the institutional set up of the SICA, nevertheless, it did highlight that the SIECA needed to be an active participant

[11] https://www.centralamericadata.com/en/search?q1=content_en_le:%22Central+American+Customs+Union%22.

[12] According to the SICA/CEPAL 2004 report, intra-regional exports represented 28% of commercial interactions. SIECA 2005 report places intra-regional exports at 30% and exports to the US at 40% of regional exports, while the PPP 2006 progress report situates this number closer to 39%. The minor discrepancies are most likely due to publication dates.

in any regional mechanism or otherwise, duplicate or opposing projects would result. The presence of Mexico in the SICA has been increasing since the inception of the PPP, particularly in the PARLACEN, where in 2006, over twenty Mexican senators were attending meetings regularly (Interview 29: 2006).

4.3 Mesoamerica "Regions"

Development Region

The Tuxtla Mechanism (Tuxtla IV: 1998), set forth the PMC (Programa Mesoamericano de Cooperación) in 1998, as the facilitator for cooperating on issues such as Agriculture, Education, Environment and Natural disasters. Each year during the Tuxtla Mechanism meetings, the attending presidents reviewed the programmes and accepted (or rejected) new proposals. The available documents are not clear regarding how the projects of the PMC worked together with the PPP from 2001 to 2008. Both the Tuxtla Mechanism reports and the PPP reports refer to the same projects. As I noted in Chapter 3, the highest criticism against the PPP was about the shortfalls of its developmental aspect. Of the eight Mesoamerican initiatives, the first three were the ones to receive the least funding and attention.

When *Proyecto Mesoamerica* replaced the PPP, development projects returned under the authority of the PMC. It is likely (though not explicit in the documentation) that some of the projects eliminated in the transition from the PPP to *Proyecto Mesoamerica* were taken over by the PMC. In 2009 the ministers of foreign affairs confirmed the eleven projects that would continue under the PMC and that nine other proposals were under consideration. Although meetings take place every two years, specific national institutions give continuity to the projects (PMC 2009–2010: 2008).

The PMC, now renamed the *Agenda Mesoamericana de Cooperación*, is the instrument designated to carry out the 2030 UN agenda for sustainable development (Tuxtla XVI: 2017). A complimentary organism, the *Programa Regional de Cooperación con Mesoamérica* also carries out development projects.[13]

[13]The 2017 accountability report shows that Colombia is leading many of these efforts and a substantial amount of funding has been secured through USAID.

Proyecto Mesoamerica limited its scope to two axes: Economic and Social. The documents of *Proyecto Mesoamerica* consider economic growth as the path to development, and as such, gives it the highest priority. However, the social axis includes areas that are not directly economic: health, environment, natural disasters, and housing (in 2015, the Mesoamerican Program to end hunger was included as the 9th area in the social axis).

It is important to note that, while the initial launch of the PPP and the "re-launch" of 2003 received quite a bit of media coverage and academic discussion, the June 2008 summit hardly made it into national newspapers. Very little has appeared subsequently, and so far, information has not been flowing outside of the institutions involved in Proyecto Mesoamerica or the periodic newsletter that is sent out to subscribers. 2018 marked its 10th anniversary, to commemorate, some videos and documents were added to the official website. Although the Mesoamerican Institute for Public Health is considered a top priority for the Proyecto Mesoamerica, very little information went public when it was launched in 2009 and when both the Fundación Grupo Carso (founded by Carlos Slim) and the Bill and Melinda Gates Foundation announced considerable financing for the project in June 2010, the announcement did not refer to the *Proyecto Mesoamerica* nor to the defunct PPP (as its predecessor). However, a different approach to financing occurred in this project. The funding bodies began financing with one-third of the funds up front, and the rest of the funds would be allotted upon receipt of progress reports and target achievement.[14] Set up as a public–private partnership, the Mesoamerican Institute for Public Health also includes a network of public health and academic research institutions aimed at giving technical and operative support to regional health systems (Tuxtla XI: 2009). The Mesoamerican Institute of Public Health is now used as a model for public–private partnerships and accountability mechanisms so that by 2017, Tuxtla XVI was recommending promoting this model for development projects as well as infrastructure projects (p. 3).

Housing is a primary concern in Mesoamerica. Many people are homeless, but even more so, people live in inadequate homes that

[14] http://www.saludmesoamerica.org/en/salud-mesoamerica-initiative/the-initiative/salud-mesoamerica-initiative-who-is-behind,2763.html.

lack essential services including access to water, electricity, and sewage (Presidencia de la República 2001). Some are improvised shelters with weak structures that could easily collapse during earthquakes, hurricanes, or even torrential rains. Some shanty homes built next to rivers (for access to water) are at risk of flooding during downpours. A housing programme was included in Proyecto Mesoamerica, spearheaded by the Central American programme for social housing. There are two unusual factors about this programme. First, that it was added due to pressure from Nicaragua's Civil Coordinator (the umbrella organisation for dozens of civil society groups).[15] The other interesting fact is that Mexico contributed 33 million dollars (reimbursable) from the funds of the San José Accord channelled through the BCIE. The San José Accord was signed in 1980 by Mexico and Venezuela committing to provide Costa Rica, Jamaica, and Nicaragua with barrels of oil to avert an energy crisis. The Accord was ratified each subsequent year and was extended to include other types of aid and to include El Salvador, Guatemala, Haiti, Honduras, Panama, and the Dominican Republic as recipients. Mexico allocated 450 million dollars to this fund between 2008 and 2009 under the supervision of the Finance Ministry.[16] The San José Accord was replaced by the Fondo Yucatán in 2011.

Economic and Monetary Region

Regional Trade

Currently, up to seven PTAs exist among countries of the MAR, as well as six formal regional arrangements along with numerous bilateral PTAs that each of the Mesoamerican countries has with external countries or regions. Mexico is a member of NAFTA and of the Latin American Integration Association (LAIA). Colombia is a member of LAIA, has a Free Trade Agreement (FTA) with Mexico, and is negotiating PTAs with several Central American countries. Not being part of either NAFTA or LAIA, Central America has its own integration mechanisms under the umbrella of SICA and recently, the Central American-Dominican

[15] "México, Centroamérica y la Sociedad Civil. Desafíos en Común" 07 Cuadernos ocasionales 2011. www.socialwatch.org/es/node/13724.

[16] "Los entretelones del Acuerdo de San José" by Claudia Villegas 15 December 2010. www.revistafortuna.com.mx/contenido/2010/12/15/los-entretelones-del-acuerdo-de-san-jose/.

Republic Free Trade Agreement with the United States (CAFTA-DR). In addition, several institutions that are part of, or associated with, SICA were designed to further integration, such as the Central American Economic Integration Bank, the Central American Parliament, and The Central American Court. Not all the Central American countries belong to all the institutions and in many cases (Mexico, along with other countries) hold an "observer" status. All nine countries have PTAs with other nations outside of the Americas. According to the Mexican Economic Ministry, Mexico, in 2007 had twelve PTAs in place covering 42 countries.[17]

Some of the various trade agreements that involve, but are not limited to, the MAR overlap (i.e., NAFTA, CAFTA, and negotiations with the EU) but each of them has its own scope and purpose, and they are not always compatible. For example, even though Mexico has a treaty with the United States and with each of the Central American countries and Central America with the United States and Mexico, these cannot easily be harmonised into one agreement that covers them all. Although many of the PTAs were signed between members in Mesoamerica, they might be causing higher trade distortion since each trade agreement has different terms. In some instances, Central America has signed trade agreements as a block, in others, as separate countries and even still with others, as smaller blocks (i.e., the Northern Triangle comprised of El Salvador, Guatemala, and Honduras). This means that sensitive products, like sugar to Guatemala or beef to Nicaragua, have different preferential treatment in each agreement. According to one analyst on trade issues from FUSADES,

> …it is absurd to set up all of these different schemes, it is absurd to think that in such a small area with such permeable borders, that just because US beef was made an exception for Nicaragua in CAFTA, due to the importance of the beef industry in Nicaragua, that it will not find its way to Nicaragua once the product enters Central America. (Interview 23: 2006)

CAFTA is used as an example of a trade agreement that produced more division than integration in Central America. Initially, the United States declared that they would be negotiating with Central America as

[17]http://www.economia.gob.mx/pics/p/p2832/Seminario_70322.pdf.

one, but then, unified stance broke down when dealing with sensitive products:

> I am under the impression that it was what the US wanted to happen with certain products, a 'divide and conquer' policy….on the surface it seems that CAFTA is a regional agreement, and it is in the general text, but it is in the annexes that we find the heart of the matter, the bilateral deals. (Interview 23: 2006)

However, the opinion of an official from the Guatemalan MFA was not that CAFTA had been a step backwards in integration, but that it had disharmonised external tariffs, not to mention, tangled the rules of origin:

> …we had already advanced quite a bit in this [tariffs] area over the past years; we were close to 94–95% harmonised when we began the negotiation process [of CAFTA], the remaining 4% are the products that are very sensitive like coffee, sugar, alcohol. We are small countries, it is hard for us to give way on many things, and we disharmonised when we did not negotiate CAFTA as a block. (Interview 3: 2006)

Unfortunately, the worst consequences of not harmonising and negotiating as a region are internal… "the largest export market is with each other internally, we [Guatemala] export approximately 30% of our total exports to El Salvador, which is a substantial proportion" (Interview 3: 2006). One interviewee commented that during the Central American Presidential Summits they all said: "…from now on we will negotiate everything together" (Interview 30: 2006) and that, as soon as they had finished the sentence, they started separate negotiations, more due to political and diplomatic reasons than to economic ones. Then come all the problems of trying to coordinate commercial policy with that "spaghetti bowl" that forms due to the different tariff schemes and rules of origin. It even complicates internal commercial relations since it can then justify intra-regional trade barriers. Although they know the advantages of negotiating as a block, they succumb to internal pressure groups. "Instead of searching to complement trade policies at a regional level and integrating productivity chains, there still exists a misunderstood competitiveness where we are unable to identify that our rivals are on the outside and not on the inside" (Interview 23: 2006).

The PPP underscored the importance of consolidating FTAs among the countries in the MAR. Its objective of "making the best use of the trading agreements in place" (Presidencia de la República 2001) proved more difficult than expected due to the existing network of trade agreements. According to several interviewees (Interviews 3, 14, 19, 20, and 42), even though proposals existed to negotiate one single FTA among the members of the PPP including Colombia and the Dominican Republic, it had not been possible. During the Tenth Summit of the Tuxtla Mechanism in 2008 (whereby the *Proyecto Mesoamerica* was announced), the presidents agreed to start negotiations towards the convergence of all the commercial treaties already in place. The goal of this convergence, according to point 47 of the Summit Declaration, was to "advance in obtaining an association agreement for Mesoamerica" (Declaración de Villahermosa 2008: 10). During this summit, they agreed to include specific points on rules of origin[18] both in the Mexico-EU agreement and the forthcoming EU-Central American association agreement, to bring some common ground to these overlapping agreements. Mexico and Central America signed a unified free trade agreement on 22 November 2011[19]; however, it did not include Panama, Colombia, or the Dominican Republic. One indirect consequence of the PPP was that it encouraged Mesoamerica to clear up what could be called an "untamed tangle of criss-crossing preferential trade agreements" (Baldwin 2006).

Financial and Monetary Regional Coordination

Financial and Monetary integration is an essential part of the Central American integration networks and institutions. The two leading institutions are the Central American Bank for Economic Integration (BCIE), founded in 1960, and the Central American Monetary Council (CMCA), established on 25 February 1964. Both of these were to provide the support necessary for future monetary union. Based in Honduras, the BCIE is the largest financial institution in Central America and the principal backer of social programmes and regional integration projects. It also supports the private sector, particularly small- and medium-sized

[18] As pointed out by Haggard (1997) and Baldwin (2006), rules of origin is where rent seeking takes place in the FTAs of the Americas.

[19] Coming into effect on 1 September 2012 with El Salvador and Nicaragua; and on 1 January 2013, with Guatemala, Costa Rica and Honduras.

enterprises (SMEs). The BCIE includes all the countries that were members of the PPP, plus Chile, Argentina, and Spain. It has worked together on projects with the World Bank (WB), IDB, CEPAL, and USAID. The BCIE worked together with the PPP throughout its 7-year existence both in funding projects and as part of the GTI.

The presidents of the Central Banks of Costa Rica, El Salvador, Guatemala, Honduras, and Nicaragua and the Governor of the Central Bank of the Dominican Republic (which became a full member in 2002) make up the CMCA. Panama does not have a Central Bank, so it is not a member of the CMCA, although the President of the National Bank is invited to participate in CMCA meetings. The Mexican Central Bank is not an official member but considered an invaluable source of cooperation for the Central Banks in the region (Interview 6: 2006). "we call Mexico and let them know if we need something, and then they come. They always help us somewhat with our institutional framework, even before we talk about financing, and they give us their perspective from the Mexican experience" (Interview 4: 2006). PPP institutional structure did not include the CMCA, nevertheless the fact that Mexico and Panama are invited to join and give input on regional financial and monetary matters could signal the potential advantages of having this respected regional organism expanded into the Mesoamerican Region.

Although the CMCA began in 1964, like many of the Central American Integration mechanisms, it was wholly amended in 1999 by the Tegucigalpa Protocol (establishing SICA). The Council was set up expressly to "encourage the regional monetary and financial integration, within a framework of macroeconomic stability" (CMCA 2006: 2). The Council President heads up the institution and rotates every year. To ensure continuity, each President first serves as vice-president the preceding year. Meetings are held three times a year, although extraordinary meetings can be called to discuss impending matters. The CMCA has a permanent Executive Ministry based in San José Costa Rica, which is responsible for monitoring its decisions, agreements, and resolutions as well as serving as the official channel for communications.

According to one Minister (2006–2009) the CMCA is an organism that works well albeit it has limited funds, because its members know each other and work towards a common goal, "Central Banks know what their functions are, they are clear. Sometimes we can resolve problems quickly, sometimes we can't, but we are a group that knows where we are going, sometimes quickly, sometimes slow, but our projects are advancing" (Interview 6: 2006). Central Banks tend to have more stability in their personnel, and the CMCA Ministry institutionalises communications between them and helps with regional integration:

> ...we are 17 people here dedicated exclusively to regional integration issues, even though advances depend on the support of the Central Banks in each country, and like in every other region of the world, we have disagree on several points, and our job is precisely to try and conciliate these points in order to advance on regional matters. (Interview 6: 2006)

The CMCA's goals in its 2007–2011 mandate were: "to encourage coordination, harmonisation, and convergence in monetary, exchange and financial policies of the member countries; to promote a single financial space in the whole region" (CMC 2006: 2).[20] The 2006–2009 Minister explained the reason for postponing the common currency, as the focus of the CMC shifted to more imminent matters of macroeconomic stability, reducing inflation, and monetary stability. In recent history, inflation rates remain under 10% in most Central American Countries, as opposed to the 80s and early 90s, where spiralling hyperinflation could reach over 200% (Interview 6: 2006). Another member of the Ministry indicated that there were additional reasons for the monetary union to lose its priority to the creation of a single financial space:

> ...there are technical reasons why monetary union has been postponed, because to form an optimal monetary zone we first have to have a customs union, one where there is complete mobility of the factors of production, and we are not there yet. There are some advances, but the customs union has been postponed and without free mobility, in the academic sense of the word, the factors of production, company movement, people, it hasn't happened, and until it does, then we cannot think of homogenising exchange rates and adopt a single currency. (Interview 4: 2006)

Alluding to the Balassa (1961) model where complete regional integration goes in stages, before adopting a single currency, a customs union needs to be in place. He stated: "let's say that academia also keeps us from thinking about a single currency, so we have to remain in the areas

[20] See also http://unpan1.un.org/intradoc/groups/public/documents/icap/unpan049986.pdf.

where we can work in the creation of a regional financial space which is not dependent on the success of the customs union" (Interview 4: 2006). So, they focused on this regional financial space, where the priorities resided in homogenising payment systems, standardising the handling of public debt and monitoring economic distortions (Interview 4: 2006). Thus, the six participating countries continue under different monetary regimes but strive to reach macroeconomic convergence using the parameters set out in 2002 by the CMCA (2006).

Environmental Region

With Mesoamerica's biodiversity, environmental issues are high on the agenda for the region. One of the eight Mesoamerican initiatives included in the PPP was sustainable development, headed by Nicaragua, which according to an official PPP report, was based on "the experiences of the Mesoamerican Biological Corridor (MBC), whose broad concept of regional development has been ratified by all the countries of the region" (Coordinación General del Plan Puebla-Panamá 2002). The MBC was the continuation of a project introduced in 1990, the *Paseo Pantera*, which initiated as an agreement of cooperation with USAID, emphasising the establishment of a corridor running from Darien (Panama) to the *Selva Maya* that extends through parts of Mexico, Guatemala, and Belize. The idea was to create a green belt to address species conservation while promoting regional cooperation.

Paseo Pantera continued through 1996 and in 1997, the region's Heads of State signed an agreement establishing the MBC. The MBC was modelled after a successful programme that took place in Costa Rica, run by the National Institute for Biodiversity (INBio), which promoted conservation through the sustainable use of resources, providing economic remuneration as well as caring for the environment. The goal of the MBC was to recover "the chain of forests that a few years ago united South and North America and which at this time appears as a series of barren patches threatened by indiscriminate felling" (CCAD-MBC 2003). Supported by the United Nations Development Programme (UNDP), the Global Environment Facility (GEF), the World Bank, and the German and Danish Governments, the MBC was lauded as a display of international cooperation.

The primary contact of the MBC in Costa Rica commented in an interview, that because they had already used environmental corridors in Costa Rica, they were able to share their experience with the rest of Central America (Interview 28: 2006). He added that they had faced resistance in other parts of Central America where protected areas were not well marked, and land was expropriated from private owners. In some cases, due to poor oversight or to the lack of long-term planning, the protected areas had just as much devastation as those not protected (Interview 28: 2006). Moreover, these protected areas were too small to make a meaningful impact on biodiversity without creating a link to others; therefore, regional cooperation was the way forward to ensure environmental conservation with a tangible impact (CCAD-MBC 2003).

This idea of regional cooperation for the environment was not new; Central American governments had previously signed a Central American Environmental Protection Agreement and had established a Central American Commission on Environment and Development (CCAD) in 1989 that then became the environmental ministry within SICA (CEPAL/SICA 2004).

According to its website, the MBC is "by no means focused exclusively on protecting the animals, plants and micro-organisms which inhabit the tropical forests but will provide benefit on a priority basis to the people who live there, to all Mesoamericans and by extension to the entire world" (accessed 5 October 2004). In Costa Rica, 33 initiatives were proposed to the local Commissions (integrated by NGOs, local population, institutions, and private companies), out of these 33, 17 made it into the MBC. Local participation was a key element to the success of the programme "…there is no point in outlining and setting a geographical limit if the people living there are not aware that they are in a Biological Corridor; the Biological Corridor only begins to function when the people or some of the people that live there begin to participate" (Interview 28: 2006). People were invited to participate in the organisation, programming, and partnership with other corridors. The role of the national coordinators was to train the people making the proposals and how to approach the donors, as well as linking the corridors with those located in the other countries.

The programme rests upon two main pillars: biodiversity conservation and the sustainable use of the region's resources. The first thing commissioned was a thorough investigation in each country, indicating the current state of its ecosystems and systems of protection. Biodiversity conservation initiative builds on the existing protected areas, creating links between them and strengthening the institutions designed for their protection. Few countries had the institutional or legal frameworks required to facilitate conservation; however, this initiative wasn't just about protecting the resources but also about using them appropriately (Interview 28: 2006).

The sustainable use of resources is an initiative that will educate people on how they can use the forests without causing them harm. The programme identified areas for activity and investment, including environmentally friendly agriculture (comprising organic food production), ecotourism, pharmaceutical prospecting, and reforestation.

The MBC is set up through a system of administrative arrangements including *core zones*, *buffer zones*, *multiple use zones*, and *corridor zones*. The core zones are areas designated to provide protection to native flora and fauna within secure habitats. Buffer zones surround the core zones to filter out any potential threats that could move into the areas. Core zones are linked together in some areas forming the Corridor Zones, which are managed to ensure that human land-uses are compatible with the maintenance of a high degree of biological connectivity—although these areas are mostly under wild cover. The Multiple-Use zones manage areas mainly intended for human use but can include broader landscapes hospitable to native species. Each type of zone should provide both ecological and socioeconomic benefits (CCAD-MBC 2005).

Although the MBC was criticised by those who claim that it promotes biopiracy and pillaging of natural resources (i.e., Barreda Marín 2002; Moguel 2001; Rioja Peregrina 2002), in general, it has been a well-received programme and viewed in a positive light by the population. Nevertheless, several organisations argued that government representatives avoided establishing the relationship between the PPP and the Mesoamerican Biological Corridor, particularly when projects were seeking economic profit from the environment (Interviews 8, 9, 16, and 20). The initial claim linking the MBC to the PPP was not entirely accurate. Although both programmes were compatible and could have been complimentary during their duration, they did not establish an ongoing dialogue of cooperation. The MBC contact in Costa Rica stated, "…people have asked me what our relationship to the Plan Puebla Panama is… Up until now, I can say that I do not have any connection to the Plan Puebla Panama. It is not that I don't know anything about it, of course, I know of it, but I have not received any calls from them (PPP), and I do not know the national coordinator of the PPP here (in Costa Rica) … In the years that I have been with the MBC, I have never been called to a meeting with anyone from the PPP" (Interview 28: 2006).

When the PPP was replaced by Proyecto Mesoamerica in 2008 most of the MBC projects had either been completed or terminated, although other projects continued in Mexico (see www.cbmm.gob.mx).[21] The initial documents of Proyecto Mesoamerica however, stated that all the activities that formed part of the MBC would continue to be committed to safeguarding the environment and promoting the sustainable use of resources (Dirección Ejecutiva Proyecto de Integración y Desarrollo de Mesoamérica 2008). Tuxtla XI (2009), established that the Central American Commission for the Environment and Development (CCAD), CEPAL, and the IDB would support the relaunching of the Mesoamerican Biological Corridor as the pillar for sustainable development. On 20 May 2013, the ministers responsible for the Mesoamerican Strategy for Environmental Sustainability signed an agreement to strengthen the MBC and confirm projects until 2020. However, they specified that it was a non-binding agreement and that each country would cooperate according to its national interest, circumstances, and laws.[22]

Security Region

The eight Mesoamerican Initiatives of the PPP did not include "security," and neither does the Proyecto Mesoamerica. It seems odd that if violence in Central America is considered a threat to Mexican national security and was identified as one of the stumbling blocks hindering development, it was left out of the multidimensional "innovative development mechanism." Containing violence was one of the main reasons for the creation of the first cooperation mechanisms—the Contadora Group and the Tuxtla Mechanism. However, security is supposed to be provided by the sovereign state, and maintaining

[21] A renewed interest in the MBC has surged since 2010, and the Director in Mexico, Pedro Álvarez Icaza is promoting the institutionalisation of the initiatives in order to promote continuity.

[22] Plan Director CBM-2020 Gestión Territorial Sostenible en el Corredor Biológico Mesoamericano 20 May 2013. http://www.proyectomesoamerica.org:8088/emsa/documentos/Proyectos/CBM/Plan%20Director%20CBM-2020%20aprob.pdf, accessed 8 September 2017.

sovereignty is of utmost importance to Mexico and Central American nations. Previous sections pointed out that the Mesoamerican countries were not willing to give up autonomy in matters of trade or even environment, and states were reluctant to sign binding agreements.

First and foremost, cooperation on matters of security, mainly on fighting drug trafficking, organised crime, and gang violence in Mesoamerica, initiated under the Tuxtla Mechanism, and included in the agenda for political cooperation. Nevertheless, regional cooperation for security matters has been forthcoming in other forums. The Merida initiative for example, announced in October of 2007 by former US President Bush and former Mexican President Felipe Calderón, is a package of US assistance for Mexico and Central America to fight organised crime and associated violence "based on principles of common and shared responsibility, mutual trust, and respect for sovereign independence."[23] The Merida initiative has been highly criticised both in the United States and in Mesoamerica since it provided resources and training to local police and armed forces that have been accused of human rights abuse on numerous occasions (Ribade 2009). Since 2007, the Merida Initiative has been refocused or expanded through the changing administrations in the region.

Within the SICA framework, Central American heads of state signed their own Central American Security Strategy in 2007, which was renewed in 2011, stating the importance of continuing with a comprehensive Central American Strategy. In January 2014, the EU offered to help Central American and Caribbean States draft a Citizen Security plan of action. The northern triangle states (Guatemala, Salvador, and Honduras) met with the (then) President of the United States, Barack Obama to formulate what was called the Alliance for Prosperity, as a response to the thousands of minors detained trying to cross illegally into the United States (Solano 2015). The Alliance for Prosperity has an active social component; investment in basic services, education, and job creation considered as crucial elements for stopping migration. The Alliance includes features to improve citizen security and access to justice through violence prevention, strengthening security institutions, and modernising the justice system (Solano 2015). The Alliance for Prosperity is structured around a consultative group (made up of the

[23] http://www.state.gov/j/inl/merida/c30128, accessed 25 November 2017.

governments of the United States and each country) and includes the participation of civil society, private enterprise, and the IDB.[24] In 2017, the Conference for Security and Prosperity in Central America was held in Miami, Florida, to address the wave of violence and organised crime that causes thousands of people to flee the region.[25] The conference convened the US and Mexican governments, and participants included the presidents of Guatemala and Honduras, the vice-president of El Salvador, and representatives from other countries like Canada, Belize, Costa Rica, Nicaragua, Panama, Colombia, Chile, the EU, and also the IDB. During this conference, John Kelly (then Minister of Homeland Security) stated that US border security starts 1500 miles to the south of the United States.[26] The 2017 meeting was convened to strengthen the Alliance for Prosperity, but this time with the support of Mexico, "an invaluable partner with a shared interest in improving conditions in Central America."[27]

4.4 Summary

Although a "spaghetti bowl" already existed in Mesoamerica prior to the PPP, the problems of having so many regional arrangements cohabiting in the same area were heightened once the PPP came into effect. The projects included in the PPP required coordination with other regional bodies as well as with national governments for their completion. The OECD report identified some of the apparent problems of coordination among Mesoamerica regional institutions, later reflected in the institutional reform leading up to *Proyecto Mesoamerica* (Table 4.6).

Moreover, institutional disarray at the regional level was probably the most evident problem of the PPP, an easily identifiable and remediable issue. The PPP and its transition to Proyecto Mesoamerica, gave priority to trade and infrastructure over all other aspects of the projects.

[24] http://www.secretariatecnica.gob.sv/alianza-para-la-prosperidad/ and https://documentop.com/plan-alianza-para-la-prosperidad-ceur-usac_59f7cef61723dd30b1b6a220.html.

[25] https://dialogo-americas.com/pt/articles/conference-security-and-prosperity-central-america.

[26] "Fixing Central America is the focus of high-level Miami summit," by Mimi Whitefield and Jaqueline Charles, *Miami Herald*, 12 June 2017.

[27] Ibid. Quote from Deputy Assistant Secretary of State John S. Creamer.

Table 4.6 Timeline: from Plan Puebla Panamá to Proyecto Mesoamerica

Year	Events
1991	• Presidential summit establishes the Tuxtla Mechanism
2000	• July: Mexican Presidential Elections • November: The Plan Puebla Panamá is presented to CA leaders • December: President Vicente Fox inaugurated
2001	• January: Madrid agenda presented • March: Plan Puebla Panamá Presented by Vicente Fox • June: Plan Puebla Panama is launched at Tuxtla extraordinary summit
2002	• June: PPP is presented to investors in Mérida , the RICAM is defined
2004	• March: PPP is relaunched during VI Tuxtla Mechanism with new institutional structure
2005	• Jaunary: Executive permanent secretariat offices installed in San Salvador • August: PPP offices are inaugurated
2006	• July: Mexican Presidential elections. Felipe Calderon declares he will strengthen the PPP • Colombia become official member
2007	• April: Summit to strengthen the PPP
2008	• June: Tuxtla X Final report of PPP is presented and Proyecto Mesoamerica is launched
2009	• Tuxtla XI: Colombia and Dominican Republic are incorporated into Tuxtla Mechanism and ratyfied as member of Proyecto Mesoamerica
2010	• Mesoamerican Cooperation Programme adopted
2011	• November: Mexico-Central America FTA (ratified between September 2012 and September 2013)
2015	• Food security added to the Human Development Pillar or Axis
2018	• Proyecto Mesoamerica celebrates 10 year anniversary • July: Mexican Presidential elections. Andrés Manuel López Obrador proposes new development projects for Mexican south and new cooperations schemes with CA

Developmental and environmental projects although included, were left to one side. Security, on the other hand, was not explicit in either project; nevertheless, regional cooperation on security has been ongoing.

Although regional institutions are important actors, as I will discuss in the following two chapters, the problems in implementing a multidimensional regional development project in Mesoamerica are not limited to its regional mechanisms, but to mechanisms throughout the different tiers of government and with other regional participants. If regionalism continues to be multifaceted in Mesoamerica, it cannot be expected to be successful if it is only designed and implemented by regional institutions and central governments. Subsequently, in Chapter 5 I will focus on the roles of national, sub-national, and local governments in regional integration and regional projects, or vertical governance; and in Chapter 6 I will highlight the activities of other players in the region, such as NGOs, civil society, trade unions, and private business.

Bibliography

Acta que institucionaliza el Mecanismo del Plan Puebla-Panamá. 2004. http://www.sieca.org.gt/Sitio-publico/OACUERDOS/83-1Acta.htm. Accessed 3 March 2006.

Balassa, Bela A. 1961. *The Theory of Economic Integration*. London: Allen and Unwin, 1962.

Baldwin, Richard E. 2006. Multilateralising Regionalism: Spaghetti Bowls as Building Blocas on the Path to Global Free Trade. *The World Economy* 29 (11): 1451–1518.

Barreda Marín, Andrés. 2002. El Plan Puebla Panamá. *Biodiversidad* 33 (Agosto): 1–8.

Bartra, Armando. 2002. Hacia una Nueva Colonización del Sureste. In *Economía Política del Plan Puebla Panamá*, ed. Alejandro Álvarez Béjar, Andrés Barreda Marín, y Armando Bartra. México: Editorial Itaca.

Bejar Alvarez, Alejandro. 2002a. The Puebla-Panama Plan: Development of a Region or a Multinational Enclave?

Bejar Alvarez, Alejandro. 2002b. El Plan Puebla-Panamá en el contexto de la integración hemisférica. *Política y cultura* 18 (otoño): 83–105.

CCAD-MBC. 2003. *Estrategia regional para la conservación y uso sostenible de la biodiversidad en Mesoamérica (ERB)*. Comisión Centroamericana de Ambiente y Desarrollo El Salvador.

CCAD-MBC. 2005. *Programa Estratégico Regional Para la Conectividad*. Comisión Centroamericana de Ambiente y Desarrollo El Salvador.

CC-SICA INFORME DE CONSULTA. 2003. *Estrategia de Modernización del Estado y Perfil de la estrategia para la Integración Regional.* San José Costa Rica: FUNPADEM.

CC-SICA. 2006. *Plan de Acción para el Fortalecimiento del CC-SICA 2006.* San José Costa Rica: FUNPADEM.

Chanona, Alejandro. 2002. Procesos de integración en el marco del Plan Puebla-Panamá (PPP). In *Lectura Crítica del Plan Puebla Panamá*, ed. Eduardo Andrés Sandoval Forero y Robinson Salazar Pérez coordinadores. Libros en Red.

Consejo Monetario Centroamericano (CMCA). 2006. *The Central American Monetary Council and its Executive Ministry* (official booklet) published July 2006.

Coordinación General del Plan Puebla-Panamá (CG-PPP). 2001. *Plan Puebla Panamá: Presentación Diagnóstico Centroamérica.* Mexico: INEGI.

Coordinación General del Plan Puebla-Panamá (CG-PPP). 2002. *Informe de Avances y Perspectivas Plan Puebla-Panamá.* Mexico: INEGI. Junio.

Curly, Jon M. 2008. Cleaning Up the Spaghetti Bowl. In *Economic Integration in the Americas*, ed. Joseph A. McKinney and Stephen Gardner. London and New York: Routledge.

Dávila Enrique, Kessel Georgina, y Levy Santiago. 2002. "El Sur también existe: un ensayo sobre el desarrollo regional de México" (originally published in Economía Mexicana Vol. XI, 2002, pp. 202–260). In *Ensayos Sobre el Desarrollo Económico y Social de México*, Santiago Levy (compilador), 2004. México: Fondo de Cultura Económica.

Declaración de Guatemala. 2000. Declaración Conjunta de la IV Cumbre de los Jefes de Estado y de Gobierno de los países integrantes del Mecanismo de Diálogo y Concertación de Tuxtla 25 de Agosto de 2000. http://www.sieca.org.gt/publico/OACUERDOS/TuxtlaIV.htm.

Declaración de Tapachula. 2001. Photocopy of text.

Declaración de Mérida. 2002. Declaración Conjunta de la quinta cumbre del Mecanismo de Diálogo y Concertación de Tuxtla 27 y 28 de junio 2002. http://sieca.org.gt/Publico/OACUERDOS/DeclaraciondeMerida.htm.

Declaración Extraordinaria. 2001. Declaración Conjunta de la Cumbre extraordinaria de los países integrantes del Mecanismo de Diálogo y Concertación de Tuxtla. http://sieca.org.gt/publico/OACUERDOS/DECLARACION_CONJUNTA_DE_LA.

Declaración de Villahermosa. 2008.

Dirección Ejecutiva Proyecto de Integración y Desarrollo de Mesoamérica. 2008. *Informe de Actividades 2008.* El Salvador. www.planpuebla-panama.org. Accessed 4 November 2008.

Dirección de Communicación del Parlamento Centroamericano. Undated Publication. ABC del PARLACEN.

ECLAC. 2007. Statistical Yearbook for Latin America and the Caribbean. www.eclac.cl/publicaciones/xml/6/32606/LCG2356B.2.pdf. Accessed 12 February 2008.

Alternativas Para el Desarrollo vol. 93, Abril–Mayo. 2005. San Salvador: FUNDE.

European Commission (EC). 2002. Regional Strategy Paper for Central America 2002–2006.

European Commission (EC). 2006. Regional Strategy Paper for Central America 2006–2013. https://eeas.europa.eu/sites/eeas/files/central_america_regional_strategy_paper_2007-2013_0.pdf.

FEMICA/SGSICA. 2009. Memorandum de Entendimiento Entre la Secretaria General del Sistema de la Integración Centroamericana (SGSICA) y la Federación de Municipios del Istmo Centroamericano (FEMICA). http://femica.org/noticias/docNoticias/Convenio_SICA_FEMICA.pdf.

FEMICA. 2008. Fortalecimiento de los Gobiernos Locales y de la Sociedad Civil. *Revista Femica* 5 (Febrero). http://www.femica.org/archivos/revista5.pdf.

Figueroa Fisher, Bruno. 2014. Breve Historia de la cooperación Internacional de México 1900–2000. *Revista Mexicana de Política Exterior* 102 (septiembre–diciembre): 29–53. https://www.gob.mx/cms/uploads/attachment/file/277450/Cien-an_os-completo_web.pdf.

FUNDE/PNUD. 2004. Asociación de Municipios y Construcción Regional para el Desarrollo. *Desarrollo Humano: Buenas Prácticas Enero* 3.

Grupo Técnico Interinstitucional (GTI). 2001. *Plan Puebla-Panamá: Iniciativas Mesoamericanas y Proyectos.* San Salvador, El Salvador: BCIE-BID-ECLAC con el apoyo del INCAE. Junio 15 de 2001.

Haggard, Stephen. 1997. The Political Economy of Regionalism in Asia and the Americas. In *The Political Economy of Regionalism*, ed. Edward D. Mansfield and Helen V. Milner. New York: Columbia University Press.

Hettne, Björn. 2003. The New Regionalism Revisited. In *Theories of New Regionalism: A Palgrave Reader*, ed. Fredrik Söderbaum and Timothy M. Shaw. Basingstoke: Palgrave Macmillan.

Hettne, Björn, and Fredrik Söderbaum. 2000. Theorising the Rise of Regionness. *New Political Economy* 5 (3): 457–472.

Hettne, Björn, and Fredrik Söderbaum. 2002. Theorising the Rise of Regionness. In *New Regionalisms in the Global Political Economy: Theories and Cases*, ed. Shaun Breslin et al. London: Routledge.

Informe Ejecutivo. 2006. El PPP: Avances retos y Perspectivas.

Informe Ejecutivo. 2008. El PPP: Avances retos y Perspectivas.

Informe Estado de la Región en Desarrollo Humano Sostenible. 2008. http://www.estadonacion.or.cr/estadoregion2008.

López Villicaña, Román. 2002. El Plan Puebla-Panamá: Historia y Geopolítica. In *Lectura Crítica del Plan Puebla Panamá*, Eduardo Andrés Sandoval Forero y Robinson Salazar Pérez coordinadores. Libros en Red.

Mansfield, Edward D., and Eric Reinhalt. 2003. Multilateral Determinants of Regionalism: The Effects of GATT/WTO on the Formation of Preferential Trading Arrangements. *International Organisation* 57 (4) (Fall): 829–862.

Martí Ascencio, Bosco. 2008. Proyecto Mesoamérica: fortaleciendo la integración y desarrollo regional. *Revista Mexicana de Política Exterior* 83: 9–39. Instituto Matías Romero.

Moguel, Julio. 2001. Claroscuros del PPP. De cómo se escamotean los derechos de los indios y se traslada el debate a los presuntos temas del desarrollo. In *Mesoamérica: Los Ríos Profundos. Alternativas Plebeyas al Plan Puebla Panamá*, ed. Armando Bartra. Mexico, DF: RMALC/El Atajo Ediciones/Instituto “Maya”, A.C.

Network Opposing the PPP (NO PPP). 2002, Assumed Date. *Batalla por el Futuro de Mesoamerica, una colección de artículos.* ACEJ/ACERCA—Handout Available Through RMALC.

OECD Territorial Reviews. 2005. *The Mesoamerican Region: Southeastern Mexico and Central America.* OECD Publishing. http://www.oecd.org/mexico/oecdterritorialreviewsthemesoamericanregionsoutheasternmexicoandcentralamerica.htm.

OECD Territoral Reviews. 2006. *The Mesoamerican Region: Southeastern Mexico and Central America.* OECD. http://www.sourceoecd.org/regionaldevelopment/9264021914, http://www.sourceoecd.org/governance/9264021914.

Office of Evaluation and Oversight (OVE). 2008. Evaluation of IDB’s Support to the Plan Puebla Panama Initiative. Interamerican Bank, August. https://publications.iadb.org/en/evaluation-idbs-support-plan-puebla-panama-initiative.

O’Keefe, Thomas Andrew. 2001. The Central American Integration System (SICA) at the Dawn of a New Century: Will the Central American Isthmus Finally Be Able to Achieve Economic and Political Unity? *Florida Journal of International Law* XIII (3, Spring): 243–261.

Payne, Anthony. 2005. The Study of Governance in a Global Political Economy. In *Globalizing International Political Economy*, ed. Nicola Phillips. New York: Palgrave Macmillan.

Phillips, Nicola. 2002. Governance After Financial Crisis: South American Perspectives on the Reformulation of Regionalism. In *New Regionalisms in the Global Political Economy: Theories and Cases*, ed. Shaun Breslin et al. London: Routledge.

Pickard, Miguel. 2004. The Plan Puebla Panama Revived: Looking Back to See What Is Ahead. *La Chronique des Ameriques avril* 12. www.americques.uqam.ca/pdf/Chro-0413-ppp-eng.pdf.

Presidencia de la República. 2001. *Plan Puebla-Panamá Capítulo México.* Documento Base. http://www.diputados.gob.mx/comisiones/asunindi/dgmxuno.pdf.

Proyecto Mesoamerica. 2011. Instrumentos financieros y presupuestarios al servicio de la integración Centroamericana.

Rioja Peregrina, Leonardo H. 2002. Biopirateria y la lucha política en el contexto del PPP. In *Lectura Crítica del Plan Puebla Panamá*, Eduardo Andrés Sandoval Forero y Robinson Salazar Pérez coordinadores. Libros en Red.

Rodríguez, Ennio. 1994. Central America, Common Market, Trade Liberalization and Trade Agreements. In *Economic Integration in the Western Hemisphere*, ed. Roberto Bauzas and Jaime Ros. University of Notre Dame Press.

Rubio, Luis. 2004. Democratic Politics in Mexico: New Complexities. In *Mexico Under Fox*, ed. Luis Rubio and Susan Kaufman Purcell. Boulder, CO: Lynne Rienner Publishers.

Saldivar, V. Americo. 2002. El Plan Puebla Panamá: Una Locomotora sin Vagones de Segunda. In *Lectura Crítica del Plan Puebla Panamá*, Eduardo Andrés Sandoval Forero y Robinson Salazar Pérez coordinadores. Libros en Red.

SG-SICA. 2010. Instrumentos Jurídicos del Sistema de Integración Centroamericana Secretaría General del Sistema de la Integración Centroamericana SG-SICA Second Edition. www.sica.int/busqueda/Libros.aspx?IDItem=28654&IdCat=35&IdEnt=1&Idm=1&IdmStyle=1.

SG-SICA. 2018. Visión Estratégica 2017–2021. http://www.sica.int/consulta/documento.aspx?idn=111508&idm=1.

SICA/CEPAL. 2004. *La Integración Centroamericana: Beneficios y Costos.* Documento Síntesis, Centroamérica, Mayo de 2004, 2a Impresión: Asesores Soluciones Integradas Impreso el 28 de junio de 2004.

SIECA. 2005. *Retos y Oportunidades del Mercado Común Centroamericano ante el DR-CAFTA.* Integración Año 6 Octubre 2005 (official publication).

SIECA. 2006. *La Unión Aduanera Centroamericana.* Guatemala, septiembre de 2006.

SIECA. 2017. *Informe Económico Regional 2016–2017 Oportunidades y riesgos para Centroamérica.* Centro de Estudios para la Integración Económica.

Tratado libre comercio México-Colombia publicado 21 mayo 2015. https://www.gob.mx/se/documentos/comercio-exterior-paises-con-tratados-y-acuerdos-firmados-con-mexico-america-latina-colombia?state=published.

Tratado libre comercio México-Panamá publicado 29 junio 2015. https://www.gob.mx/cms/uploads/attachment/file/94317/TLCMexicoPanama.pdf.

Tratado único México Centroamérica publicado 15 mayo 2015. https://www.gob.mx/se/documentos/comercio-exterior-paises-con-tratados-y-acuerdos-firmados-con-mexico-america-latina-tratado-centroamerica?state=published.

Interviews

3. Director of Integration, Ministerio de Relaciones Exteriores Guatemala, 25 September 2006, Guatemala City.

4. Economist, Consejo Monetario Centroamericano, 19 October 2006, Costa Rica.
6. Executive Secretary, Consejo Monetario Centroamericano, 19 October 2006, Costa Rica.
7. Coordinator Human Development, Dirección Ejecutiva Plan Puebla Panamá, 1 September 2006, San Salvador.
8. Centro de Estudios y Publicaciones Alforja, Costa Rica, 17 October 2006, San José.
9. Fundación Rigoberta Menchú-Guatemala, 26 September 2006.
11. Department Head on Indigenous Issues, Subsecretaría para América Latina y el Caribe, Coordinación General del Plan Puebla Panamá, 30 August 2006, Mexico.
13. International Cooperation Office, República de Costa Rica, Ministerio de Relaciones Exteriores y Culto, 17 October 2006, San José, Costa Rica.
14. Technical advisor, Dirección de Integración y Comercio, Secretaría de Integración Económica Centroamericana (SIECA), 26 September 2006, Guatemala City.
16. Regional Director of CODA international El Salvador (Project liaison with Perulapía, 6 September 2006, San Salvador, Perulapía.
19. Executive, Dirección Ejecutiva Plan Puebla Panamá, 4 September 2006, San Salvador.
20. Fundación para la Democracia (FUNPADEM) (Background information conversation not recorded), 17–19 October 2006.
21. Legislative advisor, Asamblea Legislativa, Costa Rica, Not recorded, Background information.
23. Director of International Economic Section, Departamento de Estudios Económicos y Sociales, Fundación Salvadoreña para el Desarrollo Económico y Social. FUSADES, 5 September 2006, San Salvador.
25. Economic Affairs Director, Secretaría General del Sistema de la Integración Centroaméricana (SG-SICA), 4 September 2006, El Salvador.
26. Subsecretaría para América Latina y el Caribe, Coordinación General del Plan Puebla Panamá, 30 August 2006, Mexico City.
27. PPP initiatives coordinator, Oficina local del Plan Puebla Panamá en El Salvador, Ministerio de Relaciones Exteriores El Salvador, 5 September 2006, San Salvador.
28. Representative of the Mesoamerican Biological Corridor in Costa Rica, 17 October 2006, San José.
29. Directive Cabinet, Parlamento Centroamericano, 27 September 2006, Guatemala City.
30. Executive Director, Oficina local del Plan Puebla Panamá en El Salvador, Ministerio de Relaciones Exteriores El Salvador, 5 September 2006, San Salvador.

31. Elected Deputy, Asamblea Legislativa de Costa Rica (Interview took place in room adjacent to chamber of deputies, was not allowed to record), 18 October 2006, San José, Costa Rica.
33. CEPAL, 10 October 2006, Mexico City.
34. FLACSO Regional Coordinator for Investigation and International Cooperation (Background information conversation not recorded), 18 October 2006, San José Costa Rica.
47. Assistant to the Director of Juridical reviews, 4 September 2006, San Salvador.

Conferences Attended

"Gestión integrada de programas sociales y autoridad social: experiencias latinoamericanas", Dr. Rolando Franco, Facultad Latinoamericana de Ciencias Sociales y Centro de Estudios para el Futuro FLACSO, Tuesday 17 October 2006, San José, Costa Rica, 10:00 a.m.

"Gobernabilidad Democrática y Nuevas Orientaciones Políticas en Costa Rica: escenarios a partir de las elecciones 2006," organised by Centro de Estudios Políticos, Maestría Centroamericana de Ciencias Políticas, UCR, Facultad Latinoamericana de Ciencias Sociales y Centro de Estudios para el Futuro FLACSO, 17 October 2006, 8:00 p.m.

"Indigenous People in Mexico," presented by Lynda Martinez del Campo Fonda del Claustro Mexico City, 17 March 2007.

'Multi Level Governance and Systems of Economic Organisation' Workshop, 17–19 May 2007, University of Warwick, Scarman House.

CHAPTER 5

From National to Local: Government Structures in Mesoamerica

In the previous chapter, I presented the scenario at the Mesoamerican regional level with references to how this level interacted with the rest of the Americas as part of the "spaghetti bowl." I pointed out problems that rise from the existence of overlapping regional projects, and the lack of communication and coordination among them. The implications for regional governance were that the lack of coordination among the existing official bodies gave way to duplication of efforts or initiatives falling through the cracks. The regional institutions' lack of coordination was identified both by the OECD's 2005 regional report and in the final report of the PPP in 2008.

Both reports recommend that the institutions be assessed and restructured for efficacy. Although restructuring should bring about some of the expected results, regional governance is not limited to what happens through regional institutions. As I mentioned before the regional level is affected by the global and Mesoamerica is also affected by hemispheric and Latin American integration efforts. In addition, lower levels also relate to the region.

In this chapter, I focus on government structures in Mesoamerica from national to local. Conscious of the fact that each country is different, the purpose of the examples is not to generalise, but rather to show areas that hinder policymaking and implementation through the levels of government. First, I will present some of the changes in the political scenario in Mesoamerica, and then review the levels of government—national, sub-national, and local, showing how these levels relate to one another.

A. Gamboa, *Regional Integration, Development, and Governance in Mesoamerica*,
https://doi.org/10.1007/978-3-030-25350-9_5

One of the findings of my research is that despite many decentralisation exercises, most countries remain highly centralised. Strengthening of sub-national levels of government has either only occurred on paper or has taken place in such a way where there is little accountability to both central government (budget-use) and the electorate (results).

Once I have discussed the levels of government, the next section will exemplify the supposition, with examples, that social policy tends to fall through the cracks of government structures. These examples will show a weak and fractured system of governance, through the vertical government structures, and at the horizontal level.

Vertical governance in Mesoamerica will look at how policies and projects stemming from the PPP were carried out through government or government-related bodies at the regional, national, sub-national, and local levels. In the next chapter, I will expand the focus to other actors important to governance and the regional integration process. The success of a multifaceted project does not depend on the creation of a technical ministry at the regional level or yearly presidential meetings. It requires that the actors in charge of implementing the projects share the same vision as the regional organisation and work together with it to achieve that vision. This implies that not only should these government sectors be made aware of the project and its objectives but that they should be able to contribute to the formulation of projects and the prioritisation of resource distribution. This is particularly important for the "lowest" government sectors—the local government—since this is the level that has the closest contact with the people who will be affected by these projects.

In addition, as I will demonstrate in the following chapter, many other actors that are not part of the government should be participating in the decisions affecting their interests to negotiate policies that reflect the priorities of more than one sector.

At the national level, in this chapter, I examine some of the general political tendencies of these countries and how their national government relates to the regional and local governments. Finally, at the local level, I review some case studies of local governments in the area as well as some of the cooperation schemes that border governments have designed and which, in some ways, have had better results than those developed at the regional level. The analysis of governance samples at the different levels of government provides a general panorama on the difficulty of implementing programmes in Mesoamerica.

5.1 Political Scenario in Mesoamerica

According to one analyst from FLACSO (Interview 37: 2006), the EU provided technical support to SICA to restructure Central American regional institutions and include mechanisms to decentralise power within the government's structures, as well as the methodology to include non-governmental participants into policymaking. The idea was to set up an institutional framework that would facilitate dialogue between the regional entities and the non-government actors, thus enabling them to work towards a regional vision, similar to the multilevel governance structures observed in the EU (see Chapter 2).

What the analyst depicts is that while the technical support intended to reform governance in Mesoamerica to strengthen democracy and regional integration and facilitate the participation of other actors, governments' reluctance to increase regional institutions' actual scope and enforceability rendered these efforts moot (Interview 34: 2006). However, Mesoamerican leaders' attempt to implement these recommendations at least on the surface has changed the structure of governance in the region, albeit the fact remains that little power is shared. So, whereas in the multilevel governance analysis that describes the EU there is an actual act of power sharing and policymaking, what has happened in Mesoamerica is more of a "skeletal" multilevel governance: bones, but no meat. In Mesoamerica, it is not enough to require governments to include different levels in the governmental structure for governance to be effective.

Government actions in Mesoamerica, or lack thereof, have been considered one of the main contributing factors to the failure to reach the development potential in the region. Some studies such as Dávila, Kessel and Levy's "El Sur También Existe" (The South Also Exists) (2002), urged the government to get involved and to focus on job creation, infrastructure, and development strategies in order to tap into the wealth potential of the southern states of Mexico. Other studies criticise that development has not occurred precisely because of the government being involved and exploiting these areas to its advantage (see Arreola 2006; Harvey 2006; Bartra 2001, 2004; Rioja 2002).

These studies consider that the government has used the "development" strategies to benefit big business and to fulfil the central government's priorities, to the detriment of the local population and the environment. Instances of government corruption, violent elections, and human rights abuses are rampant throughout the region and seemingly go unpunished. The studies question any "development" programmes set out by the government as having ulterior motives rather than trying to fulfil the needs of the population. In the State of Chiapas (Mexico), for example, the building of roads raises suspicions since the new roads seem to cater to the needs of the army to provide mobility and better access in case of further armed conflict, and not to the needs or desires of the people (Aguirre Rojas 2002).

So far, attempts to foment development through government-based programmes that have been carried out in most of the Mesoamerican region have brought about questionable results. With notable exceptions in Costa Rica and possibly Panama, development strategies have focused on exploiting the natural resources of the region, building extensive export-oriented infrastructure (highways, ports, electrical grids) and creating jobs that draw people away from agriculture into *maquiladoras* where wages remain low to foster competitiveness in international markets. Promises to invest in education, health, and other social services have advanced slowly or have been left on a back burner while other areas continued forward. This was true of the PPP during the seven years of its existence; there were visible results in infrastructure, electrical connectivity, and communications, whereas very little progress occurred in human development areas (See *Informe Ejecutivo* 2006, 2008; Martí Asencio 2008: 13–15).

This study identifies that at the root of the diminished ability to implement regional projects in Mesoamerica lie the lack of communication, coordination, and cooperation between regional bodies, government bodies, and non-governmental actors at different tiers in the region. Also, the lack of accountability that many government officials have for other areas of government and the voters themselves continues to bring into question the maturity of democracy in the region.[1]

[1]Although Costa Rica has been generally considered the more mature democracy in Central America, a conference was held in San José Costa Rica on 17 October 2006, titled "Gobernabilidad Democrática y Nuevas Orientaciones Políticas en Costa Rica: escenarios a partir de las elecciones 2006," to address the concern of many academics and political analysts that there was increasingly a negative tendency of becoming more like its neighbours.

In the MAR, the central or national government represents the strongest level. Even though steps have been taken to decentralise central government and/or strengthen other levels of government as per recommendations given by the World Bank and UNDP as well as the EU, many of the results have been purely symbolic. In practice, the central government is reluctant to devolve power to the higher levels (regional institutions) or, the lower levels (sub-national and local). As I showed in the previous chapter, although there are numerous regional bodies, many of them (like PARLACEN and the CACJ) have minimal power. They depend on the unanimous decisions of the Presidents for any significant policies to be put through ("unanimous meaning the dictatorship of the minority," said an interviewee from SICA) and some need additional approval from Congress. As stated by Mattli, intergovernmentalism assigns a central role to the heads of state so that regional integration becomes "a series of bargains among the political leaders of the major states in a region" (Mattli 1999: 11).

Similarly, though there are several tiers of government within each nation, few are involved in policymaking and policy implementation. The sub-national (states, departments, districts, provinces, etc.) level in Mesoamerica is the one most difficult to generalise. In some countries, there is an elected sub-national government (i.e, Mexico); whereas in others the president appoints members (El Salvador). In the context of the PPP, the Mexican sub-national governments (the eight states) were granted almost the same status as Central American national governments. In contrast, Central American sub-national governments play an insignificant role in the regional instrument. The lowest tier of government discussed in this book is that of the local government. The relationship of local governments with higher levels as well as with other local governments in the region gives an interesting dynamic. Moreover, it shows that several opportunities were missed by failing to involve local governments in designing and implementing development projects (see FUNDE/UNDP 2004).

5.2 National Government

Except for Belize (which has a parliamentary system), a president and a legislative body with support from a judicial branch head up central governments in Mesoamerica. Although each country has a legislative body separate from the executive, Belize, Colombia, Dominican Republic, and Mexico have a bicameral system whereas others have a single entity in congress. Moreover, congress is not always elected directly; in some cases, members of the legislative branch are voted directly by constituents, in others by party representation votes. They are all considered to be democracies[2] because elections take place periodically and, for the most part, international observers can participate and report anomalies. After the turbulent past of some Central American countries, tainted with military rule and guerrilla wars, and the 70-year PRI rule in Mexico, just having uninterrupted elections is a step in the right direction. However, reports of corruption, fraud, and other accusations still plague the electoral process,[3] limiting "democracy" to the periodic holding of elections without further substance (see Sanchez Bajo 2005; Carranza 2000; Arce Tena 2006; Pearce 2004). Though there is an awareness that they are not "fully democratic," most of these countries can look back at their recent history and see that they have indeed made significant strides towards having a democratic government.

The governments in Mesoamerica are highly centralised with most policymaking taking place at the national level. The closed circle of the political elite (and its economic supporters) in most of the countries tends to keep power in the central government and its dependencies. According to Pearce (2004), UNDP studies carried out in 2003,[4] revealed that even though a large proportion of people surveyed preferred democracy to other forms of government, they also preferred economic development to democracy. In addition, a staggering 44.9% of them would support an authoritarian government that resolved their economic problems (Pearce 2004: 484). These results are attributed to "the belief that regime transition from authoritarian to democratic government has in

[2]The Economist Intelligence Unit Democracy Index report 2016 classifies Colombia, Costa Rica, Dominican Republic, El Salvador, Mexico, and Panama as "Flawed democracies" and Guatemala, Honduras, and Nicaragua as "hybrid democracies." http://www.eiu.com/Handlers/WhitepaperHandler.ashx?fi=Democracy-Index-2016.pdf&mode=wp&campaignid=DemocracyIndex2016.

[3]The Presidential elections in Mexico in 2006, where supporters of the candidate that lost by a narrow margin blocked major roads throughout the nation, including an important avenue in Mexico City for several months demanding a recount; or the municipal elections of Nicaragua in 2008, where violent protests took place after international observers called it the "least transparent election in recent history" (Reforma, 10 November 2008).

[4]These studies took place in Latin America as a whole.

practice perpetuated elite rule and made little difference to large sections of the population" (Pearce 2004: 484).

Both Mexican development initiatives that were precursors to the PPP were formulated at the national level with very little input filtering up from the lower levels of government. Aside from the non-governmental Mesoamerican forums that were held each year since the launch of the PPP (which I will discuss in the next chapter), in 2002 and in 2008, the University of Quintana Roo in Cancun and the University of Tabasco in Villahermosa, respectively, organised symposiums to analyse the situation of the southern states from a "local" point of view. The first symposium dealt more with the PPP than the second, but in general, the themes and guests were the same. In addition to academics, speakers included local government officials invited to voice their opinion. The 2008 symposium titled "El Sur desde el Sur" ("the south as seen by the south"), criticised that national development programmes were formulated based on information accrued from statistics and economic indicators and not by working together with local government.[5]

All Mexican local government officials interviewed for this research considered the PPP documents (including their precursors) and the *Marcha hacia el Sur* programme to be very obviously written by people in offices in the capital of the country (Mexico City) and not by people who had spent time researching in the southern part of Mexico and who understood the complexity of the issues and problems above and beyond statistical analysis.

Representatives of the indigenous communities in Guatemala and Mexico complained that the central government tried to formulate general policies for all the indigenous communities not considering that they are all different, that they could have different priorities.

> When we ask for things that don't make sense to them [the government], so they don't consider them, they want to give the communities what they think they need, they [the government] think that they [the community members] are ignorant, that they do not know what is best for them. The government wants them to advance, to become like the rest of the country, but that is not what they want. (Interview 9: 2006)

[5] http://www.ujat.mx/eventos/2008/simposium-elsur/programa.pdf.

Former Mexican President Fox named an indigenous woman to head the Office of Indigenous Affairs in Mexico (a political appointment that in previous administrations was given to close supporters of the President). However, though this appointment was a step in the right direction, this woman had left her community to study and had foreign degrees. Critics upheld that since she had lived away from the indigenous community, the government's message was still that, to work in policymaking, you had to be "civilised," preferably abroad.

The primary expression of centralisation in Mesoamerica is in terms of budgeting and the allocation of funds. Most taxes end up in the national treasury, and the national government allocates them to its dependencies and other government tiers. Although some of the different levels of government have mechanisms to raise money, for the most part, the central government meets their budgetary needs (Interview 8: 2006).[6] Unfortunately, in most of Mesoamerica, the allocation of funds does not always transparently take place. In Mexico, for example, each state presents a budget to Congress for the following year, which will then approve or disapprove the budget and allocate the funds. Municipalities must then request money from the state government. Although there presently exists a required method for reviewing and allocating funds, until the 2008 budget exercise, states turned in their budgets in whatever format they pleased and with as much or as little detail as they wanted.[7] Until 1994, states received their funds according to the President's priorities or camaraderie with the governors, but since the break from the PRI rule, political party affiliation was more important than a well-presented budget. Similarly, in El Salvador (where the President appoints governors), the municipal authorities complain that official money given to municipalities belonging to the FMLN (then the opposition party) is the strict minimum, whereas municipalities run by ARENA (then ruling party) receive much more from the central government (Interview 44: 2006). In turn, it is likely that the municipalities belonging to the ruling party will support and facilitate the implementation of national policies (FUNDE/UNDP 2004: 13).

[6] Also see "Enfoque: Información, reflexión y cultura política;" Reforma, Num. 759, 19 October 2008, pp. 4–9.

[7] Juan E. Pardinas and Ruy Manrique: *Cuentas Estatales: Caos y Opacidad*. Reforma; revista Enfoque Num. 759, 19 October 2008, pp. 4–9.

National ministries are also the ones that formulate policies at the national level with little or no input from dependencies. The education ministries formulate nationwide policies notwithstanding the differences found throughout the country. For example, in Guatemala, where the school dropout rate is high, the government tried to implement several strategies to try to keep children in school. After these policies were found to have little impact, studies were made to try and find out why they were unable to keep children in school.[8] They found that the reasons children left school were specific to the area of the country (though all related to poverty), and so they had to design a specific strategy for each area.

As another example, Mexico's Ministry of Social Development, SEDESOL, together with IDB, formulated a nationwide programme to support some of the most vulnerable groups to try and break the cycle of extreme poverty. Households at risk were given a monthly stipend as long as the children attended school regularly, and the whole family visited a health centre periodically for check-ups. Although local offices manage the programme, the IDB hired an independent market research company to evaluate the effectiveness and shortcomings of the programme by interviewing beneficiaries nationwide. Though there were some similarities throughout, the researchers found that the complaints or satisfaction varied in the different regions of the country, enough to recommend tailoring some aspects of the programme to meet specific needs by area (Interview 45: 2008).

An important issue identified at the national level is the lack of continuity whenever an election results in a different political party taking office; this is particularly true when pursuing a long-term development plan such as the PPP. The only countries that have a professional civil service are Costa Rica and Mexico[9] (though some MFAs also have a permanent staff), so it is not just leadership that changes, but the whole government structure, including support staff.

> One further (structural) problem in our countries is that there are constant changes in governments, and the inexistence of professional civil servants has significant consequence. Each time a government changes, those

[8]Canal 7 Guatemala (TV), round table discussion on the *Acuerdo Nacional* (National Agreement) for development, aired on 27 September 2006.

[9]Mexico implemented its professional civil service in 2005. http://www.spc.gob.mx/subsistemas1.htm.

> negotiating teams change, and while they find their footing, the momentum is lost. The other countries negotiating teams take advantage of the situation and try to take a leading role in the negotiations, not because they should, but because they can. When governments change, the agenda gets side-tracked. (Interview 23: 2006)

This problem exists at different levels in different countries. For example, in Guatemala, where no political party has maintained power for more than one administration[10] since the transition from military rule back to democracy, programmes have been limited to the length of one administration.

> El Salvador is different because ARENA has been in power for three or four administrations, so there has been continuity. Most are like Costa Rica; Pacheco was moving forward with integration, and then Arias came, and there was a 180° change in policies against integration. (Interview 3: 2006)

However, the situation in El Salvador is likely to change. According to one legislator, the National Republican Alliance (ARENA) party won due to mistakes made by the Farabundo Martí National Liberation Front (FMLN) party candidate, not on its own merit (Interview 31: 2006). By the January 2009 municipal election, the FMLN managed to increase its presence substantially (La Hora; 30 January 2009).[11] But the political climate of the region is such that what wins a political party the vote into power is a platform of "change," a promise to improve the situation through radical changes in policies. Very few could win by stating that they plan to continue with the outgoing government's policies.

> In theory, it is easy to talk about having national policies that transcend governments, but national planning is challenging, particularly for developing countries. When government changes, many times, whatever projects were being done are scrapped, and then they start again at a great cost. (Interview 33: 2006)

[10]Continuing with this trend, the 2011 elections were won by the Patriotic Party and 2016 by National Convergence Front.

[11]The FMLN won national elections in El Salvador in March 2009 and again in 2014. In June 2019 a new centre-right party formed in 2010 "The Grand Alliance for National Unity" won the elections.

Investment in human capital is an example of the loss of resources after a change in government administration. Staff members receive training over four or five years, and when the administration changes, they all leave, and the skills go with them. Instead of having trained staff working on a project or programme the new administration replaces the existing team with the people who helped with campaigning; those that helped build the stage and gather people for the political rallies.

> This isn't the case of Costa Rica, where there is a trained Civil Service, but in the rest, there is not. CEPAL is trying to encourage countries to implement it (civil servants). When an administration leaves, they take everything; sometimes new administrations arrive and find that all the filing cabinets are empty and even computers are missing. (Interview 33: 2006)

PPP Ministry officials—confirmed by a member of the Costa Rican PPP team—stated that they spent quite a lot of time in meetings getting new people updated on each issue. "We are constantly dealing with new people. Every time a government changes or a particular minister changes, they change the people they send to the regional meetings" (Interview 13: 2006).

The changes not only hindered the continuity of the Plan's programmes, but they also generated uncertainty; for example, in Mexico and Nicaragua, the parties that headed the polls for the presidential elections were highly critical of the PPP and its policies. Mexico had not had a change of party in the last presidential elections of 2006 but in the months running up to the election the PPP offices outside of Mexico became very nervous about the future of the Plan. Although the Mexican government did not consistently manifest its leadership in the region, it had been the initiator and the most active supporter of the PPP (Interview 33: 2006); a victory by the opposition party (PRD) would signify shifts in the PPP or its disappearance altogether from Mexican foreign policy.

On the other hand, in Nicaragua, although the opposition Sandinista party won the presidency at the time little had changed in its policies towards the PPP. Nevertheless, the possibility that changes in national governments determine the path of a regional project continues to provide setbacks in forging a regional development strategy. "The problem, as I was telling you, is institutional; when an administration ends its term, we don't know what is going to happen next" (Interview 3: 2006). Nicaragua, however, changed its constitution to allow re-election and in 2018, with protests, uncertainty, and a call for stepping down from power[12] plagued Daniel Ortega's third term. The PPP survived several changes in national administrations (Interview 7: 2006) and survived the most determinant change, that of Mexico's government. However, the need for governments to show a break from the previous administrations did affect the PPP by changing it into *Proyecto Mesoamérica*.

Political parties play a critical role in Mesoamerican politics.[13] Since these parties do not tend to trust each other, they usually change all the personnel from a government office when they come to power. In Mexico, for example, each time there is a change in government (even when it is the same political party), all government employees turn in a letter of resignation. It is up to the new head of the dependency to accept or reject it according to how he or she would like to form the new team. Since political parties decide who will be running for which office on their behalf, close to elections, some candidates switch political parties in order to secure the candidacy they want. This also happens because re-election is not possible in most of the countries, but the same people can run for office if they belong to a different political party.

During a televised debate in Guatemala, the presenter suggested that "Guatemala does not have political parties, it has small groups that gather around people with money,"[14] a statement that was repeated by several interviewees the following days (Interviews 10, 2, 9: 2006). Guatemala is not the only country where the support of the wealthy determines the success of a candidate. Except for Mexico,[15] Costa Rica, and Panama, the main political power is held by the President, with congress taking a secondary and sometimes, ornamental role. A strong presidency means that policy can be implemented right away with little debate with other branches of government. However, in cases where

[12] Denuncian a Daniel Ortega por muerte de 34 en Nicaragua. *La Jornada*, 26 April 2018. http://www.jornada.unam.mx/ultimas/2018/04/26/denuncian-a-daniel-ortega-por-muerte-de-34-en-nicaragua-8390.html.

[13] Even though political parties are fragile, in the sense that they are easily formed and replaced, most politicians vote according to the party they belong to. A politician that goes against party lines usually changes party affiliation (i.e., Porfirio Muñoz Ledo in Mexico who started in the PRI, then went to PRD, joined PAN during Fox's campaign and later, was in congress with the PT.

[14] Guatevisión, Libre encuentro, 23 September 2006. Statement by Virgilio Alvarez, researcher at FLACSO.

[15] This has only been true for Mexico since President Zedillo's government in 1994.

Congress has the power to withhold a bill until it is approved by the majority, the stance of each political party is crucial. In Mexico, for example, deputies and senators in Congress could not be re-elected,[16] which meant little accountability to the voter. Instead, legislators were concerned with being well situated in their own political party so that when their terms are up the party considers them for a different position or candidacy.

Costa Rica allows re-election in the Senate, however, there is strong party discipline when voting on issues; a senator interviewed said: “there has to be party discipline; if everyone voted according to their conscience, we could not have governability,” (Interview 31: 2006). The problem arises, of course, when there isn’t a majority of a particular party in congress, and then voting comes to a stalemate. In Mexico, the congress—whose majority used to belong to the same party as the president, with a few token members from other parties, was considered just a formality that would rubberstamp every proposal sent by the President. During the administrations of 1994–2000, 2000–2006, and 2006–2012, there was an increase of plurality in Congress, where there has not been a party with sufficient majority to pass a bill on its own. Whereas this could provide the necessary incentive for political parties to negotiate and work together for the improvement of the country, what tends to happen is that each political party presents “their” version of a bill and they reach a stalemate.

As I discussed in the previous chapter, the PPP, like most of the regional organisms in Mesoamerica, was an intergovernmental organisation where decisions had to be unanimous. It was not a supranational body, and its highest level of decision-making rests on presidential meetings (like in SICA). The presidents, in turn, delegated to other ministries and tiers of government points of action decided upon in the meetings.

> Every President manages their agenda; there are no general guidelines at the Central American level so that the Presidents or foreign secretary can say ‘well, this is the direction we need to move on, and this is the path to take.’ Here everyone takes the path that is most convenient to them. (Interview 3: 2006)

[16]This is changing in 2018. https://politico.mx/central-electoral/elecciones-2018/reelecci%C3%B3n-inicia-en-2018-c%C3%B3mo-funcionar%C3%A1/.

The fact that each country oversaw one of the Mesoamerican initiatives meant that, for the most part, limited activities at the central government level to that initiative. Information on what was going on in other initiatives was shared during the summits and published in a progress report. Nevertheless, often presidents or ministers gave out different versions of what was going on to the press.

The lack of coordination between the national governments on PPP issues gave the press a field day; "if we are isolated when we give out information, each country gives out the bits of information it wants, and then they say 'hey, that is not what they are saying in El Salvador´" (Interview 30: 2006). The easy access to electronic information means that the regional press can compare and contrast the statements being given out by each of the countries and point out biased views or discrepancies. The consequence of misinformation was that suspicions arose as to the "true" purposes of the PPP. Even within the tiers of government, congress or state governments began to disengage themselves from anything with the PPP label. For example, two hospital buildings built as part of the PPP human development initiative later were inaugurated as initiatives of the health ministry of that country. There was no mention of the PPP at the inauguration ceremony. When the PPP offices requested an explanation, they were told that the state government would not allow the use of the PPP name or logo because of the problem it caused in that entity (one with a different political party than the President). This was not an isolated case since the PPP human development projects came out of the national budget; then a project would be credited as an initiative from the particular national or ministerial budget and not of the PPP. When asked why the PPP offices didn't clarify these cases, the response received was:

> Well, they need to work out their internal problems themselves; the PPP has to have the support of its members, not everyone believes in what we are doing, and so they are busy looking out for their own political careers over the future of the project. (Interview 7: 2006)

5.3 Sub-National Government

The recommended decentralisation process in Mesoamerican governments has been slow to take effect. The idea behind the decentralisation was to bring government closer to the people and thus make it more accountable for its actions (Interview 34: 2006). "Mesoamerica's development is hampered, in part, by a lack of local public goods and the limited capacity at the sub-national levels to effectively and efficiently provide these goods" (OECD Territorial Reviews 2005: 13). Also, a plurality of political parties at the sub-national level would give a sense to how a different party might govern.

While many steps have been taken "on paper" to decentralise, in Guatemala, El Salvador, Costa Rica, and Nicaragua, little change has taken place (Interview 8: 2006). In El Salvador, for example, the president is the one who appoints states' governors. So even if there is a certain amount of "decentralisation" at that level, the governors are likely to sympathise with the president and implement national policies regardless of the opinion of the people of that state. In Mexico, where the most considerable amount of decentralisation has taken place, the desired effect has not been forthcoming. Even though each state now has practical autonomy over its budget and legal matters (Mexico City, for example, which has the same legal status as a state, has passed laws allowing abortion and same-sex legal unions where these remain illegal in the rest of the country), sub-national government authorities still lack accountability to its citizens. Likewise, the new structures, also eliminate accountability from the states to the national government. During the 2008 budget exercise, when the Mexican states had to request budget approval from the Senate for the following fiscal year, it was publicised that the states had not presented verifiable accounts for the expenditure of the previous budget.

Moreover, each state used different criteria as to what fell under which heading and clarifying accounting methods. The same was true for the new budget that was brought forth for approval. Many states did not specify how the money requested would be used, with one state presenting its budget on a single page, only indicating its estimated amount. After the data for budget requests appeared in the media and discrepancies pointed out among the budgets, the Senate (upper chamber of Congress) decreed that state accounting should be regularised by 2012.[17] The reports that followed the initial media accounts also showed that each state reported different figures than those provided by the ministries. For example, the data published by the Ministry of Education

[17] Carole Simonnet and Armando Estrop, "Fijan reglas únicas para rendir cuentas: Deben entidades homologar contabilidad a más tardar en 2012," 26 November 2008, Reforma, front page.

regarding staff salaries in each state did not match the data reported by the school districts.[18]

The sub-national level is more relevant to the PPP in Mexico since from the beginning, it included the nine south-eastern states individually, and the state governors were invited to attend the summits. In some ways, these states held the same treatment as the Central American countries. Although some consider this a lack of respect (Bartra 2001) for the Central American nations, the reason is that the original project for Mexico that later merged with Central America, was designed for the nine states included in the Plan. However, the PPP's precursor originated in national government ministries instead of created by the nine involved states. The nine states initially welcomed the PPP as they expected an allocation of extra funds to carry out the projects. When it became clear that external funding would go to the large infrastructure projects and that the rest would have to come out of their existing budgets, they lost interest.

> At least, in the beginning, the government of Chiapas and the government of Vicente Fox went hand in hand; both governments had broken free of decades of a one-party rule… At first the PPP was well received in Chiapas with the full cooperation of the state government, however, as it became more evident that the projects were not necessarily of priority to Chiapas, then the State lost interest. (Interview 40: 2006)

Neither of the sub-national representatives interviewed, nor the PPP directives were aware of any enquiry or request from the central government to the states involved to get input prior to formulating the Mexican segment of the Plan (Interviews 40, 11, 26 and 43: 2006). In general, since the main points of the Plan were decided while Vicente Fox was President-Elect, a finished product and not a work in progress was presented to the states once he was in office. As a case in point, not one of the nine states mentioned the PPP in their published "Development Plans" during 2001–2008.[19] As one PPP director stated, "I expected to see some leadership from the Mexican states; they are supposed to

[18] Reforma, 28 November 2008, front page.

[19] Personal search of each of the State Development Plans. Projects that are part of the PPP are mentioned in some of the plans, however they appear to be of state initiative and not PPP.

participate in the meetings, but not all of them go, and they don't always participate" (Interview 7: 2006).

As part of the strategy towards decentralisation in Mexico, federal funds allocations increased for each of the states. The state government then distributed the funds to local governments as well as fulfilled the obligations presented in their budgets. Although this process began in the early 1990s, it wasn't until President Fox's term (2000–2006) that Mexico started to fit the "federalist" model that was set up in the Mexican Constitution. However, as observed by one political analyst, declaring that the states would now have greater control over their budgets and hold less accountability to the national government was not enough to become a "Federal Republic" overnight. Instead, what happened from some perspectives could be considered more a blatant bribery of the governors by the President (Interview 15: 2007). Some of the results of this change became evident several years later when in 2010, an audit of the expenditures of the state of Oaxaca showed over 254.1 million pesos missing that were supposed to be used for building hospitals in 2005 and 75 million missing in 2006.[20]

Although Mexico had been set up as a Federal Republic shortly after its independence from Spain, in practice, the governors did not have autonomy over their budgets, with the central government controlling almost all resources. After the revolution of 1910 for 70+years, that the PRI party had control of the presidency, governors, as well as local and national congresses. Until Ernesto Zedillo's administration (1994–2000), the president was also the head of the PRI party, subjecting all its members in office to party discipline. Although constitutionally the most influential power was allotted to Congress, and state governments had autonomy, because both the members of congress and the state governors had to do whatever the President requested of them, Mexico had a form of "Presidentialism" (see Rubio 2004).

President Zedillo (1994–2000), restructured some government bodies, gave the PRI an internally elected party leader and strengthened the independent electoral body (thus reducing fraud). The results of the reforms became visible towards the end of Ernesto Zedillo's presidency. In a way,

[20] "Hacen en Oaxaca obras 'fantasma'" Reforma 29 March 2009. "Hallan más desvíos en Salud de Oaxaca" Reforma 22 March 2010. Investigations began in 2009 but were hindered by state laws. In July 2010, the PRI government lost state elections and investigation of more illicit activities of that previous government continue.

he was a "victim" of the reforms, where the PRI lost several state governorships, and congress blocked or vetoed several of his proposals. The following presidential election alternated power to the National Action Party candidate, Vicente Fox (2000–2006). However, the Mexican people accustomed to having the President as the dominant government figure, perceived the inability of President Fox to pass reforms and laws through congress, as a problem caused by the President, and not congress with its newfound power. Fox himself was still under the impression his position held more power (as it had been in previous administrations) than what was given to him by law (Rubio 2004). Already facing a problematic congress and internal pressures, Fox was not about to invite problems with the state governors. He had already promised more resources and greater autonomy to them, a promise that he kept without much reserve. After launching the PPP, some extra funds were allotted to the south-eastern states to support its objectives. And although in some ways they were—hospitals were built, schools were refurbished, or teacher's salaries were raised—the governors did not mention the PPP and, instead, included these accomplishments in the state development reports.

The lack of coordination between the federal government and state governments in Mexico has produced adverse effects in implementing development projects and attaining continuity of programmes. Even more concerning is the impact it has had on the coordination of public security efforts. The Mexican Council for Foreign Relations (COMEXI) produced a White Paper on National Security for 2018,[21] where pages 21–23 describe how the power vacuums created through the changing administrations in the federal states and municipal levels have been used by crime to gain strongholds. As each head of a ministry, governor, municipal leader, judge or commander, stake out what they consider to be "their" territory, there are areas that no one administers or are disputed by several actors. These are readily taken over by criminal activity. Even more concerning, corruption has been rampant in the state governments, to the point that in 2017, there were 16 ex-governors that were either being processed or were being called to testify on counts of corruption during their administration.[22]

[21] See http://www.consejomexicano.org/index.php?s=contenido&id=2475 for full text.

[22] http://www.milenio.com/firmas/joaquin_lopez-doriga/gobernadores-presos-procesados-profugos_18_941485884.html.

Out of 16: three from Veracruz, two from Quintana Roo, two from Tamaulipas, one from Oaxaca and one from Chihuahua, among others.

5.4 Local Government

In addition to speaking with regional and national government representatives and political analysts, I interviewed local government officials to complete the section regarding governance in the region. Questions were geared to ascertain communication between local government and the people they represented, as well as the connection existing among national government and regional institutions. In some instances, the local government worked together with the national government to meet the needs of the local people. However, when the local government was of an opposing political party from that of the national government (and, in Mexico, this also applied if it was different than the state government), communication was broken, and often they worked against each other.

The OECD regional report points out that the weakest link in vertical governance in Mesoamerica is at the local level (OECD 2005). The highly centralised governments of Mesoamerica rarely devolve enough decision-making power to this essential level of government. This level is the one closest to the people, where they are likely to know personally those running for office and where they have real contact with the government officials through registrations, marriages, and other legal procedures. This is also the level that tests party loyalties, corruption is rampant, and security forces are the least trusted. In Mexico, upon finding that when administrations changed, IT equipment, telephone exchanges, and even cars go missing, new legislation was introduced to force local governments to inventory all purchases during each administration.[23] The fact that it has been going on for years and the incoming administrations do not usually denounce the missing items, shows that it is a common practice that each administration has come to consider as part of expected "fringe benefits." This is one of the reasons why national governments are reluctant to devolve more money and power to local governments: "we do not have the mechanisms to verify how they spend their budgets as it is; there is already too much corruption and embezzlement with what they get now. You see municipal presidents

[23] "Pretenden frenar saqueo en Estados," Reforma, 26 November 2008.

See also: "Opacan el gasto con fideicomisos," Reforma 9 May 2018. https://www.reforma.com/aplicacioneslibre/articulo/default.aspx?id=1390188&md5=2542afb2be298b906f39538dda9bd630&ta=0dfdbac11765226904c16cb9ad1b2efe.

buying huge houses and driving armoured cars, and then you see the roads full of holes in the municipality" (Interview 26: 2006). They argue that the government ministries should have periodic audits, making it easier to control spending.

Local governments depend on national or sub-national governments for their funding. Although there are official mechanisms for deciding the amount of funding they are meant to get, in practice, they are discretionary. In 2003, for example, a march took place in Nicaragua by the local mayors requesting a higher transfer of funds to local government. During the same year, the Municipal Association of Honduras placed a legal lawsuit against the government for not transferring the annual percentage of funds as established by law to local government (Enríquez Villacorta 2005: 23).

In both Mexico and El Salvador, some of the poorer municipalities claimed the central government overlooked them simply because they belonged to opposition parties to the ruling party. Representatives of two municipalities said that they received less funding and were not consulted when large infrastructure projects affected them (Interview 17: 2006; Interview 43: 2006). In El Salvador, for example, the national government must obtain permits from the municipal government before it can begin working on any major infrastructure. The municipal government then has the task of consulting environmental impact, making technical assessments, and consulting with the local constituents prior to granting the permits (FUNDE/UNDP 2004: 9, 13).

Of course, it doesn't always work that way. In Perulapía (El Salvador), municipal representatives gave several examples where the national government obtained the permits by providing little or no information on large constructions. When the reality of the impact of these constructions became apparent, several municipalities rallied together and protested to stop the projects. However, many times, projects only stop temporarily, and when the municipal government or the personnel change, they start again (Interview 17: 2006). In Veracruz, a representative from the municipal government of Orizaba commented that local government was not consulted on the projects that would be included in the PPP; neither were they asked if they wanted to add anything. The president and the governor negotiated the main points regarding infrastructure. The municipal government did not find out until the construction was approved and about to begin. In general, the municipal government felt unaffected by the PPP, although, there were some repercussions, as the highways that lead from Puebla to the port of Veracruz increased in affluence, particularly cargo vehicles on the roads. These transportation trucks mostly carried new cars exported from the Volkswagen plant in Puebla. The increase in traffic meant more potholes on the highway that passed by the town of Orizaba. However, since this is a toll road under concession, the national government did not allot more money for repairs and did not allow an increase in tolls (Interview 43: 2006).

Local government representatives explained that municipalities obtain funding by charging for certificates (birth, death, marriage), as well as from local business fees and a percentage of the land tax; so, municipalities that house industry, or the wealthier ones, tended to have more money to spend on services (FUNDE/UNDP 2004: 14). When municipalities face natural disasters, they do receive funds and physical aid from the national government (in addition to any foreign aid), but at times, the government does not give them their yearly stipend because they have already used over and above the allotted budget for that particular municipality (Interview 44: 2006).

The Mayor of Perulapía municipality in El Salvador mentioned that he had recently met with other mayors of the state of Cuscatlán (16 municipalities) and that these, in turn, were hoping to be in contact with the 262 other mayors in the republic to talk about their allocated government budgets. Since the President is the only one who can increase their budget, they are hoping that by joining together, they can exert enough pressure upon him. Although he mentioned that the allotted budget was not enough for any of the 262 municipalities, the reality was that municipalities that shared the same political party as the President were more likely to get more revenue than those who belonged to the opposition parties. Wealthier areas tended to receive taxes from industry and property rights, and these more affluent areas also tended to belong to the ruling party. In some areas of El Salvador, municipal governments attempted to create micro-regions by joining four or five adjacent municipalities to have more political force (Interview 44: 2006; FUNDE/UNDP 2004).

Since the opposition party municipalities had fewer resources, they decided to hold citizen's round tables to get closer to the people of the municipality and to ensure that they used their limited funds for what the people wanted the most. The round tables were a voluntary exercise that had some success, although attendance varied according to the topics addressed and how often the round tables took place. The reason for organising these round tables was:

> …to listen and to form a work plan. We have few funds; the government gives a set amount to municipalities, and it is very little. Some municipalities that are of the same ruling party can get more funds, but not us. We have a set fund and what we get from small transactions like marriage licenses. Some days we only get about nine dollars. We need bank loans to secure things like pipes for drinking water and drains. Without lending and aid, we would be lost. In the entire Republic, there is not one municipality that is not indebted; that is why we get together in microregions with two or three municipalities to work together. (Interview 44: 2006)

I found that many NGOs were working directly with municipal governments in Central America to provide services or training. Municipal governments in Mesoamerica have found that by working together, they are more likely to get their voices heard by the national government and regional organisations. Founded in 1991, the Federation of Municipalities of Central America (FEMICA, which did not include Mexico) the purpose of the FEMICA was to achieve a municipal model in Central America through strengthening their autonomy, resources, and management capabilities so that it can efficiently provide services to the local population as well as direct local development (FEMICA 2008). However, the perception of some interviewees is that they spend most of the time complaining about the lack of funding. International bodies funded the Federation, although they did not receive much for projects (Interview 44: 2006). Its main activity was to promote decentralisation at the regional level as well as cooperation between the municipal governments and civil society. Municipal government could participate in training sessions and symposiums and share their experiences. They were fighting against the status quo where:

> …local governments are marginalised, and the mayor is treated as just another employee of the central government. Local government should not replicate the lack of governance that is found in the central government, it should not be isolated from the citizens that elected it, and it should not be corrupt. (FEMICA 2008)

These statements are ideological considering the kind of problems found in municipal governments throughout Central America and Mexico; however, FEMICA has had more support since 2007. The 2008 State of the Region report included a chapter on strengthening local government, calling it the most significant challenge for Central America.[24] In addition, during the 2008 SICA summit, heads of state (which included the presidents of Mexico and the Dominican Republic) mentioned that to battle the problems facing the region—poverty, environmental degradation, climate change, etc.—local governments would have to have greater participation. To this effect, on 9 January 2009, SICA and FEMICA signed a memorandum of understanding where they agreed on nine points of cooperation and instituted three formal mechanisms for inter-institutional collaboration. As part of these nine points, the local government was recognised as a significant player in promoting a regional sense of identity as well as promoting and facilitating local development. They also acknowledged that implementing regional policies was a challenge for local government, and so, SICA agreed to provide technical support in crucial areas for the municipal governments (SICA-FEMICA 2009). On 15 June 2015, a new association was formed, "Confederación de Asociaciones Nacionales de Municipios de Centro América y el Caribe" (CAMCAYCA),[25] which includes the Dominican Republic, Panama and often has representatives from the Mexican Municipalities association attending as observers. The CAMCAYCA is being integrated into the CC-SICA to represent the needs of municipal governments in regional matters[26] and to dialogue on security issues.[27] It also receives support from VNG International's Local Government Capacity Programme to strengthen the role of local governments for the prevention of violence, agreeing on a shared vision and cooperation with other levels of government. Each country has a different strategy; some are geared to help people break away from violence, and in others, the focus is to locate young people at risk and give them opportunities through education

[24] State of the Region on Sustainable and Human Development report has been published in 1999, 2003 and 2008, 2011, and 2016 as a report from Central America for Central America, including collaborations from renowned academics and investigators in Central America and can be found on. https://estadonacion.or.cr/files/biblioteca_virtual/centroamerica/001/Prologo_I_ER-region01.pdf. https://estadonacion.or.cr/informe-iv-estado-region. https://estadonacion.or.cr/inicio/estado-region.

[25] Full text: http://www.vng-international.nl/wp-content/uploads/2017/01/Plan-Estrat.%C3%A9gico.pdf.

[26] http://fedomu.org.do/2016/09/02/camcayca-y-sica-dialogan-sobre-la-articulacion-de-los-gobiernos-locales-en-el-sistema-de-integracion-regional/.

[27] http://mjp.go.cr/Comunicacion/Nota?nom=Encuentro-Regional-para-la-prevencion-de-la-violencia-reune-a-ocho-paises-en-Costa-Rica.

or skill development to steer them away from criminal activity. VNG International states that: "…we aspire to strengthen the dialogue with this exchange of good practices, not only between local government associations but between the different layers of governments."[28]

Similarly, in Mexico, municipal governments have organised the Mexican Association of Municipalities (AMMAC) to address issues of municipal governance, funding, and decentralisation. The Municipalities that belong to the AMMAC have signed an agreement where they commit their government to transparency, efficiency, and fighting corruption (www.ammac.org.mx).

There are several projects for municipal cooperation in border areas; some government-funded binational and tri-national projects have taken place in Mesoamerica. The bulk of these border projects are proposed and led by NGOs; many of them have to do with common waterways or other environmental issues that affect both sides of a border. However, cross-border projects exist, designed expressly to further development in adjacent communities (Interviews 17, 37: 2006). The Foundation for Democracy (FUNPADEM) in Costa Rica and National Foundation for Development (FUNDE) in El Salvador have funded and supported several moderately successful projects on their borders:

> One project of a protected ecological area from Monte Rico in Guatemala to Barra de Santiago in El Salvador was taking place individually, each country doing their own thing on their side of the border, but now the governments are talking and will integrate the project into only one agenda; it makes sense for them to complement efforts. (Interview 17: 2006)

Initially, most binational efforts had to do with water or environmental issues, but cooperation has spread to other enterprises such as fishing, agriculture, and coffee, activities that can benefit from cooperation across the borders. According to an analyst from FUNDE, participation began through NGO initiatives, but local governments are starting to collaborate in these processes, including them in their agendas and allocating funds (Interview 17: 2006).

[28] http://www.vng-international.nl/blog/compendium-best-practices-local-governments-on-the-prevention-violence/.

In Central America, there are several border villages and communities where the families carry out their daily activities on both sides of the border: the mother works on one side, the father on the other, and the children study on one side, but live in the other, "…they create a series of interrelations that have to be looked into" (Interview 25: 2006). Most of these cases occur because for many years formal borders did not exist, so now they cut through houses, buildings, ranches, and even businesses.

> I personally know a family that lives on the border between Guatemala and El Salvador; they live literally on the border, they have the living room in Guatemala and the bedroom in El Salvador, they have breakfast in the morning in Guatemala, and their livestock is in El Salvador, because that is how the line was drawn. These situations need to be investigated, be regularised. (Interview 25: 2006)

During the interview, the interviewee argued that regionalisation is taking place in Central America and whether they want it to or not. Eventually, border controls will have to disappear, and commercial regulations harmonised. Borders have been a sensitive issue in Central America and a setback to integration, as was the case between Honduras and El Salvador during the "football war." The redrawing of borders has meant that some communities and even houses are found to be straddling two or more countries. SICA has facilitated two programmes, one which is the Bi-national Programme for Border Development between Honduras and El Salvador, and the other is for the Tri-border Zone between Guatemala, Honduras and El Salvador (Trifinio), to tackle the problems generated by the borders' intersecting communities. The interviewee also found amusing how, during trade negotiations, there were always discussions about the country of origin (for trade purposes) and the differences in trade agreements and tariffs in Central America, when in fact the borders are very permeable:

> There is a border post between Guatemala and El Salvador called San Cristóbal, I think that it is every Wednesday, which is market day that the post closes, customs shut down, and all the vendors pass from one side to the other. You can find whatever you want there, clothes, alcohol, perfumes, cosmetics, or whatever. The whole highway is closed; you must find another border crossing if you're going to cross. The market starts and ends at certain hours, and then, some customs police come out, throw a shot in the air, and then, they all know that it is time to close the market.

> The next day, the same trucks have to carry out all the necessary transnational paperwork for passing merchandise across the border; this is very odd. (Interview 25: 2006)

Although local government is becoming a stronger power in Mesoamerica, it still faces setbacks in becoming a key player in governance. In Costa Rica, for example, the National Congress of Communal Development Associations (CONADECO) warns that although decentralisation is an essential factor for strengthening democracy, it has to happen in an orderly fashion; "stemming from the fact that our legal framework does not possess adequate regulation for territorial decentralisation to take place" (CONADECO 2005).

This organisation advises local governments to revise their own legal frameworks, so decentralisation brings the desired results.

5.5 Governance and Trust

I have mentioned throughout this book that the objective of the PPP was to promote development and to improve the conditions of the people living in the MAR. In Chapter 3, I presented several points of view on this issue and noted that "development" could be a subjective term as it means different things for different people. A large portion of my research dealt with the difficulty of implementing the "development" proposals of the PPP due to insufficient governance mechanisms. The following examples are a sampling of many situations that take place due to the lack of communication or miscommunication among the different levels of government.

Example 1 In many areas, there is still mistrust between local representations of government and their national counterparts. For instance, during the exercise to review the effectiveness of a Mexican Ministry of Development programme that had been running for over five years, the IDB hired an independent market research company in August 2008 to interview the beneficiaries of the programme. The local managing authorities were unaware that the exercise was taking place. Although research took place nationwide, it was in the south-eastern states where they encountered the highest number of problems. In several instances the women that had agreed to participate cancelled at the last minute because the local programme office told them that if they participated, they would be dropped from the programme. Several of the women had been harassed and told not to participate or to speak badly about the programme if they wanted to continue to receive programme funds. Although they were assured by those running the study that all comments would be anonymous and that it was the programme (central) officials who wanted the feedback to improve the programme and better meet their needs, interviewees were sceptical about saying anything negative or making suggestions until the meeting was almost finished. During one session (in Córdoba, Veracruz), one of the employees of the local office showed up with the excuse that she was looking for someone and wanted to take the names of all those who were present.

What was notable in this situation was the lack of communication between the national programme directives and its local offices. The national offices had not explained to the local offices the purpose of the research. When beneficiaries of the programme began to be recruited to give their opinion, the employees in the local office heard about it and panicked, thinking that their jobs were at risk. Instead of asking the national offices for more information, they resorted to intimidating the beneficiaries to ensure that they would not say anything negative or choose not to participate.[29]

Example 2 In Tuliman, Guerrero,[30] a health centre was proposed to cater to the community of 9000 ethnic *Nahua* that lived in the village, as well as those who lived in the surrounding areas. The state of Guerrero health ministry agreed to build the centre (replacing the single room centre where a rotating medical intern, doing a required social service, sees patients) if the villagers donated the land. The community pooled together their resources and gave a piece of property in 2007, where the state began to build the promised centre. However, just one month after the construction initiated, it was suspended because according to the state government's planning director, "the federal government did not liberate the funds." From this point, the community and the ex-mayor of the town (who had proposed the centre during his term) began to

[29] I was asked to give some background information on the programme and the situation in southeast Mexico, and in return, was able to participate in one of the round tables and obtain the results of the study.

[30] Jesús Guerrero, *Abandona Guerrero clínica indígena* Reforma, 25 February 2009. Story in newspaper article.

look to various government officials that would help them secure funds and resume construction. One villager commented that they had approached the new mayor, the state senator, a congressman, and other officials to ask why the clinic was not finished. She continued to say: "it isn't fair that we each gave up to 30 or 50 pesos to pay for the land where they were going to build the health centre and up until now, we don't see any results" (Reforma 15-2-2009). After they protested at the state Governor's house, officials told them that that the construction would continue, and that the health centre would be finished by May 2009.

Even if the government kept their commitment to finish by this new completion date, the people in the village had lost their trust in the government. The former mayor said that "they just dumped the project. The company that was in charge didn't even pay the workers, and they were from the community" (Reforma 15-2-2009). The newspaper interviewed several of the government officials mentioned, and as usual, they all passed the blame. The state congressmen blamed the state health ministry, who accused the federal health ministry. And they all blamed the construction company for not paying the workers.

Example 3 One interviewee talked about the social investment funds that were in place in Costa Rica. The fund managers went to the communities and asked what was needed so they could decide where to allocate the money. Many communities requested schools and hospitals, and these were built using social funds, but they did not coordinate with the national ministries of health and education. The schools and hospitals were built, but the ministries were not able to license enough nurses and teachers to make them functional. To avoid these issues, they needed to collaborate with the departments. Sometimes communities asked for football fields and public plazas, which did not fit in with the priorities for national development (though communities thought them necessary to provide wholesome activities to young people). The national government would complain that the funds were wasted on non-essentials and wanted to end the programme. As a result, CEPAL/ECLAC is trying to promote a mechanism by which the community's immediate necessities can be made compatible with a national or regional vision (Interview 33: 2006).

There are hundreds of more examples to give, particularly in health and in education services, where government inefficiencies and bureaucracy obstruct the delivery of services to the people. In Central America, NGOs provided numerous similar examples, questioning how it was that they were supposed to trust the government when the government had turned its back on those who needed the most (Interviews 9, 16: 2006).

5.6 Summary

Although national government is reluctant to fully decentralise and devolve power to local government in Mesoamerica, it is encouraging to see municipal governments in the region pooling together to create a better form of governance. The symposiums are giving them a stronger voice with the central government, and round tables are giving them more legitimacy with the voters. All levels of government still need to tackle the problem of corruption; however, significant change is unlikely until the governments are made accountable to the citizens they represent.

For projects to be effective in Mesoamerica, all the tiers of government need to collaborate fully. From the regional to the local, governments need to communicate and cooperate instead of "defending their own turf," as one interviewee said. It is not enough for a regional institution or organisation to plan out a project, implement it, and then obtain the desired result. "Many times, it is the international organisations that come along to say what should be the priority. Logically, they do not have mechanisms to determine the priorities at a community level, and the outcome has not always been positive" (Interview 33: 2006). However, not only the communities need to get involved; it must be a comprehensive process; there needs to be coordination among all levels of government.

In most cases, this coordination is either non-existent or short-termed at best. A regional project or an integration project will only work if it can count on the input of all the levels of government as well as that of other regional actors. Government decentralisation in Mesoamerica has been happening slowly, albeit it has been gaining momentum as local governments are gathering together to strengthen their voice. SICA's intent to work with the recently formed CAMCAYCA shows promise for regional organisations to work with local government towards a regional vision. It is too early to see results from this connection, but the possibility of a region/local dualism provides an interesting shift in strategy from the highly centralised Mesoamerican governments. Although this case only involves Central American institutions, the inclusion of Mexico as an observer in both SICA and CAMCAYCA could begin cooperation efforts that could spill over into the Tuxtla Mechanism or even *Proyecto Mesoamérica*. Moreover, it is not just the previously overlooked local government tier that requests inclusion in these processes, but other actors are doing so as well. In the next chapter, I will explore the relationship of these actors with the PPP and the government structures I discussed in this chapter.

Bibliography

Aguirre Rojas, Carlos Antonio. 2002. A Modo de Introducción: Chiapas en Perspectiva Histórica. In *Chiapas en Perspectiva Histórica*, ed. Aguirre Rojas Carlos Antonio, Bolívar Echeverría, Carlos Montemayor, and Wallerstein Immanuel, 2nda edición. España: El Viejo Topo.

Arce Tena, Carlos A. 2006. *La gobernabilidad democrática: una perspective para el desarrollo*. México, D.F.: Ediciones Miguel Angel Porrúa.

Arreola Muñoz, Arturo V. 2006. Mesoamérica, el saldo actual de sus recursos naturales estratégicos. In *Geoeconomía y Geopolítica en el área del Plan Puebla Panamá*, ed. Daniel Villafuerte Solis and Xochitl Leyva Solano. México: Editorial Miguel Angel Porrúa.

Bartra, Armando (ed.). 2001. *Mesoamerica: Los Ríos Profundos: Alternativas Plebeyas al Plan Puebla Panamá*. México, D.F.: RMALC/El Atajo Ediciones/ Instituto "Maya", A.C.

Bartra, Armando. 2004. *Mesoamericanos: Recalentando una identidad colectiva*. cemos MEMORIA Revista Mensual de Política y Cultura Núm. 183 mayo 2004.

CAMCAYCA plan estratégico 2015–2020. http://www.vng-international.nl/wp-content/uploads/2017/01/Compendio-de-buenas-prácticas-CAMCAYCA-VNG.pdf.

Carranza, Mario Esteban. 2000. *South American Free Trade Area or Free Trade Area of the Americas? Open Regionalism and the Future of Regional Economic Integration in South America*. Burlington, VT: Ashgate.

CONADECO. 2005. *5to Congreso Nacional de Asociaciones de Desarrollo Comunal, Costa Rica, 29–30 de octubre de 2004 Memoria*. San José, Costa Rica: CONADECO.

Curly, Jon M. 2008. Cleaning Up the Spaghetti Bowl. In *Economic Integration in the Americas*, ed. Joseph A. McKinney and Stephen Gardner. London and New York: Routledge.

Dávila, Enrique, Georgina Kessel, and Santiago Levy. 2002 El Sur también existe: un ensayo sobre el desarrollo regional de México (originally published in Economía Mexicana, vol. 11, 202–260). In *Ensayos Sobre el Desarrollo Económico y Social de México,* compilador Santiago Levy. México: Fondo de Cultura Económica.

Dirección Ejecutiva Proyecto de Integración y Desarrollo de Mesoamérica. 2008. *Informe de Actividades 2008*. El Salvador. www.planpuebla-panama.org. Accessed 4 November 2008.

Enríquez Villacorta, Alberto. 2005. *Desarrollo local y descentralización del Estado, nuevos factores de la Integración Centroamericana*. Alternativas Para el Desarrollo N° 93 abril-mayo 2005. San Salvador: FUNDE.

FEMICA. 2008. Fortalecimiento de los Gobiernos Locales y de la Sociedad Civil. *Revista Femica*, No. 5 febrero 2008. http://www.femica.org/archivos/revista5.pdf.

FEMICA/SGSICA. 2009. Memorandum de Entendimiento Entre la Secretaria General del Sistema de la Integración Centroamericana (SGSICA) y la Federación de Municipios del Istmo Centroamericano (FEMICA). http://femica.org/noticias/docNoticias/Convenio_SICA_FEMICA.pdf.

FUNDE/PNUD. 2004. *Asociación de Municipios y Construcción Regional para el Desarrollo*. Desarrollo Humano: Buenas Prácticas eneroenero N°03.

Harvey, Neil. 2006. La disputa por los recursos naturales en el área del Plan Puebla Panamá. In *Geoeconomía y Geopolítica en el área del Plan Puebla Panamá*, ed. Daniel Villafuerte Solis and Xochitl Leyva Solano. Mexico: Editorial Miguel Angel Porrúa.

Informe Ejecutivo. 2006. El PPP: Avances retos y Perspectivas.

Informe Ejecutivo. 2008. El PPP: Avances retos y Perspectivas.

Informe Estado de la Región en Desarrollo Humano Sostenible. 2008. http://unpan1.un.org/intradoc/groups/public/documents/icap/unpan032746.pdf.

Informe Estado de la Región en Desarrollo Humano Sostenible. 2011. http://www.redalyc.org/pdf/152/15233381022.pdf.

Martí Ascencio, Bosco. 2008. Proyecto Mesoamérica: fortaleciendo la integración y desarrollo regional. *Revista Mexicana de Política Exterior* (83): 9–39. Instituto Matías Romero.

Mattli, Walter. 1999. *The Logic of Regional Integration: Europe and Beyond*. Cambridge: Cambridge University Press, New York Net Library e-book accessed through Warwick Library.

OECD Territorial Reviews. 2005. *The Mesoamerican Region: Southeastern Mexico and Central America*. OECD Publishing. http://www.sourceoecd.org/regionaldevelopment/9264021914; http://www.sourceoecd.org/governance/9264021914.

Pearce, Jenny. 2004. DEBATE Collective Action or Public Participation? Complementary or Contradictory Democratisation Strategies in Latin America? *Bulletin of Latin American Research* 23 (4): 483–504.

Rioja Peregrina, Leonardo H. 2002. Biopirateria y la lucha política en el contexto del PPP. In *Lectura Crítica del Plan Puebla Panamá*, ed. Sandoval Forero Eduardo Andrés and Robinson Salazar Pérez coordinadores. USA: Libros en Red.

Rubio, Luis. 2004. Democratic Politics in Mexico: New Complexities. In *Mexico Under Fox*, ed. Luis Rubio and Susan Kaufman Purcell. Boulder, CO: Lynne Rienner Publishers, Inc.

Sanchez Bajo, Claudia. 2005. European Union-Mercosur Interregionalism: Negotiations, Civil Society and Governance. In *The Political Economy of Regions and Regionalisms*, ed. Morten Bøås, Marianne H. Marchand, and Timothy M. Shaw. Palgrave Macmillan.

SG-SICA. 2010 Instrumentos Jurídicos del Sistema de Integración Centroamericana Secretaría General del Sistema de la Integración Centroamericana SG-SICA Second Edition. www.sica.int/busqueda/Libros.aspx?IDItem=28654&IdCat=35&IdEnt=1&Idm=1&IdmStyle=1.

SICA/CEPAL. 2004. *La Integración Centroamericana: Beneficios y Costos Documento Síntesis*, Centroamérica, mayo de 2004 2a. impresión: Asesores Soluciones Integradas Impreso el 28 de junio de 2004.

Interviews

1. Political Analyst Guatemala (Background information conversation not recorded), 25 September 2006, Guatemala City.
2. Instituto Nacional de Electrificación INDE Guatemala (Background information conversations not recorded), 25, 26, 27 September 2006, Guatemala City.
3. Director of Integration, Ministerio de Relaciones Exteriores Guatemala, 25 September 2006, Guatemala City.
4. Economist, Consejo Monetario Centroamericano, 19 October 2006, Costa Rica.
5. National Worker's Confederation (Labour Union) (Background information conversation not recorded), 30 October 2006.
6. Executive Secretary, Consejo Monetario Centroamericano, 19 October 2006, Costa Rica.
7. Coordinator Human Development, Dirección Ejecutiva Plan Puebla Panamá, 1 September 2006, San Salvador.
8. Centro de Estudios y Publicaciones Alforja, 17 October 2006, San José, Costa Rica.
9. Fundación Rigoberta Menchú, 26 September 2006, Guatemala.
10. Commercial Relations Coordinator, Cámara de Comercio de Guatemala, 27 September 2006.
11. Department Head on Indigenous Issues, Subsecretaría para América Latina y el Caribe, Coordinación General del Plan Puebla Panamá, 30 August 2006, Mexico.
12. Instituto Tecnológico Autónomo de México political Analyst (Background information conversation not recorded), 10 August 2006, Cancún Quintana Roo.

13. International Cooperation Office, República de Costa Rica, Ministerio de Relaciones Exteriores y Culto, 17 October 2006, San José, Costa Rica.
14. Technical advisor, Dirección de Integración y Comercio, Secretaría de Integración Económica Centroamericana (SIECA), 26 September 2006, Guatemala City.
15. Consultant and Analyst (Background information conversation not recorded), 2 June 2007, Acapulco, Guerrero.
16. Regional Director of CODA international El Salvador (Project Liaison with Perulapía, 6 September 2006, San Salvador, Perulapía.
17. Regional Local Area Director, Fundación Nacional para el Desarrollo (FUNDE), 5 September 2006, San Salvador.
18. Director of Economic Affairs, Cámara de Comerico e Industria de El Salvador, 1 September 2006, San Salvador.
19. Executive, Dirección Ejecutiva Plan Puebla Panamá, 4 September 2006, San Salvador.
20. Fundación para la Democracia (FUNPADEM) (Background information conversation not recorded), 17, 18, 19 October 2006.
21. Legislative advisor, Asamblea Legislativa, Costa Rica, Not recorded, Background information.
22. Director, Instituto Centroamericano de Estudios Sociales (ICAES) (CCT), 17 October 2006, San José, Costa Rica.
23. Director of International Economic Section, Departamento de Estudios Económicos y Sociales, Fundación Salvadoreña para el Desarrollo Económico y Social. FUSADES, 5 September 2006, San Salvador.
24. President Confederación Nacional de Asociaciones de Desarrollo Comunal CONADECO, 17 October 2006, San José, Costa Rica.
25. Economic Affairs Director, Secretaría General del Sistema de la Integración Centroaméricana (SG-SICA), 4 September 2006, El Salvador.
26. Subsecretaría para América Latina y el Caribe, Coordinación General del Plan Puebla Panamá, 30 August 2006, Mexico City.
27. PPP initiatives coordinator, Oficina local del Plan Puebla Panamá en El Salvador, Ministerio de Relaciones Exteriores El Salvador, 5 September 2006, San Salvador.
28. Representative of the Mesoamerican Biological Corridor, 17 October 2006, San José, Costa Rica.
29. Directive Cabinet, Parlamento Centroamericano, 27 September 2006, Guatemala City.
30. Executive Director, Oficina local del Plan Puebla Panamá en El Salvador, Ministerio de Relaciones Exteriores El Salvador, 5 September 2006, San Salvador.
31. Elected Deputy, Asamblea Legislativa de Costa Rica (Interview took place in room adjacent to chamber of deputies, was not allowed to record), 18 October 2006, San José, Costa Rica.

32. Former guerrilla leader, professor Universidad Francisco Gavidia, 1 September and 7 September 2006, El Salvador (Informal conversations, took notes, not recorded).
33. CEPAL, 10 October 2006, Mexico City.
34. FLACSO, Regional Coordinator for Investigation and International Cooperation (Background information conversation not recorded), 18 October 2006, San José, Costa Rica.
35. Director of Cooperation, fondo de Desarrollo Indígena Guatemalteco, 25 September 2006, Guatemala City.
36. FUNPADEM, 18 October 2006, Costa Rica.
37. Regional Coordinator of Investigation and International Cooperation, Secretaría General de la Facultad Latinoamericana de Ciencias Sociales (FLACSO), Costa Rica.
38. AMAP Director, Mexican Asociation for the Self-Determination of Peoples (AMAP), 22 August 2006, Mexico City.
39. Sub Coordinator of the regional office of Instituto de Fomento Municipal de Guatemala (INFON), 26 September 2006, Notes- not recorded.
40. Former candidate for governor of Chiapas, 21 September 2006, Mexico.
41. Embassy of El Salvador in Mexico City.
42. Director of Analysis and follow-up of commercial treaties with Latin America- Secretaría de Economía, 9 May 2007, Background information for context only, conversation not recorded, referred to documents.
43. Municipal Government of Orizaba, Veracruz, 26 August 2006, Mexico (Notes- not recorded).
44. Full day meeting and visit with the local government of San Bartolomé de la Perulapía municipality in El Salvador, the Mayor Guillermo Sanchez and 5 other local government representatives. All those involved in the meeting were members of the FSLN political party, 6 September 2006, El Salvador.
45. Full day participation Oportunidades/Progresa Córdoba assessment exercise, August 2008, Veracruz.
46. Director CODA international 5 and 6 September 2006 (Sessions at Perulapía recorded, informal background conversations not recorded), El Salvador.
47. Assistant to the Director of Juridical reviews, 4 September 2006, San Salvador.
48. Asociación Latinoamericana de Micro, Pequeños y Medianos Empresarios (ALAMPYME), one of the founding organisations in the Red Mexicana de Acción contra el Libre Comercio (RMALC) Interview, 29 November 2006, Mexico City.
49. General and Alternative medical doctor. Did his social service by attending medical brigades in marginalised Mexican rural communities, November 2008.
50. American student in Guatemala and El Salvador in 1969, November 2008, Mexico City.

Conferences Attended

"Gestión integrada de programas sociales y autoridad social: experiencias latinoamericanas", Dr. Rolando Franco, Facultad Latinoamericana de Ciencias Sociales y Centro de Estudios para el Futuro FLACSO, Tuesday 17 October 2006, San José, Costa Rica, 10:00 a.m.

"Gobernabilidad Democrática y Nuevas Orientaciones Políticas en Costa Rica: escenarios a partir de las elecciones 2006" organised by Centro de Estudios Políticos, Maestría Centroamericana de Ciencias Políticas, UCR, Facultad Latinoamericana de Ciencias Sociales y Centro de Estudios para el Futuro FLACSO, 17 October 2006, 8:00 p.m.

"Indigenous People in Mexico" presented by Lynda Martinez del Campo Fonda del Claustro, Mexico City 17 March 2007.

"Multi-Level Governance and Systems of Economic Organisation' Workshop" 17–19 May 2007, University of Warwick, Scarman House.

CHAPTER 6

Non-governmental Actors, Horizontal Participation in Policy

In the previous chapters, I outlined governance frameworks in Mesoamerica at the regional level and the different government tiers. However, governance implies that the "steering mechanisms" in place are not limited to the decisions and activities of the elected government officials and their offices. The ability of the government to effectively govern has meant the need to include other actors in policymaking, with specific interests embedded in the delivery of services provided by the government. In the previous chapter, I also demonstrated that policymaking is still highly centralised in Mesoamerica. Regional governments can make suggestions, sub-national and local governments can apply policies, but for the most part, it is the central government that makes and enforces policies and is in control of distributing funds according to its priorities. A similar observation can be made about horizontal governance—that which takes place between the national governments and actors at the different tiers. The notable exception, as mentioned in the previous chapter, is at the local level, where in some instances there is meaningful participation of community groups with the local government.

The recommendations made by the European Union (EU) technical support to the Central American integration efforts, as well as those issued by the OECD (2005) and CEPAL (2015), advised governments and regional bodies to include non-governmental actors in policymaking. However, in practice, non-governmental participation is just beginning to occur in policy design and policymaking in Mesoamerica. During the time

A. Gamboa, *Regional Integration, Development, and Governance in Mesoamerica*,
https://doi.org/10.1007/978-3-030-25350-9_6

of the Plan Puebla Panama (PPP), it was non-existent or just a formality. Moreover, organisations that disagree with the government or the regional policies tend not to engage in dialogue with the responsible government entity, preferring instead to keep a distance. The result seems to be a situation where governments continue to push forward policies while external organisations oppose them. Rather than developing a constructive dialogue and strategies influenced and modified by other stakeholders.

This chapter includes information gathered via interviews conducted between August and November 2006 with non-governmental organisations (NGOs), representatives of Chambers of Commerce, labour unions, and civil society organisations as well as material provided by independent regional think tanks and academics, supplemented with updates. I argue that, in addition to the difficulties of implementing the policies needed to carry out a regional development plan and projects through the different tiers of government, the ability to achieve the PPP or any other regional proposal is compromised when other regional actors are not actively involved (and some even opposed), mainly NGOs, civil society representatives, and business and trade unions.

In addition to interviewing NGOs and civil society representatives, I sent out the questionnaire to over 180 organisations in the region (see Annex B). The replies provided a sample of the diverse opinions found in the region by non-governmental actors on the most relevant issues related to them and governance in Mesoamerica.

I have divided this chapter into four sections. In the first section, I set out the main problem: that of dialogue between the actors and the government. Then I examine the main issues that arose from the questionnaire and interviews with NGOs, trade unions, and civil society. Two regional forums for civil society are then presented: the CC-SICA, which is an officially recognised advisory group that works alongside the SICA and Central American integration; and the Mesoamerican Forums, unofficial non-governmental forums that initially invited organisations based in Mesoamerica to oppose the PPP and then extended to include other regional matters. These forums show that there are other actors interested in being active participants in the shaping of regional integration. They want their views acknowledged, whether they are working with government-led integration efforts or independently. In the third section, I examine the interaction of small and medium business with the chambers of commerce. In the last part I analyse the case of local governance, where municipalities, business, government, and civil society work together towards a common goal, e.g., environment, and how they have managed to work together in border areas—bringing forth integration, even if at a smaller scale, one that is more durable.

6.1 Dialogue Between NGOs, Unions, and Regional Organisations

The notable opposition to the PPP seemed to take the government by surprise. Although they expected a certain amount of opposition from the political parties on the other side of the spectrum, they did not expect overt resistance from the people it was supposed to help, particularly since President Fox (2000–2006) had used the Mexican section of the PPP as part of the platform that got him elected. In Central America, the Madrid Agenda (2000) had been well-received; a reaction they had hoped would extend to the PPP. In this section, I explore some of the reasons why there was such a vehement reaction to the PPP and other regional proposals.

The NGOs and civil society groups that responded to the questionnaire spanned an array of activities ranging from environmental protection, human rights awareness, sustainable development, etc. (see questions 1 and 2). These groups saw an urgent need to stop the environmental degradation in the region as well as to provide the population with necessary social services and economic activities (questions 3 and 4). Even though the PPP promised to pay attention to these needs and provide the region with sustainable forms of development, the organisations polled were sceptical that the PPP was targeting the actual needs of the region and instead had ulterior motives. A representative of the Rigoberta Menchú Foundation comments that ever since the Central American Federation in the 1800s, regional integration efforts that have taken place have been the vision of the "elite" members of society, not that of general society, and certainly not the view of the poor. "These integration and regionalisation efforts and the institutions created are not aimed to impoverish society in general terms, but they focus on the economic or productive sectors and their development in (each of) the countries. So, it is only the view of this limited sector of society, not of society as a whole, so in the end, that is why there is opposition" (Interview 9: 2006).

The consensus is that NGOs and civil society groups yearn to see development policy consider the needs and wants of the poorest citizens in the region. The PPP eventually included mechanisms for consultation with civil society and NGOs, and now *Proyecto Mesoamerica* has these mechanisms in place; however, their effectiveness is questionable. To this effect, many of the questions I included in the questionnaire and posed during the interviews asked if there had been dialogue attempts with government representatives (or vice-versa) regarding the PPP, what the response had been, and what possibilities existed of a more constructive debate between the regional actors, both government and non-governmental.

Prior to the establishment of the PPP Ministry, the Inter-American Development Bank (IDB) managed the mechanisms for consulting with NGOs and civil society (Interview 7: 2006; CG-PPP 2002: 16). The IDB would hold periodic meetings with these groups to receive their input and concerns about what was happening with the PPP. This mechanism was not well-received by the groups concerned with the implementation of the PPP. The first problem was that the IDB is in Washington, DC, so it is not easily accessible. The IDB tried to solve this problem by holding meetings in different venues, but the sessions were announced through their website and only to the groups with whom they already had some contact. Some organisations only found out about meetings they could have attended after they had already taken place. In the end, the considerable opposition that surged against the PPP confirmed that the IDB mechanism was inadequate. Another problem was that the IDB suggested and set up the consults after the PPP was up and running. Naturally, the NGOs and Civil Society organisations considered this "consultation" mechanism pointless, as the PPP was a *fait accompli* and felt that the IDB was only asking them to sign off on it.

When questioned about the amount of dialogue that took place between civil society groups and those in charge of the projects, many NGOs admitted that, although they were approached, they had not accepted.[1] I inquired into their lack of involvement in the projects, and for the most part, they stated that previous experiences with government

[1]The Memoir of the "Foro Regional de Reflexión Sobre las Metas del Milenio y la Equidad de Género en el Marco del Plan Puebla-Panama" starts off with a disclosure saying that it was a challenge to produce a forum due to the stance of many organisations of NO PPP a posture that to the organisers meant "NO dialogue, NO communication, NO exchanges of expertise." Many key actors decided not to participate in this forum because of their NO PPP stance—p. 17 (SRE/UNIFEM/PNUD 2004).

officials consisted of months of discussions and round tables, but the final result reflected only government opinions, ignoring the concerns and priorities of civil society groups. Leaders of these groups, therefore considered further discussion a waste of time. Others (like Fundación Rigoberta Menchú) said that they were willing to engage in dialogue, but only if it involved the "real" decision-makers in the meetings, due to past experiences when they participated in discussions with lower civil servants who would spend the day hearing out their requests. The participants would go away feeling that their complaints and suggestions had been heard, but then, once the workshops ended, nothing would happen. When they asked the government workshop leaders about the progress on the outcome of the workshops, they answered that the dossier had been sent to the appropriate area and that they were no longer involved.

> Basically, they want to report that these workshops took place, and get more funding from international organisations. They can say, oh, this foundation and this community participated in the workshops to say that the money they request is for the people, but at the end of the day, they will do the projects that they want, whether we want them or not. (Interview 9: 2006)

The representative of the regional trade union networks argued that they did not participate in any dialogue with the PPP because they received a completed document to review and comment on (giving them less than a week for a 350-pages document). In their opinion, the fact that the document already existed meant that the governments were not asking for them to engage in dialogue, as "a dialogue happens before there is a plan, a dialogue happens when they ask if we even want a PPP and what kind of plan we want it to be" (Interview 22: 2006). One week was not enough time for their experts to analyse the documents properly and make comments on the policies proposed. Moreover, they were not going to make any modifications to the text, even if the unions did make suggestions, given the time they had before the official launch. "What they wanted was to say that we were consulted on the PPP, but they did not want to consult us, they wanted us to rubberstamp it, exactly as they proposed it" (Interview 22: 2006). In the end, the unions preferred not to review the PPP prior to its official launch. However, they assured that had they been included in the process of designing the PPP, instead of receiving a completed document—the unions would have agreed to get involved.

Not all organisations decided to remain protesting on the sidelines; some chose to engage in dialogue and debate with the PPP, and with the IDB about the PPP. However, this generated distrust between the NGOs involved in dialogue and those who did not. While some, like the Cooperation for the Guatemalan Indigenous Peoples Development Fund (FODIGUA), argue that they engaged in the discussion to learn about the projects and decide whether to support or reject them, other groups see this approach as one that has already “sold out” to the government (Interviews 35, 9: 2006).

The Director of FODIGUA cooperated with the Guatemalan commissioner for the PPP to try and involve the indigenous communities. She was not in complete agreement with the PPP but saw herself as an intermediary (Interview 35: 2006). She would lobby for information in indigenous languages, so she could take it to the communities and then relay the concerns of the community to the PPP's decision-makers. In Guatemala, where approximately 60% of the population is indigenous (divided among 23 communities) there is a long history of repression, discrimination, and marginalisation of these groups. About 40% cannot read or write, with an even higher percentage among women. The director, however, says that nowadays there will be at least one person in every family that can read and write in Spanish, so they provide families with information under this supposition.

> The FODIGUA, along with the PPP Commissioner has generated a process of information, consultation, and participation of indigenous peoples, although the term ‘consultation’ is a very sensitive term to manage here in Guatemala. People do not wish for it to be called a ‘consultation’ when they have not received a highly enriching amount of information, so instead, we manage workshops.... We try to generate spaces for dialogue, spaces, or round tables for analysis relevant to the themes presented in the Plan Puebla-Panama. Of course, if we only speak about the Plan Puebla Panama, there will be a considerable opposition. (Interview 35: 2006)

The challenge is not only to obtain the information but also to disseminate it. Although the PPP office provided plenty of information, it was very technical, and in Spanish so, the director had little to distribute to the indigenous communities. The FODIGUA tried to relay as much information as possible, and according to its director by doing so, there was greater community acceptance of PPP projects; however, that does not mean that the communities agreed to all of them (Interview 35: 2006). The director would like to see more dialogue with the communities and real consultation. FODIGUA and many community leaders had suggestions for integrating their proposals into the PPP (Interview 35: 2006). For example, there was a proposal to have traditional Maya medicine rescued by the PPP, by working together with National Universities (like the San Carlos University), the University would research traditional medicine to provide scientific endorsement and then help with obtaining the patents for community use. They also want to see more studies on the environmental impact of large infrastructure projects, since she states:

> Our main concerns about the PPP projects are the respect for nature, the respect for our culture, and the respect for human development. We have a model that in Quiché is called *ochinoj*, or the three wisdoms, and these are fundamental for development. The first wisdom is respect and reconciliation with Mother Nature, the second is authority within the community, and the third is strengthening the political voice of the people. (Interview 35: 2006)

The PPP created the Advisory Group on Indigenous and Ethnic Participation (GAPIE) to engage with the indigenous communities. Initially, it was part of the PPP Ministry in El Salvador, relocating in 2007 to Mexico City. The PPP directive that oversaw the GAPIE mentioned that:

> GAPIE was created initially as a consultative organ to the PPP, but now I am evaluating if it will continue to be so, or if it has or can evolve into a project facilitator, a generator of ideas. We have found an interesting dynamic in these meetings… we would like to arrive at a point where decision-making does not only lie in the Ministries but that we can work together with the communities in their favour. (Interview 7: 2006)

Although this directive was optimistic about the GAPIE, the director admitted that they had stacks of folders full of proposals already coming in from the meetings, but one year after its launch, they still didn't have a system in place for sorting and evaluating the feasibility of these proposals to turn them into actual projects (Interview 7: 2006).

The GAPIE did not continue with Proyecto Mesoamerica. Several of the projects that involved indigenous populations (such as bilingual education) are now under the Mesoamerican Cooperation Programme (within the Tuxtla Mechanism). The Mesoamerican Biological Corridor (MBC), set up within Proyecto Mesoamerica, does establish a framework of partnership with indigenous communities (CCAD-MBC-PM 2013: 3).

The responses to questions 6 and 7 (see Annex B) show that out of 55 organisations, only 13 tried to engage in dialogue with their government or regional representative. I followed up with other NGOs during the interviews to see why there was so little direct response to the authorities promoting these programmes. The answers given during the interviews were consistent with questionnaire findings: NGOs in this region do not trust the government, they consider it more useful to voice their opinions to the press or mobilise protests than to send communiqués to the appropriate government representatives. The organisations polled in this survey, as well as those interviewed, were direct in their statements: they would only engage in dialogue if the policymaking process will include their opinions, suggestions, and/or complaints.

Their concerns are not without foundation. As we can see with the responses to the follow up question (7), ten of the 13 organisations who sent a response to the government proposals received a reply, but only four were invited to engage in dialogue—showing the exclusion of other actors in the decision-making process. About a third of the organisations polled did participate in an official consultation group, according to question 8, but the majority (27 out of 54) did not. Replies to the questionnaire and subsequent interviews show that, although mechanisms have been set up for consultation and feedback, governments and regional organisations did not advance in convincing the NGOs and community organisations of their usefulness.

There is a modicum of acceptance of some of the regional projects (see the grid on question 10), but it is not only the government that civil society and NGOs do not trust, but there is also mistrust of the regional institutions. "PARLACEN is a clear example of an organism that is not functional because that is how the governments want to keep it, their decisions are not binding, and they don't even give any guidance for policy" (Interview 9: 2006). Several called PARLACEN a den of corruption (Interviews 9, 17, 8: 2006). Segrada and Camacho consider that the direct election of some of the deputies in PARLACEN is a step in the right direction; nevertheless, they are worried that the governments still appoint the rest. However, they do not think that these problems should mean the abolition of PARLACEN, but a reform (Segreda and Camacho 1999: 154). Alforja,[2] a regional social network and publications centre present in the region for 25 years, would also welcome a change in the institutions, "there is always great resistance to effectively modifying the integration institutions, because they have become a sort of political limbo, places of exile, and consolation prizes for the political class.... The structures of regional integration have become obsolete as they are" (Interview 8: 2006). Because of this resistance to change, they are not confident that the technical support offered by the EU will make much impact.

Moreover, since the main objective of the exercise (EU technical support) is to arrive at an association agreement between the EU and Central America, many necessary reforms will likely be overlooked. Technical support has usually consisted of proposing the same elements: political dialogue, cooperation, and trade agreements, "however, they are in a hurry to reach the trade agreement element, so the political dialogue gets watered down" (Interview 8: 2006). Instead, networks like Alforja envision a different integration process, one that would involve social processes and the environment, where transparent consultation mechanisms would allow active participation in the creation of regional integration.[3]

Several Central American NGOs compared the weak consulting process of the PPP with the well-established methods of the SICA, where a consulting body, the CC-SICA—made up of NGOs, community-based organisations, academics, and think tanks—is invited and encouraged to participate regularly.

Participatory Mechanisms in Mesoamerica

The recent history of Mesoamerica can shed light as to why this situation is taking place. During times of military governments, dictatorships, and one-party rule, harsh government repression often confronted any opposition. In many cases, as in El Salvador and Nicaragua, opposition groups

[2] http://www.redalforja.net/.

[3] See Jara, Oscar, ed. 2002. Otro Desarrollo es Posible: Sistematización de experiencias y reflexiones críticas desde la Centroamérica post-Mitch 1998–2001. Centro de Estudios y Publicaciones Alforja.

became violent in order to be acknowledged. However, when the guerrilla wars and the violence that plagued Central America (but also cases in the States of Chiapas, Oaxaca, and Guerrero in south-eastern Mexico) subsided after promises of inclusion and change, the saying applies: "*todo cambia para que todo siga igual*"[4] or everything changes so that everything can remain the same. In Nicaragua, Elías Chévez, a Sandinista legislator, said, "the revolution was like a train. People got on and off" (*Reforma*, Tuesday 25 November 2008). Although the current president is a former Sandinista revolutionary, many of his former comrades are now critical of President Daniel Ortega and accuse him of betraying their core revolutionary values.[5] These former guerrillas consider themselves true Sandinistas, followers of Augusto Sandino, the nationalist rebel leader that attacked the US occupying troops in the 1920s and 1930s. A newspaper interview with a former friend of Daniel Ortega, collaborator and revolutionary, Sergio Ramirez (vice-president of Nicaragua 1984–1990), exemplifies what went on after the revolution and why after overthrowing the Somoza dictatorship, the Sandinistas lost direction.

> What happens is that the military leaders of the revolution were not intellectually prepared. Ortega is not an intellectual; neither is Tomas Borges; they were never statesmen…. With the triumph of the Sandinista revolution in 1979, it looked like musical chairs; everyone sat down wherever they could. Some in the police force, others in the government or the army, and some didn't get a chair. Some of the great strategists of the revolution did not have any abilities besides being revolutionaries. The triumph of the revolution was their downfall; some committed suicide, others became alcoholics. (*Reforma*, 2 December 2008)[6]

In El Salvador, a former guerrilla leader explained that the demise of the revolution happened once the peace agreements were signed. Before

[4]Called 'gatopardismo' as it is derived from Guissepe Tomasi di Lampedusa's novel "Il Gatopardo" circa 1954–1957.

[5]Constitutional reform has allowed him to stay in power for three terms, https://www.reuters.com/article/oukwd-uk-nicaragua-ortega-idAFTRE59J11820091020; https://www.washingtonpost.com/news/worldviews/wp/2016/11/05/nicaraguas-daniel-ortega-headed-for-third-consecutive-term-amid-questions-about-democracy/?noredirect=on&utm_term=.8c929c94f295.

[6]*A Ortega lo atrapó el poder*, Silvia Isabel Gámez *Reforma*, 2 December. Entrevista con Sergio Ramírez.

signing these documents, he said, the revolutionaries had the upper hand. But once the papers were signed and the guerrilla disarmed, then the promises made on behalf of the government were either weakened or postponed (Interview 32: 2006). The "victory" obtained was then clouded by the lack of tangible results. Another problem, as stated by another interviewee from El Salvador, is that the peace agreements were not a result of dialogue. Instead, they were agreements that took place between two sectors, the government and the Farabundo Martí National Liberation Front (FMLN). The people did not get to participate. "The FMLN did not represent all the people; it represented certain armed groups of that time, but not the general population. People ended up disappointed with the results of this 'dialogue'" (Interview 22: 2006).

Similarly, in Guatemala, a member of the Rigoberta Menchú foundation[7] commented that government officials were quick to make promises when international representatives were around, but when it was time for them to act, they were very slow to carry through on anything (Interview 9: 2006). Segreda and Camacho (1999) note that the Esquipulas II peace treaty[8] does include a "democratisation" clause whereby governments commit to promoting social justice, however, this clause is buried into just a few lines of the agreement (Segreda and Camacho 1999: 153). They consider that at least in the case of Central America, "formal" democracy has been one of the biggest obstacles for civil society to have access to government and particularly regional integration processes. The treaties signed to implement the integration process were supposed to impact domestic laws; instead, they only managed to change regional trade laws (i.e., export tariffs). Also, the new integration agenda (post-1990), minimised social benefits. Instead it was more concerned with "exporting labour" (through the *maquilas* without leaving its borders) than job creation.

[7] Rigoberta Menchú was awarded the Nobel Peace prize for her efforts to bring equality and dignity to the indigenous peoples of Guatemala. She denounced the human rights abuses that were taking place and obtained international support for her cause. Her foundation continues to fight for the human rights of indigenous peoples, not only in Guatemala, but also in the rest of Mesoamerica.

[8] The Esquipulas process established a framework of peaceful conflict resolution as set up by the Contadora group to settle the military conflicts in Central America. The Esquipulas II accord was signed in 1987 by the five presidents.

For this reason, "integration did not obtain much following from the population it excluded, and it was seen more as a cause to their problems than as a solution" (Segreda and Camacho 1999: 150–151). Although these authors spoke about the renewed Central American integration agenda of the 1990s, their observations are relevant to the PPP process as well. They conclude that the "formal" democratic process left out civil society, so it had to join in with NGOs in order to actively participate in national and regional politics (Segreda and Camacho 1999: 151–152).

6.2 CC-SICA

Article 12 of the Tegucigalpa Protocol (1991) ascribes the CC-SICA as the consultative body "integrated by the business, labour, academic, and other principal living forces of the central American isthmus; representative of the economic, social, and cultural sectors that are committed to the integration efforts of the isthmus" (CC-SICA 2006). It started with 18 regional social networks that filled the criteria defined in the Tegucigalpa Protocol and involved the same geographical span. These groups later increased to 26 with the representatives chosen by organised civil society groups and not by the government. Although part of the function of the CC-SICA is to participate in meetings with other SICA organisms, its main activities focus on analysing policies and documents concerning integration and development in Central America. Even if it does not participate in formulating these documents or policies, the CC-SICA provides a thorough analysis of each of them and publishes its comments, agreements, and disagreements.

Notwithstanding that they are the official consultative group, their comments are not always considered. Segreda and Camacho find that CC-SICA has an "important, but limited role" and maintain the importance of including other types of "formal" participation in the integration process (Segreda and Camacho 1999: 153). Among the most notable successes of the CC-SICA, is the Alliance for Sustainable Development (ALIDES).[9]

[9] In the CC-SICA's own literature, there are also several examples of unsuccessful attempts to change documents or project proposals. In general, they attribute these failures to the fact that CC-SICA did not manage to reach consensus or consolidate their position, giving them little leverage in the negotiations.

Unhappy with the original proposal (precursor to ALIDES), social organisations pressured CC-SICA to set forth an integral scheme that directly related to the interests of the inhabitants of Central America. The input from the CC-SICA challenged the original project, which had been "The Joint Declaration between Central America and the United States" (CONCAUSA) and shifted the focus from a statement of intent between the two entities to an integral development programme (CC-SICA 2006). The strategy for strengthening the regional integration institutions as part of the Central American Regional Integration Support Program (PAIRCA) signed between the SG-SICA, and the EU recognises the CC-SICA as an essential element of the integration process in Central America.

Also, the CC-SICA was an active participant of the Madrid Agenda 2000 (Central America facing the twenty-first century, a precursor to the PPP) setting forth proposals given by the regional social networks, integrated into a total of 24 projects. Once the Madrid Agenda formed part of the PPP, the CC-SICA was driven to the sidelines and was no longer invited to be an active participant in the agenda.

> Once the PPP took over, and the PPP was not an endogenous project, it comes from Mexico, then all sorts of agendas took over: the PPP agenda, the CAFTA agenda, and the EU agenda. What is no longer clear is what Central America's development model is going to be. There is no longer a regional vision; only agendas and some are just plain opportunistic. (Interview 22: 2006)

According to one of the representatives from the Foundation for Peace and Democracy (FUNPADEM)—also one of the original members of the CC-SICA—, the IDB viewed the PPP as a more viable project than Central American Integration, which is why they financially backed the PPP more readily than the Madrid Agenda. The FUNPADEM, though, considers that the PPP debilitates the Central American integration process since the SG-SICA was included as an organism of technical support and not as one of the pillars of the Plan (Interview 36: 2006). Similarly, the CC-SICA did not necessarily welcome the use of new consultation mechanisms. According to one of the CC-SICA interviewees, these mechanisms violate the Tegucigalpa Protocol, which establishes the CC-SICA as the only mechanism. He considered that these external processes were created only to say that a consultation took place, "but it is a process created by them, not by us, and we are not represented, even if CC-SICA is unable to represent everyone, it is independent, and it is taken seriously" (Interview 22: 2006).

One of the most prominent criticisms by the CC-SICA is the proliferation of Free Trade Agreements (FTAs) in Central America, "because we are in favour of integration, we are not in favour of FTAs; instead of integrating us, they disintegrate us" (Interview 22: 2006). According to this interviewee, who was the director of the Central American Confederation of Workers (CCT), to really integrate, Central America needed to focus on integrating economically, socially, politically, and culturally.[10] He stated that they could not consider CAFTA or any other FTA as an instrument of integration, or as one that would promote development. From their point of view, in an FTA the strongest member always wins. Hence it is a weak argument to say that it will produce employment, growth, development, or wealth distribution. "For example, those in favour of CAFTA say that it will mean more employment. They cannot guarantee more employment; it does not include an employment policy; these things don't just happen. Even less can they guarantee decent employment and salaries, which is what the Unions want" (Interview 22: 2006).

The CC-SICA reiterates this position on integration whenever it's asked to comment on documents and proposals. For example, one consultation conducted in 2002 on an IDB paper titled "Regional Integration Strategy Profile" criticises the definition of "regional integration" used in the document. The consultation considers that the concept of "regional integration," as used in the reviewed document as an equivalent to free trade, is more of a strategy for the insertion into the "globalised world economy" than for regional integration. However, the CC-SICA recognises that "regional integration" has many connotations and definitions. The fact that they are made up of organisations that "practice the regional integration of the Central American civil society and expects integration to bring forth concrete results in the social,

[10]The CCT, which at the time had the presidency of the CC-SICA (2006–2007), has a parallel organisation, the Central American Institute for Social Studies (ICAES), which is responsible for much of the investigation used by the CCT in its recommendations. The ICAES has produced a substantial amount of literature on integration, which can be found at www.cct-icaes.org.

productive, business, educational, labour, and cultural, etc., areas" (CC-SICA, FUNPADEM 2003).

The CC-SICA considers that regional integration needs to be viewed more holistically and tailored according to what Central Americans want. It

> ...should not be reduced to a market economy vision; instead, it should be an integral development strategy oriented to improve the quality of life of the citizens and where commercial policies should give equal importance to intra-regional trade as they do to extra-regional trade. (CC-SICA, FUNPADEM 2003: 53)

The CC-SICA, through its publications and its regional representations, is pushing the Central American integration institutions to widen their definition of integration from the one engrained in most of the regional institutions (limited to economic integration). According to one representative in the CC-SICA, "integration that occurs through civil society, instead of leaving it up to the governments, this integration can be a powerful force, one that transcends government changes –that audits government and opens up spaces for dialogue between the various sectors" (Interview 36: 2006). The CC-SICA has been lobbying the Central American regional institutions to widen their definition of integration to include what they consider more important—the social, labour, and cultural areas, as well as economic areas and the promotion of development. Although the PPP was supposed to do precisely this as a regional development programme, it was unable to convince the CC-SICA that it was promoting the "regional integration" that they want to see.

6.3 Integration from Below: The Mesoamerican Forums

Many Central American NGOs have had a longstanding relationship with Mexican NGOs since there was a lot of support coming from Mexico during their era of civil war. These close ties translated into the Mesoamerican Forums that took place from the launch of the PPP until 2011. The first one convened on 12 May 2001 in Tapachula, Mexico, shortly after the PPP was launched. Though some organisations believed that the forums promoted more unity and solidarity (Interviews 8, 38: 2006), others complained that all that came out of the discussions were watered-down declarations and that they did not further integration, cooperation, or solidarity among those who attended. These dissenting groups argued that time and resources should be spent helping the most vulnerable communities and not on complaining (Interview 9: 2006).

The closing declarations, published after each forum, were clear on what the approximately 500 organisations did not want; however, project proposals or petitions for government action were few. The impact of these declarations is almost as empty as those made by the presidents each year during the Tuxtla Mechanism.

The Mesoamerican forums included representatives of somewhere between 400 and 500 organisations (according to the list of those that signed the forum declarations, but some organisations claim that more were present) that gathered to discuss the common problems faced in Mesoamerica as well as discuss the PPP and, from 2008, Proyecto Mesoamerica. They rejected the PPP and all the trade agreements that had been signed or were in the process of being approved by the Mesoamerican Countries (i.e., CAFTA-DR at the time of negotiations). The organisations represented were mostly NGOs and community organisations, but they also included indigenous groups, small agricultural communities, and artisan workers. When I asked one of the organisers if they invited any government officials to participate, he said that they did not see any usefulness in doing so and, on the contrary, having them there could cause uneasiness and problems. Some of the indigenous groups and other Central American organisations still remember the harsh government repression during the civil war period, and they would not voice their opinions freely if they knew government officials were present (Interview 38: 2006). So, it is not only the government that does not include other actors in their decision-making processes; the forum organisers also decided not to include government representatives at their meetings.

The Second Mesoamerican Forum was held on 24 November 2001 in Guatemala, as a call to urgent action against the PPP. From then until December 2005, the forums were held once a year rotating among the Mesoamerican countries. Each panel was divided into large conferences and concurrent subject- specific round table discussions. At the end, an official declaration was produced, reiterating the rejection of the PPP and other regional projects, and highlighting the important points that came out of the conference. The first five forums focused on the PPP and its projects.[11] One representative from the AMAP affirmed that the forums managed to have several projects removed from the original PPP list, including two hydroelectric plants and corresponding dams (Interview 38: 2006). However, the PPP directives from several countries and the PPP Secretariat assured that those projects never formed part of the PPP (Interviews 3, 27, 19: 2006).

Interestingly, neither of these affirmations were confirmed through documentation, to prove or to negate the existence of these projects. The ministries of foreign affairs (MFA) in El Salvador said they had documentation of the original projects but were not able to find them as they had changed offices and the files were still in boxes. The 2006 PPP progress report published an official "revised" list of 99 projects, which did not include any hydroelectric plants (CG-PPP 2006). Regardless of whether these assertions are correct, the organisers of the forums had the satisfaction of a perceived victory.

According to the AMAP organisation in December 2005, the 6th Mesoamerican Peoples' Forum held in San José, Costa Rica included over 1300 delegates from 600 social organisations. This forum urged opposition to the implementation of CAFTA, which had been signed but was still being ratified by each country. For many of the participants, there was still not enough clarity about the relationship between the PPP and other regional projects, as well as the FTAs among the Mesoamerican countries. Many of the protests against the PPP attacked free trade, notwithstanding that the FTAs were in place before the PPP or were being negotiated independently from the PPP. Several of the NGOs interviewed had been part of the forums since the beginning. AMAP and UZICONI, for example, helped organise the conferences and attended all of them. They mentioned that it was inspiring to be with so many organisations that shared a common purpose: to help achieve "real development" in Mesoamerica and to stop the exploitation of its resources by big business.

Two and a half years expired before the next forum was held on 14–16 July 2008, in Managua, Nicaragua as a response to the replacement of the PPP with Proyecto Mesoamerica, nevertheless the panels prioritised discussions on the upcoming CAFTA as well as to the Association

[11] Information on the forums used to be found on www.foro-mesoamericano.org/resena-historica, now a dead link. RMALC still has several documents available in its historical archives. http://www.rmalc.org/historico/ppp/foros.php.html; http://www.rmalc.org/historico/eventos/viii_foro_mesoamericano/declaracion-minanitlan.htm.

Agreement with the European Union (Declaración VII Foro 2008). The official statement produced by the 7th Forum shows clear signs of improvement, in length and content, compared with its predecessors. Although it is still a document that states what the forum is against (90% of it), it does call for actions. In addition to supporting individual initiatives (like same-sex marriage in Costa Rica), its pleas for agrarian reform and greater democracy are more specific. Concerning agricultural reform, the statement argues that it should not just include land distribution, but also policies that support small and medium agriculture, rescuing native seeds, and prohibiting the use of genetically modified seeds (Declaración VII Foro 2008: 6). The declaration also suggests including initiatives to empower young people in the democratic process.

Out of the 54 organisations that responded to question 9 about attendance to the Mesoamerican Forums, only eight were unaware of the existence of these forums, which shows that there was effective communication between the forum organisers and their target audience. The majority had attended at least one of the forums (22) although only four had participated in all six until that point. Most interesting is that 21 organisations had not been able to attend but wanted to.

A representative of the Rigoberta Menchu Foundation (which did not answer the questionnaire), stated that the Guatemala branch of the foundation did not participate in the first six forums. The reason for not joining was that they had not seen any results from the first forums. They stated that they were not interested in large gatherings that produced declarations and workshops but no actions (Interview 9: 2006).

The declaration from the 8th Forum asserted that it contributed to the construction of thought and collective action through discussions and debates they could use to create an alternative regional social project. It reaffirms the commitment to continue deepening the relationship between social groups and movements in Mesoamerica and calls for:

> …the construction of a Mesoamerican model to govern from the bottom up, without any distinctions. To manage our own regional agenda, we need to advance with our own concepts of democracy and governance, and for that, we need to consolidate a true Mesoamerican Social Movement. (Declaración VII Foro 2008: 6)

The declaration's closing remarks reiterate the consolidation of a Mesoamerican Social Movement, so the forum would not be the main event, but part of the process. Although the next forum was scheduled to take place in Mexico in 2009, the date or city was not specified. Due to the military coup that took place in Honduras in 2009,[12] the organisers suspended the forum in favour of mobilising groups supporting President Zelaya to demonstrate "unity in the struggle against oppression." The 8th Forum was rescheduled to take place in Chiapas, Mexico, on 12–14 November; however, it didn't take place until 8, 9, and 10 April 2011, in Minatitlán, Veracruz. The 8th Forum focused on food security and declared that the organisations present "would defend native seeds and traditional knowledge" (Declaración VIII Foro 2001). Although introduced in 2015, Proyecto Mesoamerica includes food security as the 9th line of action within the social axis. Contrasting with the Forum Declaration, the Proyecto Mesoamerica fights hunger by providing technical support for family farms and distributing "conditioned" seeds.[13]

In addition to discussing food security, the 8th Forum also showed concern for the persecution faced by young people "for the only reason of being young" (Declaración VIII Foro 2001), referring to arbitrary detentions of young people that form part of the strategy against the *Maras* in Central America and Mexico, without evidence of their involvement in criminal activity.

During this encounter, the Movimiento Mesoamericano de los Pueblos was instituted as the official movement for the defence of the Mesoamerican people and called for a day of "mobilization" on 12 October 2011 for all organisations from Darien, Panamá to Tijuana, Mexico. The forums stopped taking place after 2011. Some of the organisations I contacted mentioned a lack of consensus regarding the way to proceed with the movement. A representative of Sipaz, in Chiapas (2018) said that organisations were dealing with more pressing matters, such as the displacement of peoples due to mining activities, territorial disputes, and violence. The Mexican Commission for the Defence and Promotion of Human Rights reports that in 2017, 20,390 people were

[12] 28 June 2009, President Zelaya was ousted and sent to Costa Rica, and a provisional government was put in place. Zelaya proposed changes to the Constitution that Congress rejected. For more information see http://www.derechos.org/nizkor/honduras/golpe/; http://www.latimes.com/world/mexico-americas/la-fg-a-honduran-coup-20150427-story.html.

[13] 2016 Avances del Proyecto Mesoamerica. The official report of 2017 calls them 'sustainable seeds' and says that "bean seeds adapted to withstand drought were distributed in El Salvador", p. 23.

forcibly displaced in Mexico; of these, 6090 displacements occurred in Chiapas, 5948 in Guerrero, 2700 in Oaxaca, and 60.44% belong to indigenous population (in Chiapas 100%).[14]

Two of the main organisers of the Mesoamerican Forums—AMAP and RMALC—stopped being active around 2014. However, one former directive of RMALC assures that the partner organisation that was active in the Mesoamerican forums (i.e., UZICONI) continues to fight against "deathly megaprojects and defending the land, constructing new alliances, and common fronts to coordinate efforts" (Interview 51: 2018). There are three organisations that seem to be filling the void, although they may not be related to the original Mesoamerican forums: (1) The M4, Movimiento Mesoamericano contra el Modelo Extractivo Minero (Mesoamerican Movement against the Extractive Mining Model), an umbrella organisation housing 70 NGOs (62 from Mesoamerica and 8 external), positioned against extractive mining, but also dealing with other issues (www.movimientom4.org). (2) Red Mesoamericana de Educación Popular Alforja, now expanded to include Mexico. This network focuses on publishing educational material to raise awareness on pressing issues for the region and supporting social movements. Red Alforja has ten (member) centres in the area, but it also holds workshops called "Escuela Mesoamericana," where non-member regional organisations gather to share their experiences and struggles (http://www.redalforja.net/). (3) Movimiento Mesoamericano Alternativas Populares al Capitalismo (MAPCA), began meeting in September 2011 hosting between 30 and 50 organisations each time. Most of the information about MAPCA can be found on the websites of member organisations or their Facebook page (https://www.facebook.com/AlternativasPopularesAlCapitalismo/).

As a final comment before moving on to business groups, replies to question 5 of the questionnaire show that the organisations polled prefer that development in Mesoamerica is tackled regionally rather than nationally. Sixteen out of 54 respondents were in favour of the governments of the eight countries (Colombia and the Dominican Republic were not full members at the time) working out a development strategy together, and 33 were in favour of them working "together including NGO's and International Organisations." Only 3 out of the 54 favoured

[14]For full report: http://www.cmdpdh.org/publicaciones-pdf/cmdpdh-informe-de-desplazamiento-interno-masivo-en-mexico-2017.pdf.

that each country worked out its development strategy on its own. The objections to many of the regional programmes then are not due to an overall opposition to regionalism or regional cooperation; instead, they oppose the methods that were used. NGOs and community groups would like to see the most vulnerable and marginalised populations taken into consideration when regional projects are drawn up or funds allocated. They want to see more actions and fewer governmental meetings. They agree with a model of integration that steers away from free trade and dependence on foreign funds (ICAES, FUNDE, Equipo Maiz).

6.4 Business

The business sector is by no means homogeneous, nor does it present a unified voice in regional policy. One reason why I used the term "governance" in my research rather than the preferred term by Latin American authors of "democratic governability" is since this term can include "private" or business actors. This inclusion is important because business is an important regionalising actor in the "new regionalism," not only at the macroregional level but also at the micro-regional level (see Gamble and Payne 1996; Breslin and Hook 2002; Hettne et al. 2000 as examples). As discussed in Chapter 3, many of the critics of the PPP felt that the real winners of the development project would be big business, particularly multinationals, and not the population represented in the region.

Bartra (2002) considers that only transnational (business) capital interests are being looked after in the PPP, an assertion seconded by others (see López Castellanos 2009). Rocha (2006) considers that large Mexican companies will also gain from the project, more so than their Central American Counterparts. Just a year after its launch, in June 2002, international and regional firms were invited to a meeting in Mérida (Mexico), so they could assess the "investment opportunities" in 28 PPP projects. Abel Pacheco, then President of Costa Rica said: "…in reality the presidents will not carry any weight in this meeting, only the businessmen interested in investing" (*Nación*, 26 June 2002).[15] Ultimately it was not a very successful meeting, leaving most of the financing up to the IDB, BCIE, CAF, and other international

[15] Presidentes centroamericanos buscan financiamiento para el Plan Puebla Panamá, article in *Nación* newspaper Costa Rica, published 26 June 2002 (www.nación.com).

organisations. The 2002 PPP progress report mentions ambiguously that a change would take place in financing mechanisms to "adapt to the nature of this process" (CG-PPP 2001: 21).

In the light of assertions that only sizeable national business would benefit from FTAs and such treaties, the two major Mexican business agglomerations, the Business Coordination Council (CCE) and the Industrial Chamber Confederation (Concamin), met with the Minister of Economy in 2006 to discourage the continuance of what they considered "light treaties." Both associations signalled that neither big nor small business was gleaning any benefits from the numerous trade agreements signed without their input. They requested that the government include the private sector in reviewing current trade agreements to find ways for Mexican industry to benefit from them, and in the negotiation of any new trade agreements (*Reforma*, 2 October 2006).[16]

The PPP 2002 report explained that the 5th Mesoamerican initiative, "Enabling commercial exchange," was to disburse the idea that "big business" was the priority. The report revealed that in addition to working with existing trade agreements and modernising customs procedures, this initiative would help SMEs find business opportunities in the MAR. To this end, three mechanisms were set up. First, gave technical assistance to the formation of clusters; second, promoted business opportunities through the dissemination of information online (including publishing information on regional trade fairs), and the third, increased "regional dialogue" through the creation of a virtual network of government entities that help the development of SMEs (CG-PPP 2001: 29–30). The Mesoamerican Competitive Council became a part of this initiative.

Conversations with the representatives of the Chambers of Commerce and the Mexican group ALANPYMES revealed that they believed that only groups of influential businessmen were consulted on matters of trade and had any input in the design of trade policy and PTAs and FTAs (Interviews 10, 18, 48: 2006). The Chambers, made up chiefly of medium and small enterprises, were not consulted but were later informed of the outcomes of these meetings. Even so, the chambers consider themselves in favour of integration, a stance that a regional organisation of chambers of commerce that operates on the Central America level, known

[16] "Rechazan empresarios firma de tratados 'light'", article by Dayna Meré in *Reforma*, printed edition, Monday, 2 October 2006.

as the Federation of Chambers of Commerce of the Central American Isthmus (FECAMCO) confirms. The FECAMCO initially included all Central America and recently incorporated the Dominican Republic and Colombia. The main topic on the agenda of their 45th reunion was that of integration followed by the discussion of the commercial agreements signed by the Central American countries (Interview 10: 2006).

Unlike the NGOs, the Chambers welcomed the infrastructure developments of the PPP. The representative of the Chamber of El Salvador mentioned that the time needed to transport goods in Central America had been cut considerably due to the improvements made to the Pan-American Highway. The consolidation of a Mesoamerican electrical grid (SIEPAC) together with the communications highway (fibre optic), benefited businesses. Both projects symbolised improvements in making businesses more competitive and efficient. Even though they have contact with the people of the PPP (this representative knew the Executive Secretary of the PPP personally), she had not approached the chamber in a working relationship. The chamber was invited to participate in the inauguration of projects (like the Pan-American Highway), but not in the decision-making processes; "…a workshop or something like that where we could propose something? No, we were given very little space" (Interview 18: 2006). They do receive invitations from SICA, but "they are not so frequent, and most of the people that go are government officials. I must admit that we don't always go; sometimes these meetings last several days, and you have to stay there, and that is difficult for us. The few times I have gone they are about 85 to 90% government officials" (Interview 18: 2006).

The representative from the Guatemalan chamber mentioned that they had a closer relationship with SIECA, based in Guatemala. "In general, when there is a meeting that involves a specific area of business, then they discuss the more political themes there [In SIECA], and we discuss them at the same time" (Interview 10: 2006). The chambers of commerce, in general, house SMEs and are usually not taken into consideration in these matters, whereas more significant and transnational business are sought out for their opinion or support.

Both chambers were positive about Central America starting to negotiate as a block (as encouraged by the EU) so that they could have better negotiating teams and a growing presence. "When Mexico or Colombia go to the WTO, they have teams of 35 or 40 people; but we can barely get a team of 15" (Interview 18: 2006). Getting a unified team to negotiate was difficult, and most of those interviewed blamed Costa Rica, who vetoed the inclusion of negotiators from Nicaragua in the group (Interview 23: 2006). As much as they welcomed the trade agreements, they felt that these would not give Central America commercial leverage. One mentioned that El Salvador had always been at a disadvantage when trading with the United States or Mexico, so a trade agreement made little difference in their trade relations; "...what it does do is set the rules; we have rules to play by, and so do they, and when they break the rules we have mechanisms to straighten things out" (Interview 18: 2006).

Though dispute settlement is a role that should be filled by the World Trade Organisation (WTO), to them it is evident that bilateral or regional trade agreements are more efficient, "it used to be that if we had a problem and we could not resolve it amicably, then it was supposed to be taken to the WTO, but then we would think that it would never get resolved or would take too long and cost a lot more than it was worth, so we only did it for very, very large problems" (Interview 18: 2006). Although in Costa Rica there was higher resistance and controversy over the ratification of CAFTA-DR, in both El Salvador and Guatemala, their view was that Central America had already been open to US exports for some time, just like it had been open to Mexican products, but both the United States and Mexico had placed many obstacles to Central American products. The PTA signed with Mexico had already helped with certain Central American exports, "for example, pharmaceuticals. Mexican products entered Central America without any problems, but we could not export; it took two years to resolve, but now it is solved; before the PTA it was unthinkable, you really couldn't export to Mexico" (Interview 18: 2006).

Even though they welcomed the advances in infrastructure that had taken place as part of the PPP initiatives, they were surprised to hear about other aspects of the PPP that dealt with business and commerce. For example, when I asked about the effectiveness of the Mesoamerican Competitive Council (CMC), which had been set up as part of the 5th Mesoamerican Initiative, they had not heard about it. The National Chambers of Commerce of two of the countries had not been approached or received any training from the CMC whereas, in the PPP offices, I was told that it was a great mechanism that was having a considerable impact on regional trade with outside blocks. It seemed strange that a tool aimed at helping regional businesses (particularly

SMEs) to be more competitive had not approached the chambers or the FECAMCO (the Guatemala Chamber held the presidency at the time of the interview) for input in its design, nor had they offered expertise or training.

The transition to Proyecto Mesoamerica increased the emphasis on trade and infrastructure. The economic pillar included projects in the following categories: transport, energy, telecommunications, trade facilitation, and competitiveness. The latter began with facilitating border controls and customs crossings and creating a database with competitiveness indicators. As the 10th anniversary of Proyecto Mesoamerica approached in January 2018, representatives of the FECAMCO were invited to a meeting with representatives of Proyecto Mesoamerica to "understand the regional work they each do, agree on their alliance and cooperation, and dialogue on the creation of the Mesoamerican Business Council."[17]

6.5 Horizontal Governance at the Local Level

Regionalism in Mesoamerica has tended to concentrate its efforts on region-wide projects or intergovernmental cooperation at the national level. The PPP, SICA, Proyecto Mesoamerica, Tuxtla Mechanism, and even the MBC focus on projects with a broad scope. As I previously discussed, regional projects are mostly designed and implemented at the national level of government, with little input from the lower levels of government and with little power given to the regional institutions. Similarly, other actors like civil society organisations, NGOs, and chambers of commerce are granted a reduced space for participating or even to provide feedback. Although the SICA system does have mechanisms for participation, these are still undergoing reforms and have ways to go before being considered inclusive. Finding themselves left out of the official regional consults, these groups have organised alternative networks to meet needs that surpass their scope. These regional networks tend to take place in parallel to the official institutions and do not include government participation in their activities.

However, at the local level, in several cases, there was a shift away from the separatist dynamic. Notwithstanding the numerous claims of

[17] http://www.proyectomesoamerica.org/index.php/comunicacion/seccion-noticias/20-noticiaspm/articulos-noticias/260-noticias-enero-2018.html.

corruption and lack of governance that occur at the local level, there is a new generation of municipal governments that are breaking away from past practices and want to demonstrate that governmental accountability is possible. These municipalities find themselves in the same situation as most other municipalities, in that they are allotted few resources and have little power. For these municipal governments to achieve anything beyond registering births and handing out death and marriage certificates, they form coalitions or alliances with NGOs, local commerce, and civil society groups to get the support they need. In Perulapía, El Salvador, the municipal government sought financial assistance from NGOs to carry out public works, provide employment possibilities, and offer political awareness workshops. The municipal government showed the NGOs that their proposals were congruent with the needs and wants of the local people by presenting the results from "round tables" held periodically with any citizen that wanted to attend. The NGOs requested transparent accounting and reserved their right to audit any accounting or assess the projects. This municipal government showed that even though it did not receive much support from the central government, it could network with other municipalities in Central America (Chapter 5) as well as NGOs to provide governance to its inhabitants (Interview 44: 2006).

Although this positive example of local governance cannot be generalised to all Mesoamerica, it is a practice that has been on the upswing in the region. Several local and regional groups like FUNDE (El Salvador), Alforja (regional network), and FUNPADEM (Costa Rica) are working with municipal governments to carry out projects. Some of the projects limit their scope to working with one municipal government and providing one specific service or need. However, several of their most successful projects have involved more than one municipality, often across national borders (Interviews 8, 17, 20: 2006). They range from environmental protection, agriculture (mostly coffee and livestock), border trading, water, and even financial matters, particularly in municipalities that receive many remittances from abroad. A representative of FUNDE, in charge of the "Regional, Local Area," mentioned that at the time of the interview, formal government policy or state strategy did not exist for these kinds of projects and partnerships, even though they began on a small scale since around 1995.

> For the most part, the NGOs initiate the processes, and then the governments recognise them and include them in their agenda and develop strategies... now the projects are taking on a different orientation, instead of vertical, a little more horizontal, though when there is more intervention by the states, then they give less space to civil society. (Interview 17: 2006)

Environmental issues are usually the ones that traverse national borders; the Gulf areas and common protected areas generate the most projects. Communities and municipal authorities tend to accept these projects often financed through NGOs and sometimes international organisations.

> In protected areas, we work with the people to ensure that they care for the environment, while also finding ways for them to carry out economic activities. You see some of the poorest people in the protected areas because they do not have access to the resources. Finding ways to care for the environment that also generate wealth is even more important in border areas, where authorities are weaker. (Interview 8: 2006)

The main issues that hinder cooperation between the government and non-governmental actors at the local level are similar to those between the regional level and the central government. The first is the lack of professional civil service, suggesting that changes in government structure can derail an entire project.

> As happens in all the local governments, not just in the [Gulf] area, many of the setbacks of the binational programme were because there were elections in El Salvador in 2006 and there was a change of government in Honduras in 2005, so it weakened the process because we had to explain what was happening to the new Mayors; the other groups kept working, but the government was immobilised for some time. (Interview 17: 2006)

Second, when municipal governments belong to different political parties, they do not always agree to participate in a project. In El Salvador, where municipal associations have become popular (Enríquez Villacorta 2005: 28), political party discipline has become a problem "when political party policy states that they cannot get together and think like Mayors, instead they must think as members of their political party, over and above their role as municipal governments" (Interview 17: 2006). The third problem is that the government is still centralised, so projects remain very limited, "we cannot do this without national decentralisation processes. We cannot work on development processes along the borders or the rural areas until there is a national policy of decentralisation; in fact, there should be a regional decentralisation policy" (Interview 8: 2008).

Projects along the borders of the states in the region have been on the rise. Alforja credits some of this increase to the EU which has encouraged development in the border areas.[18] One model developed by municipalities that share borders was to create a fund for local development and then, foment exchanges between the local institutions, businesses, and population so that close links exist in all areas. Costa Rica has had several multidimensional projects across its borders with Nicaragua and Panamá. There were varied results even though the projects were similar in nature; projects with Panamá were more successful. Although projects with both countries (mostly environmental) have the same elements, government relations between Costa Rica and Panamá are better than those between Costa Rica and Nicaragua, resulting in different outcomes (Interview 8: 2006).

One author, active with FUNDE, indicates that a "transborder local development" project entails joint cooperation of various local, regional, national, and international actors as well as local government, national government, civil society, NGOs, and business (which she says should include micro, small, medium, and macro business) (Gernaert Willmar 2006: 2). The project that exemplifies their activities is in the border area called "Trifinio," which includes the border areas of Honduras, Nicaragua, and El Salvador; this is a clear tri-national strategy that is part of the government's policy and has the support of local government, NGOs, business and civil society (Interview 17: 2006).[19] This cross-border project signed in 1986, was part of the peace process supported by the OAS and the American Institute for Cooperation on Agriculture. The success of these projects has to do with a congruent policy that has the input and support of its inhabitants, local government, NGOs, and business as well as that of the central government of the three countries who, though not the initiator, has been a facilitator. The Trifinio Plan was reviewed and strengthened in 2004 and

[18] The BCIE and the EU launched a development programme for border areas, which is developed in nine micro-regions, five are cross-border municipalities and four are shared river basins (OECD 2005; www.sica.org).

[19] See www.sica.int/trifinio.

incorporated into the SICA framework. The OECD regional report considers that the "Trifinio Plan has greatly contributed to the physical integration of the borderland belt and the promotion of socio-economic development and the conservation of the Montecristo Cloud Forest and the Fraternity Biosphere Reserve" (OECD 2005: 184). It estimates that the project has benefited nine municipalities directly and 22 indirectly.

6.6 Summary

Governance across the horizontal level is the weakest sphere of governance in the MAR (OECD 2005), albeit it is a crucial element to give policies and projects the legitimacy, accountability, and cooperation required. Although some examples of successful governance can be found, particularly at the local level, these are the exception and not the rule. Governance in Mesoamerica is characterised (noting that there are exceptions to this statement) by a lack of "formal" participatory mechanisms. As pointed out by authors such as Vargas Roldán (1999), Segreda and Camacho (1999), and Arce Tena (2006), a lack of mechanisms for participation in governance leads to involvement by other means, such as through NGOs or resistance movements. Even though these provide essential forums for expressing views other than the government's, they do not make up a "participatory democracy."

As I have pointed out, resistance movements may represent a minority of the population, but one that is well organised and vocal. Civic associations (referring here to global civic associations but can be applied to regional) do not necessarily mean greater democracy, where "in the south as well as the north, many NGOs are self-elected and follow no formal procedures to ensure transparency of their operations and accountability towards those whom they claim to serve" (Scholte 2001: 30). In this chapter, I have shown that when there are "formal" participatory mechanisms, as with the CC-SICA and the creation of the ALIDES, they have positive outcomes. CC-SICA is not always successful in changing or influencing policy, but it has had some success in including some changes as well as proposing[20] themes and issues that they would like to see added. The Mesoamerican forums have provided

[20]For more information, see www.sica.int/ccsica as well as CC-SICA publications as outlined in the Bibliography.

additional points for discussion and have brought forth greater awareness to the problems facing the region. However, they have not engaged in dialogue with policymakers, so they have had less influence on policy. I argue, from my observation of the course of events, that they have played a role in removing the PPP out of the spotlight so that groups after 2005 had first to state that the PPP was still marching forth, before denouncing undesired PPP activity (see López Castellanos 2009).

Participation of the business sector in governance is not as easy to define, even though some authors (Chapter 3) stipulated that the PPP was created for big business and, for many, *Proyecto Mesoamerica* confirmed this premise. The lack of increased business investments in Mesoamerica and the complaint by some business associations on the direction of trade policy show that this is not necessarily the case. Also, as this investigation points out, the SMEs were not only not consulted on the PPP projects; many were not even aware of the projects specifically designed to help them "seek out the business opportunities in the region and create business networks" (CG-PPP 2001: 30). *Proyecto Mesoamerica* has maintained trade and infrastructure at the forefront of its projects; however, it was almost ten years later in January 2018, that it sought partnerships with regional players.

Bibliography

Acta que institucionaliza el Mecanismo del Plan Puebla-Panamá. 2004. http://www.sieca.org.gt/Sitio-publico/OACUERDOS/83-1Acta.htm. Accessed 3 March 2006.

Arce Tena, Carlos A. 2006. *La gobernabilidad democrática: una perspectiva para el desarrollo*. México, D.F.: Ediciones Miguel Ángel Porrúa.

Available on http://web.archive.org/web/20071029105130; http://www.planpuebla-panama.org/.

Bartra, Armando. 2002. Hacia una Nueva Colonización del Sureste. In *Economía Política del Plan Puebla Panamá*, ed. Alejandro Álvarez Béjar, Andrés Barreda Marín, and Armando Bartra. México: Editorial Itaca.

Breslin, Shaun, and Glenn D. Hook (eds.). 2002. *Microregionalism and World Order*. New York: Palgrave Macmillan.

CCAD-MBC. 2003. *Estrategia regional para la conservación y uso sostenible de la biodiversidad en Mesoamérica (ERB)*. Comisión Centroamericana de Ambiente y Desarrollo El Salvador.

CCAD-MBC. 2005. *Programa Estratégico Regional Para la Conectividad*. Comisión Centroamericana de Ambiente y Desarrollo El Salvador.

CCAD-MBC-PM. 2013. *Plan Director CBM 2020.* Gestión territorial sostenible en el Corredor Biológico Mesoamericano.

CC-SICA. 2006. *Plan de Acción para el Fortalecimiento del CC-SICA 2006.* San José, Costa Rica: FUNPADEM.

CC-SICA Informe de Consulta. 2003. *Estrategia de Modernización del Estado y Perfil de la estrategia para la Integración Regional.* San José, Costa Rica: FUNPADEM.

CEPAL. 2015. *Una mirada a los países del Proyecto Mexoamèrica.* Documento de Proyectos, Estudios e Investigaciones—Sede subregional México. Documento elaborado para la XV Cumbre del Mecanismo de Diálogo y Concertación de Tuxtla Ciudad de Guatemala Guatemala Viernes, 26 de junio de 2015. Naciones Unidas, Impreso en México D.F. LC/MEX/L.1183. http://repositorio.cepal.org.

CONADECO. 2005. *5to Congreso Nacional de Asociaciones de Desarrollo Comunal, Costa Rica, 29–30 de Octubre de 2004 Memoria.* San José, Costa Rica: CONADECO.

Coordinación General del Plan Puebla-Panamá (CG-PPP). 2001. *Plan Puebla Panamá: Presentación Diagnóstico Centroamérica.* México: INEGI. http://web.archive.org/web/20071029105130/; http://www.planpuebla-panama.org/.

Coordinación General del Plan Puebla-Panamá (CG-PPP). 2002. *Informe de Avances y Perspectivas Plan Puebla-Panamá Junio 2002.* México: INEGI.

Coordinación General del Plan Puebla-Panamá (CG-PPP). 2006. *Informe de Avances y Perspectivas Plan Puebla-Panamá Junio 2006.* Mexico: INEGI. http://web.archive.org/web/20071029105130/; http://www.planpuebla-panama.org/.

Coordinadora regional de los altos de Chiapas de la sociedad civil en resistencia. 2002. Plan Puebla – Panamá: Un proyecto de "Desarrollo" …¿Para quién? http://www.nadir.org/nadir/initativ/agp/free/colobmia/puebla/pueblapanama.htm.

Dávila Enrique, Kessel Georgina, and Levy Santiago. 2002. El Sur también existe: un ensayo sobre el desarrollo regional de México (originally published in Economía Mexicana, vol. 11, 202–260). In *Ensayos Sobre el Desarrollo Económico y Social de México*, compilador Santiago Levy. México: Fondo de Cultura Económica.

Declaración de Guatemala. 2000. Declaración Conjunta de la IV Cumbre de los Jefes de Estado y de Gobierno de los países integrantes del Mecanismo de Diálogo y Concertación de Tuxtla, 25 de Agosto de 2000. http://www.sieca.org.gt/publico/OACUERDOS/TuxtlaIV.htm.

Declaración de Mérida. 2002. Declaración Conjunta de la quinta cumbre del Mecanismo de Diálogo y Concertación de Tuxtla, 27 y 28 de junio 2002. http://sieca.org.gt/Publico/OACUERDOS/DeclaraciondeMerida.htm.

Declaración de Tapachula. 2001. Photocopy of Text.

Declaración Extraordinaria. 2001. Declaración Conjunta de la Cumbre extraordinaria de los países integrantes del Mecanismo de Diálogo y Concertación de Tuxtla. http://sieca.org.gt/publico/OACUERDOS/DECLARACION_CONJUNTA_DE_LA.

Declaración Política del VII Foro Mesoamericano de los Pueblos ¡Mesoamerica en Resistencia, no al neocolonialismo del libre comercio! 2008. http://Chiapas.indymedia.org/local/webcast/uploads/declaracion_vii_mesoamericano.pdf.

Declaración VIII Foro. 2001. VIII Foro Mesoamericano de los Pueblos. Declaración de Minatitlán 13 de abril de 2011 Minga informativa de Movimientos Sociales. http://movimientos.org.

Delgado-Wise, Raúl. 2004. The Hidden Agenda of Mexico's Fox Administration. *Latin American Perspectives* 31 (5): 146–164.

Dirección Ejecutiva Proyecto de Integración y Desarrollo de Mesoamérica. 2008. Informe de Actividades 2008. El Salvador. www.planpuebla-panama.org. Accessed 4 November 2008.

Enríquez Villacorta, Alberto. 2005. Desarrollo local y descentralización del Estado, nuevos factoes de la Integración Centroamericana. *Alternativas Para el Desarrollo* 93 (Abril–Mayo). FUNDE San Salvador.

European Commission (EC). 2002. Regional Strategy Paper for Central America 2002–2006.

FUNDE/PNUD. 2004. *Asociación de Municipios y Construcción Regional para el Desarrollo*. Desarrollo Humano: Buenas Prácticas Enero 2004 N°03.

Gamble, Andrew, and Anthony Payne (eds.). 1996. *Regionalism and World Order*. London: Macmillan Press Ltd.

Gernaert Willmar, Silvina. 2006. *Desarrollo Local Transfronterizo: territorios, fronteras e integración centroamericana*. Segunda Parte Alternativas Para El Desarrollo No. 97 Enero-Febrero-Marzo 2006 FUNDE.

Guevara Bermúdez, José Antonio (ed.). 2018. Episodios de Desplazamiento Interno Forzado Masivo en México. Informe 2017 CDMPDH, PADF, USAID. http://www.cmdpdh.org/publicaciones-pdf/cmdpdh-informe-de-desplazamiento-interno-masivo-en-mexico-2017.pdf.

Hettne, Björn, András Inotal, and Osvaldo Sunkel (eds.). 2000. *The New Regionalism and the Future of Security and Development*. London: Macmillan.

Informe Ejecutivo. 2006. El PPP: Avances retos y Perspectivas. http://web.archive.org/web/20071029105130/; http://www.planpuebla-panama.org/.

Informe Ejecutivo. 2008. El PPP: Avances retos y Perspectivas. http://web.archive.org/web/20071029105130/; http://www.planpuebla-panama.org/.

Informe Estado de la Región en Desarrollo Humano Sostenible. 2008. http://www.estadonacion.or.cr/estadoregion2008.

López Castellanos, Nayar. 2009. *Del Plan Puebla-Panamá al Proyecto Mesoamérica: un espejo de la globalización*. México: Neoliberal Plaza y Valdés Editores.

OECD Territoral Reviews. 2005. *The Mesoamerican Region: Southeastern Mexico and Central America*. OECD. http://www.oecd.org/mexico/oecdterritorialreviewsthemesoamericanregionsoutheasternmexicoandcentralamerica.htm.

Proyecto Mesoamérica. 2017a. Informe Estado de Proyectos PM 2008–2016. http://www.proyectomesoamerica.org/index.php/comunicacion/kit-de-comunicaciones-pm/comunicados-de-prensa.html.

Proyecto Mesoamérica. 2017b. Resumen Ejecutivo de Proyecto Mesoamérica 2008–2017. http://www.proyectomesoamerica.org/index.php/comunicacion/kit-de-comunicaciones-pm/comunicados-de-prensa.html.

Proyecto Mesoamérica. 2017c. Proyecto de Integración y Desarrollo de Mesoamérica y los Objetivos de Desarrollo Sostenible. http://www.proyectomesoamerica.org/index.php/comunicacion/kit-de-comunicaciones-pm/comunicados-de-prensa.html.

Rocha, Alberto. 2006. La geopolítica de México en Centroamérica: ¿una hegemonía regional? In *Geoeconomía y Geopolítica en el área del Plan Puebla Panamá*, ed. Daniel Villafuerte Solis and Xochitl Leyva Solano. México: Editorial Miguel Angel Porrúa.

Scholte, Jan Aart. 2001. The Globalization of World Politics. In *The Globalization of World Politics: An Introduction to International Relations*, ed. John Baylis and Steve Smith, 2nd ed. Oxford: Oxford University Press.

Segreda, Luis, and Daniel Camacho. 1999. El Papel de la ONG en el Proceso de la Integración Centroamericana, Democracia y Derechos Humanos: La experiencia del CODEHUCA. In *Hacia una Integración desde Abajo. Participación, Sociedad Civil e Integración Centroamericana*, ed. Ricardo Grinspun, Carlos Alvarenga, and Shamsie Yasmine. San Salvador: Talleres Gráficos UCA.

SRE/UNIFEM/PNUD. 2004. *Foro Regional de Reflexión Sobre las Metas Del Milenio y la Equidad de Género en el Marco del Plan Puebla-Panamá: Memoria*. ISBN:0-912917-95-4. SRE/UNIFEM/PNUD Impreso en México.

Vargas Roldán, Jorge. 1999. Corrupción, Gobernabilidad y Sociedad Civil en Centroamérica. In *Hacia una Integración desde Abajo. Participación, Sociedad Civil e Integración Centroamericana*, ed. Ricardo Grinspun, Carlos Alvarenga, and Shamsie Yasmine. San Salvador: Talleres Gráficos UCA.

Interviews

3. Director of Integration, Ministerio de Relaciones Exteriores Guatemala, 25 September 2006, Guatemala City.

7. Coordinator Human Development, Dirección Ejecutiva Plan Puebla Panamá,1 September 2006, San Salvador.
8. Centro de Estudios y Publicaciones Alforja, 17 October 2006, Costa Rica, San José.
9. Fundación Rigoberta Menchú, 26 September 2006, Guatemala.
10. Commercial Relations Coordinator, Cámara de Comercio de Guatemala, 27 September 2006.
16. Regional Director of CODA International El Salvador (Project liaison with Perulapía), 6 September 2006, San Salvador, Perulapía.
17. Regional Local Area Director, Fundación Nacional para el Desarrollo (FUNDE), 5 September 2006, San Salvador.
18. Director of Economic Affairs, Cámara de Comerico e Industria de El Salvador, 1 September 2006, San Salvador.
19. Executive, Dirección Ejecutiva Plan Puebla Panamá, 4 September 2006, San Salvador.
20. Fundación para la Democracia (FUNPADEM) (Background information conversation not recorded), 17, 18, 19 October 2006.
22. Director, Instituto Centroamericano de Estudios Sociales (ICAES) (CCT), 17 October 2006, San José, Costa Rica.
27. PPP Initiatives Coordinator, Oficina local del Plan Puebla Panamá en El Salvador, Ministerio de Relaciones Exteriores El Salvador, 5 September 2006, San Salvador.
32. Former Guerrilla Leader, Professor, Universidad Francisco Gavidia, 1 September and 7 September 2006, El Salvador (Informal conversations, took notes, not recorded).
35. Director of Cooperation, Fondo de Desarrollo Indígena Guatemalteco, 25 September 2006, Guatemala City.
36. FUNPADEM, 18 de Octubre 2006, Costa Rica.
38. AMAP Director, Mexican Association for the Self-Determination of Peoples (AMAP), 22 August 2006, Mexico City.
44. Full day meeting and visit with the local government of San Bartolomé de la Perulapía municipality in El Salvador, the Mayor Guillermo Sanchez and 5 other local government representatives. All those involved in the meeting were members of the FSLN Political Party, 6 September 2006, El Salvador.
45. Full day participation Oportunidades/Progresa Córdoba assessment exercise, August 2008, Veracruz.
48. Asociación Latinoamericana de Micro, Pequeños y Medianos Empresarios (ALAMPYME), one of the founding organisations in the Red Mexicana de Acción contra el Libre Comercio (RMALC) Interview, 29 November 2006, Mexico City.

49. General and Alternative Medical Doctor. Did his social service by attending medical brigades in marginalised Mexican rural communities, November 2008.

51. Informal correspondence with former members of CIEPAC and RMALC on what happened to the Mesoamerican forums, February–March 2017.

Conferences Attended

"Gestión integrada de programas sociales y autoridad social: experiencias latinoamericanas", Dr. Rolando Franco, Facultad Latinoamericana de Ciencias Sociales y Centro de Estudios para el Futuro FLACSO, Tuesday 17 October 2006, San José, Costa Rica, 10:00 a.m.

"Gobernabilidad Democrática y Nuevas Orientaciones Políticas en Costa Rica: escenarios a partir de las elecciones 2006" organised by Centro de Estudios Políticos, Maestría Centroamericana de Ciencias Políticas, UCR, Facultad Latinoamericana de Ciencias Sociales y Centro de Estudios para el Futuro FLACSO, 17 October 2006, 8:00 p.m.

"Indigenous People in Mexico" presented by Lynda Martinez del Campo Fonda del Claustro, Mexico City, 17 March 2007.

"Multi-level Governance and Systems of Economic Organisation' Workshop", 17–19 May 2007, University of Warwick, Scarman House.

CHAPTER 7

Conclusion

Mesoamerica is host to a web of regionalisms, regionalisation, and networks; so many that it has been impossible to cover all of them in this volume. Throughout this research, I was constantly referred to another network, organisation, or publication centre in the region. And there is a whole other realm of (negative) regional networking in Mesoamerica that I barely touched upon in this book: that of organised crime, people smuggling, drug trafficking, *Maras*, etc. What became evident is that the MAR is becoming more intricately linked through its regional institutions and informal networks. Governance is a growing problem, particularly when it involves decision-making at the regional level and implementation at the local level. As in the case of PARLACEN (described in Chapter 4), instead of effectively reforming the institution, parliamentarians in Central America meet and discuss items with a regional impact in a different venue (Interview 31: 2006). The inefficiencies of the governments and regional institutions, coupled with their unwillingness to allow full participation of those outside the political class, has encouraged many sectors to create alternative regional networks. There are business, agricultural, indigenous, publication, and regional studies networks. Beyond the 20+regional forums a year in Mesoamerica (though some only involve Central America) linked to its regional institutions (Interview 19: 2006), the various networks frequently hold regional symposiums, conferences, and workshops. The Mesoamerican forums hosted representatives of up to 600 organisations

A. Gamboa, *Regional Integration, Development, and Governance in Mesoamerica*,
https://doi.org/10.1007/978-3-030-25350-9_7

in their regional meetings. Thus, it can safely be assumed that these organisations and networks sense that they can reach their objectives if they group with similar regional groups. Small organic coffee growers from southern Mexico to Costa Rica network together to share techniques and compare prices. NGOs like the Rigoberta Menchu Foundation have extended their offices from Guatemala to Mexico to address the problems faced by the Maya community and raise awareness in both countries (Interview 9: 2006).

I set out to draw out observations and reflect on the experience of regionalism, development, and security in Mesoamerica introduced through the PPP regional project and continued through Proyecto Mesoamerica. To do so I introduced both the MAR and the PPP in the first chapter. I provided some background information on the origins of the PPP as well as the influence of the relationship of the MAR with the United States. I aimed to look at the relationship between regionalism and regionalisation during the seven years of the PPP.

Chapter 2 shifted from the specific issue of the PPP to the broader subject of regions, regionalism, regionalisation, and regionness. I defined these terms in order to classify the different schemes and movements in a clear manner (Gamble and Payne 1996; Hettne 2000). Regions could expand and contract at different times; they were constructed by several actors and could change direction (see Grugel and Hout 1999; Hettne 2000). I explored part of the history of Latin American regionalism to know how the "spaghetti bowl" phenomenon came about, as well as the debates between hemispheric integration versus Latin American integration. I discussed an overview of literature on regionalism, and I presented three commonalities as a useful tool to identify what is meant by "new regionalism." From this understanding, I introduced the New Regionalism Approach as a framework that would help situate the extent of the regionalisation of the MAR at the point of the creation of the PPP through the use of the "degrees of regionness" (see Hettne and Söderbaum 2000, 2002). I based this framework on the more recent writings of Hettne and Söderbaum, with an emphasis on the constructivist elements of their approach. The "return to the political" (Hettne 2003) was a significant element, as the importance of the internal workings of a region is brought back into the equation in contrast to the earlier versions that emphasised the changing world order (Hettne et al. 1999, 2000). Considering there are varying "degrees of regionness," I explored the relationship between regionalism and regionalisation.

I explained some of the debates regarding governance as a concept, as well as its uses in Latin America. I then demonstrated, by using the governance analytical framework, that governance is an intermediary variable because it produces effects on a dependent variable and depends itself on independent variables. It is "a tool to systematise the social, political, and institutional complexity of the process for formulating and implementing collective decision" (Hufty 2009: 1). Instead of using the theoretical debates on governance, I discussed the current modes of governance to show how they were influential in the process of regionalisation.

In Chapter 3 I reviewed the issues and debates that surrounded the PPP or the MAR, noting that although the literature regarding each of the countries or Central America as a whole was plentiful and provided valuable information, it did not contribute to the objectives of this research. As most of the literature written about the MAR and the PPP focuses on debates and issues, I formatted the chapter to address the main issues and debates highlighting the importance of these without engaging in them. The purpose was not to reach a verdict on the PPP, but to draw insights pertinent to the study of regions and how regions are made and unmade. However, the relevant criterion applied in this research pertains to the overlapping of regional schemes as well as the applicability of a multidimensional and multifaceted scheme in the MAR.

One subject that is not as readily available in the literature is that of governance. While most authors focused on the issues or pointed out the weaknesses of the PPP, in a region where so many different regional arrangements co-exist, overlap, and interact with many other actors, effective modes of governance are required to coordinate and implement policies. The OECD (2005) report shows many issues of ineffective governance and recommends striving for effective "multi-level governance" through institutional reform. However, the findings of this research question whether institutional restructuring is enough to bring about effective governance in Mesoamerica or whether external players can put multilevel governance into place.

Chapter 4 honed in on the MAR and the regionalism that is taking place in a context of overlapping regional projects. What is becoming known as "spaghetti bowl" regionalism (see Vega 2006) is clearly present in the MAR, where individual countries are members of several different regional institutions, each with a different scope or timespan. This complicates the overall effectiveness of subscribing to the regional institutions since there is a lack of homogeneity in policies and best practice.

Adding the PPP to the existing regional institutions created confusion as to which organism is responsible for the different areas of regional cooperation and how to best utilise their resources.

The PPP did not initiate regionalism in Mesoamerica. It did not create the MAR, nor did it drive the networks that are expanding from south-eastern Mexico down to Colombia. However, it did change the *modus operandi* of many of these organisms in Mesoamerica. The PPP highlighted the inefficiencies of having a web of regional arrangements operating in the same area (OECD 2005). I noted that the lack of coordination and communication with other regional institutions often caused duplicate efforts or took away funding from another organisation. Instead of pooling their efforts to maximise their impact on regional integration and development projects, the prevailing outcome was competition between them—they were more rivals than partners.

In Chapter 4, I introduce some of the regional instruments that had been in place prior to the PPP and explain how these interacted with it. As an intergovernmental organisation, most decisions needed to be unanimous: one interviewee called this a "dictatorship of the minority" (Interview 25: 2006). Outcomes will often represent the lowest common denominator or the position of the least advanced member state (Jachtenfuchs 2001: 251).

In this chapter I also highlight institutional changes made during the PPP's timespan as a reaction to the problems that arose, as well as the restructuring that formed part of the transformation to *Proyecto Mesoamerica*. Nevertheless, the issues involved with implementing the PPP were not solely due to the institutional weaknesses at the regional level, and therefore the attempts made by *Proyecto Mesoamerica* to remedy the problems at this level did not guarantee success. As I have emphasised, the PPP was multidimensional and multifaceted. It was a regional instrument based on eight very diverse initiatives and required the involvement of several government departments to deal with the areas included.

In Chapter 4, I categorise four "regions": economy and trade; developmental; environmental; and security. The PPP was designed to have a positive impact on trade and economic integration in the MAR as well as motivate development and safeguard the environment. These three "regions," however, matured at different rates. While interconnectivity and trade facilitation were a priority; trade relations improved along with road construction, infrastructure, and border coordination.

Environmental projects through the MBC also improved significantly (though not precisely through PPP initiatives), and the MBC was chosen as the appropriate instrument to continue overseeing environmental issues in *Proyecto Mesoamerica*. However, due to problems implementing the social development aspects of the PPP, such as healthcare, education, and access to basic services, there was little impact. *Proyecto Mesoamerica* eliminated several projects (the Mesoamerican Cooperation Programme took over some of them) and reorganised others. One new approach for the health initiative was to use a public–private partnership to fund and monitor the activities of the programme. The security region was more difficult to assess since the PPP did not include "security" under its scope.

Nevertheless, regional security is one of the most pressing issues in Mesoamerica today, and so several efforts at regional cooperation have been undertaken. Mexico, for example, has asked to be included in SICA meetings discussing the *Maras* problem and has been a critical player in the Alliance for Prosperity and the Conference on Prosperity and Security in Central America. Notwithstanding these mechanisms, regional cooperation on security was not institutionalised; collaboration still takes place on a case-by-case occurrence.

In Chapter 5, I deal with the area of governance. I note that some of the countries in the MAR had recently returned to democratic governments, but in some cases their level of democracy only reached as far as holding periodic elections. Even these are questionable with recent examples in the controversial Mexican 2006 elections, the violent elections in 2009 in El Salvador, and the coup ousting the government of Manuel Zelaya in Honduras in 2009. In addition to claims of corruption and undemocratic practices (such as rigged elections), there is also a problem of vertical governance and coordination within the government structures. At the central government level, I note that the different government ministries often "protected their own corner" (Interview 3: 2006) and did not fully cooperate. In general, party politics influence legislative bodies more than the voting citizen.

At the sub-national level, the Mexican states were the primary example, since initially they were given the same status as the Central American countries. Mexican state governments were not involved in creating the PPP and, though initially they were excited about receiving extra funds for projects, they did not necessarily use the funds for their intended purposes. Even in cases where the funds had their intended use (i.e., building a hospital), the state governor would inaugurate the project as a state initiative without mentioning the PPP. Local governments had been even less involved in the creation of the PPP. Although local governments should have been the most engaged in implementing the project in areas of health, disaster prevention, and education, the plan did not reach this level in most of the MAR. On the other hand, I note the lack of resources given to the local government to carry out the delivery of public goods, while many municipal governments opted for joining with others to pool their existing resources or obtain more from external sources. This situation takes place among municipalities within national borders as well as across them. In conclusion, I establish in this chapter that government structure would have been better placed to get involved in implementing an instrument like the PPP if:

1. Those expected to carry out the project were involved in creating it, integrating their needs and priorities, and
2. They were provided with the resources required and were held accountable for their use.

One of the most notable signs that there were problems with the PPP was that numerous groups of NGOs and civil society networks gathered explicitly to oppose the regional project. In Chapter 6, I propose that in addition to having the different levels of government involved in creating a multifaceted and multidimensional regional project, other actors also need to get involved. The PPP tried to engage other participants through the Consultative Committee (created more as an afterthought) once it was up and running. Moreover, the testimonies of those interviewed explain why the PPP directives were unable to explain the practical application of the outcome from the consults. I present the concerns of non-governmental actors towards the purpose and creation of the PPP. The NGOs, civil society networks, trade unions, and chambers of commerce that I interviewed were favourable to the idea of a regional development strategy and the strengthening of regional cooperation. As they pointed out, they had their alternative regional networks in place. Their primary complaint related to the fact that they were not engaged in the process that created regional policy (such as in the PPP). These groups reciprocated by not inviting any government representatives to participate in their forums and workshops. There seemed to be little willingness for dialogue from these non-governmental actors.

The main culprit for the absence of dialogue was the lack of trust, a consequence of past experiences and broken promises.

My interviews with chambers of commerce and an SME network, presented in Chapter 6, show that they thought that only big business, tied in politically with national governments was invited to participate in policymaking (Interview 10: 2006). Although the chambers welcomed the advance in infrastructure and the formalisation of trade rules established through commercial agreements, there were issues vital to them that had been left out. One example was the homogenising of the border crossings throughout Central America. Notwithstanding the permeable borders, formal transport had to go through complicated networks and customs revisions. These caused delays and financial loss. To bring this issue to attention, they had to use different regional mechanisms, such as the FECAMCO (Interviews 10, 18: 2006). Proyecto Mesoamerica has made progress in revising and simplifying the customs process (Proyecto Mesoamérica 2017a), but it was not until 2018 that representatives of Proyecto Mesoamerica and the FECAMCO started to work together.

In Chapter 6, I also note that there are more fluid modes of governance at the local level, where NGOs have proposed projects to municipal governments, sometimes across national borders, to address impending issues. It is at this government level that some projects have proved successful. Having several of the local actors participating with the government has produced positive results in proposing and implementing projects. In some instances, as in El Salvador and Costa Rica, adjacent municipal governments joined together to maximise their resources (Interviews 24, 44: 2006).

This study goes beyond other books and articles written about the PPP. Most literature deals with analysing the PPP's approach to development in Mesoamerica and either agrees or disagrees with fomenting development through the stimulation of a market economy using the principles of neoliberal economics. I contend that although it is important to evaluate the effectiveness of a specific project, it is also necessary to analyse the conditions under which it operates. In this case, the PPP was set up under less than optimal conditions. Whether the project was good or bad is difficult to ascertain since it was never implemented in the form that it was designed. Apart from a lack of communication from the project leaders to the communities surrounding it, there exist substantial communication gaps between PPP directives and the other projects being carried out in the area, along with the discrepancies among regional bodies, national governments, and local governments in Mesoamerica. The participatory mechanisms for non-governmental actors (and even sub-national government actors) were installed after the project was already running, and in my opinion, this was one of the governance failures in the region. These actors did not want to engage in the process after the regional project was in place; they wanted to be part of creating the sections relevant to them. This implementation of participatory mechanisms triggered responses by non-governmental actors. Still, if nothing happens with the proposals resulting from this participation, it becomes harder to encourage them to continue participating.

7.1 Regionalism

The MAR is under construction; its boundaries and scope are constantly shifting and changing throughout centuries. During the time frame analysed—the duration of the PPP, 2001–2008—, the borders expanded from the original south-eastern Mexico area down to Panama and on to include Colombia and, later, the Dominican Republic. The scope of the MAR evolved during those seven years; the ambitious initial plan of the PPP to integrate Mesoamerica in eight significant areas was reduced to three major infrastructure projects (RICAM, SIEPAC, and AMIST see Annex A). However, under *Proyecto Mesoamerica*, the scope shifted once more to include more areas of cooperation. The construction of the MAR is taking place in different spheres: the political sphere, through government initiatives; the social sphere, through the efforts of civil society and NGO regional networks; and the commercial sphere, through the business and trade union networks. Each has a different vision of what they would like to emerge from regional cooperation. There is communication between the political and commercial spheres, as well as between the social and commercial spheres; however, the political and social spheres appear to be working in isolation from one another.

1. The MAR can be best assessed through the "New Regionalism Approach," bringing out its multidimensionality and the multifaceted aspects of the regionalisms and the regionalisation taking place. The overlapping of the PPP, MBC, SICA, and other regionalisms show the extent to which regional integration and cooperation can be broadened beyond the economic aspect, to include environmental programmes, infrastructure, and other issues. Moreover, in the MAR, it can be seen how previously independent regional networks can band together quickly for a specific purpose and become part of the process without engaging in it. As a result of the multidimensionality and multifaceted aspects of the MAR, governance becomes an important issue. The cohabitation of so many levels of regionalisms and regional networks has resulted in increased difficulty in reaching points of agreement. The shortfalls of the government in meeting people's basic needs (health, education, security, home, employment, adequate housing, etc.) have highlighted the need for governance in Mesoamerica at all levels.

2. Regionalism is only as effective as its modes of governance. Both the OECD report and the EU technical support encourage multilevel governance in Mesoamerica. Whereas this form of governance has emerged more naturally in regions like the EU, it is still debatable whether it can be designed and made to work in Mesoamerica. First, as I show in Chapter 4, the attempts at achieving regional institutions with supranational power have been rejected by the governments; none of the national governments are willing to give up control. In addition, the regional institutions themselves do not encourage input from other regional actors for policymaking. Consultation processes take place after an initiative has already been designed and presented. National governments have not decentralised effectively to different levels of government. They have either decentralised only on paper, where in practice the lower levels of government are still treated as employees of the central government without any decision-making powers or financial capabilities, or they have decentralised and devolved power without setting up structures for accountability and transparency. The Mexican states are an example of the latter, where the decentralisation has not translated into better government. Instead, it has meant that the states are merely no longer accountable to the central government. In Costa Rica, this situation was identified by the CONADECO; this organisation notes that the country's regions and municipalities do not have the adequate legal framework or organisational structures necessary for decentralisation to be useful or desirable.

Regionalisation

With few exceptions, like the AMAP (which was created specifically to oppose the PPP), most of the NGOs and civil society networks in the region predated the PPP. It was interesting to note that many of these groups were not specific to Central America or Mexico but included both. Several NGOs had initiated contact during the Central American civil wars, where Mexican groups had been supporting them and their efforts to help the refugees (Interview 38: 2006). Other groups, such as the CCT, had included both for practical reasons: "our confederation covers all of Latin America, but we divided into chapters, so we have the Southern Cone and Central America, and that would leave Mexico on its own, so instead it was included with Central America" (Interview 22: 2006). Individual networks span specific areas, according to their interests and concerns. For example, those that pertain to ethnic groups span the areas where these exist (i.e., Maya, Kuna), as do those relating to specific crops (small coffee growers association).

These organisations have spontaneously emerged throughout the MAR and seem to be proliferating exponentially. However, they have not really shaped the region by merely existing. Although there was a conscious regional interdependence, particularly since Hurricane Mitch, where

> ...November 1998 demonstrated that the region is one in the environmental context; there exists a decisive interdependence between our countries and our peoples. The river beds, environmental impacts, government policies, international politics, affect all the population in this small corner of the planet, America's waistline, where over all there vibrates an enormous creative capacity of a people a thousand times punished and a thousand and one times has overcome. (Jara 2003: 7)

Hurricane Mitch showed that collective efforts brought forth results. This disaster caused Central America to formulate the Madrid agenda, later incorporated into the PPP. The PPP itself had a different effect on these groups; it pushed them to join for a specific purpose: to oppose the PPP and its projects. I propose that this "reactive" regionalism that came about through the Mesoamerican forums is forming into a coherent political voice, one that could begin to shape the region if it combines its efforts towards policy and project proposals.

My research suggests that non-governmental regional actors would like to be more involved in policymaking, not only at the regional level but at all levels. Results varied; whereas the regional networks that make up the CC-SICA worked with the regional institutions of the SICA, the regional networks of the Mesoamerican Forums did not. Even though CC-SICA could only recommend and make observations on the policies and proposals presented by the SICA, they were sometimes able to get these proposals reshaped (like the ALIDES) into something more acceptable. The representatives that I approached for this research acknowledged that the CC-SICA mechanism could be improved insofar as being able to present proposals and not solely a reaction to what the SICA was doing. But they felt that it was better to be involved and make changes than to do nothing at all. My research shows that in contrast, the Mesoamerican forums formed to resist the PPP did not have any interaction with government representatives. Many felt that participating in consultative processes, where the outcome was not likely to make a difference to the existing proposals, was a waste of time and would allow the government or regional institutions to use these processes as proof that there had been participation from NGOs or civil society networks.

The Mesoamerican forums had high participatory numbers during the 2008 and 2011 conferences, including workshops and round tables, in addition to the general meetings. The purpose of this expanded format was to shift from being a purely reactive force to becoming a proactive force, bringing forth policy and project proposals.[1] According to CIEPAC (Centre of Economic Investigation and Community Action Policy), the resistance had to do with the imposition of the PPP plans. Mexican civil society wanted to be in full participation, both in the planning and implementation phases of regional development plans (Pickard 2004). Other networks, such as CCT and the FECAMCO, which also predated the PPP, would have preferred to give more input on their specific concerns but chose to remain on the sidelines of the government-proposed projects. However, they have had regionalising roles, as they used their networks as a platform to put forward proposals (CCT through CC-SICA) or influence policies (i.e., FECAMCO on customs border posts), even if on a smaller scale.

Governance

It is worth mentioning again that multilevel governance does not exist in the MAR. The inference, as I stated previously, is that "new regionalisms need new forms of governance." In the classical approach to regional

[1] However, a formal member of CIEPAC in 2018 said that part of the demise of the Mesoamerican forums had to do with lack of agreement on proposals, having groups spanning over many interests, their greatest common denominator was opposing the projects.

economic integration, central governments are the ones that make the game changing decisions. It was only after achieving full economic integration that political integration would be forthcoming (Balassa 1961). Economic integration would happen through the choices of specific government ministries, albeit in some cases other actors had input as to the design of the instruments or agreements. But at the end of the day, it was the economic and commercial ministries that implemented the protocols. Conversely, the complete implementation of a project such as the PPP required the participation of all levels of government as well as of non-governmental actors.

In Chapter 5, I contend that even though the PPP and other regional projects did not permeate through the levels of government, at the local level, particularly in the poorer municipalities, a glimpse of multilevel governance can be perceived. These local, almost forgotten, municipalities are willing to share what little governing power they have with NGOs, business, and civil society in exchange for cooperation and funding. Municipal governments in these cases are held accountable to funding bodies, submitting their expenses for review. They are also accountable to their constituents, as many NGOs require feedback from the people involved before continuing to fund a project. Local businesses also get involved at this level, providing funds or employment in exchange for policy shaping or infrastructure design. This is not to say that there are not cases of corruption or poor governance at the local level. A doctor who went on medical brigades in rural parts of Mexico mentioned a particular case in Guerrero, where one mayor "had set up a financial institution for the people, for them to save. He charged them 12 pesos to the dollar, while the real exchange rate was less than ten at that time. He also had a small store and would charge more than double for things … it was a very remote village, the people there didn't know any better" (Interview 49: 2009).

While one cannot assume that all local governments in the MAR show effective governance, cases of cooperation and communication have been found at this level.

Vision

Mesoamerica has a network of regional projects and networks, entangled and overlapping, and not necessarily working towards the same objectives. Though on paper most countries have a division of powers and governing actors that are accountable to each other and society, in practice this isn't usually the case. Although labour unions, civil society groups, and chambers of commerce have influence within their sectors, they were kept from the decision-making process and can only influence government decisions through opposition and resistance. Having horizontal and vertical actors is not enough for effective governance, they need to engage. The region is being built in spurts and stalls because each actor has a different vision of what the region should be. Although they each seem to include regional integration, many of these visions are quite opposing and thus bring about a stalemate.

With so many different schemes in the region, it is difficult to form a "regional vision." Each project has a different perspective on where the region should be heading, and these schemes are not always compatible. Although there is a common sense that with Mesoamerica being a relatively small and rather homogeneous territory, it should work as a region, it seldom does.

> At the Central American level, there is supposed to be a regional function in health; there was even a regional epidemiologic vigilance system set up and everything. That worked for about a year –you can find the statistics on the Internet. They are still stuck in 1998, and it has not been updated. That is the main problem –they have good initiatives that work for a while, and then there is no continuity. So 'regional' functions very little. (Interview 33: 2006)

In 2006, 23 uncoordinated Central American Forums took place, each dealing with different topics. According to a PPP directive, this reveals the absence of a shared vision at the regional level. "There is no regulatory framework. The resolutions at the presidents' summit usually get lost because they are not made by the different sectors, it is easy for the presidents to promise [....] Also, there exists a divorce between the state and civil society, and they need to work together in order to have a regional vision" (Interview 19: 2006).

The discourse of many of those working with Central American regionalism emphasises similarities in the culture, economies, and population of the region (usually with a few asides, mainly regarding Belize, Panama, and to some extent, Costa Rica). Books such as *Central America, one nation divided* give the sense that at one point they were unified and had a will for integration but that it was sabotaged by external meddling and by the interests of the wealthy few. The manifests of the Mesoamerican Forums, which I discussed in Chapter 6, also gives a sense that the people of the MAR are united for common goals and have certain camaraderie. Benedicte Bull (2005) even asks if PPP opposition was in some way, creating regionalisation from below.

My research suggested that many of those interviewed thought that the new policies in the region are hindering rather than furthering integration. Interviewees questioned the possibility of forging a regional vision when "FTA's are fragmenting, these are just commercial exercises and are taking away from the Tegucigalpa treaty. We had a regional vision with the Central American Common Market; we are destroying it" (Interview 22: 2006). This same interviewee explained that one of the main reasons for opposing CAFTA was its role in detracting from the regional integration process. Also, many Central Americans object to Mexico or Colombia being a part of the regional vision (Interviews 17, 1, 36: 2006). Some thought that the involvement of Mexico and Colombia (and to some extent, that of Panama and Belize) in Central America distracted away from their integration process. Although they did not oppose the participation of these countries entirely, they felt that a regional vision was forthcoming for Central America: adding more players would cause it to lose focus and direction.

7.2 Development

Promotors of PPP called it an "innovative development project," a solution that would help insert south-eastern Mexico and Central America into the world economy. The projects that advanced: building roads; modernising ports; and hooking up electric distribution and communications networks focused on promoting economic activity and trade in Mesoamerica. The PPP wagered that given the right incentives, industry would move towards Mesoamerica, providing jobs and transporting goods efficiently through the region. My analysis of the data suggests that the PPP advanced infrastructure projects, disregarding the protests and concerns of civil society organisations. The opposition argued that the development model could result in economic growth, but it would not bring "development" as they envisioned it for the people. Electric connectivity would surely help the regional distribution of electricity, but it was not providing marginalised homes with electrical power or running water. The big highways did connect cities and facilitate the transport of goods, but they did not connect marginalised communities or help them take community-produced products to markets. In addition, some of the highways were poorly planned and divided communities to the effect that children had to cross them to get to school, putting them in danger. Industry did move south in the form of *maquiladoras* that maintained low wages and had little impact on the local economy.

The PPP included an ambitious range of projects under the headings of sustainable development, human development, disaster prevention, and tourism promotion (see Table 1.1 in Chapter 1). However, there is little data to support advancement in these four initiatives during the seven-year existence of the PPP. First, their funding came out of each country's existing budget. The lack of coordination between the regional programme, national governments, and local providers resulted in the national government (or state government) receiving the credit for any progress achieved.

After seven years, the PPP was transformed into *Proyecto Mesoamerica*, reducing the number of projects and their scope. *Proyecto Mesoamerica* shows that lessons were learned from its predecessor, as mentioned in the previous section. Better coordination with regional networks was set up, and free trade agreements among its members were encouraged. *Proyecto Mesoamerica* intensified efforts to finish electric and highway connectivity, communications networks, and facilitate customs procedures. By reducing its scope of projects, it would be more effective in accomplishing its goals. The health initiative involved a public–private partnership as a means of obtaining funds, but with it also came independent monitoring that was not present in the PPP. The Mesoamerican Biological Corridor was continued as part of the environment initiative. Natural disaster prevention and mitigation was done through the construction of a regional database of vulnerable areas and sharing information. Recent disasters have confirmed that *Proyecto Mesoamerica* has neither a central coordinator for natural disasters nor a fund for disaster relief. The earthquakes in Chiapas and Oaxaca in September of 2017 brought forth aid (Colombia, Panama, El Salvador, Honduras, and Costa Rica pledged assistance and support), but this was given individually, not as part of the regional mechanism.[2]

[2] http://www.milenio.com/internacional/sismo_mexico-magnitud-terremoto-solidaridad-puebla-eu-milenio-noticias_0_1033096992.html.

On a positive note, *Proyecto Mesoamerica* included the housing initiative proposed by a civil society network in Nicaragua (the mechanism that produced this initiative is not clear). It has also added a new initiative: that of eliminating hunger, which, according to internal reports, has been well-received by the population (Proyecto Mesoamérica 2017c). It is important to note the removal or relocation of projects that required large amounts of coordination from the regional level to the local level. Several of the relocated projects ended up under the *Programa Mesoamericano de Cooperación*, where projects take place locally and then biennial reports are compiled and presented to the Tuxtla Mechanism.

7.3 Security

Regional security was an initial motivator for regional cooperation in Mesoamerica. Violence and armed conflict caused waves of refugees to flee to southern Mexico and with these, the increased social malaise in Mexico and concern about the spill over of violence and social conflict. The Tuxtla Mechanism formalised after the Central America peace accords were signed and became the regional forum for cooperation and dialogue. Nevertheless, when the PPP was proposed and accepted within the Tuxtla Mechanism, regional security was not included in the proposal. Considering that the PPP was a development project, it perplexed some people that it did not include mechanisms to ensure regional security since violence and organised crime hinder economic activity cause much of the forced migration from the region. Violence resulting from organised crime and increasing gang activity has proliferated in Central America and Mexico. The highly porous borders (as we saw with the movement of merchandise in Chapter 4) also allow the flow of gang activity and criminal organisation—The Central American Security Commission created within the framework of the SICA, is the only formal institutionalised mechanism for cooperation on regional security, but it does not encompass Mesoamerica. Even though Mexico can request to participate when regional issues (such as the *Maras*) are on the agenda. Mexico and Colombia are active participants, along with the United States, in specially created regional forums on security. There is a heightened sense that security is a regional affair; Colombia and Mexico are stepping up to provide technical support and training to their Central American neighbours albeit they too are dealing with security difficulties. Although it was not addressed explicitly in any document, nor mentioned during interviews, I infer that regional security was left out of the PPP and Proyecto Mesoamerica due to sensitivity in matters pertaining to national sovereignty. Interviews with SICA and PARLACEN representatives specified that Central American countries were very protective of their sovereignty. Thus, all voting must be unanimous on regional matters in the SICA, and PARLACEN only has an advisory role where its decisions are not binding. The suggestion of having a Mesoamerican Integration System was disregarded, possibly due to fears of Mexico taking over (Interviews 17, 1, 36: 2006). Security cooperation takes place through external actors, as with the Merida initiative and the Conference for Prosperity and Security, and even the Alliance for Prosperity (although it is an alliance of the northern triangle countries, the United States, IDB, and Mexico participate with technical support), but always with a disclosure that national sovereignty is maintained. Institutionalising regional security in Mesoamerica, particularly under the banner of the PPP and later *Proyecto Mesoamerica,* could cause further division and controversy of the projects. So regional security has only been institutionalised through Central American Security Commission and to a lesser extent in the Alliance for Prosperity. The Tuxtla Mechanism and the regional conferences provide mechanisms for dialogue and agreements on cooperation and support, but in an intergovernmental and non-binding scenario. As pressure increases from the United States to curb illegal migration, it becomes evident that violence and lack of personal security require immediate attention. The most recent migrant caravan proceeding from Central America through Mexico and seeking asylum in the United States has underscored the dimension of the problem.[3] Many people travelling with the group said that the *Maras* threatened to kill them if they remained in their home/town. They undertake the journey because they have nothing to lose: they prefer to take their chances of going into a bleak unknown than remain and face certain death.[4] The government of Honduras has legitimacy issues; Guatemala's government is uncovering corruption scandals in the military, and Nicaragua's President Ortega is trying to regain

[3]Further information: Understanding the Central American Refugee crisis, special report February 2016. https://www.americanimmigrationcouncil.org/research/understanding-central-american-refugee-crisis.

[4]http://www.jornada.unam.mx/ultimas/2018/04/11/caravana-de-migrantes-es-recibida-en-casa-refugio-de-la-ciudad-de-mexico-2343.html.

control after protests against social security reform turned violent and resulted in government oppression.[5] Mexico is still trying to find out what happened in Guerrero when, in 2014, 43 students disappeared after clashing with the police[6]; months turned to years, and in 2019 the case remains unsolved to the satisfaction of their parents or human rights groups. Mesoamerican countries are having difficulties resolving internal security issues; they tackle security with security forces accused of human rights abuses, corruption, and even close cooperation with organised crime.

7.4 Heritage of the PPP

In Chapter 4, I discussed an article by Martí Asencio in which he shared his view on the "legacy of the PPP." He argued that the PPP (1) nurtured the Tuxtla Mechanism, (2) interested financial institutions in Mexico and Central America, and (3) placed the south-eastern region of Mexico on the national agenda. The research presented in this work does not contradict any of these statements, but I do not concur that this is the legacy of the PPP.

I believe that the PPP leaves a heritage behind. After the creation, implementation, and replacement of the PPP, Mesoamerica is not back to the way it was before its installation. Although others will surely find more topics of interest as a result of the PPP, I would like to point out the following three:

First, the PPP highlighted the problem of the "spaghetti bowl" of regionalism in Mesoamerica. While the entangled regionalisms were present in the area before the PPP; it was the attempt of the PPP to pull them together that made the bowl overflow. Its proposal to use "the existing Free Trade Agreements" (Presidencia Documento Base 2001) to promote intra-regional trade was found to be inoperable given the entanglement of FTAs in the MAR. The transition to Proyecto Mesoamerica urged the consolidation of the existing FTAs, and though there is not a unified Mesoamerican FTA, a Mexico-Central America

[5] https://www.nytimes.com/2018/04/26/world/americas/nicaragua-uprising-protesters.html.

[6] https://www.nytimes.com/2017/07/10/world/americas/mexico-missing-students-pegasus-spyware.html.

(El Salvador, Nicaragua, Guatemala, Costa Rica, and Honduras) agreement was consolidated. Bilateral agreements continue between Mexico and Panama and between Mexico and Colombia (revised in 2015). The Dominican Republic is a full member of CAFTA-DR and has a free trade agreement with Panama, but not with Mexico or Colombia.

The PPP formed over an existing web of regionalisms, some commercial and others more complicated like the SICA. Over time, it was clear that it could not achieve its agenda isolated from these other instruments. Whatever SICA, MBC, or SIECA were doing, this affected the PPP and vice versa, either through the competition for funding, creating an overlap in projects, or in obstructing them outright. Regional projects, joining late in the game, need to engage with the existing regionalisms, evaluate whether some "untangling" needs to take place and coordinate with established institutions. Prior to establishing a "new" form of regionalism, my research suggests it would be worthwhile to analyse if existing mechanisms and institutions can expand or restructure to reach the desired objectives.

Second, regionalisation resulted from the regional project, either in a positive or negative form. In the MAR, social groups were quick to accept the "Mesoamerican" identity set out by the PPP and group together as a region. Mesoamerican regionalisation, manifested through the Mesoamerican forums, took place hand in hand with the PPP, forming to oppose it and expanding with it (including Colombian groups after Colombia became a member). The declarations that resulted from their yearly forums showed the opinions and reactions of their members on the advances and proposals of the PPP. However, beginning with the 7th Mesoamerican Forum, they included workshops so that participants could generate proposals instead of only reacting to the activities of the PPP. Still, this exercise showed that the organisations that joined together against the PPP and Proyecto Mesoamerica had different priorities and concerns and could not produce unified proposals. Nevertheless, regional networks are robust and becoming more engaged in mobilising and organising society to demand participation in matters that concern them (development, environment, security). Nonetheless, it will require a willingness from both parts—non-governmental regional networks and the regional institutions—to negotiate alternatives and make compromises, instead of the "all or nothing" approach that has routinely taken place.

Third, governance matters. Central American and Mexican politics have been evolving quickly since the 1980s. Many of the Central American countries settled down after civil wars and conflict, while Mexico came out of 70+years of a one-party rule. Most of the countries have highly centralised governments as a result. Even though some decentralisation has taken place, the results have yet to become evident in the day-to-day running of government. Democracy is not just the periodic holding of elections; it requires informed voters, transparency, and trust in government processes and institutions; in this sense, democracy is still maturing in Mesoamerica.

Even if central governments agreed with a regional proposal, implementing a multifaceted proposal required the participation of other levels of government. Moreover, as civil society groups, NGOs, and businesses become more organised, they also expect and need to be included in the participation and implementation of instruments such as the PPP.

7.5 Further Research

My purpose in this book has been to discuss regionalism, development, and governance in Mesoamerica using the Plan Puebla Panama as a case study and drawing observations from 2001 to 2008, and then, from its replacement as Proyecto Mesoamerica. This book could not go into detail on every aspect of Mesoamerican regionalism, development, and security. Nevertheless, the seven years of the PPP and subsequent modifications for Proyecto Mesoamerica can provide enriching observations for regionalism studies. Mesoamerica will continue to change as a region; some issues will continue to be addressed regionally, while others may revert to bilateral cooperation or to a multilateral hemispheric (i.e. CEPAL, OAS) or global (UN) forum. However, it is unlikely that Mesoamerican countries will be able to address many of the issues discussed here on their own. Natural disasters and climate change do not have borders, neither do violence and organised crime. There will be plenty to be said and analysed about Mesoamerica for years to come.

During the process of this research, several questions arose that I could not fully address but may provide an entry point into further research. One has to do with the micro-regions that are noticeably forming throughout the MAR through the cooperation of municipal governments. Government, civil society, and NGOs were cooperating, sometimes across borders, to provide public services or in some cases, address environmental issues. I was only able to review eight cases of such cooperation documented by FUNDE or FUNPADEM, aside from the interviews in the municipality of San Bartolomé de la Perulapía in El Salvador (who did not participate in cross-border micro-regions but did have cooperation networks with municipal governments in Nicaragua). However, I noted that in these cases, where local governments were working together with NGOs, the municipal governments belonged to opposition left-wing political parties.

Additionally, all these municipalities had little revenue coming in from their services or the central government. Questions arise from these observations. Does the political affiliation of a local government influence its willingness to cooperate with other parties like NGOs? Do NGOs approach mostly left-wing governments to participate in joint projects? Are the micro-regions forming because they do not have resources? In other words, if these governments were not lacking resources and power, or had central government support, would they still be willing to cooperate with adjacent municipalities and other participants?

A second issue warranting further investigation was that of identity, particularly in the construction of Mesoamerica. Although I touched upon Mesoamerican identity in this study, the results obtained were contradictory, and so more in-depth research could expand understanding of this topic.

Third, it could be interesting to analyse interregionalism of the MAR with NAFTA (now T-MEC), or EU and other regions with which it regularly interacts (Bäert et al. 2014). Although I discussed some of these interactions, their extent is vaster and could provide further observations on the nature and outcomes of interregional activities. A case could also be made to compare the MAR experience with that of other regions and draw observations of similarities or differences.

Much remains to be researched about the Mesoamerican region, as about regions themselves. This volume brings out some observations on the experience of the MAR with two regional projects, I hope that it will raise further interest in the MAR and regional studies.

Bibliography

Acta que institucionaliza el Mecanismo del Plan Puebla-Panamá. 2004. http://www.sieca.org.gt/Sitio-publico/OACUERDOS/83-1Acta.htm. Accessed 3 March 2006.

Baert, Francis, Tiziana Scaramagli, and Fredrik Söderbaum. 2014. Introduction: Intersecting Interregionalism. In *Intersecting Interregionalism, Regions, Global Governance and the EU*, ed. Francis Baert, Tiziana Scaramagli, and Fredrik Söderbaum. www.researchgate.net/publication/259580409. Downloaded 6 December 2017.

Balassa, Bela A. 1961. *The Theory of Economic Integration*. London: Allen and Unwin.

Bull, Benedicte. 2005. Between Bush and Bolivar: Change and Continuity in the Remaking of Mesoamerica. In *The Political Economy of Regions and Regionalisms*, ed. Morten Bøås, Marianne H. Marchand, and Timothy M. Shaw. Basingstoke, Hampshire: Palgrave Macmillan.

Dirección Ejecutiva Proyecto de Integración y Desarrollo de Mesoamérica. 2008. *Informe de Actividades 2008*. El Salvador. www.planpuebla-panama.org. Accessed 4 November 2008.

Gamble, Andrew and Anthony Payne (eds.). 1996. *Regionalism and World Order*. London: Macmillan.

Grugel, Jean and Wil Hout. 1999. *Regionalism Across the North-South Divide State Strategies and Globalization*. London and New York: Routledge.

Hettne, Björn. 2000. The New Regionalism: A Prologue. In *National Perspectives on the New Regionalism in the South*, ed. Björn Hettne, András Inotal, and Osvaldo Sunkel. London: Macmillan.

Hettne, Björn. 2003. The New Regionalism Revisited. In *Theories of New Regionalism: A Palgrave Reader*, ed. Fredrik Söderbaum and Timothy M. Shaw. Basingstoke: Palgrave Macmillan.

Hettne, Björn, and Fredrik Söderbaum. 2002. Theorising the Rise of Regionness. In *New Regionalisms in the Global Political Economy Theories and Cases*, ed. Shaun Breslin et al. London and New York: Routledge.

Hettne, Björn, András Inotal, and Osvaldo Sunkel (eds.). 1999. *National Perspectives on the New Regionalism in the South*. London: Macmillan.

Hettne, Björn, András Inotal, and Osvaldo Sunkel (eds.). 2000. *The New Regionalism and the Future of Security and Development*. London: Macmillan.

Hettne, Björn, and Fredrik Söderbaum. 2000. Theorising the Rise of Regionness. *New Political Economy* 5 (3): 457–472.

Hufty, Marc. 2009. The Governance Analytical Framework. www.north-south.unibe.ch/content.php/publications/Infosystem/On-line%20Dokumente/Upload/GovernanceFrameworkE.pdf. Accessed 15 July 2010.

Informe Ejecutivo. 2006. El PPP: Avances retos y Perspectivas. https://web.archive.org/web/20071029105130/http://www.planpuebla-panama.org/.
Informe Ejecutivo. 2008. El PPP: Avances retos y Perspectivas. https://web.archive.org/web/20071029105130/http://www.planpuebla-panama.org/.
Jachtenfuchs, Markus. 2001. The Governance Approach to European Integration. *Journal of Common Market Studies* 39 (2) (June): 245–264.
Jara, Oscar (ed.). 2003. *Otro Desarrollo es Posible: Sistematización de experiencias y reflexiones críticas desde Centroamérica*. Costa Rica: Centro de Estudios y Publicaciones Alforja.
OECD Territorial Reviews. 2005. *The Mesoamerican Region: Southeastern Mexico and Central America*. OECD Publishing. http://www.oecd.org/mexico/oecdterritorialreviewsthemesoamericanregionsoutheasternmexicoandcentralamerica.htm.
Pickard, Miguel. 2004. The Plan Puebla Panama Revived: Looking Back to See What Is Ahead. *La Chronique des Ameriques*, avril num 12. www.americques.uqam.ca/pdf/Chro-0413-ppp-eng.pdf.
Presidencia de la República. 2001. *Plan Puebla-Panamá Capítulo México*. Documento Base.
Proyecto Mesoamérica. 2017a. Informe Estado de Proyectos PM 2008–2016. http://www.proyectomesoamerica.org/index.php/comunicacion/kit-de-comunicaciones-pm/comunicados-de-prensa.html.
Proyecto Mesoamérica. 2017b. Resumen Ejecutivo de Proyecto Mesoamérica 2008–2017. http://www.proyectomesoamerica.org/index.php/comunicacion/kit-de-comunicaciones-pm/comunicados-de-prensa.html.
Proyecto Mesoamérica. 2017c. Proyecto de Integración y Desarrollo de Mesoamérica y los Objetivos de Desarrollo Sostenible. http://www.proyectomesoamerica.org/index.php/comunicacion/kit-de-comunicaciones-pm/comunicados-de-prensa.html.
Vega, Francisca Santiago. 2006. *Integración al Pesto* América Economía Edición Aniversario 20 Años en América Latina del 6 al 19 de octubre 2006 AMERICAECONOMIA Santiago de Chile, 36–38.

Interviews

1. Political Analyst Guatemala (Background information conversation not recorded), 25 September 2006, Guatemala City.
3. Director of Integration, Ministerio de Relaciones Exteriores Guatemala, 25 September 2006, Guatemala City.
9. Fundación Rigoberta Menchú, 26 September 2006, Guatemala
17. Regional Local Area director, Fundación Nacional para el Desarrollo (FUNDE), 5 September 2006, San Salvador.

18. Director of Economic Affairs, Cámara de Comerico e Industria de El Salvador, 1 September 2006, San Salvador.
19. Executive, Dirección Ejecutiva Plan Puebla Panamá, 4 September 2006, San Salvador.
22. Director, Instituto Centroamericano de Estudios Sociales (ICAES) (CCT), 17 October 2006, San José Costa Rica.
24. President Confederación Nacional de Asociaciones de Desarrollo Comunal CONADECO, 17 October 2006, San José Costa Rica.
25. Economic Affairs Director, Secretaría General del Sistema de la Integración Centroaméricana (SG-SICA), 4 September 2006, El Salvador.
31. Elected Deputy, Asamblea Legislativa de Costa Rica (Interview took place in room adjacent to chamber of deputies, was not allowed to record), 18 October 2006, San José Costa Rica.
33. CEPAL, 10 October 2006, Mexico City.
36. FUNPADEM, 18 de Octubre 2006, Costa Rica.
38. AMAP Director, Mexican Asociation for the Self-Determination of Peoples (AMAP) 22 August 2006, Mexico City.
49. General and Alternative Medical Doctor, Did his social service by attending medical brigades in marginalised Mexican rural communities, November 2008.

Conferences Attended

"Gestión integrada de programas sociales y autoridad social: experiencias latinoamericanas", Dr. Rolando Franco, Facultad Latinoamericana de Ciencias Sociales y Centro de Estudios para el Futuro FLACSO, Tuesday 17 October 2006, San José Costa Rica 10:00 a.m.

"Gobernabilidad Democrática y Nuevas Orientaciones Políticas en Costa Rica: escenarios a partir de las elecciones 2006" Organised by Centro de Estudios Políticos, Maestría Centroamericana de Ciencias Políticas, UCR, Facultad Latinoamericana de Ciencias Sociales y Centro de Estudios para el Futuro FLACSO 17 October 2006 8:00 p.m.

"Indigenous People in Mexico" Presented by Lynda Martinez del Campo Fonda del Claustro, Mexico City, 17 March 2007.

"'Multi-Level Governance and Systems of Economic Organisation' Workshop", 17–19 May 2007, University of Warwick, Scarman House.

ANNEX A

ASSESSING THE ACHIEVEMENTS OF THE PPP AND PROYECTO MESOAMERICA

Gauging the PPP's achievements is a difficult task. The Plan did not establish baselines or indicators to measure its progress towards achieving its development objectives and goals. Since the PPP did not set priorities nor measurable outcomes to be met, the Plan has been pursuing its objectives without a coherent operational guideline. More worrisome is the fact that the PPP does not have an overall system of monitoring and supervision of its project portfolio. Instead, both the Plan administrators and third-party stakeholders have reported little more than sporadic execution information about individual projects on its website and printed reports. (OVE 2008: 10)

A. Gamboa, *Regional Integration, Development, and Governance in Mesoamerica*,
https://doi.org/10.1007/978-3-030-25350-9

8 Initiatives of PPP	*Main Project*	*Advance 2001–2008*	*Advance 2008–2018*
Sustainable development initiative	Mesoamerican biological corridor	Many completed projects in 2005 but remained independent from PPP	Relaunched MBC as the main pillar for sustainable development
Transportation initiative	RICAM 13,132 km	6629 km 50%	3244 km 75%
Energy integration	SIEPAC 1800 km	30% Mexico-Guatemala	Continue with SIEPAC, Mexico-SIEPAC-Colombia interconnectivity in progress Include renewable energy as a pillar
Telecommunication initiative	AMI 1800 km	Progress together with SIEPAC as they use the same infrastructure	Now AMIST (Agenda Mesoamericana de la Información de los Servicios de Telecomunicaciones) handled by REDCA (private sector)
Trade and competitiveness initiative	Mesoamerican Competitiveness Council (CMC)	4-year delay	Harmonized trade agreements 2011, CMC relaunched
Human development initiative	Health, education	3 hospitals built in Mexico	Results based Health initiative Housing initiative Food Security initiative launched 2009
Natural disaster mitigation initiative	Map of risk zones	Considered failed in the design phase (OVE: 2008)	2015 announced a Mesoamerican GIS that was to be launched in 2017—not yet running
Tourism initiative	Mundo Maya	Increased coordination as a themed tourist destination	Not included as a separate initiative

IDB's evaluation of the PPP acknowledged that the only projects that were complete in 2008 when the transition to Proyecto Mesoamerica occurred were 3 hospitals that were built by Mexico. However, even these they considered difficult to assess because they could not compare against initial targets, since these did not exist (OVE 2008: 11). The transition to Proyecto Mesoamerica in some ways wiped the slate clean, not all projects that were in progress continued to form part of Proyecto Mesoamerica, some were relocated to other organisms, others discontinued and still others, renamed.

For up to date information on the advancement or status of Proyecto Mesoamerica and other Mesoamerican projects please visit:

Proyecto Mesoamerica official website: http://proyectomesoamerica.org/index.php.

Central American Economic Integration (SIECA) official website: https://www.sieca.int/.

Central American Integration (SICA) official website: https://www.sica.int/.

Sources

Office of Evaluation and Oversight (OVE) Interamerican Bank Evaluation of IDB's support to the Plan Puebla Panama Initiative August 2008. https://publications.iadb.org/en/evaluation-idbs-support-plan-puebla-panama-initiative.

Informe Ejecutivo (2008)-El PPP: Avances retos y Perspectivas. http://portal2.sre.gob.mx/ppp/dmdocuments/Informe_Tuxtla_final.pdf. Downloaded 5 June 2009.

Proyecto Mesoamérica (2017): Informe Estado de Proyectos PM 2008–2016. http://www.proyectomesoamerica.org/index.php/comunicacion/kit-de-comunicaciones-pm/comunicados-de-prensa.html. Downloaded 25 April 2018.

Proyecto Mesoamérica (2018): Informe Estado de Proyectos PM 2008–2017. http://www.proyectomesoamerica.org/index.php/comunicacion/kit-de-comunicaciones-pm/comunicados-de-prensa.html. Downloaded 25 April 2018.

Annex B

Questionnaire sent out via www.surveymonkey.com from 1 March 2006–30 July 2006.

1. The best description for your organisation is:

1. Local independent NGO	8
2. Local NGO, with ties to NGO's in Mexico and Central America	14
3. Local NGO, with ties to International NGOs from the US, Canada, or Europe	17
4. International NGO based outside of Mexico and Central America	5
5. Organized social movement	1
6. Community-based organisation	5
7. Other	11
Total responses	61
Skipped this question	0

The category other included 4 NGOs that fit the above profiles, but adding specificity to their activities, 4 civil society networks, 1 indigenous organisation affiliated to its national government, 1 association of municipalities, and one that just denominated itself as "independent."

A. Gamboa, *Regional Integration, Development, and Governance in Mesoamerica*,
https://doi.org/10.1007/978-3-030-25350-9

2. The main activities of your organisation are: (select up to 3)

1. Community development	29
2. Defence of Human Rights/Women's Rights	18
3. Poverty reduction	10
4. Support of Indigenous communities	15
5. Environmental Protection	20
6. Sustainable Development	23
7. Other	29
Total responses	60
Skipped this question	1

Other included, political awareness, democracy and participation 16, Environmental education/awareness 3, defence of specific human rights causes 4, documenting and communicating social struggles in the region 4, Defence of micro and small businesses interests1, community health development 1.

3. What are the main problems facing Mesoamerica according to your organization? Select the two most important.

1. Environmental degradation	26
2. Economic stagnation	20
3. Lack of social services (i.e., education, healthcare)	20
4. Natural disasters	2
5. Lack of infrastructure	5
6. Unemployment	14
7. Human rights abuses	18
8. Other	16
Total responses	54
Skipped this question	7

Other includes: 10 responses linked all of the above as interdependent and noted that they had to be tackled jointly, 3 of these included corruption as the main ingredient. The remaining 6 responses included, discrimination, racism and gender bias 1, Children's rights 1, Democratic governance 1, Regional integration independent from the US 1, Rural development 1 and Double standards from the West 1.

4. What are the greatest needs of the people you represent? Please choose two

1. Access to clean water	15
2. Access to electricity	2
3. Access to quality education	28
4. Access to quality healthcare	22
5. Access to quality housing	12
6. Access to formal employment	30
7. Other ______________	16
Total responses	54
Skipped this question	7

Other: All of the above 5, sustainable development 1, legal rights of indigenous peoples 1, Bilingual and bicultural education 1, justice 1, security 1, democracy 1, enabling citizen participation 1, opportunities for children at risk 1, help and development of micro and small businesses 2, injustice of western culture 1.

5. In order to encourage regional development, the governments of Belize, Costa Rica, El Salvador, Guatemala, Honduras, Mexico, Nicaragua, and Panama should....

1. Work out their development strategies independently and according to the needs of each country	3
2. Work out their development strategies independently (at the nation al level, but encourage NGO's and International Organisations (i.e., UN, World Bank, IMF, IaBD) to attack problems at a regional level	2
3. Work out a regional strategy for development as well as other areas that affect the region as a whole (i.e., natural disasters)	16
4. Work out a regional development strategy together, including NGO's and International Organisations	33
Total responses	54
Skipped this question	7

6. Has your organisation been in communication with Government representatives about current government development and integration policy in the Region (ie Commercial FTA Agreements, Plan Puebla Panama, Tegucigalpa Protocol (SICA) Mesoamerican Biological Corridor, etc)?

1. Yes we sent an initial response to Government policy	13
2. No, we have aired our response to the media and our members only	15
3. No, we have not aired any official response, we work independent of Government policy and do not voice opinions to Government policy	12
4. Other	14
Total responses	54
Skipped this question	7

Other: 4 stated that they had given specific initial responses, 4 stated that they sent in proposals pertaining to these subjects, 2 said that they participated in reunions where they talked about the subject, 2 stated that their sister organisations in Central America had done so, but they did not directly. 1 stated that it did not deal with these projects and 1 said that the government has no shame.

7. If your answer was 1 to Question 6, did you receive a prompt government response to your comments?

1. Yes, the Government replied promptly and invited us to dialogue	4
2. Yes, the Government replied but did not invite further dialogue	6
3. No, we never received a Government reply	3
Total responses	13

8. Is your organisation represented in any official consultation group?

1. Yes, with the InterAmerican Development Bank	6
2. Yes, with our home government (in the region)	8
3. Yes, with our home government (outside the region)	0
4. Yes, with several governments	2
5. No	24
6. other	14
Total responses	54
Skipped this question	7

Other: 3 specified why they did not participate, 2 participate in mechanism within the Organisation of American States, 1 in the CC-SICA, 1 with the Mexican Government, and 4 are part of civil society networks.

9. Has your organisation been represented through attendance to one of the VI Mesoamerican Social Forums?

1. Attended 1 or 2 Forums	13
2. Attended 3 or 4 Forums	5
3. Attended all Forums I–VI	4
4. Have not attended any, but would have liked to	21
5. Have not attended any and would not like to	3
6. Was unaware of the Mesoamerican Social Forums	8
Total responses	54
Skipped this question	7

10. Please tick the box that would best represent the position of your organisation towards the following project.

Project	*Eliminate and not replace*	*Eliminate and replace with alternative*	*Maintain the concept, but change the content*	*Maintain with some modifications*	*Maintain and continue with program*	*Do not know enough about project*
Mesoamerican Biological Corridor	8	9	5	12	5	14
Tegucigalpa Protocol (SICA)	6	3	13	14	8	8
Tuxtla Mechanism for Dialogue	6	5	5	7	2	28
Plan Puebla Panama	16	16	9	3	2	7
Plan Nuevos Horizontes	8	3	1	0	1	40
FTA Mexico-Northern Triangle	16	11	2	3	3	18
FTA Mexico-Costa Rica	9	8	5	5	6	20

Project	*Eliminate and not replace*	*Eliminate and replace with alternative*	*Maintain the concept, but change the content*	*Maintain with some modifications*	*Maintain and continue with program*	*Do not know enough about project*
FTA Mexico-Panama	10	8	5	4	6	20
FTA Central America-US	20	13	3	8	2	7
Total responses						53
Skipped this question						8
Any other comment?						

Annex C

Resources

Interviews

1. Political Analyst Guatemala (Background information conversation not recorded), 25 September 2006, Guatemala City.
2. Instituto Nacional de Electrificación INDE Guatemala (Background information conversations not recorded), 25, 26, 27 September 2006, Guatemala City.
3. Director of Integration, Ministerio de Relaciones Exteriores Guatemala, 25 September 2006, Guatemala City.
4. Economist, Consejo Monetario Centroamericano, 19 October 2006, Costa Rica.
5. National Worker's Confederation (Labour Union) (Background information conversation not recorded), 30 October 2006.
6. Executive Secretary, Consejo Monetario Centroamericano, 19 October 2006, Costa Rica.
7. Coordinator Human Development, Dirección Ejecutiva Plan Puebla Panamá, 1 September 2006, San Salvador.
8. Centro de Estudios y Publicaciones Alforja, 17 October 2006, San José, Costa Rica.
9. Fundación Rigoberta Menchú, 26 September 2006, Guatemala.
10. Commercial Relations Coordinator, Cámara de Comercio de Guatemala, 27 September 2006.

A. Gamboa, *Regional Integration, Development, and Governance in Mesoamerica*,
https://doi.org/10.1007/978-3-030-25350-9

11. Department Head on Indigenous Issues, Subsecretaría para América Latina y el Caribe, Coordinación General del Plan Puebla Panamá, 30 August 2006, Mexico.
12. Instituto Tecnológico Autónomo de México political Analyst (Background information conversation not recorded), 10 August 2006, Cancún Quintana Roo.
13. International Cooperation Office, República de Costa Rica, Ministerio de Relaciones Exteriores y Culto, 17 October 2006, San José, Costa Rica.
14. Technical advisor, Dirección de Integración y Comercio, Secretaría de Integración Económica Centroamericana (SIECA), 26 September 2006, Guatemala City.
15. Consultant and Analyst (Background information conversation not recorded), 2 June 2007, Acapulco, Guerrero.
16. Regional Director of CODA international El Salvador (Project Liaison with Perulapía, 6 September 2006, San Salvador, San Bartolomé Perulapía.
17. Regional Local Area Director, Fundación Nacional para el Desarrollo (FUNDE), 5 September 2006, San Salvador.
18. Director of Economic Affairs, Cámara de Comerico e Industria de El Salvador, 1 September 2006, San Salvador.
19. Executive, Dirección Ejecutiva Plan Puebla Panamá, 4 September 2006, San Salvador.
20. Fundación para la Democracia (FUNPADEM) (Background information conversation not recorded), 17, 18, 19 October 2006.
21. Legislative advisor, Asamblea Legislativa, Costa Rica, Not recorded, Background information.
22. Director, Instituto Centroamericano de Estudios Sociales (ICAES) (CCT), 17 October 2006, San José, Costa Rica.
23. Director of International Economic Section, Departamento de Estudios Económicos y Sociales, Fundación Salvadoreña para el Desarrollo Económico y Social. FUSADES, 5 September 2006, San Salvador.
24. President Confederación Nacional de Asociaciones de Desarrollo Comunal CONADECO, 17 October 2006, San José, Costa Rica.
25. Economic Affairs Director, Secretaría General del Sistema de la Integración Centroaméricana (SG-SICA), 4 September 2006, El Salvador.
26. Subsecretaría para América Latina y el Caribe, Coordinación General del Plan Puebla Panamá, 30 August 2006, Mexico City.
27. PPP initiatives coordinator, Oficina local del Plan Puebla Panamá en El Salvador, Ministerio de Relaciones Exteriores El Salvador, 5 September 2006, San Salvador.
28. Representative of the Mesoamerican Biological Corridor, 17 October 2006, San José, Costa Rica.

29. Directive Cabinet, Parlamento Centroamericano, 27 September 2006, Guatemala City.
30. Executive Director, Oficina local del Plan Puebla Panamá en El Salvador, Ministerio de Relaciones Exteriores El Salvador, 5 September 2006, San Salvador.
31. Elected Deputy, Asamblea Legislativa de Costa Rica (Interview took place in room adjacent to chamber of deputies, was not allowed to record), 18 October 2006, San José, Costa Rica.
32. Former guerrilla leader, professor Universidad Francisco Gavidia, 1 September and 7 September 2006, El Salvador (Informal conversations, took notes, not recorded).
33. CEPAL, 10 October 2006, Mexico City.
34. FLACSO, Regional Coordinator for Investigation and International Cooperation (Background information conversation not recorded), 18 October 2006, San José, Costa Rica.
35. Director of Cooperation, fondo de Desarrollo Indígena Guatemalteco, 25 September 2006, Guatemala City.
36. FUNPADEM, 18 October 2006, Costa Rica.
37. Regional Coordinator of Investigation and International Cooperation, Secretaría General de la Facultad Latinoamericana de Ciencias Sociales (FLACSO), Costa Rica.
38. AMAP Director, Mexican Asociation for the Self-Determination of Peoples (AMAP), 22 August 2006, Mexico City.
39. Sub Coordinator of the regional office of Instituto de Fomento Municipal de Guatemala (INFON), 26 September 2006, Notes- not recorded.
40. Former candidate for governor of Chiapas, 21 September 2006, Mexico.
41. Embassy of El Salvador in Mexico City.
42. Director of Analysis and follow-up of commercial treaties with Latin America- Secretaría de Economía, 9 May 2007, Background information for context only, conversation not recorded, referred to documents.
43. Municipal Government of Orizaba, Veracruz, 26 August 2006, Mexico (Notes- not recorded).
44. Full day meeting and visit with the local government of San Bartolomé de la Perulapía municipality in El Salvador, the Mayor Guillermo Sanchez and 5 other local government representatives. All those involved in the meeting were members of the FSLN political party, 6 September 2006, El Salvador.
45. Full day participation Oportunidades/Progresa Córdoba assessment exercise, August 2008, Veracruz.
46. Director CODA international 5 and 6 September 2006 (Sessions at Perulapía recorded, informal background conversations not recorded), El Salvador.

47. Assistant to the Director of Juridical reviews, 4 September 2006, San Salvador.

48. Asociación Latinoamericana de Micro, Pequeños y Medianos Empresarios (ALAMPYME), one of the founding organisations in the Red Mexicana de Acción contra el Libre Comercio (RMALC) Interview, 29 November 2006, Mexico City.

49. General and Alternative medical doctor. Did his social service by attending medical brigades in marginalised Mexican rural communities, November 2008.

50. American student in Guatemala and El Salvador in 1969, November 2008, Mexico City.

Conferences Attended

"Gestión integrada de programas sociales y autoridad social: experiencias latinoamericanas", Dr. Rolando Franco, Facultad Latinoamericana de Ciencias Sociales y Centro de Estudios para el Futuro FLACSO, Tuesday 17 October 2006, San José, Costa Rica, 10:00 a.m.

"Gobernabilidad Democrática y Nuevas Orientaciones Políticas en Costa Rica: escenarios a partir de las elecciones 2006" organised by Centro de Estudios Políticos, Maestría Centroamericana de Ciencias Políticas, UCR, Facultad Latinoamericana de Ciencias Sociales y Centro de Estudios para el Futuro FLACSO, 17 October 2006, 8:00 p.m.

"Indigenous People in Mexico" presented by Lynda Martinez del Campo Fonda del Claustro, Mexico City, 17 March 2007.

Fonda del Claustro, Mexico City, 17 March 2007.

"Multi-level Governance and Systems of Economic Organisation' Workshop", 17–19 May 2007, University of Warwick, Scarman House.

Useful Websites

PPP: http://www.sre.gob.mx/ppp.

PPP/Proyecto Mesoamerica: http://www.planpuebla-panama.org, October 2006–February 2009, www.proyectomesoamerica.org, March 2009–July 2010, www.mesoamerica.sre.gob.mx, August 2010–present.

Mesoamerica Resiste: http://www.mesoamericaresiste.org. Last accessed February 2007, domain no longer available.

RMALC: http://www.rmalc.org.mx.

SICA: http://www.sica.int.

PAIRCA: http://www.sica.int/pairca.

CC-SICA: http://www.sica.int/ccsica.

CCAD: http://www.sica.int/ccad.
Comisión trinacional del plan Trifinio: http://www.sica.int/trifinio.
PARLACEN: http://www.parlacen.org.gt/.
Corte Centroamericana de Justicia: http://www.ccj.org.ni/index.html.
SIECA: http://www.sieca.org.gt/SIECA.htm.
Programa mesoamericano de cooperación: http://www.sica.int/busqueda/busqueda_basica.aspx?IdCat=47&IdMod=8&IdEnt=847&IdEntStyle=401&Idm=1&IdmStyle=1.
MBC: http://www.biomeso.net/. Last Accessed October 2006, domain no longer available.
MBC-Mexico: http://www.cbmm.gob.mx/.
INEGI: http://www.inegi.org.mx/inegi/default.aspx.
Mexican Ministry for Trade and Finance: http://www.economia.gob.mx/.
Mexican Government main portal: http://www.gob.mx/wb/egobierno/temas.
El Salvador Government main portal: http://www.elsalvador.gob.sv/.
Costa Rica Government main portal: http://www.gobiernofacil.go.cr/weblinks/index.aspx.
Nicaragua Government main portal: http://www.migob.gob.ni/.
Honduras Government main portal: http://www.gob.hn/.
Colombia Government main portal: http://www.gobiernoenlinea.gov.co/home_principal.aspx.
Panama Presidency: http://www.presidencia.gob.pa/.
Belize Government main portal: http://www.governmentofbelize.gov.bz/.
Guatemala Government main portal: http://guatemala.gob.gt.
Consejo Monetario Centroamericano: http://www.secmca.org/Indice.html.
Interamerican Development Bank: http://www.iadb.org.
Mexican Municipalities Association (AMMAC): http://ammac.org.mx.
Federation of Municipalities of the Central American isthmus (FEMICA): http://www.femica.org.
Mesoamerican Forums: www.foro-mesoamericano.org.
VIII Foro Mesoamericano: http://www.albatv.org/Se-convoca-el-VIII-Foro.html.

Bibliography

Acta que institucionaliza el Mecanismo del Plan Puebla-Panamá. 2004. http://www.sieca.org.gt/Sitio-publico/OACUERDOS/83-1Acta.htm. Accessed 3 March 2006.

Adler, Emmanuel. 1994. Imagined (Security) Communities. Annual Meeting of the American Political Society 1–4 September, New York.

Aguirre Rojas, Carlos Antonio. 2002. A Modo de Introducción: Chiapas en Perspectiva Histórica. In *Chiapas en Perspectiva Histórica*, ed. Aguirre Rojas Carlos Antonio, Bolívar Echeverría, Carlos Montemayor, and Wallerstein Immanuel, 2nda edición. España: El Viejo Topo.

Alvarez Béjar, Alejandro. 2002a. El Plan Puebla-Panamá en el contexto de la integración hemisférica Política y Cultura Núm. 18, 83–105. UNAM, otoño.

Alvarez Béjar, Alejandro. 2002b. The Puebla-Panama Plan: Development of a Region or Multinational Enclave? In *Economía Política del Plan Puebla Panamá*, ed. Alejandro Álvarez Béjar, Andrés Barreda Marín, y Armando Bartra. Mexico: Editorial Itaca.

Alvarez Béjar, Alejandro. 2002c. Sies Factores Estructurales que explican la estrategia del Plan Puebla Panama. In *Economía Política del Plan Puebla Panamá*, ed. Alejandro Álvarez Béjar, Andrés Barreda Marín, y Armando Bartra. México: Editorial Itaca.

Alvarez Béjar, Alejandro, Andrés Barreda, and Armando Bartra (eds.). 2002. *Economía Política del Plan Puebla Panamá*. México: Editorial Itaca.

Ángeles Cruz, Hugo, and Santiago Martínez Junco. 2006. Violencia social y pandillas. Las maras en la región fronteriza del Soconusco, Chiapas In *Geoeconomía y Geopolítica en el área del Plan Puebla Panamá*, ed. Daniel

A. Gamboa, *Regional Integration, Development, and Governance in Mesoamerica*,
https://doi.org/10.1007/978-3-030-25350-9

Villafuerte Solis and Xochitl Leyva Solano. México: Editorial Miguel Angel Porrúa.

Arce Tena, Carlos A. 2006. *La gobernabilidad democrática: una perspectiva para el desarrollo*. México: Ediciones Miguel Angel Porrúa.

Ardila Ardila, Martha. 2015. El regionalismo mexicano en la Alianza del Pacífico y el Proyecto Mesoamérica. *Carta Económica Regional Año* 27 (116) (Julio-Diciembre), 36–62.

Arreola Muñoz, Arturo V. 2006. Mesoamérica, el saldo actual de sus recursos naturales estratégicos. In *Geoeconomía y Geopolítica en el área del Plan Puebla Panamá*, ed. Daniel Villafuerte Solis and Xochitl Leyva Solano. México: Editorial Miguel Angel Porrúa.

Bache, Ian, and Matthew Flinders. 2004. Themes and Issues in Multi-level Governance. In *Multilevel Governance*, ed. Bache Ian and Flinders Matthew. New York: Oxford University Press.

Bacon, David. 2003. The Wages of Death: Why Immigrant Workers Need a Better Contract with America. *The American Prospect* (July/August) 40+. http://www.questia.com/.

Baert, Francis, Tiziana Scaramagli, and Fredrik Söderbaum. 2014. Introduction: Intersecting Interregionalism. In *Intersecting Interregionalism, Regions, Global Governance and the EU*, ed. Francis Baert, Tiziana Scaramagli, and Fredrik Söderbaum. www.researchgate.net/publication/259580409. Downloaded 6 December 2017.

Balassa, Bela A. 1961. *The Theory of Economic Integration*. London: Allen and Unwin, 1962.

Baldwin, Richard E. 2006. Multilateralising Regionalism: Spaghetti Bowls as Building Blocas on the Path to Global Free Trade. *The World Economy* 29 (11): 1451–1518.

Banco Popular. 2002. *Normas Básicas de la Asamblea de Trabajadores y Trabajadoras del Banco Popular y de Desarrollo Comunal*. Publicación Oficial.

Barbossa, Rubens Antonio. 1991. *América Latina em perspectiva: A Integraçao Regional Da Retórica à Realidade*. Sao Paulo: Ediçoes Aduaneiras Ltda.

Barreda Marin, Andrés. 2001. Los Peligros del Plan Puebla Panama. In *Mesoamerica: Los Ríos Profundos. Alternativas Plebeyas al Plan Puebla Panamà*, ed. Armando Bartra. Mexico: RMALC/El Atajo Ediciones/ Instituto "Maya", A.C.

Barreda Marín, Andrés. 2002a. Los Objetivos del Plan Puebla Panamá. In *Economía Política del Plan Puebla Panamá*, ed. Alejandro Álvarez Béjar, Andrés Barreda Marín, y Armando Bartra. Mexico: Editorial Itaca.

Barreda Marín, Andrés. 2002b. El Plan Puebla Panamá. *Biodiversidad* 33 (Agosto): 1–8.

Bartra, Armando (ed.). 2001a. *Mesoamerica: Los Ríos Profundos. Alternativas Plebeyas al Plan Puebla Panamà*. Mexico: RMALC/El Atajo Ediciones/ Instituto "Maya", A.C.

Bartra, Armando. 2001b. SUR, Megaplanes y utopías en la América equinoccial. In *Mesoamerica: Los Ríos Profundos. Alternativas Plebeyas al Plan Puebla Panamà*, ed. Armando Bartra. Mexico: RMALC/El Atajo Ediciones/Instituto "Maya", A.C.

Bartra, Armando. 2002. Hacia una Nueva Colonización del Sureste. In *Economía Política del Plan Puebla Panamá*, ed. Alejandro Álvarez Béjar, Andrés Barreda Marín, y Armando Bartra. México: Editorial Itaca.

Bartra, Armando. 2004. Mesoamericanos: Recalentando una identidad colectiva cemos. *MEMORIA Revista Mensual de Política y Cultura Numero 183*, Mayo.

Bauzas, Roberto, and Jaime Ros (eds.). 1994. *Economic Integration in the Western Hemisphere*. Notre Dame: University of Notre Dame Press.

Baylis, John, and Steve Smith. 2001. *The Globalization of World Politics: An Introduction to International Relations*, 2nd ed. Oxford: Oxford University Press.

Bilial, Sanoussi. 2005. *The Coherence of Multi-Level Negotiations: Challenges for Developing Countries*. UNU-CRIS e-Working Papers W-2004/11. www.ecdpm.org. Accessed 12 May 2005.

Blatter, Joachim. 2004. From 'Spaces of Place' to 'Spaces of Flows'? Territorial and Functional Governance in Cross-Border Regions in Europe and North America. *International Journal of Urban and Regional Research* 28 (3) (September): 530–548.

Blejer, Mario I. 1984. Economic Integration: An Analytical Overview. In *Social and Economic Progress in Latin America, Special Report: Economic Integration*, 5–34. Washington, DC: Inter-American Development Bank.

Bøås, Morten, Marianne H. Marchand, and Timothy M. Shaw. 1999. The Weave-World: Regionalisms in the South in the New Millennium. *Third World Quarterly* 20 (5): 1061–1070.

Bøås, Morten, Marianne H. Marchand, and Timothy M. Shaw. 2003. The Weave-World: The Regional Interweaving of Economies, Ideas and Identities. In *Theories of New Regionalism: A Palgrave Reader*, ed. Fredrik Söderbaum and Timothy M. Shaw. Basingstoke: Palgrave Macmillan.

Bøås, Morten, Marianne H. Marchand, and Timothy M. Shaw (eds.). 2005a. *The Political Economy of Regions and Regionalisms*. Basingstoke: Palgrave Macmillan.

Bøås, Morten, Marianne H. Marchand, and Timothy M. Shaw. 2005b. The Political Economy of Regions and Regionalism: An Introduction to Our Critical, Revisionist Inquiries. In *The Political Economy of Regions and Regionalisms*, ed. Morten Bøås, Marianne H. Marchand, and Timothy M. Shaw. Basingstoke: Palgrave Macmillan.

Bøås, Morten, Marianne H. Marchand, and Timothy M. Shaw. 2005c. Conclusion: Possible Projections for the Political Economy of Regions and Regionalisms. In *The Political Economy of Regions and Regionalisms*, ed.

Morten Bøås, Marianne H. Marchand, and Timothy M. Shaw. Basingstoke: Palgrave Macmillan.

Booth, John A., and Thomas W. Walker. 1999. *Understanding Central America*. 3rd ed. Boulder, CO: Westview Press.

Bougher, Kathy. 2003. Women's Lives for Sale: Free Trade and Education in El Salvador. *Off Our Backs* 33 (11) (November–December): 15–18.

Bowles, Paul. 2002. Regionalism and Development After (?) the Global Financial Crises. In *New Regionalisms in the Global Political Economy: Theories and Cases*, ed. Shaun Breslin et al. London: Routledge.

Braga, Carlos Primo. 1996. Comments on the Proliferation of Regional Integration Arrangements. *Law and Policy in International Business* 27 (4): 963–968. http://www.questia.com/.

Breslin, Shaun. 2000. Decentralisation, Globalisation and China's Partial Re-engagement with the Global Economy. *New Political Economy* 5 (2): 205–226.

Breslin, Shaun. 2010. Regions and Regionalism in World Politics. In *Issues in Twenty-First Century World Politics*, ed. Mark Beeson and Nick Beesley, 33–51. Basingstoke: Palgrave.

Breslin, Shaun, and Glenn D. Hook (eds.). 2002. *Microregionalism and World Order*. New York: Palgrave Macmillan.

Breslin, Shaun, Christopher W. Hughes, Nicola Phillips, and Ben Rosamond (eds.). 2002. *New Regionalisms in the Global Political Economy: Theories and Cases*. London: Routledge.

Breslin, Shaun, Richard Higgot, and Ben Rosamond. 2002. Regions in Comparative Perspective. In *New Regionalisms in the Global Political Economy: Theories and Cases*, ed. Shaun Breslin et al. London: Routledge.

Broome, André. 2014. *Issues and Actors in the Global Political Economy*. New York: Palgrave Macmillan.

Bull, Benedicte. 1999. New Regionalism in Central America. *Third World Quarterly* 20 (5): 957–970.

Bull, Benedicte. 2005. Between Bush and Bolivar: Change and Continuity in the Remaking of Mesoamerica. In *The Political Economy of Regions and Regionalisms*, ed. Morten Bøås, Marianne H. Marchand, and Timothy M. Shaw. Basingstoke: Palgrave Macmillan.

Bull, Benedicte, and Morten Bøås. 2003. Multilateral Development Banks as Regionalising Actors: The Asian Development Bank and the Inter-American Development Bank. *New Political Economy* 8 (2) (July): 245–260.

Bulmer-Thomas, Victor. 1998. The Central American Common Market: From Closed to Open Regionalism. *World Development* 26 (2): 313–322.

Bulmer-Thomas, Victor. 2001. Introduction. In *Regional Integration in Latin America and the Caribbean: The Political Economy of Open Regionalism*, ed. Victor Bulmer Thomas. London: University of London.

Bulmer-Thomas, Victor, and Douglas A. Kinkaid. 2000. *Central America 2020: Towards a new regional development model*. http://www.netamericas.net/Researchpapers/Documents/Bulmer-Thomas/Bulmer-Thomas1.pdf.

Burnel, Peter. 2000. Democracy Assistance: The State of the Discourse. In *Democracy Assistance: International Cooperation for Democratization*, ed. Peter Burnel. London: Frank Cass.

Burnham, Peter, Karin Gilland, Wyn Grant, and Zig Layton-Henry. 2004. Research Methods.

Cabrera, Jorge and Pedro Cuc. 2002. *Ambiente, conflicto y cooperación en la Cuenca del río Usumacinta*. FUNPADEM.

Call, Wendy. 2002. Plan Puebla-Panamá: Done Deal or Emerging Flashpoint? *International Journal of Public Administration* 9 (April).

CAMCAYCA. diciembre 2015. *Plan Estratégico Confederación de Asociaciones de Municipios de Centroamérica y el Caribe CAMCAYCA 2015–2020.*

Capdepont Ballina, Jorge Luis. 2011. Mesoamérica o el Proyecto Mesoamérica: La Historia como Pretexto. *Revista LiminaR. Estudios Sociales y Humanísticos año* 9 (1) (junio). ISSN: 1665-8027.

Carr, Archie III. 2002. A Plait of Three Colors. *Americas* 54 (July–August): 64. http://www.questia.com/.

Carranza, Mario Esteban. 2000. *South American Free Trade Area or Free Trade Area of the Americas? Open regionalism and the future of regional economic integration in South America*. Farnham: Ashgate.

CCAD-MBC. 2003. *Estrategia regional para la conservación y uso sostenible de la biodiversidad en Mesoamérica (ERB)*. Comisión Centroamericana de Ambiente y Desarrollo El Salvador.

CCAD-MBC. 2005. *Programa Estratégico Regional Para la Conectividad*. Comisión Centroamericana de Ambiente y Desarrollo El Salvador.

CC-SICA Informe de Consulta. 2003. *Estrategia de Modernización del Estado y Perfil de la estrategia para la Integración Regional*. San José, Costa Rica: FUNPADEM.

CC-SICA. 2006. *Plan de Acción para el Fortalecimiento del CC-SICA 2006*. San José, Costa Rica: FUNPADEM.

CEPAL. 2015. *Una mirada a los países del Proyecto Mexoamèrica*. Documento de Proyectos, Estudios e Investigaciones—Sede subregional México. Documento elaborado para la XV Cumbre del Mecanismo de Diálogo y Concertación de Tuxtla Ciudad de Guatemala Guatemala Viernes, 26 de junio de 2015. Naciones Unidas, Impreso en México D.F. LC/MEX/L.1183. http://repositorio.cepal.org.

Chanona, Alejandro. 2002. Procesos de integración en el marco del Plan Puebla-Panamá (PPP). In *Lectura Crítica del Plan Puebla Panamá*, coordinadores Eduardo Andrés Sandoval Forero y Robinson Salazar Pérez. Buenos Aires: Libros en Red.

Chomsky, Noam. 1985. *Turning the Tide: U.S. Intervention in Central America and the Struggle for Peace*. Boston: South End Press.

COMEXI Grupo de Trabajo de Seguridad Pública. 2018. *Una estrategia de Seguridad Pública para proteger a la ciudadanía*. Consejo Mexicano de Asuntos Internacionales.

CONADECO. 2005. *5to Congreso Nacional de Asociaciones de Desarrollo Comunal, Costa Rica, 29–30 de Octubre de 2004 Memoria*. San José, Costa Rica: CONADECO.

Consejo Monetario Centroamericano (CMCA). 2006a. *The Central American Monetary Council and its Executive Ministry* (official booklet) published July 2006.

Consejo Monetario Centroamericano (CMCA). 2006b. Informe Económico Regional 2005, Junio 2006 publicación oficial.

Cooper, Andrew F., Christopher W. Hughes, and Phillippe De Loambaerde. 2008. *Regionalisation and Global Governance: The Taming of Globalisation?* London and New York: Routledge.

Coordinación General del Plan Puebla-Panamá (CG-PPP). 2001. *Plan Puebla Panamá: Presentación Diagnóstico Centroamérica*. México: INEGI.

Coordinación General del Plan Puebla-Panamá (CG-PPP). 2002. *Informe de Avances y Perspectivas Plan Puebla-Panamá junio 2002*. México: INEGI.

Coordinadora regional de los altos de Chiapas de la sociedad civil en resistencia. 2002. Plan Puebla – Panamá: Un proyecto de "Desarrollo" …¿Para quién? http://www.nadir.org/nadir/initativ/agp/free/colobmia/puebla/pueblapanama.htm.

Curly, Jon M. 2008. Cleaning Up the Spaghetti Bowl. In *Economic Integration in the Americas*, ed. Joseph A. McKinney and Stephen Gardner. London and New York: Routledge.

Dávila Enrique, Kessel Georgina, and Levy Santiago. 2002. El Sur también existe: un ensayo sobre el desarrollo regional de México (originally published in Economía Mexicana, vol. 11, 202–260). In *Ensayos Sobre el Desarrollo Económico y Social de México*, compilador Santiago Levy. México: Fondo de Cultura Económica.

Declaración de Guatemala. 2000. Declaración Conjunta de la IV Cumbre de los Jefes de Estado y de Gobierno de los países integrantes del Mecanismo de Diálogo y Concertación de Tuxtla, 25 de Agosto de 2000. http://www.sieca.org.gt/publico/OACUERDOS/TuxtlaIV.htm.

Declaración de Tapachula. 2001. Photocopy of Text.

Declaración de Mérida. 2002. Declaración Conjunta de la quinta cumbre del Mecanismo de Diálogo y Concertación de Tuxtla, 27 y 28 de junio 2002. http://sieca.org.gt/Publico/OACUERDOS/DeclaraciondeMerida.htm.

Declaración Extraordinaria. 2001. Declaración Conjunta de la Cumbre extraordinaria de los países integrantes del Mecanismo de Diálogo y

Concertación de Tuxtla. http://sieca.org.gt/publico/OACUERDOS/DECLARACION_CONJUNTA_DE_LA.

Declaración de Villahermosa. 2008. *Declaración Conjunta de la décima cumbre del Mecanismo de Diálogo y Conceración de Tuxtla*, 28 de junio de 2008. http://sieca.org.gt/publico/OACUERDOS/DeclaraciondeVillahermosa.htm.

Declaración Política del VII Foro Mesoamericano de los Pueblos ¡Mesoamerica en Resistencia, No al neocolonialismo del libre comercio! 2008. http://Chiapas.indymedia.org/local/webcast/uploads/declaracion_vii_mesoamericano.pdf.

Declaración VIII Foro. 2001. VIII Foro Mesoamericano de los Pueblos. Declaración de Minatitlán 13 de abril de 2011 Minga informativa de Movimientos Sociales. http://movimientos.org.

Delgadillo Macías, Javier. 2006. El cálculo de un índice de desarrollo socioeconómico para la región del sur-sureste de México. In *Los espacios de reserva en la expansión global del capital: El sur-sureste mexicano da cara al Plan Puebla-Panamá*, Felipe Torres Torres y José Gasca Zamora (coordinadores). Barcelona, España: Universidad Nacional Autónoma de México y Plaza y Valdés S.A de C.V.

Delgado-Wise, Raúl. 2004. The Hidden Agenda of Mexico's Fox Administration. *Latin American Perspectives* 31 (5) (September): 146–164.

De Lombaerde, Philippe, Antoni Estevadeordal, and Kati Suominen. 2008. Governing Regional Integration for Development: Introduction. In *Governing Regional Integration for Development*, ed. Philippe De Lombaerde, Antoni Estevadeordal, and Kati Suominen. Aldershot: Ashgate.

De Lombaerde, Philippe, and Luis Jorge Garay. 2006. New Regionalism in Latin America and the Role of the US. UN-CRIS Occasional Papers O-2006/10.

De Lombaerde, Philippe, and Luk Van Langenhove. 2004. Indicators of Regional Integration: Conceptual and Methodological Issues. UN-CRIS Occasional Papers O-2004/15.

Devlin, Robert, and Antoni Estevadeordal. 2001. What's New in the New Regionalism in the Americas? In *Regional Integration in Latin America and the Caribbean: The Political Economy of Open Regionalism*, ed. Victor Bulmer Thomas. London: University of London.

Dirección Ejecutiva Proyecto de Integración y Desarrollo de Mesoamérica. 2008. *Informe de Actividades 2008*. El Salvador. www.planpuebla-panama.org. Accessed 4 November 2008.

Dirección de Comunicación del Parlamento Centroamericano. n.d. ABC del PARLACEN.

Eckerberg, Katarina, and Marko Joas. 2004. Multi-level Environmental Governance: A Concept Under Stress? (Guest Editorial). *Local Environment* 9 (5) (October): 405–412.

ECLAC. 1994. *Open Regionalism in Latin America and the Caribbean*. Santiago, Chile: United Nations Economic Commission for Latin America and the Caribbean.

ECLAC. 2007. Statistical Yearbook for Latin America and the Caribbean. www.eclac.cl/publicaciones/xml/6/32606/LCG2356B.2.pdf. Accessed 12 February 2008.

Edelman, Marc. 1998. Transnational Peasant Politics in Central America. *Latin American Research Review* 33 (3): 49–86.

Enríquez Villacorta, Alberto. 2005. Desarrollo local y descentralización del Estado, nuevos factores de la Integración Centroamericana. *Alternativas Para el Desarrollo* 93 (Abril–Mayo). FUNDE San Salvador.

European Commission (EC). 2002. Regional Strategy Paper for Central America 2002–2006.

Fawcett, Louise, and Andrew Hurrell (eds.). 1995. *Regionalism in World Politics: Regional Organization and International Order*. New York: Oxford University Press.

FEMICA. 2008. Fortalecimiento de los Gobiernos Locales y de la Sociedad Civil. Revista Femica No 5 febrero 2008. http://www.femica.org/archivos/revista5.pdf. Downloaded 24 February 2010.

FEMICA/SGSICA. 2009. Memorándum de Entendimiento Entre la Secretaria General del Sistema de la Integración Centroamericana (SGSICA) y la Federación de Municipios del Istmo Centroamericano (FEMICA). http://femica.org/noticias/docNoticias/Convenio_SICA_FEMICA.pdf.

Fernández, Sara Yaneth, y Carlos Iván Pacheco. 2011. Macroproyectos, desplazamiento y guerra en Colombia: apropiación de territorios y de los cuerpos como referentes simbólicos de dominio. In *Planes Geoestratégicos, Desplazamientos y Migraciones Forzadas en el Área del Proyecto de Desarrollo e Integración Mesoamérica*, coordinadores Juan Manuel Sandoval Palacios, Raquel Álvarez de Flores, and Sara Yaneth Fernández Moreno. Mexico: Seminario Permanente de Estudios Chicanos y de Fronteras, DEAS-INAH; Venezuela: Centro de Estudios de Fronteras e Integración, Universidad de Los Andes-Táchira; Colombia: Departamento de Trabajo Social, Facultad de Ciencias Sociales y Humanas, Universidad de Antioquia. http://www.academia.edu/7454005/PLANES_GEOESTRATÉGICOS_DESPLAZAMIENTOS_Y_MIGRACIONES_FORZADAS_EN_EL_ÁREA_DEL_PROYECTO_DE_DESARROLLO_E_INTEGRACIÓN_DE_MESOAMÉRICA.

Fregosi, Renée. 2008. Gobernabilidad y Gobernanza Global: desafíos teóricos y políticos. In *II Escuela Chile-Francia: Transformaciónes del Espacio Público*, ed. Ximena Póo. Chile: Documento de Recopilación de Ponencias Cátedra Chile-Francia "Michel Foucoult".

Frohmann, Alicia. 2000. The New Regionalism and Collective Diplomacy in Latin America. In *National Perspectives on the New Regionalism in the South*, ed. Bjorn Hettne, Andreas Inotal, and Osvaldo Sunkel. London: Macmillan.

FUNDE/PNUD. 2004. *Asociación de Municipios y Construcción Regional para el Desarrollo*. Desarrollo Humano: Buenas Prácticas Enero 2004 N°03.

Gamble, Andrew, and Anthony Payne (eds.). 1996a. *Regionalism and World Order*. London: Macmillan.

Gamble, Andrew, and Anthony Payne. 1996b. Conclusion: The New Regionalism. In *Regionalism and World Order*, ed. Andrew Gamble and Anthony Payne. London: Macmillan.

Gamble, Andrew, and Anthony Payne. 2003. The World Order Approach. In *Theories of New Regionalism: A Palgrave Reader*, ed. Fredrik Söderbaum and Timothy M. Shaw. Basingstoke: Palgrave Macmillan.

Gellert, Paul K., and Barbara D. Lynch. 2003. *Mega-Projects as Displacements*. Oxford: Blackwell.

George, Stephen. 2004. Multi-level Governance and the European Union. In *Multilevel Governance*, ed. Ian Bache and Matthew Flinders. New York: Oxford University Press.

Gernaert Wilmar, Silvina. 2005. *Desarrollo Local transfronterizo: territorios, fronteras e integración centroamericana*. Primera parte Alternativas Para El Desarrollo No. 96 Octubre-Noviembre-Diciembre 2005 FUNDE.

Gernaert Wilmar, Silvina. 2006. *Desarrollo Local transfronterizo: territorios, fronteras e integración centroamericana*. Segunda parte Alternativas Para El Desarrollo No. 97 Enero-Febrero-Marzo 2006 FUNDE.

Gomáriz Moraga, Enrique. 2006. *Democracia, ciudadanía y desarrollo local*. Alternativas Para El Desarrollo No. 97 enero-febrero-Marzo 2006 FUNDE.

Grinspun, Ricardo, Carlos Alvarenga, and Shamsie Yasmine (eds.). 1999. *Hacia una Integración desde Abajo. Participación, Sociedad Civil e Integración Centroamericana*. Talleres Gráficos UCA.

Grugel, Jean. 1996. Latin America and the Remaking of the Americas. In *Regionalism and World Order*, ed. Andrew Gamble and Anthony Payne. London: Macmillan.

Grugel, Jean B. 2004. New Regionalism and Modes of Governance—Comparing US and EU Strategies in Latin America. *European Journal of International Relations* 10 (4): 603–626.

Grugel, Jean, and Wil Hout. 1999. *Regionalism Across the North-South Divide State Strategies and Globalization*. London and New York: Routledge.

Grupo Técnico Interinstitucioinal (GTI). 2001. *Plan Puebla-Panamá: Iniciativas Mesoamericanas y Proyectos*. San Salvador, El Salvador: BCIE-BID-ECLAC con el apoyo del INCAE.

Guevara Bermúdez, José Antonio (ed.). 2018. Episodios de Desplazamiento Interno Forzado Masivo en México. Informe 2017 CDMPDH, PADF,

USAID. http://www.cmdpdh.org/publicaciones-pdf/cmdpdh-informe-de-desplazamiento-interno-masivo-en-mexico-2017.pdf.

Haas, E.B. 1964. *Beyond the Nation-State: Functionalism and International Organization*. Stanford, CA: Stanford University Press.

Haggard, Stephen. 1997. The Political Economy of Regionalism in Asia and the Americas. In *The Political Economy of Regionalism*, ed. Edward D. Mansfield and Helen V. Milner. New York: Columbia University Press.

Hansen, Tom. 2001. El neoliberalismo como fundamento del PPP. In *Mesoamerica: Los Ríos Profundos. Alternativas Plebeyas al Plan Puebla Panamà*, ed. Armando Bartra. Mexico: RMALC/El Atajo Ediciones/ Instituto "Maya", A.C.

Harvey, Neil. 2006. La disputa por los recursos naturales en el área del Plan Puebla Panamá. In *Geoeconomía y Geopolítica en el área del Plan Puebla Panamá*, ed. Daniel Villafuerte Solis and Xochitl Leyva Solano. México: Editorial Miguel Ángel Porrúa.

Hernández Navarro, Luis, and Laura Carlsen. 2001. El Plan Puebla Panamá, Pueblos Indígenas y Café. In *Mesoamerica: Los Ríos Profundos. Alternativas Plebeyas al Plan Puebla Panamà*, ed. Armando Bartra. Mexico: RMALC/El Atajo Ediciones/Instituto "Maya", A.C.

Hettne, Björn. 1995. *Development Theory and the Three Worlds: Towards an International Political Economy of Development*, 2nd ed. Harlow: Longman.

Hettne Björn. 2000a. The New Regionalism: A Prologue. In *National Perspectives on the New Regionalism in the South*, ed. Björn Hettne, Andreas Inotal, and Osvaldo Sunkel. London: McMillan Press Ltd.

Hettne, Björn. 2000b. Global Market Versus Regionalism. In *The Global Transformations Reader*, ed. David Held and Anthony McGrew. Cambridge: Polity Press.

Hettne, Björn. 2003. The New Regionalism Revisited. In *Theories of New Regionalism: A Palgrave Reader*, ed. Fredrik Söderbaum and Timothy M. Shaw. Basingstoke: Palgrave Macmillan.

Hettne, Björn. 2005. Beyond the 'New' Regionalism. *New Political Economy* 10 (4): 543–571.

Hettne, Björn, András Inotal, and Osvaldo Sunkel (eds.). 2000a. *National Perspectives on the New Regionalism in the South*. London: Macmillan.

Hettne, Björn, András Inotal, and Osvaldo Sunkel (eds.). 2000b. *The New Regionalism and the Future of Security and Development*. London: Macmillan.

Hettne, Björn, and Fredrik Söderbaum. 1998. The New Regionalism Approach. www.unisa.ac.za. Last accessed 22 March 2010.

Hettne, Björn, and Fredrik Söderbaum. 2000. Theorising the Rise of Regionness. *New Political Economy* 5 (3): 457–472.

Hettne, Björn, and Fredrik Söderbaum. 2002. Theorising the Rise of Regionness. In *New Regionalisms in the Global Political Economy: Theories and Cases*, ed. Shaun Breslin et al. London: Routledge.

Hettne, Björn, András Inotal, and Osvaldo Sunkel (eds.). 1999. *Globalism and the New Regionalism*. Basingstoke: Macmillan.

Hiernaux-Nicolas, Daniel. 2002. El Plan Puebla Panamá: ¿una nueva visión del desarrollo regional? *Lectura Crítica del Plan Puebla Panamá*, coordinadores Eduardo Andrés Sandoval Forero y Robinson Salazar Pérez. Buenos Aires: Libros en Red.

Higgot, Richard, and Simon Reich. 1998. *Globalisation and Sites of Conflict: Towards Definition and Taxonomy*, CSGR Working Paper. University of Warwick, Centre for the Study of Globalisation and Regionalism. Accessed 01 March 1998.

Hooghe, Liesbet, and Gary Marks. 2003. Unraveling the Central State, but How? Types of Multi-level Governance. *American Political Science Review* 97 (2) (May): 233–243.

Hook, Glenn, and Ian Kearns (eds.). 1999. *Subregionalism and World Order*. Basingstoke: Macmillan.

Hurrell, Andrew. 1995. Regionalism in Theoretical Perspectiva. In *Regionalism in World Politics*, ed. Andrew Hurrell and Louise Fawcett. Oxford: Oxford University Press.

Hufty, Marc. 2009. The Governance Analytical Framework. www.north-south.unibe.ch/content.php/publications/Infosystem/On-line%20Dokumente/Upload/GovernanceFrameworkE.pdf. Accessed 15 July 2010.

Informe Ejecutivo. 2006. El PPP: Avances retos y Perspectivas.

Informe Ejecutivo. 2008. El PPP: Avances retos y Perspectivas.

Informe Estado de la Región en Desarrollo Humano Sostenible. 2008. http://www.estadonacion.or.cr/estadoregion2008.

Íñiguez, Martín. 2005. Los Maras ¿Problema de seguridad pública o nacional? Territorio y Economía Número Especial 4/2005. México: Frontera Sur, Sistema de Información Regional de México, 19–26.

Jachtenfuchs, Markus. 2001. The Governance Approach to European Integration. *Journal of Common Market Studies* 39 (2) (June): 245–264.

Jara, Oscar (ed.). 2003. *Otro Desarrollo es Posible: Sistematización de experiencias y reflexiones críticas desde Centroamérica*. Costa Rica: Centro de Estudios y Publicaciones Alforja.

Jessop, Bob. 2003. The Political Economy of Scale and the Construction of Cross-Border Micro-Regions. In *Theories of New Regionalism: A Palgrave Reader*, ed. Fredrik Söderbaum and Timothy M. Shaw. Basingstoke: Palgrave Macmillan.

Kooiman, Jan. 2008. Exploring the Concept of Governability. *Journal of Comparative Policy Analysis* 10 (2): 171–190.

Labrecque Marie France. 2005. Cultural Appreciation and Economic Depreciation of the Mayas of Northern Yucatán, Mexico. *Latin American Perspectives* 32 (4) (July): 87–105.

Levy, Santiago (compilador). 2004. *Ensayos Sobre el Desarrollo Económico y Social de México*. Mexico: Fondo de Cultura Económica.

Levy, Santiago, y Rodríguez Evelyne. 2003. IV. El Programa De Educación Salud y Alimentación, Progresa-Programa de Desarrollo Humano Oportunidades. In *Ensayos Sobre el Desarrollo Económico y Social de México*, compilador Santiago Levy. México: Fondo de Cultura Económica.

López, Miguel Angel. 2008. Gobernabilidad y Democracia en America Latina: La Institucionalización Partidiaria. In *II Escuela Chile-Francia: Transformaciónes del Espacio Público*, ed. Ximena Póo. Chile: Documento de Recopilación de Ponencias Cátedra Chile-Francia "Michel Foucoult".

López-Calva, Luis F., and Nora Lustig. 2003. *Social Protection and Inclusive Trade: Strengthening the Sources of Convergence Within FTAA*. Universidad de Las Americas Working Paper No. 2003–06.

López Castellanos, Nayar. 2009. *Del Plan Puebla-Panamá al Proyecto Mesoamérica: un espejo de la globalización*. México: Neoliberal Plaza y Valdés Editores.

López Villicaña, Román. 2002. El Plan Puebla-Panamá: Historia y Geopolítica. In *Lectura Crítica del Plan Puebla Panamá*, coordinadores Eduardo Andrés Sandoval Forero y Robinson Salazar Pérez. Buenos Aires: Libros en Red.

Lora Cam, Jorge, and Sanchez R. Jose Luis. 2002. La recolonización del Angelopolis, el TLC, el Plan Puebla Panamá y el ALCA. In *Lectura Crítica del Plan Puebla Panamá*, coordinadores Eduardo Andrés Sandoval Forero y Robinson Salazar Pérez. Buenos Aires: Libros en Red.

Lybecker, Donna, and Stephen P. Mumme. 2002. Decentralization and Environmental Protection on Mexico's Northern and Southern Boundaries. *Journal of Environment & Development* 11 (4) (December): 402–429.

Malamud, Andrés. 2004. Regional Integration in Latin America: Comparative Theories and Institutions. *Sociologia* 44: 135–154. ISSN: 0873-6529.

Mansfield, Edward D., and Helen V. Milner. 1997a. The Political Economy of Regionalism: An Overview. In *The Political Economy of Regionalism*, ed. Edward D. Mansfield and Helen V. Milner. New York: Columbia University Press.

Mansfield, Edward D., and Helen V. Milner (eds.). 1997b. *The Political Economy of Regionalism*. New York: Columbia University Press.

Mansfield, Edward D., and Eric Reinhalt. 2003. Multilateral Determinants of Regionalism: The Effects of GATT/WTO on the Formation of Preferential Trading Arrangements. *International Organisation* 57 (4) (Fall): 829–862.

Marchand, Marianne H., Morten Bøås, and Timothy M. Shaw. 1999. The Political Economy of New Regionalisms. *Third World Quarterly* 20 (5): 897–910.

Marks, Gary. 1993. Structural Policy and Multilevel Governance in the EC. In *The State of the European Community Vol. 2: The Maastritcht Debates and Beyond*, ed. A. Cafruny and G. Rosenthal. Boulder, CO: Lynne Riener.

Marras, Sergio. 1992. *América Latina: Marca Registrada*. Buenos Aires: Grupo Editorial Zeta.

Martí Ascencio, Bosco. 2007. ¿Por qué retomar y reposicionar el Plan Puebla Panamá? *Revista Bien Común* 152 (August).

Martí Ascencio, Bosco. 2008. Proyecto Mesoamérica: fortaleciendo la integración y desarrollo regional. *Revista Mexicana de Política Exterior* 83: 9–39.

Mattli, Walter. 1999. *The Logic of Regional Integration: Europe and Beyond*. New York: Cambridge University Press. Net Library e-book accessed through Warwick Library.

Maxwell, Joseph A. 2005. *Qualitative Research Design: An Interactive Approach*, 2nd ed. London: Sage.

Meyer, Carrie A. 1999. *The Economics and Politics of NGOs in Latin America*. Westport, CT: Praeger.

Miguel Velasco, Andrés, and Armando Heredia González. 2004. Regiones competitividad y Desarrollo en México *Problemas del Desarrollo: Revista Latinoamericana de Economía* 35 (138) (julio–septiembre).

Milner, Helen. 1997. Industries, Governments, and Regional Trade Blocs. In *The Political Economy of Regionalism*, ed. Edward D. Mansfield and Helen V. Milner. New York: Columbia University Press.

Mistry, Percy S. 2000. Regional Integration and Economic Development. In *National Perspectives on the New Regionalism in the South*, ed. Bjorn Hettne, Andreas Inotal, and Osvaldo Sunkel. London: Macmillan.

Mistry, Percy S. 2003. New Regionalism and Economic Development. In *Theories of New Regionalism: A Palgrave Reader*, ed. Fredrik Söderbaum and Timothy M. Shaw. Basingstoke: Palgrave Macmillan.

Mitrany, David. 1975. *The Functional Theory of Politics*. New York: St. Martins Press.

Mittelman, James H. 1996. Rethinking the "New Regionalism" in the Context of Globalization. *Global Governance* 2: 189–213.

Moguel, Julio. 2001. Claroscuros del PPP. De cómo se escamotean los derechos de los indios y se traslada el debate a los presuntos temas del desarrollo. In *Mesoamerica: Los Ríos Profundos. Alternativas Plebeyas al Plan Puebla Panamà*, ed. Armando Bartra. Mexico: RMALC/El Atajo Ediciones/Instituto "Maya", A.C.

Montemayor, Carlos. 2002. La Guerrilla Recurrente. In *Chiapas en perspectiva histórica*, ed. Carlos Antonio Aguirre Rojas. España: Ediciones de Intervención Cultural.

Muñoz Martínez, Hepzibah. 2004. State, Capital and "Second Nature": Re-Territorialization in the Plan Puebla Panama. *Capitalism Nature Socialism* 15 (1) (March) London: Routledge.

Neumann, Iver B. 2003. A Region-Building Approach. In *Theories of New Regionalism: A Palgrave Reader*, ed. Fredrik Söderbaum and Timothy M. Shaw. Basingstoke: Palgrave Macmillan.

NoPPP (Network Opposing the PPP). 2002 assumed date. Batalla por el Futuro de Mesoamerica, una colección de artículos. ACEJ/ACERCA—Handout available through RMALC.

OECD Territorial Reviews. 2005. *The Mesoamerican Region: Southeastern Mexico and Central America*. OECD Publishing. http://www.oecd.org/mexico/oecdterritorialreviewsthemesoamericanregionsoutheasternmexicoandcentralamerica.htm.

Offenheiser, Raymond C. 1998. Transforming Central America After Hurricane Mitch. *Foreign Policy* (Fall 1999), 8. http://www.questia.com/.

Office of Evaluation and Oversight (OVE) Interamerican Bank Evaluation of IDB's support to the Plan Puebla Panama Initiative August 2008. https://publications.iadb.org/en/evaluation-idbs-support-plan-puebla-panama-initiative.

O'Keefe, Thomas Andrew. 2001. The Central American Integration System (SICA) At the Dawn of a New Century: Will the Central American Isthmus Finally Be Able to Achieve Economic and Political Unity? *Florida Journal of International Law* XIII (3) (Spring): 243–261.

Orantes, Isaac Cohen. 1981. The Concept of Integration. In *CEPAL Review*. Santiago: Publicaciones Naciones Unidas.

Ornelas Delgado, Jaime. 2002. El Plan Puebla Panamá y la globalización neoliberal. In *Lectura Crítica del Plan Puebla Panamá*, coord. Sandoval Forero, Eduardo Andrés, and Robinson Salazar Pérez. Buenos Aires: Libros en Red.

Orozco, Marcela. 2011. Mesoamérica: Integración y Tratados de Libre Comercio. In *Planes Geoestratégicos, Desplazamientos y Migraciones Forzadas en el Área del Proyecto de Desarrollo e Integración Mesoamérica*, coordinadores Juan Manuel Sandoval Palacios, Raquel Álvarez de Flores, and Sara Yaneth Fernández Moreno. Mexico: Seminario Permanente de Estudios Chicanos y de Fronteras, DEAS-INAH; Venezuela: Centro de Estudios de Fronteras e Integración, Universidad de Los Andes-Táchira; Colombia: Departamento de Trabajo Social, Facultad de Ciencias Sociales y Humanas, Universidad de Antioquia. http://www.academia.edu/7454005/PLANES_GEOESTRATÉGICOS_DESPLAZAMIENTOS_Y_MIGRACIONES_FORZADAS_EN_EL_ÁREA_DEL_PROYECTO_DE_DESARROLLO_E_INTEGRACIÓN_DE_MESOAMÉRICA.

Pacheco, Carlos. 2003. Los Callejones del desarrollo en Centroamérica: del Mitch al Plan-Puebla Panamá y el ALCA. In *Otro Desarrollo es Posible: Sistematización de experiencias y reflexiones críticas desde Centroamérica*, ed. Oscar Jara. Alforja, Costa Rica: Centro de Estudios y Publicaciones.

Pardinas, Juan. 2004. Fighting Poverty in Mexico: Policy Changes. In *Mexico Under Fox*, ed. Luis Rubio and Susan Kaufman Purcell. Boulder: Lynne Rienner.

Payne, Anthony. 1996. The United States and Its Enterprise for the Americas. In *Regionalism and World Order*, ed. Andrew Gamble and Anthony Payne. London: Macmillan.

Payne, Anthony (ed.). 2004a. *The New Regional Politics of Development*. London: Palgrave Macmillan.

Payne, Anthony. 2004b. Rethinking Development Inside International Political Economy. In *The New Regional Politics of Development*, ed. Anthony Payne. London: Palgrave Macmillan.

Payne, Anthony. 2004c. Concluding Thoughts and Next Steps. In *The New Regional Politics of Development*, ed. Anthony Payne. London: Palgrave Macmillan.

Payne, Anthony. 2005. The Study of Governance in a Global Political Economy. In *Globalizing International Political Economy*, ed. Nicola Phillips. New York: Palgrave Macmillan.

Payne, Anthony, and Andrew Gamble. 1996. Introduction: The Political Economy of Regionalism and World Order. In *Regionalism and World Order*, ed. Andrew Gamble and Anthony Payne. London: Macmillan.

Payne, Anthony and Nicola Phillips. 2010. *Development*. Cambridge, UK: Polity Press.

Paz Paredes, Lorena. 2001. La Costa Grande de Guerrero, laboratorio de la promoción concertada del desarrollo regional. In *Mesoamérica: Los Ríos Profundos. Alternativas Plebeyas al Plan Puebla Panamá*, ed. Armando Bartra. México: RMALC/El Atajo Ediciones/Instituto "Maya", A.C.

Pearce, Jenny. 2004. DEBATE Collective Action or Public Participation? Complementary or Contradictory Democratisation Strategies in Latin America? *Bulletin of Latin American Research* 23 (4): 483–504.

Pellicer, Olga (ed.). 1998. *Regional Mechanisms and International Security in Latin America*. New York: United Nations University Press.

Peters, Guy B., and Jon Pierre. 2001. Developments in Intergovernmental Relations: Towards Multi-level Governance. *Policy and Politics* 29 (2): 131–135.

Phillips, Nicola. 2001. Regionalist Governance in the New Political Economy of Development: 'Relaunching' the Mercosur. *Third World Quarterly* 22 (4): 565–583.

Phillips, Nicola. 2002. Governance After Financial Crisis: South American Perspectives on the Reformulation of Regionalism. In *New Regionalisms in the Global Political Economy: Theories and Cases*, ed. Shaun Breslin et al. London: Routledge.

Phillips, Nicola. 2003. Hemispheric Integration and Subregionalism in the Americas. *International Affairs* 79 (2): 327–349.

Phillips, Nicola. 2004. The Americas. In *The New Regional Politics of Development*, ed. Anthony Payne. London: Palgrave Macmillan.

Phillips, Nicola (ed.). 2005. *Globalizing International Political Economy.* New York: Palgrave Mcmillan.

Pickard, Miguel. 2004. The Plan Puebla Panama Revived: Looking Back to See What Is Ahead. *La Chronique des Ameriques*, avril num 12. www.americques.uqam.ca/pdf/Chro-0413-ppp-eng.pdf.

Pisani, Michael J., and Wayne A. Label. 2003. Plan Puebla-Panama: Toward FTAA or regionalism? *Business Horizons* (September–October): 33–40.

Pollack, Mark A. 2001. International Relations Theory and European Integration. *Journal of Common Market Studies* 39 (2) (June): 221–244.

Ponce de León, Juana. 2001. *Our Word Is Our Weapon: Selected Writings Subcomandante Insurgente Marcos.* New York: Seven Stories Press.

Preciado Coronado, Jaime, and Aarón Villarruel Mora. 2006. México y Centroamérica: hegemonía mundial, resistencias y visibilidad social. In *Geoeconomía y Geopolítica en el área del Plan Puebla Panamá*, ed. Daniel Villafuerte Solís and Xochitl Leyva Solano. Mexico: Editorial Miguel Ángel Porrúa.

Presidencia de la República. 2001. *Plan Puebla-Panamá Capítulo México.* Documento Base.

Proyecto Mesoamérica. 2017a. Informe Estado de Proyectos PM 2008–2016. http://www.proyectomesoamerica.org/index.php/comunicacion/kit-de-comunicaciones-pm/comunicados-de-prensa.html. Downloaded 24 April 2018.

Proyecto Mesoamérica. 2017b. Resumen Ejecutivo de Proyecto Mesoamérica 2008–2017. http://www.proyectomesoamerica.org/index.php/comunicacion/kit-de-comunicaciones-pm/comunicados-de-prensa.html. Downloaded 24 April 2018.

Proyecto Mesoamérica. 2017c. Proyecto de Integración y Desarrollo de Mesoamérica y los Objetivos de Desarrollo Sostenible. http://www.proyectomesoamerica.org/index.php/comunicacion/kit-de-comunicaciones-pm/comunicados-de-prensa.html. Downloaded 24 April 2018.

Red Regional de Social Watch. 2004. *Pobreza y Sociedad Civil: Análisis y Desafíos desde la perspectiva de la Sociedad Civil en Centroamérica y México.* CIDEP San Salvador.

Rioja Peregrina, Leonardo H. 2002. Biopiratería y la lucha política en el contexto del PPP. In *Lectura Crítica del Plan Puebla* Panamá, coordinadores Eduardo Andrés Sandoval Forero y Robinson Salazar Pérez. Buenos Aires: Libros en Red.

Robinson, William I. 2002. Globalisation as a Macro-Structural-Historical Framework of Analysis: The Case of Central America. *New Political Economy* 7 (2): 221–250.

Robson, Peter. 1980. *The Economics of International Integration.* London: George Allan & Unwin Ltd.

Rocha, Alberto. 2006. La geopolítica de México en Centroamérica: ¿una hegemonía regional? In *Geoeconomía y Geopolítica en el área del Plan Puebla Panamá*, ed. Daniel Villafuerte Solis and Xochitl Leyva Solano. México: Editorial Miguel Angel Porrúa.

Rodríguez, Ennio. 1994. Central America, Common Market, Trade Liberalization and Trade Agreements. In *Economic Integration in the Western Hemisphere*, ed. Roberto Bauzas and Jaime Ros. Notre Dame, IN: University of Notre Dame Press.

Rojas Aravena, Francisco (ed.). 2000. *Multilateralismo: Perspectivas Latinoamericanas*. Flacso-Chile Editorial Nueva Sociedad.

Romero Contreras, Tonatiuh, and Lorena Ávila Ramos. 1999. Mesoamérica: Historia y reconsideración del Concepto. *Ciencia Ergo Sum* 6 (3): 233–242. http://redalyc.uaemex.mx/redalyc/src/inicio/ArtPdfRed.jsp?iCve=10401602. Downloaded 9 August 2010.

Rosenau, James N. 2000. Governance in a Globalizing World. In *The Global Transformations Reader*, ed. David Held and Anthony McGrew. Cambridge: Polity Press.

Rozental, Andrés. 2004. Fox's Foreign Policy Agenda: Global and Regional Priorities. In *Mexico Under Fox*, ed. Luis Rubio and Susan Kaufman Purcell. Boulder: Lynne Rienner.

Rubio, Luis. 2004. Democratic Politics in Mexico: New Complexities. In *Mexico Under Fox*, ed. Luis Rubio and Susan Kaufman Purcell. Boulder: Lynne Rienner.

Rubio-Fabián, Roberto. 2003. *El marco macroeconómico de la integración centroamericana*. Alternativas para el Desarrollo N° 82 marzo-abril 2003 FUNDE El Salvador.

Salazar Pérez, Robinson. 2002. El vínculo militar del Plan Colombia y el Plan Puebla Panamá. In *Lectura Crítica del Plan Puebla Panamá*, coordinadores Eduardo Andrés Sandoval Forero y Salazar Pérez. Buenos Aires: Libros en Red.

Saldivar, V. Americo. 2002. El Plan Puebla Panamá: Una Locomotora sin Vagones de Segunda. In *Lectura Crítica del Plan Puebla Panamá*, coordinadores Eduardo Andrés Sandoval Forero y Robinson Salazar Pérez. Buenos Aires: Libros en Red.

Sanchez Bajo, Claudia. 2005. European Union-Mercosur Interregionalism: Negotiations, Civil Society and Governance. In *The Political Economy of Regions and Regionalisms*, ed. Morten Boas, Marianne H. Marchand, and Timothy M. Shaw. Basingstoke: Palgrave Macmillan.

Sancho, Eduardo. 2005. *Impacto de los Tratados de Libre comercio en la integración regional de América Central,* Realidad y Reflexión Año 5 N° 12 mayo-agosto 2005. San Salvador: Universidad Francisco Gavidia.

Sancho, Eduardo. 2006. *Turismo: Desarrollo Sostenible de La Región*, Realidad y Reflexión Año 6 N° 16 enero-abril 2006. San Salvador: Universidad Francisco Gavidia.

Sandoval Forero, Eduardo Andrés. 2002. El Plan Puebla Panamá y la globalización de los indios. In *Lectura Crítica del Plan Puebla Panamá*, coordinadores Eduardo Andrés Sandoval Forero y Robinson Salazar Pérez. Buenos Aires: Libros en Red.

Sandoval Forero, Eduardo Andrés y Robinson Salazar Pérez. 2002. *Lectura Crítica del Plan Puebla Panamá*. Libros en Red.

Sandoval García, Carlos. 2004. Contested Discourses on National Identity: Representing Nicaraguan Immigration to Costa Rica. *Bulletin of Latin American Research* 23 (4) (October): 434–445.

Sandoval Palacios, Juan Manuel. 2001a. *El Plan Puebla-Panamá Como Regulador de la Migración Laboral Centroamericana y del Sur-Sureste de México*. Foro de Análisis, Información y Propuestas Xela. http://www.usuarios.lycos.es/celaju/pronencia3-parte1.htm. Downloaded 10 August 2010.

Sandoval Palacios, Juan Manuel. 2001b. El Plan Puebla Panamá como regulador de la migración laboral mesoamericana. In *Mesoamerica: Los Ríos Profundos. Alternativas Plebeyas al Plan Puebla Panamà*, ed. Armando Bartra. Mexico: RMALC/El Atajo Ediciones/Instituto "Maya", A.C.

Sandoval Palacios, Juan Manuel. 2006. Migración y seguridad nacional en las fronteras norte y sur de México. In *Geoeconomía y Geopolítica en el área del Plan Puebla Panamá*, ed. Daniel Villafuerte Solis and Xochitl Leyva Solano. México: Editorial Miguel Angel Porrúa.

Sandoval Palacios, Juan Manuel. 2011a. Introducción. In *Planes Geoestratégicos, Desplazamientos y Migraciones Forzadas en el Área del Proyecto de Desarrollo e Integración Mesoamérica*, coordinadores Juan Manuel Sandoval Palacios, Raquel Álvarez de Flores and Sara Yaneth Fernández Moreno. Published by: Seminario Permanente de Estudios Chicanos y de Fronteras, DEAS-INAH (México), Centro de Estudios de Fronteras e Integración, Universidad de Los Andes-Táchira (Venezuela), and Departamento de Trabajo Social, Facultad de Ciencias Sociales y Humanas, Universidad de Antioquia (Colombia). e-book: http://www.academia.edu/7454005/PLANES_GEOESTRATÉGICOS_DESPLAZAMIENTOS_Y_MIGRACIONES_FORZADAS_EN_EL_ÁREA_DEL_PROYECTO_DE_DESARROLLO_E_INTEGRACIÓN_DE_MESOAMÉRICA. Downloaded 9 February 2018.

Sandoval Palacios, Juan Manuel. 2011b. El proyecto de Integración y Desarrollo de Mesoamérica (Proyecto Mesoamérica) en el marco de la Alianza para la Seguridad y Prosperidad de América del Norte (ASPAN), la política de Seguridad Democrática y la Iniciativa Mérida. In *Planes Geoestratégicos, Desplazamientos y Migraciones Forzadas en el Área del Proyecto de Desarrollo e Integración Mesoamérica*, coordinadores Juan Manuel Sandoval Palacios,

Raquel Álvarez de Flores and Sara Yaneth Fernández Moreno. Published by: Seminario Permanente de Estudios Chicanos y de Fronteras, DEAS-INAH (México), Centro de Estudios de Fronteras e Integración, Universidad de Los Andes-Táchira (Venezuela), and Departamento de Trabajo Social, Facultad de Ciencias Sociales y Humanas, Universidad de Antioquia (Colombia). e-book: http://www.academia.edu/7454005/PLANES_GEOESTRATÉGICOS_DESPLAZAMIENTOS_Y_MIGRACIONES_FORZADAS_EN_EL_ÁREA_DEL_PROYECTO_DE_DESARROLLO_E_INTEGRACIÓN_DE_MESOAMÉRICA. Downloaded 9 February 2018.

Sandoval Palacios, Juan Manuel, Raquel Álvarez de Flores, and Sara Yaneth Fernández Moreno (coordinadores). 2011. *Planes Geoestratégicos, Desplazamientos y Migraciones Forzadas en el Área del Proyecto de Desarrollo e Integración Mesoamérica*. Published by: Seminario Permanente de Estudios Chicanos y de Fronteras, DEAS-INAH (México), Centro de Estudios de Fronteras e Integración, Universidad de Los Andes-Táchira (Venezuela), and Departamento de Trabajo Social, Facultad de Ciencias Sociales y Humanas, Universidad de Antioquia (Colombia). e-book: http://www.academia.edu/7454005/PLANES_GEOESTRATÉGICOS_DESPLAZAMIENTOS_Y_MIGRACIONES_FORZADAS_EN_EL_ÁREA_DEL_PROYECTO_DE_DESARROLLO_E_INTEGRACIÓN_DE_MESOAMÉRICA. Downloaded 9 February 2018.

Santiso, Carlos. 2000. Towards Democratic Governance: The Contribution of the Multilateral Development Banks in Latin America. In *Democracy Assistance: International Cooperation for Democratization*, ed. Peter Burnel. London: Frank Cass.

Savenije, Wim. 2004. La mara Salvatrucha y el Barrio 18 St. Fenómenos sociales transnacionales, respuestas represivas nacionales *Foreign Affaires en Español abril/junio*. http://www.foreignaffairs-esp.org/20040404 01faenespessay040205/winsavenije/la-mara-salvatrucha.htm.

Savenije, Wim. 2007. Las pandillas transnacionales o "maras": violencia urbana en Centroamérica. *Foro Internacional* 47 (3) (July–September): 637–659.

Saxe-Fernández, John, and Gian Carlo Delgado-Ramos. 2004. Denationalization of Mexico: The World Bank in Action. In *Globalization and Antiglobalization: Dynamics of Change in the New World Order*, ed. Henry Veltmeyer. Burlington, VT: Ashgate.

Segreda, Luis, and Daniel Camacho. 1999. El Papel de la ONG en el Proceso de la Integración Centroamericana, Democracia y Derechos Humanos: La experiencia del CODEHUCA. In *Hacia una Integración desde Abajo. Participación, Sociedad Civil e Integración Centroamericana*, ed. Ricardo Grinspun, Carlos Alvarenga, and Shamsie Yasmine. San Salvador: Talleres Gráficos UCA.

Scholte, Jan Aart. 2001. The Globalization of World Politics. In *The Globalization of World Politics: An Introduction to International Relations*, ed. John Baylis and Steve Smith, 2nd ed. Oxford: Oxford University Press.

Shaw, Timothy M. 2002. New Regionalisms in Africa in the New Millennium: Comparative Perspectives on Renaissance, Realisms and/or Regressions. In *New Regionalisms in the Global Political Economy: Theories and Cases*, ed. Shaun Breslin, Christopher W. Hughes, Nicola Phillips, and Ben Rosamond. London: Routledge.

SG-SICA. 2010. Instrumentos Jurídicos del Sistema de Integración Centroamericana Secretaría General del Sistema de la Integración Centroamericana SG-SICA Second Edition. www.sica.int/busqueda/Libros.aspx?IDItem=28654&IdCat=35&IdEnt=1&Idm=1&IdmStyle=1.

SICA/CEPAL. 2004. *La Integración Centroamericana: Beneficios y Costos.* Documento Síntesis, Centroamérica, Mayo de 2004, 2a Impresión: Asesores Soluciones Integradas Impreso el 28 de junio de 2004.

SIECA. 2005. *Retos y Oportunidades del Mercado Común Centroamericano ante el DR-CAFTA.* Integración Año 6 Octubre 2005 (official publication).

SIECA. 2006. *La Unión Aduanera Centroamericana.* Guatemala, septiembre de 2006.

SIECA. 2017. *Informe Económico Regional 2016–2017 Oportunidades y riesgos para Centroamérica.* Centro de Estudios para la Integración Económica.

Söderbaum, Fredrik. 2003. Introduction: Theories of New Regionalism. In *Theories of New Regionalism: A Palgrave Reader*, ed. Fredrik Söderbaum and Timothy M. Shaw. Basingstoke: Palgrave Macmillan.

Söderbaum, Fredrik. 2005. The International Political Economy of Regionalism. In *Globalizing International Political Economy*, ed. Nicola Phillips. New York: Palgrave Macmillan.

Söderbaum, Fredrik. 2016. *Rethinking Regionalism.* New York: Palgrave Macmillan.

Söderbaum, Fredrik, and Timothy M. Shaw. 2003. *Theories of New Regionalism: A Palgrave Reader.* Basingstoke: Palgrave Macmillan.

Söderbaum, Fredrik, and Timothy M. Shaw. 2004. Conclusion: What Futures for New Regionalism? In *Theories of New Regionalism: A Palgrave Reader*, ed. Fredrik Söderbaum and Timothy M. Shaw. Basingstoke: Palgrave Macmillan.

Solà, Amadeu. 2000. Colaboraciones: La traducción de governance. *Puntoycoma*, No. 65 (septiembre–octubre). www.europa.eu.int/comm/translation/bulletins/puntoycoma/65/pyc652.htm. Accessed 15 August 2009.

SRE/UNIFEM/PNUD. 2004. *Foro Regional de Reflexión Sobre las Metas Del Milenio y la Equidad de Género en el Marco del Plan Puebla-Panamá: Memoria.* ISBN:0-912917-95-4. SRE/UNIFEM/PNUD Impreso en México.

Sunkel, Osvaldo. 2000. Development and Regional Integration in Latin America: Another Chance for an Unfulfilled Promise? In *National Perspectives on the New Regionalism in the South*, ed. Bjorn Hettne, Andreas Inotal, and Osvaldo Sunkel. London: Macmillan.

Talcott, Molly. 2014. "Together We Have Power" Personal Traumas and Political Responses among Activist Oaxaqueñas. *Latin American Perspectives* 41 (1) (January): 72–88. http://www.jstor.org/stable/24573977.

Tedesco, Laura. 2004. Democracy in Latin America: Issues of Governance in the Southern Cone. *Bulletin of Latin American Research* 23 (1) (January): 30–42.

Thrift, Nigel. 2001. Forum: Perspectives on the New Political Economy: Chasing Capitalism. *New Political Economy* 6 (3): 375–380.

Toly, Noah J. 2004. Globalization and the Capitalization of Nature: A Political Ecology of Biodiversity in Mesoamerica. *Bulletin of Science, Technology &Society* 24 (1) (February): 47–54.

Toussaint, Mónica, and Marisol Garzón. 2017. El Proyecto Mesoamérica: ¿Éxito o Fracaso? Límites de la Cooperación de México hacia Centroamérica Entre Diversidades. *Revista de Ciencias Sociales y Humanidades* 0 (8) (enero-junio): 15–52.

Tratado libre comercio México-Panamá publicado 29 junio 2015. https://www.gob.mx/cms/uploads/attachment/file/94317/TLCMexicoPanama.pdf.

Tratado único México Centroamérica publicado 15 mayo 2015. https://www.gob.mx/se/documentos/comercio-exterior-paises-con-tratados-y-acuerdos-firmados-con-mexico-america-latina-tratado-centroamerica?state=published. Downloaded 12 April 2018.

Tratado libre comercio México-Colombia publicado 21 mayo 2015. https://www.gob.mx/se/documentos/comercio-exterior-paises-con-tratados-y-acuerdos-firmados-con-mexico-america-latina-colombia?state=published. Downloaded 12 April 2018.

Vargas Roldán, Jorge. 1999. Corrupción, Gobernabilidad y Sociedad Civil en Centroamérica. In *Hacia una Integración desde Abajo. Participación, Sociedad Civil e Integración Centroamericana*, ed. Ricardo Grinspun, Carlos Alvarenga, and Shamsie Yasmine. San Salvador: Talleres Gráficos UCA.

Väyrynen, Raimo. 2003. Regionalism Old and New. *International Studies Review* 5 (1): 25–51.

Vega Santiago, Francisca. 2006. *Integración al Pesto* América Economía Edición Aniversario 20 Años en América Latina del 6 al 19 de Octubre 2006 AMERICAECONOMIA Santíago de Chile 36–38.

Velásquez José Martín. 2005. La Defensa del Patrimonio Territorial Frente al Plan Puebla-Panamá. In *Culturas en Resistencia Frente al Libre Comercio*, Red Mexicana de Acción Frente al Libre Comercio (RMALC) editor with Maria Atilano Uriarte as editorial compilator and coordinator. Foro Internacional Resistencias y Alternativas RMALC.

Veltmeyer, Henry (ed.). 2004a. *Globalization and Antiglobalization: Dynamics of Change in The New World Order*. Aldershot: Ashgate.

Veltmeyer, Henry. 2004b. Restructuring Latin America and Labour and the World Bank. In *Globalization and Antiglobalization: Dynamics of Change in The New World Order*, ed. Henry Veltmeyer. Aldershot: Ashgate.

Villafuerte Solis, Daniel. 2004a. Mas allá del Plan Puebla-Panamá: del TLCAN al ALCA. *Comercio Exterior* 54 (4) (abril): 283–284. revistas.bancomext.gob.mx/rce/magazines/65/2/villa0404.pdf.

Villafuerte Solis, Daniel. 2004b. *Los problemas del desarrollo en la frontera sur.* Territoria y Economía Número Especial 3 / Chiapas Sistema de Información Regional de México, 51–59.

Villafuerte Solís, Daniel. 2006a. Integraciones en el Norte y Sur de México: del NAFTA al CAFTA. In *Geoeconomía y Geopolítica en el área del Plan Puebla Panamá*, ed. Daniel Villafuerte Solís and Xochitl Leyva Solano. México: Editorial Miguel Ángel Porrúa.

Villafuerte Solís, Daniel. 2006b. Reflexiones Finales. In *Geoeconomía y Geopolítica en el área del Plan Puebla Panamá*, ed. Daniel Villafuerte Solís and Xochitl Leyva Solano. México: Editorial Miguel Ángel Porrúa.

Villafuerte Solís, Daniel, and Xochitl Leyva Solano (eds.). 2006. *Geoeconomía y Geopolítica en el área del Plan Puebla Panamá*. México: Editorial Miguel Ángel Porrúa.

Villegas, Claudia. 2011. Vulnerabilidad Social, desastres y migración forzada: el caso de migrantes climáticos. In *Planes Geoestratégicos, Desplazamientos y Migraciones Forzadas en el Área del Proyecto de Desarrollo e Integración Mesoamérica*, coordinadores Juan Manuel Sandoval Palacios, Raquel Álvarez de Flores and Sara Yaneth Fernández Moreno. Published by: Seminario Permanente de Estudios Chicanos y de Fronteras, DEAS-INAH (México), Centro de Estudios de Fronteras e Integración, Universidad de Los Andes-Táchira (Venezuela), and Departamento de Trabajo Social, Facultad de Ciencias Sociales y Humanas, Universidad de Antioquia (Colombia). e-book: http://www.academia.edu/7454005/PLANES_GEOESTRATÉGICOS_DESPLAZAMIENTOS_Y_MIGRACIONES_FORZADAS_EN_EL_ÁREA_DEL_PROYECTO_DE_DESARROLLO_E_INTEGRACIÓN_DE_MESOAMÉRICA.

Viner, Jacob. 1950. *The Customs Union Issue*. New York: Carnegie Endowment of International Peace.

Welch, Stephen, and Caroline Kennedy-Pipe. 2004. Multi-level Governance and International Relations. In *Multilevel Governance*, ed. Ian Bache and Matthew Flinders. New York: Oxford University Press.

Wendt, Alexander. 1994. Collective Identity Formation and the International State. *The American Political Science Review* 88 (2): 384–396.

Wilson, Japhy. 2008. The New Phase of the Plan Puebla Panama in Chiapas (Parts 1, 2, 3) Bulletins of CIEPAC "Chiapas Day by Day", 22 May 2008, No. 560. http://www.ciepac.org/boletines/chiapas_en.php?id=560. Accessed 10 August 2009.

Wilson, Japhy. 2011. Contesting the Plan Puebla Panama: Henri Lefebvre and the Politics of Space in Southern Mexico. In *Planes Geoestratégicos, Desplazamientos y Migraciones Forzadas en el Área del Proyecto de Desarrollo e Integración Mesoamérica*, coordinadores Juan Manuel Sandoval Palacios, Raquel Álvarez de Flores and Sara Yaneth Fernández Moreno. Published by: Seminario Permanente de Estudios Chicanos y de Fronteras, DEAS-INAH (México), Centro de Estudios de Fronteras e Integración, Universidad de Los Andes-Táchira (Venezuela), and Departamento de Trabajo Social, Facultad de Ciencias Sociales y Humanas, Universidad de Antioquia (Colombia). e-book: http://www.academia.edu/7454005/PLANES_GEOESTRATÉGICOS_DESPLAZAMIENTOS_Y_MIGRACIONES_FORZADAS_EN_EL_ÁREA_DEL_PROYECTO_DE_DESARROLLO_E_INTEGRACIÓN_DE_MESOAMÉRICA.

Woodward, Ralph Lee, Jr. 1985. *Central America: A Nation Divided.* London: Oxford University Press.

Woodward, Ralph Lee. 1988. *Central America: Historical Perspectives on the Contemporary Crises.* New York: Greenwood Press.

Zebadúa, Emilio. 2005. *La Frontera Sur: una aproximación inicial* Territorio y Economía Número Especial 4/2005 Frontera Sur, Sistema de Información Regional de México, México 2–6.

FSC
www.fsc.org
MIX
Papier | Fördert gute Waldnutzung
FSC® C083411

Kolibri 360 GmbH
Ferdinand-Jühlke-Straße 7
99095 Erfurt, Deutschland
produktsicherheit@kolibri360.de